Chattanooga Great Places

After you've seen the ChooChoo, there's more to do!

The where-to-go guide to Chattanooga's great restaurants, arts, entertainment, recreation, sports, tours, outings, shopping, lodgings and services

Plus a Hundred Miles

& Atlanta, Birmingham, Huntsville, Knoxville, Nashville

by
Linda L. Burton

with illustrations by
Betty H. Harrelson

Phase II: Publications
Chattanooga, Tennessee

Printed in the United States of America.

First edition published in 1995.

Library of Congress Catalog Card Number 95-69855
       Burton, Linda L.
             Chattanooga Great Places: an indispensable guide to a captivating city; Chattanooga's great places to eat, go, shop, stay and use, plus a hundred miles; first edition.
             Includes index.
ISBN 0-9644760-0-2. $11.95.

Cover and chapter illustrations by Betty H. Harrelson
Assistance with cover layout by Beth Close, LPI
Color separations by Compu-Color
Editing by Shelagh Lane
Editing assistance and research by Winston Brooks
Research assistance by Willa Ibach

This is a personal guidebook, with evaluations based on numerous reports from locals and traveling inspectors. Final judgments are made by the publisher. Our inspectors never identify themselves (except over the phone) and never take free meals or other favors during reviews. The publisher welcomes information conveyed by users of this book, as long as they have no financial connection with the establishment concerned. A report form is provided at the end of the book.

All prices and hours open listed in the book are subject to change without notice.

All guidebooks published by Phase II: Publications are available at bulk discounts for corporate gifts, conventions, and fund-raising sales for clubs and organizations.

Published by Phase II: Publications
5251-C Hwy 153, # 255
Chattanooga, Tennessee 37343
Voice 615-875-4795 Fax 615-877-4089

Dedication

**This book is dedicated with love
to my parents
Ivous Sizemore Burton
&
Craig Sherer Burton
who never fail to stick by me.
Thanks for that heredity and environment thing:
good stock, good example and good raising.
It was your Chattanooga honeymoon
that started it all!**

Thanks and Love are in order for these Very Important People

- ♦ To my brother Craig Burton Jr, who has traveled more than half the 50 states with me, and can be counted on to be where he's needed;
- ♦ To my brother Hal Burton, who flies around the world, but stayed close with an extra helping hand in May so I could complete the book;
- ♦ To my son Michael Shumate, who calmly keeps my computer updated and running fast, and always helps me when I need helping;
- ♦ To my son Richard Shumate, who keeps me pumped with his smiling sweet enthusiasm, and always has a kind and listening ear;
- ♦ To my son Scott Shumate, who led us west of the Mississippi so many years ago, and always urges me to do what's right for me;
- ♦ To my daughters-by-love-and-law Karen Shumate and Tess Shumate, who make my sons happy, and make our family a better place;
- ♦ To my special southern friends, Betty Harrelson and Jay Jones, who have shared over a quarter-century's worth of raising families and living life, and, knowing my best and worst sides, like me anyhow;
- ♦ To my special Seattle friends, Gayle Gilbert and Shelagh Lane, who have shared so many walks around the lake and ferry rides and big-life plans, and who never stop encouraging me;
- ♦ And littlest, but not least, to my grandsons Jeffrey, Jason, Justin and Matthew Shumate, who are inside their G-Mom's heart and beside her on the trail, with years of going still ahead. This book was written because of them.

G-Kids, and all readers of this book, stay curious, keep exploring, and have fun. Remember, life is a giant possibility place. Enjoy!

Linda L. Burton

Chattanooga Plus a Hundred Miles
✪ ✪ ✪ ✪

X marks the spot! Chattanooga is centrally located in the southeast.
You'll find easy freeway access to Atlanta, Birmingham, Nashville and
Knoxville via I-75, I-59 and I-24; and to Huntsville on US72.

If you live in one of our sister cities, anywhere in between, or far beyond,
note how easy it is to get to Chattanooga! The welcome mat is always out.

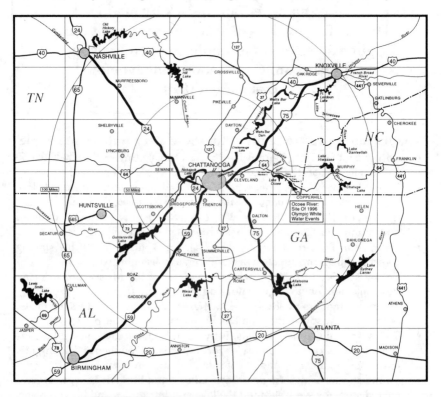

Emergency Assistance in City or County
Ambulance, Fire or Medic   **911**
Emergency Highway Assistance
Alabama Highway Patrol	**205-546-6385**
*HP for Mobile Phones	
Georgia Highway Patrol	**706-638-1400**
North Carolina Highway Patrol	**704-298-4252**
Tennessee Highway Patrol	**615-821-5151**
*THP for Mobile Phones	

Chattanooga Region
✪ ✪ ✪ ✪

Time Zones
Alabama Central. Georgia Eastern.
Middle Tennessee Central. East Tennessee & Chattanooga Eastern.
Area Codes
North Alabama 205. North Georgia 706.
Tennessee 615. East Tennessee is 423 after September 1995.

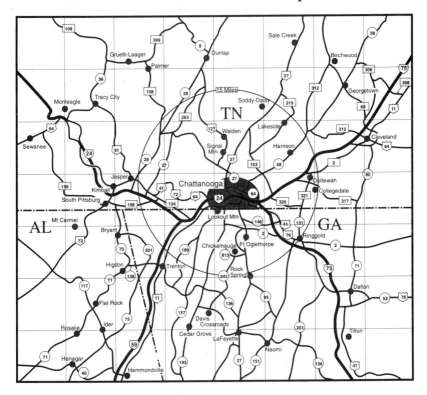

Climate
Summer Temperatures
Lows average 69. Highs average 89.
Winter Temperatures
Lows average 32. Highs average 50.
Precipitation
Averages 52 inches of rain and 4 inches of snow annually.
Spring and fall are pleasant here
and the trees and flowers are spectacular!

Chattanooga Downtown
✪ ✪ ✪ ✪

1990 Population 152,466. Metro Population 433,210.
Elevation
Downtown 685 feet. Lookout Mountain 2,100 feet.
Signal Mountain 1,900 feet. Raccoon Mountain 1,800 feet.
Missionary Ridge 1,100 feet. Big Ridge 1,000 feet.
Area Code
615 before September 1995, afterwards it is 423.
Time Zone
Eastern

What is Chattanooga's real name? You may know it as ChooChoo City, due to the train song; of course it's River City, and takes superb advantage of the fact with river boats, walks and festivals. No one will dispute its Scenic City title, and lately it's getting to be known as the Environmental City. But everyone agrees on one name for it: a Captivating City! On the following page is one such opinion.

People Who Love Chattanooga
Dalton Roberts

"How can you keep from loving it?" Dalton says simply. "It's a beautiful place with beautiful people. It's a small town with big-city conveniences. Whenever I'm away from Chattanooga for a while, I develop a hunger for the mountains and rivers. It must be the Indian coming out in me. I feel in harmony with the place. I was raised on the banks of Chickamauga Creek, swam and fished in it, ran my trot lines, it's in my blood. I grew up drinking from a spring flowing from within Missionary Ridge, as a Scout I camped in caves and breathed the air inside the mountains. Chattanooga is a part of me."

Dalton Roberts has lived most of his life in Chattanooga, Tennessee. He taught in the city schools, was hired as supervisor of special education, was appointed County Manager, and was elected County Executive, where he served for 16 years. His musical career has run parallel to these accomplishments, the Martin guitar being a part of his life since age 15. Today he concentrates on songwriting and recording, writing a column for The Chattanooga Times, and teaching at UTC. And you might catch him playing and singing at a benefit, political rally, or musical event.

Perhaps no one reflects the whole of the community and a connection with virtually everything you'll read about in this book more completely than Dalton Roberts. Many places in the Restaurants, Shopping and Lodgings sections have benefited by Dalton's efforts to create jobs and promote business and tourism in Hamilton County. As a musician, writer, and radio personae, he's been center-stage and supportive of Arts and Entertainment events as long as folks can remember; his zest for enjoying the mountains and rivers and his efforts to develop parks and greenways ties into Recreation, Sports and Outings you'll read about. With a masters degree in special education and years of teaching and working with community services, he's helped numerous organizations listed in the Services section of the book. What were the beginnings of a person so immersed in community?

"Our home was the center of the neighborhood," Dalton recalls with a smile. "It was wide open to kids; even hoboes came by to eat. Mother was a very nurturing woman, always with time to help someone else, maybe because her grandfather was a full-blooded Cherokee. Daddy wrote Mother a love note every day. He cooked breakfast every morning, too. Mother would read into the night, and Daddy would get up early and fix her breakfast. Daddy was a minister, he pastored Methodist and Nazarene churches over the years."

Dalton grew up surrounded by books. His mother not only loved to read, she wrote letters, with pen pals all over the world. She's no longer living, but Dalton still writes to some of those who loved his mother most. There was always music in Dalton's house; his Uncle Van loved Jimmy Rodgers' songs and would come over with his guitar for family-singing evenings. When Dalton was 13, his uncle taught him to play three chords; by the time he was 15 his fingers were callused enough to convince his Daddy that he should have his own guitar.

Dalton's raising took place in East Chattanooga, in a community called Watering Trough, so named because of a cool spring-water outlet. It's believed Civil War soldiers and their horses drank from the Missionary Ridge spring. Years later a pipe was installed and the trough was bricked in to cool milk or a summer melon. Thousands of travelers and residents can tell you about drinking from the spring; it's still there today, on Harrison Pike at Meadow Lane; take your jug or cup and refresh yourself, as Dalton still does.

All this produced a man who learned to be reasonable, responsible, and responsive; steady as a rock; a man who will tell the truth. Sometimes he lays it out in song; sometimes on the editorial page, upper-center spot; sometimes in the classroom, in a let's-think-it-out discussion. With Dalton, a conversation is round-trip; he talks and he listens in a words-and-meanings exchange; you walk away feeling understood, even if you didn't agree. He's good with good-old-boy chatter too; much sought to fill the after-dinner speaking slot, when the crowd hankers for a tale with a salty-peppered twist.

Dalton was born with a special pair of crap-filtering looking-glasses; blessed with magical powers, they bend and fold into periscope or telescope, allowing viewing privileges around corners or into the future to the "possibilities" plane; the how-things-could-be level of thinking; otherwise known as visionary. As elected head of county government, he reorganized and redirected departments and staff in national-award-winning fashion; setting the stage for a county-benefiting stream of positive events: county-city cooperation for downtown revitalization, creation of industrial parks and new jobs, development of recreational complexes, a county sewer authority. He chose to leave politics in '94, the same year one of his long-fought-for changes was voted into being -- county-city school consolidation; a happy moment for this former school-teacher who had worked so many years inside the system.

Dalton hit the retirement-from-politics road in a writing-talking-singing blaze; devoting more time to his music; writing eleven songs about Bessie Smith and recording his first blues album, *The Blues in Black and White;* making a benefits-the-school music video with Orange Grove students, singing and sharing love in *A Little Christmas Every Day.* Dalton has written "a couple of hundred" songs, he says, since he got that Martin guitar; more than 75 have been recorded by himself or by other artists.

But has he really left politics? The University of Tennessee at Chattanooga has established a Dalton Roberts Professorship in Political Science; Dalton's influence on the political scene will continue through his teachings there, as he explains the intricacies of local government and promotes his get-yourself-involved attitude towards community service. And into the future? "Sometimes I get frustrated thinking our culture is slow to change," says Dalton. "But we need to keep working . I'd still like to see consolidated governments, and there's always something you can do to make a town better. There's no end to how much quality of life you can build into a community."

Table of Contents

Chattanooga Great Places

• *Plus a Hundred Miles*

Great Places to Eat

Great Places to Go

Great Places to Shop

Great Places to Stay

Great Places to Use

Introduction

About the Cover

Blue skies and Lookout Mountain, watching over every city scene. The gold-topped Dome Building, built in 1892 for *The Chattanooga Times*. The Faxon-Thomas Mansion, a historic landmark now housing the Hunter Museum of American Art. A Civil War cannon, as you can see at Point Park or Missionary Ridge. Dogwood blossoms, mountain glory in the spring. Father Rock, according to the legend of a dying Chief and a raging storm. Golden foliage for autumn cruises through the gorge. The First Baptist steeple, reaching skyward in a city of churches. The glass and highrise Marriott doing duty by the Convention and Trade Center. River City's riverboat, the Southern Belle. The largest fresh-water aquarium in the world, Chattanooga's pride and joy. The longest pedestrian walkway over water in the world, the Walnut Street Bridge. The mighty Tennessee, home to more species of fish than any river in North America. And underneath it all, one version of a Chattanooga ChooChoo, like the kind that rode the rails in song.

About the Illustrator

Betty Higginbotham Harrelson did the watercolor for the cover, as well as the Little People in the seven illustrations inside. Born in Madison, Georgia, Betty did her first watercolor at age 12 and has been painting and drawing ever since. She has lived in Chattanooga for more than 30 years; her family numbers husband Reuben, children Angie, Karen, Margie, Martin and all their spouses, and her mother, Marjorie Higginbotham; all contributed to the book. Betty has a great eye for humor as well as design; see how she captures the gentility of southern living with just a hint of a barbeque-eating grin!

About the Author

Linda L. Burton (that's me), was born in Jasper, Alabama. The first vacation trip I recall as a kid was to Chattanooga with a ride on the Incline and stops at Rock City and Ruby Falls. I wound up moving to Chattanooga when my three sons were small; they grew up here. I went to Little League and Pinewood Derby and parents night at PTA. We played at Lake Winnie and picnicked at Pops in the Park and flew kites by the dam and locked through Chickamauga Lock in a small, I said *small*, boat. I was in the new UTC's first graduating class; I taught at UTC; and I owned a business that had me writing about Chattanooga people and places from a corporate view. Somewhere along in there I traveled to all 50 states, most all National Parks, and worked at the University of Washington in Seattle for 13 years. When I returned to Chattanooga in 1993, I was WOWED! I went to the store to buy a book about all the new stuff I could do with my grandkids; the Aquarium, museums, bridges, and greenways everywhere. There wasn't one, so I decided to write it! My sincere thanks to the hundreds of you who talked glowingly about the city you love, and who stopped what you were doing to get information for me; you know who you are. My experiences and yours are here.

How to Use This Book

Are you a long-time resident? A new resident? A visitor? Thinking about visiting? Then, this book was written just for you! Notice, it's the first edition of Chattanooga's authoritative guidebook. Keep a copy near your kitchen phone, on your desk at work, and crammed in your purse, coat pocket, or travel bag. Make notes in it for your reference, and send us your suggestions for the next edition. It is not a coffee table book, it's meant to be used.

This is a book with no advertisers or sponsors; no reviewer accepted any free meals or favors from anyone mentioned in the book. Trust the reviews to be honest opinions. Obviously every great place isn't in here; after all, there are over 900 restaurants in the area. The fact that a place was not included does not imply adverse criticism.

So how did we choose the places that are in it? Hundreds of restaurants were visited and hundreds of people were interviewed. "Tell me five of your favorite places to eat," was asked. Restaurants we heard about over and over obviously were included. Others were selected simply because they do what they do well, be it fast food or fancy. This is not a food critique, it's information that tells you what to expect. Is it noisy or quiet? Do they pamper kids? Do they pamper me? Do they serve alcohol? Is there a nice view? Where should I go when I'm in a hurry? The category listings are by location and then by type; find the place or type you want, then turn to the alphabetical reviews and read about what you will find when you get there.

We put "meals served" rather than "hours open"; hours often change seasonally; check before you go. One "$" sign translates roughly to $5 for your basic meal; appetizers, desserts and drinks add more, of course. Information about prices and days open was obtained directly from the establishments listed. Some changes are inevitable, and Phase II: Publications cannot be responsible for any variations from the information printed.

As to the Arts, Entertainment, Sports, Recreation and Tours, we tried to select things that have a broad family appeal and that won't break the bank. We note things that are FREE and that are especially great for KIDS. We believe in exploring new places; even if you've lived here forever, you can find something new to do just about every weekend. Jump into the spirit of it all!

Shopping and Services are meant to get you started; you should develop your own criteria about the specific places that suit your needs. Lodgings were selected to provide a broad range of choice, from camping-on-the-ground to crystal ballrooms. There's a location and type index for them too.

If you're looking for a particular spot, check the full index at the back of the book. It's a long list of Great Places! Phone numbers are local unless otherwise indicated.

People Who Love Chattanooga
Grady Foster

"I had already gone to Baking School at the University of Paris when I arrived in Chattanooga in 1960," says Grady Foster. Today he is a member of Chaine des Rotisseurs, the worldwide French food society that was founded in 1248. Chaine members love good food, and more, they devote time to the study of it. The local Chattanooga chapter meets several times a year for food fêtes at such varied spots as riverboats, wineries, downtown restaurants, and antebellum mansions.

The art of preparing good food has fascinated Grady for a long time. "I used to watch my grandmother make hoecakes. She just poured the batter into the skillet and they turned out fine. One day when she was out of the kitchen, I tried it myself. Mine flopped. She shook her head when she saw the mess, but she took the time to show me how."

Curiosity and this risk-taking bent have propelled Grady throughout his life. "Watch someone who does something well; then try it," he believes. And he is intensely interested in sharing what he knows, in ways such as teaching commercial cooking classes in the public schools for a number of years. "I was very strict with my students. You can't have a bad day in the restaurant business. That customer who comes in for a meal expects good food and good service, and they have a right to get it. 'Sweetheart, if you don't feel like working today, go home,' I would tell them. 'Here, we're going to do it right.'"

Beginning his food service career in Chattanooga selling beer and potato chips, Grady soon started working in restaurants in private country clubs. He was manager of Rock City Restaurant for 17 years, earning a degree in culinary arts while working, and taking a leadership role in his community. Today, his house is filled with awards and plaques symbolizing the recognition and appreciation he has been shown over the years for his contributions, his involvement ranging from Scout troop leader to president of both the Chattanooga and the Tennessee Restaurant Association, and board member of the National Restaurant Association.

Grady Foster is a member of the Food Services Committee which oversees banquet planning for the Chattanooga-Hamilton County Trade Center. He also does special-events catering and is busy collecting recipes he has developed over the years for inclusion in a book. Another book he has in mind is entitled "Who Says Blacks Can't Make It In Chattanooga?"

Grady is pleased with the direction the food service industry is taking today. "We are very conscious of good nutrition. Fast-food restaurants are becoming heart-smart and publishing literature about how their food is prepared. Everywhere, better cooks are preparing better food. In many restaurants the waitstaff is trained to suggest a good meal to the customer. Maybe it's competition that has brought us here, but we've really tuned in to why people choose a restaurant. People want to feel comfortable in a place and they want food that tastes good and is eye-appealing. They want value for their money. Chattanoogans have some good choices today."

Restaurants

Contents

She: You're looking very handsome tonight! Have you been working out?
He: No, I've been eating out! Maybe it's like Grandma says: "Southern cooking makes you good looking."

LOCATION BY AREA

Battlefield: Chickamauga, Ft Oglethorpe. Hamilton: Hamilton Place, Collegedale, East Brainerd. Lookout: Lookout/Raccoon Mountain. Northlake: Hixson, Soddy-Daisy. Northriver: North Shore, Red Bank, Signal Mtn. Ridge: Brainerd, East Ridge, Rossville. Southlake: Hwy 58 E of Hwy 153.

BATTLEFIELD

Arby's Roast Beef
Armando's
Buck's Pit Barbeque
Captain D's
Central Park
Dairy Queen
Golden Corral
KFC
Krystal
Little Caesar's Pizza
McDonald's
Papa John's
Pizza Hut
Shoney's
Sonic Drive In
Subway
Taco Bell
Wendy's

DOWNTOWN

Back Inn
Big River Grill
Blue Cross Cafeteria
Brass Register
Cafe Francais
Cafe Tazza
ChooChoo Diner
ChooChoo Espresso
ChooChoo Gardens
ChooChoo Station
Clearwater
Comfort Hotel Seasons
Daryl's Sandwich Shop
David's
El Cancun Mexican
El Meson Mexicano
Figgy's Sandwich Shop
Fix's
Flatiron Deli
Greek Roma Grill
Hot Sauce Charlie
HRH Dumplin's
KFC
Kilroy's Coffeehouse
Krystal
Le Doux's Bluff View
Margaret's
Marriott Ashley's
Marriott Cafe Chat.
Marriott Terrace
Mary's Deli
McDonald's
Mom's Italian
Pickle Barrel
Pizza Hut
Porker's BBQ
Provident Cafeteria
Radisson Bistro
Radisson Green Room
Radisson Coffee
Rembrandt's
Sandbar
Shapiro's
Shoney's
Sneakers
Soup Kitchen
Southside Grill
Steamboat
Subway
TGI Fridays
Thai Food
Two Twelve Market
Vine St Market
Warehouse Row Food
Wendy's
Yellow Submarine

HAMILTON

Applebee's
Arby's Roast Beef
Armando's
Back Yard Burgers
Blimpie Subs & Salads
Buckhead Roadhouse
Captain D's
Central Park
Chick-Fil-A
China Coast
Chop House
Cirrus Garden
Country Place
Cracker Barrel
El Cancun Mexican
El Meson Mexicano
Gianni's Little Italy
Golden Dragon
Gondolier Italian
Grady's Goodtimes
Imperial Garden
Kanpai of Toyko
Kenny Rogers Roasters
KFC
Krystal
Little Caesar's Pizza
McDonald's
Morrison's Cafeteria
Mozzarella's
O'Charley's
Old Country Buffet
Olive Garden Italian
Outback Steakhouse
Papa John's
Pizza Hut
Ruby Tuesday
Ryan's Family Steak
S & S Cafeteria
Shoney's
Sonic Drive In
Steak-Out
Subway
Taco Bell
TGI Fridays
Waffle House
Wendy's

LOOKOUT

Buck's Pit Barbeque
Captain D's
Cracker Barrel
Hot Sauce Charlie
La Cabriole
Mt Vernon
Riverside Catfish
Shoney's
Soup's On
Subway
Taco Bell
Waffle House

NORTHLAKE

Applebee's
Arby's Roast Beef
Aris' Lakeshore
Armando's
Baywatch Waterfront
Blimpie Subs & Salads
Captain D's
Central Park
Checkers
Chick-Fil-A
Chuck E Cheese's
Dockside
Glen-Gene Deli
Home Folks
Hy's Barbecue
In Good Taste
Karl's Family
Kenny Rogers Roasters
KFC
Little Caesar's Pizza
Mandarin Garden
McDonald's
O'Charley's
Panda's Chinese
Piccadilly Cafeteria
Pizza Hut
Red Lobster
Roy Peppers Porch
Ryan's Family Steak
Sonic Drive In
Steak Express
Subway
Taco Bell
Waycrazy's Bar-B-Que

NORTHRIVER

Arby's Roast Beef
Armando's
C. C. Loy's
Captain D's
Central Park
Country Place
Dairy Queen
Dolphin Dan's Italian
Durty Nelly's
El Cancun Mexican
Fehn Brothers
Formosa
Ichiban Japanese Steak
Just Delicious
KFC
Krystal
Las Margaritas
Little Caesar's Pizza
Loft
Madhatters
McDonald's
Mudpie Coffeehouse
Nikki's Drive Inn
Noodles
Padrino's Mexican
Papa John's
Pizza Hut
Pizza Place

Shoney's	Blimpie Subs & Salads	Las Margaritas	Uncle Bud's Catfish
Shuford's Smokehouse	Captain D's	Little Caesar's Pizza	Veg-Out
Sonic Drive In	Central Park	Longhorn Steaks	Waffle House
Sportsman's BarBQ	Checkers	Los Reyes Mexican	Wendy's
Subway	Chick-Fil-A	McDonald's	**SOUTHLAKE**
Taco Bell	Chili's Grill	Papa John's	Arby's Roast Beef
Town & Country	ChooChoo BBQ	Peking	Captain D's
Typhoon of Toyko	Country Life Veg	Pizza Hut	Central Park
Vittles	Cracker Barrel	Red Lobster	El Cancun Mexican
Waffle House	Dairy Queen	Rib & Loin	KFC
Way It Was	Eidson	Roy's Grill	Krystal
Waycrazy's Bar-B-Que	Epicurean	Ryan's Family Steak	Little Caesar's Pizza
Wendy's	Fifth Quarter	Shoney's	McDonald's
RIDGE	Glen-Gene Deli	Sonic Drive In	Pizza Hut
Arby's Roast Beef	Gulas	Steak & Ale	Subway
Armando's	J. R.'s Country	Steak-Out	Taco Bell
Bea's	Kenny Rogers Roasters	Subway	Waffle House
Bennigan's	KFC	Taco Bell	Wendy's
Birdland	Krystal	Trip's Seafood	

SERVICES OFFERED

DELIVERY	**LINE/COUNTER/**	Little Caesar's Pizza	Bennigan's
Buck's Pit Barbeque	**BUFFET**	Marriott Cafe Chat.	Big River Grille
El Meson	Arby's Roast Beef	Marriott Terrace	Birdland
Figgy's Sandwich Shop	Armando's	Mary's Deli	Brass Register
Panda's Chinese	Back Yard Burgers	McDonald's	Buckhead Roadhouse
Papa John's	Blimpie Subs & Salads	Morrison's Cafeteria	Cafe Francais
Pizza Hut	Blue Cross Cafeteria	Mudpie Coffeehouse	Chili's Grill
Pizza Place	Buck's Pit Barbeque	Old Country Buffet	China Coast
Shapiro's	C. C. Loy's	Piccadilly Cafeteria	ChooChoo Diner
Soup Kitchen	Cafe Tazza	Pizza Place	ChooChoo Garden
Soup's On	Captain D's	Provident Cafeteria	ChooChoo Station
Southside Grill	Checkers	Radisson Coffee	Chop House
Steak Express	Chick-Fil-A	Rembrandt's	Cirrus Garden
Steak-Out	ChooChoo Espresso	Ryan's Family Steak	Clearwater
Steamboat	Chuck E Cheese's	S & S Cafeteria	Comfort Hotel Seasons
Vine St Market	Comfort Hotel Seasons	Shapiro's	Country Place
Yellow Submarine	Country Life Veg	Shoney's	Cracker Barrel
DRIVETHROUGH	Country Place	Shuford's Smokehouse	David's
Arby's Roast Beef	Dairy Queen	Soup Kitchen	Dockside
Armando's	Daryl's Sandwich Shop	Soup's On	Durty Nelly's
Back Yard Burgers	Dolphin Dan's Italian	Sportsman's BarBQ	Eidson
Buck's Pit Barbeque	Figgy's Sandwich Shop	Steamboat	El Cancun Mexican
Captain D's	Fix's	Subway	El Meson Mexicano
Central Park	Flatiron Deli	Taco Bell	Epicurean
Checkers	Glen-Gene Deli	Thai Food	Fehn Brothers
Dairy Queen	Golden Corral	Trip's Seafood	Fifth Quarter
J. R.'s Country	Golden Dragon	Vine St Market	Formosa
Kenny Rogers Roasters	Gondolier Italian	Warehouse Row Food	Gianni's Little Italy
KFC	Greek Roma Grill	Wendy's	Golden Dragon
Krystal	Home Folks	**TABLE SERVICE**	Grady's Goodtimes
McDonald's	In Good Taste	Applebee's	Gulas
Sonic Drive In	Kenny Rogers Roasters	Aris' Lakeshore	HRH Dumplin's
Taco Bell	KFC	Back Inn	Hy's Barbecue
Veg-Out	Kilroy's Coffeehouse	Baywatch Waterfront	Ichiban Japanese Steak
Wendy's	Krystal	Bea's	Imperial Garden
			In Good Taste

J. R.'s Country
Kanpai of Toyko
Karl's Family
La Cabriole
Las Margaritas
Le Doux's Bluff View
Loft
Longhorn Steaks
Los Reyes Mexican
Madhatters
Mandarin Garden
Margaret's
Marriott Ashley's
Marriott Terrace
Mom's Italian
Mozzarella's
Mt Vernon

Nikki's Drive Inn
Noodles
O'Charley's
Olive Garden Italian
Outback Steakhouse
Padrino's Mexican
Panda's Chinese
Peking
Pickle Barrel
Pizza Hut
Porker's BBQ
Radisson Bistro
Radisson Green Room
Red Lobster
Rib & Loin
Riverside Catfish
Roy Peppers Porch

Roy's Grill
Ruby Tuesday
Sandbar
Shoney's
Sneakers
Southside Grill
Sportsman's BarBQ
Steak & Ale
TGI Fridays
Town & Country
Trip's Seafood
Two Twelve Market
Uncle Bud's Catfish
Vine St Market
Vittles
Waffle House
Way It Was

Waycrazy's Bar-B-Que
Yellow Submarine

TAKEOUT ONLY

Back Yard Burgers
Central Park
ChooChoo BBQ
Fix's
Little Caesar's Pizza
Papa John's
Sonic Drive In
Steak Express
Steak-Out
Veg-Out

MEALS SERVED

BREAKFAST

Cafe Tazza
Chick-Fil-A
ChooChoo Garden
Comfort Hotel Seasons
Country Place
Cracker Barrel
Fix's
Flatiron Deli
Golden Corral
Gulas
J. R.'s
Just Delicious
Karl's Family
Kilroy's Coffeehouse
Krystal
Margaret's
Marriott Cafe Chat.
Marriott Terrace
Mary's Deli
McDonald's
Nikki's Drive Inn
Old Country Buffet
Provident Cafeteria
Radisson Bistro
Radisson Coffee
Rembrandt's
Roy's Grill
Shoney's
Vittles
Waffle House

BRUNCH

Back Inn
Big River Grille
Cafe Francais
O'Charley's
TGI Fridays

Two Twelve Market

LUNCH

Applebee's
Arby's Roast Beef
Armando's
Back Inn
Back Yard Burgers
Baywatch Waterfront
Bea's
Bennigan's
Big River Grille
Birdland
Blimpie Subs & Salads
Blue Cross Cafeteria
Brass Register
Buck's Pit Barbeque
Buckhead Roadhouse
C. C. Loy's
Cafe Francais
Captain D's
Central Park
Checkers
Chick-Fil-A
Chili's Grill
China Coast
ChooChoo BBQ
ChooChoo Garden
Chop House
Chuck E Cheese's
Cirrus Garden
Clearwater
Comfort Hotel Seasons
Country Life Veg
Country Place
Cracker Barrel
Dairy Queen
Daryl's Sandwich Shop
David's

Dockside
Dolphin Dan's Italian
Durty Nelly's
Eidson
El Cancun Mexican
El Meson
Epicurean
Fehn Brothers
Fifth Quarter
Figgy's Sandwich Shop
Fix's Sandwich Shop
Flatiron Deli
Formosa
Gianni's Little Italy
Glen-Gene Deli
Golden Corral
Golden Dragon
Gondolier Italian
Grady's Goodtimes
Greek Roma Grill
Gulas
Home Folks
Hot Sauce Charlie
HRH Dumplin's
Hy's Barbecue
Ichiban Japanese
Imperial Garden
In Good Taste
J. R.'s
Just Delicious
Kanpai of Toyko
Karl's Family
Kenny Rogers Roasters
KFC
Krystal
Las Margaritas
Le Doux's Bluff View
Little Caesar's Pizza

Loft
Longhorn Steaks
Los Reyes Mexican
Madhatters
Mandarin Garden
Margaret's
Marriott Terrace
Mary's Deli
McDonald's
Mom's Italian
Morrison's Cafeteria
Mozzarella's
Mt Vernon
Mudpie Coffeehouse
Nikki's Drive Inn
Noodles
O'Charley's
Old Country Buffet
Olive Garden Italian
Padrino's Mexican
Panda's Chinese
Papa John's
Peking
Piccadilly Cafeteria
Pickle Barrel
Pizza Hut
Pizza Place
Porker's BBQ
Provident Cafeteria
Radisson Bistro
Red Lobster
Rembrandt's
Rib & Loin
Riverside Catfish
Roy Peppers Porch
Roy's Grill
Ruby Tuesday
Ryan's Family Steak

S & S Cafeteria	Bennigan's	Gulas	Pickle Barrel
Sandbar	Big River Grille	Home Folks	Pizza Hut
Shapiro's	Birdland	Hot Sauce Charlie	Pizza Place
Shoney's	Blimpie Subs & Salads	Hy's Barbecue	Porker's BBQ
Shuford's Smokehouse	Brass Register	Ichiban Japanese Steak	Radisson Bistro
Sneakers	Buck's Pit Barbeque	Imperial Garden	Radisson Green Room
Sonic Drive In	Buckhead Roadhouse	In Good Taste	Red Lobster
Soup Kitchen	C. C. Loy's	Just Delicious	Rib & Loin
Soup's On	Cafe Francais	Kanpai of Toyko	Riverside Catfish
Southside Grill	Captain D's	Karl's Family	Roy Peppers Porch
Sportsman's BarBQ	Central Park	Kenny Rogers Roasters	Roy's Grill
Steak & Ale	Checkers	KFC	Ruby Tuesday
Steak-Out	Chick-Fil-A	Krystal	Ryan's Family Steak
Steamboat	Chili's Grill	La Cabriole	S & S Cafeteria
Subway	China Coast	Las Margaritas	Sandbar
Taco Bell	ChooChoo BBQ	Le Doux's Bluff View	Shoney's
TGI Fridays	ChooChoo Diner	Little Caesar's Pizza	Shuford's Smokehouse
Thai Food	ChooChoo Garden	Loft	Sneakers
Town & Country	ChooChoo Station	Longhorn Steaks	Sonic Drive In
Trip's Seafood	Chop House	Los Reyes Mexican	Southside Grill
Two Twelve Market	Chuck E Cheese's	Madhatters	Sportsman's BarBQ
Typhoon of Toyko	Cirrus Garden	Mandarin Garden	Steak & Ale
Uncle Bud's Catfish	Comfort Hotel Seasons	Marriott Ashley's	Steak Express
Veg-Out	Country Place	Marriott Kicks	Steak-Out
Vine St Market	Cracker Barrel	Marriott Terrace	Subway
Vittles	Dairy Queen	McDonald's	Taco Bell
Waffle House	David's	Mom's Italian	TGI Fridays
Warehouse Row Food	Dockside	Morrison's Cafeteria	Town & Country
Way It Was	Durty Nelly's	Mozzarella's	Trip's Seafood
Waycrazy's Bar-B-Que	Eidson	Mt Vernon	Two Twelve Market
Wendy's	El Cancun Mexican	Mudpie Coffeehouse	Typhoon of Toyko
Yellow Submarine	El Meson	Nikki's Drive Inn	Uncle Bud's Catfish
DINNER	Epicurean	Noodles	Vine St Market
Applebee's	Fehn Brothers	O'Charley's	Vittles
Arby's Roast Beef	Fifth Quarter	Old Country Buffet	Waffle House
Aris' Lakeshore	Formosa	Olive Garden Italian	Warehouse Row Food
Armando's	Gianni's Little Italy	Outback Steakhouse	Way It Was
Back Inn	Glen-Gene Deli	Padrino's Mexican	Waycrazy's Bar-B-Que
Back Yard Burgers	Golden Corral	Panda's Chinese	Wendy's
Baywatch Waterfront	Golden Dragon	Papa John's	Yellow Submarine
Bea's	Gondolier Italian	Peking	
	Grady's Goodtimes	Piccadilly Cafeteria	

FOOD AND OTHER FEATURES

ALCOHOL-NO	ChooChoo BBQ	Greek Roma Grill	La Cabriole
Arby's Roast Beef	Chuck E Cheese's	Home Folks	Little Caesar's Pizza
Armando's	Cirrus Garden	Hot Sauce Charlie	Margaret's
Back Yard Burgers	Country Life Veg	HRH Dumplin's	Mary's Deli
Bea's	Country Place	Hy's Barbecue	McDonald's
Blimpie Subs & Salads	Cracker Barrel	In Good Taste	Morrison's Cafeteria
Blue Cross Cafeteria	Dairy Queen	J. R.'s Country	Noodles
Buck's Pit Barbeque	Daryl's Sandwich Shop	Just Delicious	Old Country Buffet
Cafe Tazza	Dockside	Karl's Family	Panda's Chinese
Captain D's	Figgy's Sandwich Shop	Kenny Rogers Roasters	Papa John's
Central Park	Fix's Sandwich Shop	KFC	Piccadilly Cafeteria
Checkers	Flatiron Deli	Kilroy's Coffeehouse	Pizza Place
Chick-Fil-A	Golden Corral	Krystal	Provident Cafeteria

Radisson Coffee
Rembrandt's
Riverside Catfish
Roy's Grill
Ryan's Family Steak
S & S Cafeteria
Shoney's
Sonic Drive In
Soup Kitchen
Soup's On
Sportsman's BarBQ
Steak Express
Steak-Out
Steamboat
Subway
Taco Bell
Thai Food
Typhoon of Toyko
Veg-Out
Vittles
Waffle House
Warehouse Row Food
Waycrazy's Bar-B-Que
Wendy's

BAKERY
Dolphin Dan's Italian
Fehn Brothers
Fix's
HRH Dumplin's
In Good Taste

BAR
Applebee's
Aris' Lakeshore
Baywatch Waterfront
Bennigan's
Big River Grille
Birdland
Brass Register
Buckhead Roadhouse
Cafe Francais
ChooChoo Station
Chili's Grill
China Coast
Chop House
Clearwater
Comfort Hotel Seasons
David's
Durty Nelly's
El Cancun Mexican
El Meson Mexicano
Fifth Quarter
Gianni's Little Italy
Grady's Goodtimes
Kanpai of Toyko
Las Margaritas
Loft

Longhorn Steaks
Los Reyes Mexican
Mandarin Garden
Marriott Kicks
Mozzarella's
O'Charley's
Olive Garden Italian
Outback Steakhouse
Padrino's Mexican
Peking
Radisson Bistro
Radisson Green Room
Red Lobster
Roy Peppers Porch
Ruby Tuesday
Sandbar
Southside Grill
Steak & Ale
TGI Fridays
Town & Country
Two Twelve Market

BARBECUE
Buck's Pit Barbeque
ChooChoo BBQ
Hot Sauce Charlie
Hy's Barbecue
Porker's BBQ
Rib & Loin
Roy Peppers Porch
Shuford's Smokehouse
Sportsman's BarBQ
Waycrazy's Bar-B-Que

CATERING
Back Inn
Back Yard Burgers
Blimpie Subs & Salads
Buck's Pit Barbeque
Cafe Francais
ChooChoo BBQ
Country Place
Daryl's Sandwich Shop
Dolphin Dan's Italian
El Meson Mexicano
Gulas
Hot Sauce Charlie
HRH Dumplin's
Hy's Barbecue
In Good Taste
J. R.'s Country
Just Delicious
La Cabriole
Le Doux's Bluff View
Mary's Deli
Olive Garden Italian
Pickle Barrel
Porker's BBQ

Rib & Loin
Sandbar
Shapiro's
Shuford's Smokehouse
Soup's On
Southside Grill
Steamboat
Trip's Seafood
Two Twelve Market
Uncle Bud's Catfish
Vine St Market
Waycrazy's Bar-B-Que

CHINESE
China Coast
Formosa
Golden Dragon
Imperial Garden
Mandarin Garden
Panda's Chinese
Peking
Warehouse Row Food

COUNTRY
Bea's
Clearwater
Country Place
Cracker Barrel
Gulas
Home Folks
J. R.'s Country
Karl's Family
Morrison's Cafeteria
Old Country Buffet
Piccadilly Cafeteria
S & S Cafeteria
Veg-Out
Vittles

DELI/SAND/SOUP
Arby's Roast Beef
Blimpie Subs & Salads
C. C. Loy's
Daryl's Sandwich Shop
Dolphin Dan's Italian
Figgy's Sandwich Shop
Fix's Sandwich Shop
Flatiron Deli
Glen-Gene Deli
Mudpie Coffeehouse
Pickle Barrel
Shapiro's
Soup Kitchen
Soup's On
Steamboat
Subway
Vine St Market
Yellow Submarine

ENTERTAINMENT
Aris' Lakeshore
Birdland
Brass Register
Cafe Francais
Cafe Tazza
ChooChoo Station
Chuck E Cheese's
Clearwater
Durty Nelly's
El Meson Mexicano
Las Margaritas
Marriott Ashley's
Marriott Cafe Chat.
Marriott Kicks
Sandbar
Town & Country
Two Twelve Market

ESPRESSO
Cafe Tazza
ChooChoo Espresso
Kilroy's Coffeehouse
Marriott Cafe Chat.
Mudpie Coffeehouse
Radisson Coffee
Rembrandt's

FIREPLACE
Buckhead Roadhouse
Chop House
Cracker Barrel
Dockside
Loft
Steak & Ale

FRENCH
Cafe Francais
ChooChoo Diner
La Cabriole
Le Doux's Bluff View

GERMAN
Way It Was

GREEK
Epicurean
Greek Roma Grill

IRISH
Durty Nelly's

ITALIAN
Back Inn
Chuck E Cheese's
Dolphin Dan's Italian
Gianni's Little Italy
Gondolier Italian
Little Caesar's Pizza
Mom's Italian

Mozzarella's
Olive Garden Italian
Papa John's
Pizza Hut
Pizza Place
Warehouse Row Food

JAPANESE
Ichiban Japanese Steak
Kanpai of Toyko
Typhoon of Toyko

KID FRIENDLY
Back Yard Burgers
Baywatch Waterfront
Buck's Pit Barbeque
Buckhead Roadhouse
Captain D's
Central Park
ChooChoo Station
Checkers
Chick-Fil-A
Chili's Grill
China Coast
Chuck E Cheese's
Country Life Veg
Cracker Barrel
Dairy Queen
Dockside
El Cancun Mexican
El Meson Mexicano
Golden Corral
Gondolier Italian
Grady's Goodtimes
Home Folks
In Good Taste
Karl's Family
Kenny Rogers Roasters
KFC
Krystal
Las Margaritas
Little Caesar's Pizza
Loft
McDonald's
Morrison's Cafeteria
Mt Vernon
Mudpie Coffeehouse
O'Charley's
Old Country Buffet
Olive Garden Italian
Outback Steakhouse
Papa John's
Piccadilly Cafeteria
Pizza Hut
Red Lobster
Rib & Loin
Riverside Catfish

Roy Peppers Porch
Ryan's Family Steak
Shoney's
Sneakers
Sonic Drive In
Taco Bell
TGI Fridays
Town & Country
Trip's Seafood
Uncle Bud's Catfish
Vittles
Waffle House
Warehouse Row Food
Waycrazy's Bar-B-Que
Wendy's
Yellow Submarine

LATE NIGHT
Applebee's
Arby's Roast Beef
Bennigan's
Big River Grille
Birdland
Brass Register
Cafe Tazza
Captain D's
Central Park
Chili's Grill
Comfort Hotel 4th St
David's
Durty Nelly's
El Cancun Mexican
Krystal
Marriott Kicks
O'Charley's
Radisson Bistro
Roy Peppers Porch
Sandbar
Shoney's
Steak-Out
Taco Bell
Two Twelve Market
Waffle House

MEXICAN
El Cancun Mexican
El Meson Mexicano
Las Margaritas
Los Reyes Mexican
Padrino's Mexican
Taco Bell

OUTDOOR DINING
Back Inn
Baywatch Waterfront
Brass Register
C. C. Loy's
Cafe Tazza

Cirrus Garden
Comfort Hotel Seasons
David's
El Cancun Mexican
Flatiron Deli
Grady's Goodtimes
Kilroy's Coffeehouse
Las Margaritas
Mary's Deli
McDonald's
Mozzarella's
Mudpie Coffeehouse
Outback Steakhouse
Pickle Barrel
Radisson Bistro
Rembrandt's
Riverside Catfish
Ruby Tuesday
Sandbar
Shuford's Smokehouse
Southside Grill
TGI Fridays
Two Twelve Market

PRIVATE ROOMS
Bennigan's
Brass Register
Buck's Pit Barbeque
Buckhead Roadhouse
Country Place
David's
Eidson
El Cancun Mexican
Epicurean
Fehn Brothers
Fifth Quarter
Formosa
Golden Corral
Home Folks
Ichiban Japanese Steak
In Good Taste
J. R.'s Country
Karl's Family
La Cabriole
Loft
Mandarin Garden
Mt Vernon
Peking
Red Lobster
Roy Peppers Porch
Ryan's Family Steak
Town & Country
Trip's Seafood
Two Twelve Market
Uncle Bud's Catfish

SEAFOOD/FISH

Captain D's
Nikki's Drive Inn
Red Lobster
Riverside Catfish
Sandbar
Trip's Seafood
Uncle Bud's Catfish

SOUTHWEST
Chili's

STEAK
Fifth Quarter
Ichiban Japanese Steak
Loft
Longhorn Steaks
Outback Steakhouse
Radisson Green Room
Ryan's Family Steak
Steak & Ale
Steak Express
Steak-Out
Town & Country

THAI
Thai Food

VIEW
Aris' Lakeshore
Back Inn
Baywatch Waterfront
Blue Cross Cafeteria
Cirrus Garden
Dockside
Epicurean
Figgy's Sandwich Shop
La Cabriole
Le Doux's Bluff View
Madhatters
Marriott Cafe Chat.
Pickle Barrel
Provident Cafeteria
Rembrandt's
Riverside Catfish
Sandbar
Trip's Seafood

NOTE
Only specialty
restaurants were
categorized, all other
full-service restaurants
have a variety of beef,
chicken and fish and
serve a broad range of
American fare.

Applebee's Neighborhood Grill & Bar
875-8353, 356 Northgate Mall
499-1999, 2342 Shallowford Village Dr
Open daily lunch/dinner, $$

It's wood and brass and noise and bustle, like a neighborhood grill ought to be. Folks pile in after the softball game, after work, before the movie, between shopping and more shopping. The menu varies during the year, with lighter fare in the summertime and more hearty dishes when winter arrives. Typical winter specialties for stoking up are riblet platters, steaks marinated in Cajun spices, chilis and soups and a bacon-cheese-chicken grill; big apple-honey cobbler and apple-cheese-caramel crunch.

You can hang around the bar for gathering-time specials, or get a family booth over at the side. The one at Northgate is in the mall; eat and oversee the shoppers strolling by. Shallowford Village Grill is in the midst of other eateries and motels; right handy for tourists staying near Exit 5 who are looking for a backhome neighborhood atmosphere.

Aris' Lakeshore
877-7068, 5600 Lake Resort Terrace at Lakeshore complex
Open Mon-Sat, dinner, $$$

Just opening in January '95, it's a new venture in a location that's been around for years. Dinner only, six nights, a fairly simple menu of steaks and fish, and reasonable prices; they've started out fine and are staying very busy. Regulars who love the Lakeshore location are delighted to be back in that dining-by-the-lake setting; it's the only one of its kind in the city. If you've never been, picture this: three distinctive mountains in the distance, the nightlit downtown skyline tucked carefully in front, and just below, silver-moonlight water, a mile across.

Visitors to the city, head north on Hwy 153, cross the dam, exit right immediately to Access Road, left at the first light, go under the big bridge and follow Lake Resort Drive a mile or so to the big Lakeshore Restaurant sign, on your right. Up the hill and down and you're there; you won't get lost. There's a lake-view bar; music and dancing week nights and weekends.

Arby's Roast Beef Restaurant
894-7478, 5420 Brainerd Rd   *892-5984, 4766 Hwy 58*
899-6035, 2100 Hamilton Place Blvd   *866-5874, 2100 Lafayette Rd*
875-4048, 501 Northgate   *499-6332, 6302 Ringgold Rd*
870-5488, 3903 Hixson Pike   *899-2660, 7314 Shallowford Rd*
Open daily lunch/dinner, $

Kids and grownups love Arby's for those thinly-sliced piled-high-on-a-bun roast beef meals and odd-shaped little cakes of potatoes. Add some horsey sauce or Arby's own special, and you feel like you're eating out-of-the-ordinary. Chicken, ham and cheese sandwiches available too, in different combinations. The new stores are bright; service is fast.

Armando's

899-3705, 8018 E Brainerd Rd
629-9218, 1814 E Main
877-4495, 4509 Hixson Pike
842-0479, 7330 Hixson Pike

861-2252, 1105 Lafayette Rd
855-0772, 7032 Lee Hwy
622-1889, 4340 Ringgold Rd

Open Mon-Sat lunch/dinner, $

Each Armando's is individually owned and has an individual style -- but all sell burgers and like-minded stuff. Check the one nearest you when that's what you're looking for. Two are reviewed.

♦ **Armando's 4509 Hixson Pike**: There's a whole lotta frying going on in this 50's looking spot on Hixson Pike. The blue-white sign greets and directs you to "Place Your Order Here," and crowds line up to do just that, for taking out and for eating in. The friendly staff is busy hauling baskets of burgers and fries to customers seated in the 12 open, airy booths; they keep checking on you too, in table-service style. Get a shake, for goodness sake -- it comes piled with whipped cream, cherry-topped.

♦ **Armando's 7053 Hixson Pike**: Wander through the front room and down a corridor to place your order in this UT sportsy-looking place. Then they take good care of you, with table service and a smile. There's stuff from the grill, and ice-box pies. And that front room is a completely separate nonsmoking space, rare in smaller restaurants. Handy to Chester Frost Park, at the end of a day of fishing or riding around in the boat.

Back Inn Cafe

757-0108, 412 E 2nd
Open Mon-Sat lunch/dinner, Sun Brunch, $$$

Two outside decks give river views; have a glass of wine, or maybe minted tea. There's a sculpture garden across the street; perhaps you'll stroll over when you're finished. For now, you're just relaxing. Nice, isn't it?

Though heaters offer outdoor dining when it's chilly so you can stay near that view, the inside space has its appeal. This basement bistro in a 1920's home atop a bluff is bricked and cozy; local art adorns the walls. The smells of sauces, garlic, cheeses urge you to stay, and eat. Mama Mia, Pasta, Pizza; fill your body and your soul! More elegant dining upstairs in several rooms, a part of Bluff View B and B; just down the parking lot in Rembrandt's you can order coffee and dessert. Or stay right where you are, and watch the great blue herons flying at the river's edge.

Back Yard Burgers

499-0955, 2000 Gunbarrel Rd
Open daily lunch/dinner, $

Fast gourmet burgers are cooking here, in this almost-in-the-backyard corner near Wal-Mart. Fresh-ground meat and fancy combinations of mushrooms, cheddar, bacon and more are sided with chili or slaw and, if you like, tried-and-true fries or, for a kick, kiddie kool-aid. Specialties are charbroiled chicken salad and a great-in-the-summer BLT; top it all off with fresh baked cobbler and a scoop of ice cream. You can drive-thru or walk up and sit at the umbrella-topped picnic tables. Back Yard will come to your back yard too: they bring grills, staff, and a full menu to meet your catering needs.

Baywatch Waterfront Eatery & Bar
843-3100, 9718 Hixson Pike
Open Wed-Sun lunch/dinner, $$$
A deck on the main river channel? Yes! Relax at a big round table; during the day watch folks fishing; at night watch the harbor lights. Inside, a center-of-the-room bar has windows all around, perfect for an after-work or after-fishing unwind. There are plenty of pull-up spaces at the dock and Harbor Lights Marina is just behind on the slough. Perfect for Saturday lunch when you're out for an admire-the-dogwoods drive; perfect for Sunday evening supper, to bring the weekend to a fitting close. Sandwiches at lunchtime, including one catfish-style; in the evening order steaks, seafood, chicken or pasta; the dessert list is long. From Hwy 153, it's nine miles east on Hixson Pike; make a right at Harbor Lights Marina for this look-at-me-I'm-on-the-water spot.

Bea's Restaurant
867-3618, 4500 Dodds Avenue
Open Wed-Sun lunch/dinner, $ all-you-can-eat
It's been there more than 40 years, on Dodds near Rossville, at the bottom of the Ridge. Round tables offer get-acquainted seating -- the lazy Susan serving lets you dip and pass it on to someone else. There's no menu here, the table's set; fried chicken, mashed potatoes, beans and greens in home-cooked southern style. Season up with pepper sauce, hot sauce, ketchup -- all within your reach; then butter up your cornbread, and those great yeast rolls. Finish off with cobbler, and another glass of tea. The ladies waiting tables keep the bowls and platters filled and bring your check -- one price for all.

Bennigan's
899-5650, 5621 Brainerd Rd
Open daily lunch/dinner, $$$
The big square bar near the front door sets the mood in this darkish, upbeat, busy Brainerd place. In addition to the standards, drinks include Lynchburg lemonade, with the Jack Daniels touch, and non-alcohol bananaberry blast, filled with strawberries, bananas, and cream of coconut. Charleston chicken salad or Caesar shrimp are good for lunch, many sandwiches too; for dinner, great steaks or seafood can fill your needs. End it all with Death by Chocolate, a killer dessert! A separate room for parties up to 50.

Big River Grille
267-2739, 222 Broad St
Open daily lunch/dinner, $$$
The Big River is Chattanooga's first brew pub. Order the sampler; you get a small glass of each type that's brewed, set down before you on a paper mat

that tells what's what. This big bricked place is in the old bus barn, near the River, to be sure. The wide-open bar looks squarely at the brew-tanks; wooden half-walls section off some spots for quieter dining in the middle of it all.

They make sausage too -- spicy pork, lean lamb, apple pecan. Get a Trolley Sausage Platter or taste it teamed with okra in Big River Gumbo. You can order big Gulf shrimp battered in beer and coconut and fried; the spinach salad, bacon-topped, comes with chunks of apple, raisins, orange. Pasta, chicken, fish and ribs are hearty, tasty eating in this have-a-good-time place. The appetizer list is long; desserts include Big River Brownies, fresh-baked every day. Non-alcohol special drinks are homemade root beer, cream soda, or ginger ale.

Birdland Restaurant & Lounge
697-7484, 2510 E Main St
Open daily lunch/dinner/latenight, $$
Jazz, and more. Drop by for lunch. Open-faced sandwiches include the steak, pork loin, grilled chicken, and memories-of-home ham; there are sides of salads, including fruit; choose from chili, stew or soup of the day; top it with a treat-yourself-right apple pie. Drop by after work. Owner John McManus says he's "tried to create a place where people have a respite from our hurry-up way of living," and the intimate burgundy-rose setting has a comfortable feel. There's a spacious bar; note the clever and unusual art. The jazz is Live on Saturday Night; Mondays and Fridays too; listen to the all-jazz juke box other days.

Blimpie Subs and Salads
899-0160, 5746 Brainerd Rd   *499-8444, 6940 Lee Hwy*
877-0702, 5450 Hwy 153
Open daily lunch/dinner, $
You can watch while they slice fresh turkey, or ham, or whatever you choose to have stacked on the freshly baked Italian or whole wheat bread. There's a veggie pocket too, and tuna salad, and pickles, and saucer-size cookies for dessert. The place is bright and pleasant for staying a while; but if you want they'll fix your food to go and even make up trays of subs or cookies for your office meeting or at-home get-together.

Blue Cross Cafeteria
755-5969, 801 Pine St, 10th floor
Open Mon-Fri lunch, $
Go early enough to browse the latest display of art in the spacious lobby of this big bronzed-glass building; then ride the bubble elevator to the 10th floor for lunch. The cafeteria offers salads, soups, sandwiches, and a variety of hot entrees; desserts too; get your drinks and silverware and pick out a table by floor-to-ceiling window-walls with one of the finest views in town. Great skyline peeks over the city; a good, good value for the money. Visitors

staying downtown, you might want to take advantage of this not-visible-from-the-street luncheon spot.

Brass Register
265-2175, 618 Georgia Ave
Open Mon-Sat lunch/dinner, $$$
It's been compared to "Cheers," and surely there are those whom everybody knows by name; regulars come for weekday lunches, happy hours, and evening music weekdays and weekends. The has-a-history cash register is brass (ask them about it), the worn-out wooden floor well trod. This downtown favorite fronts Georgia Avenue with outdoor dining too when weather's good. The appetizer menu lets you choose from famous fried mushrooms, buttered potato skins, spicy hot peppers; the big menu offers steaks and burgers and homemade soups. Plan your party here, there's room for sit-down.

Buckhead Roadhouse
894-9700, 7015 Shallowford Rd
Open daily lunch/dinner, $$$
No kidding, the top of the menu reads "If you hit it or hook it we'll smoke it or cook it," and you can order a Redneck Margarita as soon as you sit down. But it has a classy hunting-lodge look about it, with beautiful oversized dark furniture, a huge stone fireplace, and the obligatory mounted deerhead. The aroma of barbecue and smoked beef surrounds you; go ahead and enjoy; there's an assortment of lighter pastas and fish dishes too. And the most delicate lemon custard cake you'll find anywhere, topped with fresh, sweet strawberries.

They serve espresso and cappuccino; there's a nice bar; and there's upper-loft-area seating too. It's not too noisy, even though there is a juke box by the door; it's not too quiet, fine for kids of just about any age; you're almost guaranteed that even the stodgiest will have a good time here.

Buck's Pit Barbeque Restaurant
866-2204, 345 Battlefield Pkwy, Ft Oglethorpe
*267-1390, 3146 Broad St ***
Open daily lunch/dinner, $$
*Five-year-old Jason wanted a burger, but the smoky smell wafting all the way to the street and into our car from Buck's gave this never-eaten-barbecue boy a hankering to stop, quick. "We'll get a picnic," he said to me, "and eat it when we get to the duck pond." Inside, in line to order, he tugged my hand. "Can we eat here? Puh-lease!" The log cabin with its wooden stairway had his eye.

A table at the top of the stairs, a first barbecue sandwich for a little boy. He ate it all, smiling while he chewed. You will too! Get a plate of ribs, or a sandwich platter, with a slew of sides. Try the Brunswick stew, and lemonade. It's too good not to go; and handy to all the Lookout Mountain tourist stuff. The Buck's in Ft Oglethorpe is close to the Battlefield attractions, though there's no log cabin there.

Cafe Français
267-7411, 1265 Market St
Open daily, lunch/dinner, Sun brunch, $$$
It snowed during the February '95 opening week, as if a restaurant grand opening weren't challenging enough in itself. Nevertheless, the balloons were flying out front, and the pianist came in on Saturday night. Next to Mom's Italian and Porkers Uptown, the opening of Cafe Français is quickly transporting the 1200 block of Market Street into a concentrated eclectic dining destination. This new spot has two rooms; red-checked tables and a counter filled with fresh French bread for lunchtime; an elegant softly-carpeted-grand-pianoed room for dinner, and for Sunday brunch. The snow has melted by now, you'll want to go see. Parking available behind the building.

Cafe Tazza
265-3032, 1010 Market St
Open Mon-Fri 7AM-midnight; Sat-Sun 2PM-midnight, $
This big little spot has been drawing coffee lovers and coffee converts in droves since it opened in the former lobby of the Park Plaza Hotel a year or so ago. Bagels and pastries are good, but not the star. It's coffee, cappuccino, latte, mocha, macchiato; gourmet brews to test your senses, make you want to linger, talk, or read. Used books are stacked along the back hall wall; out front, musicians gather on the sidewalk after dark. Tazza is a central downtown place, next to Miller Park.

Owners Orin Kilgore and sister Amy will explain the different blends if they're new to you; they'll also sell you beans to take home. They have studied at the master's knee -- checking out Seattle, the bastion of coffeedom, and other coffee towns before opening Chattanooga's first real coffeehouse.

Captain D's
861-4592, 309 Battlefield Pkwy	*855-5178, 2008 Gunbarrel Rd*
698-1518, 3821 Brainerd Rd	*870-4601, 5106 Hixson Pike*
877-1227, 3510 Dayton Blvd	*892-3896, 5001 Oakhill Rd*
629-1352, 1690 E 23rd	*266-1129, 3614 Tennessee Ave*

Open daily lunch/dinner, $
Seafood: get it fried or get it broiled in heart-smart style. Rice, green beans and salads are on the low-cal side; of course there are hush puppies and fries if you go for the traditional fish-fry stuff. Several good desserts including ice-box lemon pie. This family place has lower prices for seniors on Wednesdays; Thursdays kids under 10 eat free.

Inspectors and reviewers for Chattanooga Great Places *accept no free meals or favors; the book has no sponsors or advertisers.*

C. C. Loy's Sandwiches & Sweets, Etc.
266-2362, 141 N Market St
Open Mon-Sat lunch/dinner, $
The plants are dead and the juke box is out of order. Magazines are rowed up on the counter and everything's a-clutter. But folks line up to order Polish-on-a-bun and a Coke float or chicken-on-wheat with a cherry Canadian to eat out on the latticed porch or maybe scrunched in a wooden booth inside. On North Market in the Town and Country Shopping Center, it basks in good location.

The soup and sandwich counter is only half the draw; sweets fill the other side of the store. Fine chocolates packaged in ornate and lovely tins, cards and other gifts are there to choose. Buy your mother a present here.

Central Park
629-9356, 3604 Brainerd Rd
875-6113, 3601 Dayton Blvd
624-5449, 2401 E 23rd
892-5617, 7910 E Brainerd Rd
875-0283, 5119 Hixson Pike
894-0174, 4631 Hwy 58
866-6329, 318 Lafayette Rd
894-0476, 6301 Ringgold Rd
867-1981, 4190 Rossville Blvd
855-3957, 6009 Shallowford Rd
490-0680, 7308 Shallowford Rd
Open daily, lunch/dinner, $
Take your big-ole-bubba hay-baling appetite to Central Park for a driveup and driveout bag of big burgers and spicy fries. Those tiny lights around the green and yellow signs are blinking all over town; close enough to relieve your hungries within minutes. The only-slightly-hungry are welcome too.

Chattanooga ChooChoo Holiday Inn Restaurants
266-5000, 1400 Market St, Holiday Inn Downtown
A variety of unusual food services in the ChooChoo complex, all designed to take full advantage of the historical nature of the terminal and the warehouses used in the time of the trains.

Cafe Espresso
♦ *Open daily, all day, $*
♦ Next to the gift shop, you can pop in here for gourmet coffee, bottled waters or a snack for your sweet tooth, such as cappuccino torte or Bourbon Street pecan pie.

Dinner in the Diner
♦ *Open daily, dinner, $$$$*
♦ Just as the name implies, you board an honest-to-goodness authentic dining car for a romance-of-the-rails meal. Make your reservation in advance at the main lobby desk. Not many opportunities like this left in the US, especially with such grand Victorian ambiance. Your car doesn't leave the complex, but it's a fine journey, nonetheless. Plan on this for a special treat, when you're looking for attention and a little adventure.

Gardens Restaurant

♦ *Open daily breakfast/lunch/dinner, $$*

♦ Go back in time. Nothing could be finer than the trip to Carolina you're about to take; you just got your ticket in the terminal under a dome soaring 85 feet over your head; now you're hurrying towards the tracks, ready to board. Halfway in between, where the baggage handling used to happen, is the Gardens Restaurant today. Enclosed and latticed, garden-like with plants, food is served here all day long. Go for the reminiscing, at the very least. This is a very historic place.

Station House

♦ *Open Mon-Sat, dinner, $$$*

♦ Entertainment here, courtesy of your waitstaff. They bring your drinks, take your order, and take your request. Look up on the stage! There's your waitperson, mike in hand, belting out country-rock-pop, apron hanging on a nail. Apron back on, presto-chango, and here they are with your prime rib and a smile. Tell them how great they are; it's easy to see they're having fun; they do their best to make sure you do too. This railroad-warehouse-turned-restaurant has an interesting decor; gilt-framed portraits of long-skirted-and-parasoled ladies hang on the old-brick walls; wooden tables and chairs are positioned so everyone has a good view of the stage. Kids really like the informal happy atmosphere in here; let staff know if there's a birthday at your table; you-know-what will happen.

Victorian Lounge

♦ *Open daily*

♦ Just off the grand dome lobby; cocktails at the bar or in a cozy chair under huge old-fashioned brass chandeliers.

Checkers

870-3638, 5200 Hwy 153
622-7120, 4348 Ringgold Rd
Open daily lunch/dinner, $

American flags are flapping in the breeze, waving you to the double drive-through windows beside the bright red posts. Stop and place an order at the speaker phone. Drive home with a bag of burgers, shakes, or hotdogs, chili-filled. Seasoned fries are so, so good! This is a sleek little place, checkered black and white, with a few inside stools and outside picnic tables.

Chick-Fil-A

894-6368, Eastgate Mall
894-3181, Hamilton Place Mall
875-4771, Northgate Mall
Open Mon-Sat, breakfast/lunch/dinner, $

Try the little sample-on-a-toothpick and you're hooked. The chicken, pressure-cooked in peanut oil, then marinated and grilled, is almost free of fat, but full of flavor. Daily-from-scratch fresh salads and cole slaw; fresh-squeezed lemonade and fresh-brewed iced tea; lemon meringue pie; good prices in these handy mall-stops. They'll do party trays to order.

Chili's Grill and Bar
855-0376, 5637 Brainerd Rd
Open daily lunch/dinner, $$$

The volume is always set on high in this busy Brainerd place, so if you're feeding noisy kids or just want to party, come on in. The near-the-front-door bar is set off from the dining area; this makes for private spots. Southwest terra cotta and sunwashed green backdrop plant-filled baskets everywhere; your table, ceramic-tiled, is soon set up with quesadillas or tostada chips.

They've got good salads -- southwest with guacamole, or smoked chicken Frisco style. Main meal fare from the grill runs to steak, chicken and fish, plus a variety of burgers. The low-fat guiltless gives you broiled chicken several ways, a veggie pasta too. They're famous here for Awesome Blossom -- an onion sliced into a flower and fried. Yogurt smoothies are worth a trip; try, at least, the piña chilada. A kiddie menu too.

China Coast
954-1041, 2200 Bams Dr
Open daily lunch/dinner, $$$

It's huge but intimate. From the "Nin Hau Ma?" greeting at the front door to the Jing Jing platter, you get a welcome-home feeling, true southern-hospitality style. Drink your hot tea, learn to eat with your kwai dz, admire the gorgeous jade jars and the fiery dragons. Snuggle in your cozy space. How can it seat 325? The pretty little rooms are here, there, everywhere.

Try one of the regional specialties: from Peking and the north, Beef and Scallops in Oyster Sauce -- marinated steak, sea scallops and fresh broccoli; from Szechuan and the west, Sea, Wind and Fire -- shrimp, scallops and chicken stir-fried with broccoli, mushrooms and baby corn; from Canton and the south, Hong Kong Steak -- chargrilled, sliced and topped with peppercorn sauce. Get the children Dragon Bones (BBQ ribs) or Chinese Chicken Nuggets with sweet and sour sauce to dip. Their meals include the Jing Jing platter too -- that's egg roll, bread, vegetable munchies and crispy Chinese noodles. It's bottomless, refilled as often as you want. Two items worthy of note: they use no MSG in anything they prepare, and unlike most Chinese restaurants, they have an awesome selection of desserts, such as Great Wall of Chocolate and Double Happiness Cheesecake. "Xie xie ni for coming," you'll hear as you leave.

ChooChoo BBQ
622-1802, 2612 Amnicola Hwy
892-5572, 7968 E Brainerd Rd
Open daily, lunch/dinner, $

Stop by the little red caboose and get a hearty BBQ plate to take home for supper. Two friends own these two quickstop places. Their specials offer large portions and big tall drinks; also good for hard-working folks looking for a fill-me-up lunch. A few picnic tables by the road.

The Chop House
892-1222, 2011 Gunbarrel Rd
Open daily lunch/dinner, $$$
The Chop House, believe it or not, is a restaurant specializing in chops. Big hunks of meat like a 20-ounce T-bone, a 16-ounce prime rib, a 14-ounce pork chop. You can get them with an Idaho baked or a Big Orange potato (that's a yam). Smoky Mountain barbecue ribs come with Kentucky baked beans and spiced applesauce; the tenderest pork tenderloin you'll ever eat is served with cornbread dressing.

There's a good-sized bar, and you'll probably wind up waiting in it, although they do handle call-ahead seating. The crowds are coming fast to this noisy striped-awning eatery; coolers near the door display the big, thick chops; you can feel the purpose in the air: let's get some food. Start with a bucket of beer or a blackberry juice and a plate of colossal onion rings. Lighter eaters, order hickory smoked chicken salad or the catch of the day, grilled.

Chuck E Cheese's Pizza
870-3215, 22 Northgate Park
Open daily, lunch/dinner, $$
Grownups, do you ever have problems eating out with kids? Do they get fidgety before you're done? Go to Chuck E Cheese's and everyone can be happy! The pizza is good plus there's all-you-can eat salad and keep-on-filling drinks. And this non-smoking, non-alcohol place puts the premium on family entertainment. Claim a booth on the high side and the kids will eat while charmed with the robotics show; there are dancing critters and strumming banjos; then a switch to TV graphics in a fast-move mode. Two-year-old Justin forgot what he was doing and ate four pieces of pizza, his little blond head bobbing in time to the music.

After eating, start the token dole. You get some with your food, and it's worth the fun to buy more. Give the little ones a few at a time and they can play while you relax. There are kiddie rides for the smaller ones and skill games for the older crew. Prizes are tickets, and tickets can be swapped for hundreds of items such as neon-orange pencils, creepy-black-plastic spider rings, or scary, clawy, fake red nails. The crawl-through-the-balls toy house handles high-energy needs. Chuck E, a six-foot gray mouse wearing hat and tie, walks around dispensing hugs and handshakes to delighted kids.

If you're on vacation and the kids can't sit in the car another minute, pull off the freeway and head north on Hwy 153 for Chuck E's. If you're babysitting grandkids and your place is small, if it's family night at your house, or if you want a fresh, inexpensive salad bar in a clean and friendly place, come to Chuck E's. It's fun.

You'll find restaurants indexed by neighborhood and by cuisine at the beginning of this chapter.

Cirrus Garden Cafe
396-3717, 9413 Apison Pike
Open Mon-Fri lunch/dinner; Sat dinner, $$$
Need a little pampering? Drive out to Cirrus Garden Cafe, located at the foot of beautiful White Oak Mountain in Collegedale. No, no, no, it's not too far; if you're on the Georgia or Tennessee side of the line, on Lookout or Signal Mountain, north of the lake or squarely downtown; wherever you are, make the drive; you'll see. There's a garden patio for fine mountain-gazing, but inside is garden-like too; it's furnished patio style with glass-topped tables; a fountain bubbles peacefully; vases lavishly stuffed with armloads of lilies and lilacs are placed just where the eye needs them to be. You get a sense of abundance in this wide-windowed place; there's enough space, enough time, enough attention, and, you'll soon discover, wonderful food.

It's fairly new, so the menu may adjust again; but count on such items as salmon in dill sauce, tournedos of beef, and carefully prepared veal and chicken dishes. There's a truly fine selection of pastas; mushroom-lovers can get stirfry with lots of shittake mushrooms or fresh oyster mushrooms sautéed with leeks and baby carrots. The recipe for the raspberry-purée-topped cheesecake is a carefully guarded secret; not New York style, it's a Cirrus special, delicately done. Your drinks are virgin, mocktails such as the Shaved Navel, Jamaican cola, or not-so-Innocent Passion, built at the big bar where they put the lime in the coconut.

Cirrus accepts reservations and there's plenty of parking available. Locals and visitors, seek out this fine new place. Going north on I-75, exit 7A towards Collegedale; it's about two miles to the stop sign; hang right on Apison Pike; another two miles to the traffic light; watch for Cirrus in the white building on the left; you'll also find Liesl's gorgeous flower-gift-garden shop, the Cirrus flower-supplier.

Clearwater Cafe
266-0601, 1301 Chestnut St
Open Mon-Fri lunch, $
Named after that city in Florida, the owner has decked his land-bound restaurant with fishing memories; there's a marlin on the wall and hats and lures behind the bar; the focus, however, is today's lunch: meat and three at a good price with a Monday-Friday daily special -- fried chicken, pot roast, meatloaf, turkey and dressing, fish; the menu has sandwiches too. Service is fast in this classy-informal stained-wood-and-dark-green place with the straight-back wooden chairs. Wednesday and Friday, come at 6 for the music; a small group in a comfortable setting; great after-work camaraderie going on.

Practically in the back door of the TVA office complex, it's handy for downtown workers and visitors. Off-the-beaten-path by just a block, look for Ken Garner Mfg., Coker Tire, and Chattanooga Electric Supply nearby; Chattanooga Photoengraving is just around the corner. Plenty of parking.

Comfort Hotel Restaurants
266-7808, 407 Chestnut Street
Seasons Restaurant
♦ *Open daily, breakfast/lunch/dinner, $$$*
♦ Seasons is a spacious, pleasant dining room off the main lobby of the hotel. It's certainly handy if you're staying there, but even if you're not, you might want to give it a try. Near the Creative Discovery and Regional History Museums you might be touring, and handy for folks who occupy the downtown office buildings each day, it offers buffet and menu service at breakfast, lunch and dinnertime.
4th Street Cafe
♦ *Open daily, afternoon/late evening*
♦ Lounge area off the lobby; can order food here from Seasons menu.

Country Life Natural Foods & Vegetarian Restaurant
622-2451, 3748 Ringgold Rd
Buffet open Sun-Thu, lunch, $
A place with taste! Maybe you want the low-fat, no-cholesterol lifestyle, but fear you'll have to give up taste. Here's a deal for you: in a neat shopping-center restaurant on Ringgold Road you'll find a daily buffet salad bar that offers 25 fruit and vegetable choices, two entrees, two vegetables, long-grain rice and beans. You won't find any animal products, however, in anything. Try herbed tofu cream cheese, tabouli salad, eggplant Mediterranean style, hearty corn soup and fresh baked rolls; for dessert there's non-dairy rice cream, vanilla flavored, with four toppings to choose from.

It's relaxing here; this restaurant-in-a-store looks like a garden oasis tucked in the middle of the shopping aisles; classical music plays softly while a table of businessmen talk business over there; a baby smiles from his stroller in a two-kids-family group; a jogging-suited grandma and granddaughter pop in for a bowl of soup; a pregnant lady enjoys a cup of herbal tea.

Many aisles to browse-and-buy as you leave; this is one of the most complete health-food stores in town with cooler, frozen and bulk foods, vitamins and herbs; they sell cookbooks, health books and small appliances such as breadmakers and juicers; knowledgeable staff available to answer questions.

Country Place Restaurant
875-0741, 5025 Dayton Blvd
855-1392, 7320 Shallowford Rd
Open daily, breakfast/lunch/dinner, $$
Local folks like to gather at the Dayton Boulevard Country Place; it's been in operation for 18 years and is family owned and operated. The newer spot on Shallowford is a gathering place too, for hungry tourists staying in the Exit 5 motels or shoppers headed for Hamilton Place. You'll find true southern cooking here, such as chicken tenders, country-style steak, and lots and lots of vegetables. The Shallowford place has a covered drive-up-to-the-door entry

for rainy days; inside, cozy country wallpaper cheers the room and a cute model train rides the rails above your head. Buffets are available at handy times, such as Saturday morning breakfast and Sunday after church. Large private rooms can be reserved.

Cracker Barrel Old Country Store
825-5885, 50 Birmingham Hwy, I-24 Exit 174
899-5729, 1460 Mack Smith Rd, I-75 Exit 1
892-0977, 2346 Shallowford Village Dr, I-75 Exit 5*
Open daily, breakfast/lunch/dinner, $$
*Is it a restaurant or is it a store? It's both, in splendid form. You don't even mind a wait because browsing hooks you, fast. There are games and gifts and decorating things, plus foods already packaged to take home -- Vidalia onion relish, chocolates, hams, jars of jellies and preserves. The big stone fireplace blazes away winter chills as you get seated in the straight-backed wooden chairs. This place is proudly southern style; but foods are brought from everywhere to serve the best that can be found, like Florida for fresh-squeezed orange juice, the Northwest for strawberries, blackberries, and grapes for the preserves. Sorghum molasses come from Tennessee; Kentucky cures the hams.

Breakfast is all day, every day; a sampler plate gets you eggs, grits, gravy, fried apples, hash brown casserole, country ham, smoked sausage, bacon, and biscuits with butter and jam! Dinner items are farm-raised catfish, roast beef, chicken n' dumplins, pork chops, and barbecue, to name a few. Vegetables are plenteous, or just get beans n' greens served with onion, relish and corn muffins. Maybe you'd prefer a rib-eye steak. If you still can eat more, they'll bring you bread pudding, or apple pie. If you don't already love country food, you'll get converted here. Headquartered in Lebanon, Tennessee, this chain has spread to 22 states.

Dairy Queen
866-2253, 204 Battlefield Pkwy   *756-2834, 1002 McCallie Ave*
877-2253, 5433 Hwy 153
Open daily, lunch/dinner, $
The queen of the soft-cream cone has expanded its menu considerably over the years; you can still get the butterscotch sundae with nuts and whipped cream, but now there's a range of frosty treats, such as tall-cup blizzards mixed with heath bars or chunky fruit. They have hot dogs, burgers and chicken for a full-meal stop. Need a pretty, tasty ice-cream birthday cake? Get it here.

Daryl's Sandwich Shop
267-6819, 9 W 8th
Open Mon-Fri, lunch, $
Daryl gives fair warning: try it once and you'll be hooked for lunch. His favorite is ham and bacon and swiss, served up with lettuce and mayo on a

steamed hoagie bun. Croissants and pitas are choices you can make; salads too, including a waist watcher with sliced tomato and cucumber. Enter from 8th, or Market, or the Chattanooga Bank Building lobby, order at the counter, then take a table in this longish room done up in pink. Great catering for office parties and business meetings; meat, salad, sandwich or dessert travs as well as bag lunches.

David's Restaurant
267-6418, 422 Vine St
Open daily, lunch/dinner, $$
Go to David's for pizza and cheer. If there's a college hangout in town, this is it. David's has a worn and comfy look, familiar like a favorite chair; good for students away from home. The air is juicy with conversation, students and profs; it's good here before the game, or after the term paper has been turned in. Kind of dark and roomy, it has a big bar, big-screen tv's, video games and green-striped awnings, inside, for effect. Awnings are outside too, where wrought-iron fences keep the street away from stone-paved patios, filled with folks from David's on those hot and muggy have-a-cool-beer days; in winter months you'll find Kilroy's coffee drinkers from next door, enjoying fresh air and a late-day latte.

Dockside Restaurant
332-4098, 1145 Poling Circle, Pine Harbor Marina, Soddy
Open Wed-Sun, lunch/ dinner, $$$
Sitting near the dock on the bay of Soddy Creek, this restaurant-for-boaters is for downtowners too; after a scenic drive north on Hwy 27, it's just a mile out Hixson Pike and left at the shrimpboat by car; by boat, it's Mile Marker 487.5. Easy to find, it is a find, set among tall, swaying pines, waterside, with a porch bench inviting you to stay. Inside it's nautical red, white and blue; fishing nets and oars are strung about; lots of windows overlook the boats out on the lake; it feels like summertime all the time; a stone fireplace keeps you warm in winter months. Sandwiches and burgers and salads for lunch; evening meals are chicken, steak and fish; for dessert derby or apple pie. This place posts their Health Department ratings for all the world to see -- a clue, my friends, that it's spic and span. The Marina has 200 slips and a ships store; everything's open year round.

Dolphin Dan's Italian Deli
877-4007, 4812 Hixson Pike
Open Mon-Fri lunch, $$
You almost don't notice it on busy Hixson Pike. Slow down! Dan, the owners' son, is a Dolphins fan from Florida; hence the name. Marilyn Pye, the owner/chef, knows her Italian stuff, apprenticing in Italy after growing up on Mediterranean cuisine. The menu varies day-to-day. There may be bow-tie pasta in white wine clam sauce topped with chicken, or tri-colored tortellini with scampi. Maybe tomato basil pie, spaghetti with meat sauce, chicken Français, spinach ravioli with gorgonzola cheese. You order at the

counter; the small dining space is pleasant, forest green and white. Go in for lunch; take home a loaf of pepperoni bread. They do weddings, parties, a Lovers Basket for Two. Do you know someone who's ill? Order a Hospital Stay Basket, made up to please. Their desserts are legend -- chocolate mousse pie with Grand Marnier, tiramisu, eclairs, Kahlua cream cakes covered with whipped cream. And if you do nothing else this year, have the carrot cake.

Durty Nelly's
265-9970, 109 N Market St
Open Mon-Sat lunch/dinner, $$
An Irish Pub specializing in chili? Well, yes. Patterned after the original Durty Nelly's in County Clare, this place puts its unique twist to the luck of the Irish with chilis like Nelly's Wild, O'Flaherty's White, and Dublin Market Vegetable. Other things follow tradition: the decor is green and the noise level is pleasantly rowdy; Irish tunes are going and there's a broad range of beers at the bar -- in fact, they claim the most complete selection of imported beers in town. Favorite snacks are the Durty Fries, and the Nacho Colosso, loaded down with cheeses and, of course, Wild Irish Chili. Get a Durty Burger, Durty Chicken, or if you're not too hungry, the Shannon, a meal-of-goodies salad.

Of course you'll come for the St Paddy's Day party, but don't miss the Halfway-to-St-Patrick's-Day one that's just as much fun in September. If your sense of humor has been taking a beating, drop in at Durty's and start smiling again. This is a major after-work gathering spot; very busy on weekends too, when it's open late-night.

Eidson Restaurant
867-1742, 5308 Ringgold Rd
Open Mon-Sat lunch/dinner, $$
Fried green tomatoes, sugar-cured ham, and just-browned-at-the-edges baked yams are a few of the standards that have kept folks coming to the Eidson for over 40 years. It's a popular spot, a white-shuttered brick building that feels friendly and comfortable and kind of homey; the menu offers a wide selection of southern-style favorites and very good desserts. Rooms can be reserved for your own private gathering.

El Cancun Mexican Restaurant & Cantina
266-1461, 1809 Broad Street   *499-8181, 4762 Hwy 58*
875-9785, 5307 Hwy 153 *   *894-1942, 7010 Lee Hwy*
Open daily, lunch/dinner, $$
*The waiters look crisp in their white shirts and black pants, and they move so fast, you soon are settled in with your bowl of munchy chips and whatever you like to drink. Not too long after you've placed your order, your plate is set in front of you with a warning: Hot, very hot! Fajitas are especialidades at Cancun; marinated chicken, beef or shrimp sizzled with onions and peppers; steaks come in several flavors -- with hot sauce or without. Hearty Chile

Colorado is served with rice and beans; there are vegetarian combos and plates for children too. Express lunches include the tostaguac. Lively colored piñatas, swinging overhead, invoke a happy mood. Linger, if you like.

El Mesón Restaurante Mexicano
267-6544, 3210 Broad St
894-8726, 2204 Hamilton Place Blvd*
Open daily lunch/dinner, $$
*The restaurant at Hamilton Place is big, big, big, and the menu is too. Besides the standard chicken and beef, fajitas even come in catfish style! Pedro Munoz, the owner, guarantees your satisfaction; chips, tortillas and salsas are homemade and fresh every day; the cantina is well-stocked; one of the dishes is even Mama's recipe: red snapper grilled over mesquite and covered with Mama's Veracruz sauce.

It's pretty here, stuccoed and tiled in old-mission style; the interior courtyard is nicely fountained; brick walls backdrop portraits of dancing cabaleros wooing lovely senoritas; dark wooden booths add to the Spanish look. Service is prompt and friendly; there's a full bar, a tortilleria bar, and live mariachi on Thursday nights. Order ahead by fax if you're in a hurry; they'll even deliver; catering is available too.

Epicurean
622-4139, 4301 Ringgold Rd
Open Mon-Sat lunch/dinner, $$$
Go just to admire the gorgeous mural of the hills of Athens on the restaurant's rear wall. Dream of travel, and far-away places. Order layered moussaka, lasagna or a gyro plate. They bring you tiropetakia for starters, flaky cheese rolls you will love. Or you can order steak or lobster, lamb chops Epicurean or chicken parmesan, or the specials of the day. Honeyed baklava for dessert, or sherry peaches supreme. It's been on Ringgold Road for umpteen years, and has a devoted following. Rooms for parties too.

Fehn Brothers Restaurant
877-1615, 5435 Hwy 153
Open Tue-Sat lunch/dinner, $$
They moved from a prime waterfront location across the river from the Hunter to a parking lot near a cemetery in Hixson. It didn't faze anyone -- the Friday night lines are as long as ever with folks who can't wait to get in for clam chowder and macaroon pie. Fehn's is one of the most beloved names in Chattanooga dining. Today's location has a contemporary look, soft in mauves and blues. And the menu is still packed with seafoods and steaks, numerous chicken dishes, and a good variety of vegetables. The bakery makes and packages breads and rolls for you to take home too; stock up.

For an explanation of price ranges,
see "How to Use This Book."

Fifth Quarter Restaurant
899-0181, 5501 Brainerd Rd
Open daily lunch/dinner, $$$
One of the biggest and most complete salad bars in town waits for you at the Fifth Quarter. Don't keep it waiting too long, and while you're there go for the specialty -- a sumptuous hunk of prime rib, done just the way you want it. This busy restaurant on busy Brainerd Road has been keeping folks happy for over twelve years with nicely prepared steaks, chicken and vegetables, good service, and a well-stocked bar. Lots of cozy, quiet booths for sitting and talking a while; private rooms and kids' menu too.

Figgy's Sandwich Shop
266-8675, 20 W 8th
Open Mon-Fri lunch, $
Soup's on every day at Figgy's; creamy broccoli or potato, chicken noodle, vegetable, and on Thursday, tasty Wisconsin cheese. Are you a little hungry, or a lot? Add roast beef on an onion roll, or turkey on whole wheat. How about chicken, tuna, or pasta salad? You'll know if they're baking brownies while you're there. Grab a table near the front door and enjoy the 8th Street buildings view; the modern Blue Cross bronze provides a backdrop for the historic James. Wisteria surrounds; a wisp of a bloom on every table; vines are painted on the wall, climbing to the second floor. From the balcony tables you look down on the muraled wall below: lavender mountains, trees the softest green. You can't have a bad afternoon after lunch at Figgy's.

Fix's Old-Fashioned Bakery and Sandwich Shop
756-3497, 850 Market St
Open Mon-Fri breakfast/lunch, $
Stop by this little shop for a filled coffee ring when it's your turn to treat the office. Or stop for breakfast, or lunch, any weekday. Get a turkey sandwich, fresh-made, to eat outside in Miller Plaza; pick up bread for tonight's dinner, stuffed with chicken salad or spinach and cheese. It's a wonderland at Christmas: fruitcakes from Tennessee whiskey to southern-style amaretto; cookie tins filled with spicy pfeffernuesse; cranberry, banana and pumpkin breads; great-for-gifts stollen, filled with raisins, apricots and pecans. Gingerbread houses come in two sizes -- the larger one with a tub of icing and candies for a perfect at-home project with the kids.

The owners are two northern transplants who chose Chattanooga for its warmth -- both kinds. Stop in to say hello; you'll probably wind up taking home a chocolate-raspberry-truffle torte. Gift baskets are available too.

Flatiron Deli
266-2620, 706 Walnut St
Open Mon-Fri breakfast/lunch, $
Some places put a lot of effort into being charming; some are charming because they didn't try to be. The Flatiron's charm is 100% natural. Near the

courthouse, this smallish triangular building was constructed in the early 1900's and has been apartment, retail, and office. A replica of the famous New York City structure, it once boasted a 60-foot electronic Coca-Cola sign along its side. Just down the street, in 1899, the first Coke was bottled.

Go in today and eat, surrounded by bricks that could tell tales. It's pleasant -- newspapers and plants are strewn about and service is friendly. Breakfast is biscuits and muffins, sausage and eggs; lunch is rotisserie chicken with fresh corn muffins, every day; plus sandwiches like the torpedo, rocket, sub -- various combinations of turkey, ham, salami, and cheese. No need to hurry. Just like this place, let yourself hang around a while.

Formosa Restaurant
875-6953, 5425 Hwy 153
Open daily lunch/dinner, $$$
Read the letters from satisfied customers framed and hanging in the small front lobby. You'll want to write one too, after you enjoy a meal in this well-established Hixson place.

Food gets star billing here. Choose from nine soups and ten appetizers to start; the Happy Family dinner for two combines king crab, scallops, lobster, shrimp, beef, chicken, and pork with Chinese vegetables and rice. Oh, a fortune cookie too. One of the chef's specialties is five-flavor shrimp with pecan, marinated in white wine; another is orange peel beef, sautéed with ginger and hot peppers. Red snapper crispy fish is fried and topped with hot brown sauce; get pineapple chicken if you prefer the sweet.

Out-of-town visitors will love this red-boothed, white-clothed, friendly place, with an emphasis on good food, but locals, count your blessings, because you can come back again and again. Need a banquet for a crowd? Call ahead, they'll arrange.

Gianni's Little Italy
499-4242, 2122 Gunbarrel Rd
Open daily, lunch/dinner, $$$
There is no Fay Wray. The ceiling-high 3-D King Kong hovering over New York City's skyline has a fist-full of spaghetti and meatballs! Sit in the shadow of the giant gorilla and enjoy your pasta Gianni, with tomato cream sauce and Italian sausage, or choose from combos: for lunch Sophia's, Rocky's, Vinny's; for dinner Valentino's, Frankie's, Sal's -- favorite family dishes of parmigiana, lasagna, fettucine, and spaghetti combined to fill you up.

Have a seat at the dark-wood bar in the center section and watch the action in the kitchen. Number One, coming up! Portions are huge and service fast in this very, very lively place. The restaurant walls are decked with steamy New-York's-Little-Italy-in-the-30's scenes. Opened December '94.

Glen-Gene Deli
894-0581, Eastgate Mall
870-8872, Northgate Mall
Open daily lunch/dinner, $
Handy for a mall meal; fill up on a burger or shrimp basket or grilled cheese and fries; pop in for coffee on your afternoon break. Almost everyone who goes to the mall stops in at Glen-Gene's every now and then -- it's a habit!

Golden Corral
866-7514, 327 Battlefield Pkwy
Open daily breakfast/lunch/dinner, $$
This family place promotes value for your money. Walk in and pay, then take your tray back through the line as much as you need. Good meat selections, plenty of vegetables, even french-fried sweet potatoes; salad and dessert bars too. Or you can order steak cooked to order. Handy for locals or visitors touring the battlefields.

Golden Dragon Chinese Restaurant
899-0181, 6231 Perimeter Rd
Open daily lunch/dinner, $$
The pleasant exotic aroma of Chinese seasonings welcomes you into the Golden Dragon; their popular buffet offers chicken teriyaki, crab, pork, pepper steak, eggroll, a variety of vegetables, and, of course, fried rice. They specialize in the spicy Hunan style here, and Chattanoogans keep coming back for more. Handy location, in the shopping center at the intersection of Hwy 153 and Lee Hwy.

Gondolier Pizza
899-8100, 6901 Lee Hwy
Open daily lunch/dinner, $$
What a deal! Buy one pizza and get one free. Add a salad from the list of six and a refillable drink and you are set for a long, long time. Yes, six salads, from antipasto to tossed. The Gondolier special is a Greek salad with gyro meat. And there's a Greek salad with chicken, provolone topped. Don't want pizza? Would you prefer veal parmesan, with a side of spaghetti? Sandwiches include homemade meatballs on a hoagie bun and a vegetarian sub. Cheeseburgers too. Order at the counter in this red-striped family-friendly place. Desserts include black forest cheesecake, if you can eat another bite. Oh, go ahead. Take that second pizza home for breakfast; you know pizza in the morning is just cheese toast.

Grady's Goodtimes
894-4663, 2020 Hamilton Place Blvd
Open daily lunch/dinner, $$$
This is a true good-time place with a high decibel level; snazzily decorated, ingeniously located, and clever enough to offer very well-prepared American cuisine. Popular entrees include mesquite grilled salmon, slow-roasted prime

rib and baby back ribs. Pastas are good too, and varied; portions are take-half-of-it-home-in-a-box size. There are some unusual sandwich combinations and good grief to the desserts: chocolate cake made with Hershey bars, and topped with Haagen Daz ice cream and hot fudge, or Tennessee Heaven with ice cream and Jack Daniels sauce. They have a kids' menu and balloons; they have a big, noisy bar; they have outdoor dining; they have ample parking; what else could you want?

Greek Roma Grill
266-0320, 11 W 8th
Open Mon-Fri lunch, $
Regulars come in regularly, for a gyro platter with Greek salad and pita bread. Gyro meat is an absolutely delicious blend of lamb and beef, spiced and blended with the lightest touch, and then combined with onions, tomatoes and green peppers on the grill. The biggest bowl of lettuce you have ever seen begins the salad base; soon it's topped with olives, tomatoes, feta cheese. Souvlaki top sirloin sandwiches are a favorite too, as well as chicken divine; both are served with onions, green peppers, and the special cucumber sauce. A few stools and tables, some in the bank building lobby, but takeout is most popular in this authentic Greek carry-out shop.

Gulas Restaurants
894-2241, 5665 Brainerd Rd   *894-2521, 6002 Lee Hwy*
Open daily breakfast/lunch/dinner, $$ *Open daily, lunch/dinner, $$*
These two restaurants are under different ownership, but share the same family name. It's a name well-known to Chattanooga diners, as the first Gulas restaurant was opened in the 40's. People come in for charcoal-broiled ribeye, tender fried chicken, and vegetables that have a down-home flavor. At the Lee Highway spot, chairs on rollers let you cozy right up to the table; have an extra cup of coffee and dessert. There's a large crowd of regulars, but they welcome new customers too. Special prices for senior citizens, special menu for kids. On Brainerd Road they begin serving breakfast at 6.

Home Folks Restaurant
332-5724, 8981 Dayton Pike, Soddy-Daisy
Open Tue-Sun lunch/dinner, $$
If you've moved here from some other part of the country and want to learn about real southern country cooking, drive up Dayton Pike to the Home Folks, and as their sign suggests, set a spell. On a really rainy day I was warmly welcomed, quickly seated, and invited to get a plate and go through the buffet line. Five meats and ten vegetables every day -- from hominy to creamed corn, and green beans to pinto; salad and dessert bars too.

At the foot of Walden Ridge, it's worth driving the distance if you aren't lucky enough to live nearby. A good place to eat if you've been hiking the North Chickamauga Pocket Wilderness trails. Look for the blue-white sign out front. Fixed price for lunch and dinner, every day.

Hot Sauce Charlie
756-7888, 832 Georgia Ave   *265-2827, 3625 Tennessee Ave*
Open Mon-Fri breakfast/lunch, $ *Open daily lunch/dinner, $*

Join the little piggies and head for Hot Sauce Charlie; two locations. Breakfast is offered at the Georgia Avenue spot beginning at 7; lunch at both is bar-b-q, of course, sandwiches or plates, with sides. The buffet line downtown serves fried chicken too, and has a wide variety of vegetables steaming in the pots. Visitors to Lookout Mountain can feed on Charlie's food from the takeout trailer on Tennessee Avenue; and you can catch it every summer, hot and spicy like the music, at a sidestreet tent along the Strut.

Note: The Bessie Smith Strut is the city's biggest block party; a Monday-night gathering during Riverbend Festival when M. L. King Boulevard is wall-to-wall music, food and fun. It happens in June, every year!

HRH Dumplin's
756-3522, 701 Broad St
Open Sun-Fri lunch, $$

A favorite of the after-church lunch bunch, and weekday workers too; this place offers several fitness choices, including low-cal banana split dessert. There's chicken n' dumplins, of course, and a homemade casserole every day, plus a range of salads and sandwiches. Fresh-baked cake-of-the-day might be Italian coconut, Reese's peanut butter, or mandarin orange. The specialty, to carry out the theme, is an apple dumplin -- the choice of HRH, the king! Next door to the Tivoli, catering available too.

Hy's Barbecue and Catering
842-3195, 5720 Hixson Pike
Open Tue-Sat lunch/dinner, $$

It seems a bit incongruous, when you think about it. A barbecue place with gold-rimmed china plates hanging on the walls, floral-print valances at the windows, and yes, the tablecloths are pink! But have a seat, and never fear. The barbecue is so good you swear you'll come back tomorrow for some more, and the vegetables are really fine. Did you notice those magnificent mile-high meringue pies at the front counter?

They will cater any size party you want to have. Rumor has it a mystery career woman who wants her boyfriend to think she cooks has Hy's cater for her: in addition to the well-prepared meal, Hy's provides eggshells and potato peelings too, which that mystery person puts right into her garbage can, for nice effect. That's service, wouldn't you say? Middle Valley residents, slow down and stop at the curve on Hixson Pike for a great meal -- eat in on pink tablecloths or take it with you. And if you need potato peels, they can probably oblige.

Wondering what we look for in a Great Place?
See "How to Use This Book."

Ichiban Japanese Steak House
875-0404, 5425 Hwy 153
Open daily lunch/dinner, $$$$

Ichi-ban means "first" in Japanese. And this is a first-rate restaurant, with five pretty and intimate softly-matted rooms, set up hibachi-style for preparing and serving your meal right before your eyes. The chef will entertain you as he makes your evening meal -- knives are twirled and brandished with a chop-chop here and a chop-chop there until your food is done and set upon your plate.

Dinners of steak and chicken, shrimp, or scallops come with soup, salad, steamed rice and hibachi vegetables, plus Japanese tea and your fortune cookie. A great place for a special party; dress up and go. Lower prices for kids; for sure they'll love the show. When you ask for something, please say "dozo" (please); you'll hear "arigato" when you go.

Visitors staying downtown or in the Hamilton area, you may want to make the drive north on Hwy 153 for this one; it's in a shopping mall on your left, just-a-ways after you pass Northgate mall and cross under Hixson Pike -- not too hard to find. The excellent Formosa Restaurant is next door; both good choices.

Imperial Garden Chinese Restaurant
499-9333, 2288 Gunbarrel Rd
Open daily, lunch/dinner, $$$

This is a place for relaxing, quiet enough for good conversation. The tinkling fountain, muted colors, and gracious service urge you to linger. Tables are set with pink linens and black lacquered chairs; there's a cozy feel in the high-backed turquoise booths; floral screens are elegantly oriental.

Food is served with flair on large and lovely Chinese plates. Champagne shrimp is slightly hot, fried with scallions; Peking chicken sweet and sour. Kung pao beef is cooked with peanuts, Szechuan twice-cooked pork is boiled, then hot-sauced and stir-fried much like a southern style. The menu is long, especially with seafood dishes; they also have chow mein (crunchy noodles), lo mein (soft noodles) and fried rice. And although they have takeout, in a place so pretty, why not stay?

In Good Taste
877-7196, 5110 Hixson Pike
Open Mon-Sat lunch/dinner, $$

It's a tea room on one side, a few pretty-in-pink tables for ladies lunching; or you can stop at the counter on the other side for sandwiches, cookies, pies and frozen entrees to take home. Some of the best casseroles are broccoli and chicken, chicken tetrazzini, and shepherd's pie. The main ticket here is catering, though; with special birthday parties for children. They'll do your wedding cake too.

J. R.'s Country Cooking Restaurant
629-6538, 3208 Amnicola Hwy
Open Mon-Sat breakfast/lunch, $

J.R.'s Country Cooking sits off the road on Amnicola between the Police Services Center and the Fire Training Facility, near the truck terminal. Open early for breakfast and closing mid-afternoon, J. R.'s means to satisfy a hungry appetite. The crowded parking lot hints it's popular; there's a drive-through too, where you can order a fried bologna sandwich, burgers and fries, or vegetables and cornbread. Salmon patties and mashed potatoes are as good as Mom used to make and of course you can get sweet tea. Their beef stew is so hearty it will get you well no matter how bad you may be feeling. Service is friendly in this informal place, where the main point seems to be getting folks fed.

Just Delicious
886-7210, 1309 Taft Hwy, Signal Mountain
Open Mon-Sat breakfast/lunch/dinner, $$

Aptly named, this spiffy black-and-white-checked little shop on Signal Mountain offers unique family recipes. Brownies are most popular, but don't let that cause you to miss the cream cheese Danish, cinnamon-sour cream coffee cake or coconut cake with pineapple. Dinner entrees? Marzetti, lasagna, chicken divan, and on and on. The catering menu is long, long, long; be sure to plan your party while sitting in there so you can enjoy the smells of delicious food cooking; it will help you think.

Kanpai of Toyko
855-8204, 2200 Hamilton Place Blvd
Open daily, lunch/dinner (no lunch Sat), $$$

This Japanese steakhouse is right in the middle of everything, at Hamilton Place; dining rooms are set up with two hibachi tables in each; you know, of course, that you are seated to watch the cooking show. Crowds are moved through the process rapidly; your steak and shrimp are laid sizzling on your plate; the food tastes fine down to the rainbow sherbet for dessert, but you'll need to do your lingering in the separate bar.

Karl's Family Restaurant
875-5506, 5100 Hixson Pike
Open daily breakfast/lunch/dinner, $$

A true daily bread place, Karl's can feed you every meal, every day, and provide you with a copy of "The Daily Bread"; it's on the counter for anyone to pick up. With the distinction of being the oldest existing restaurant in Hixson, Karl's maintains a real family atmosphere. No liquor here, and a note on the menu requests that you "Please refrain from using profanity."

Starting at 6, you can get breakfast all day long: country ham with gravy and grits, homemade biscuits, even porkchops or ribeye steak. Lunch and dinner fare include such standards as chicken and dressing; the vegetable list is very long, get your fried okra and squash right here. A super-friendly atmosphere prevails; they seem genuinely happy you stopped by. Native American art and artifacts for sale, ask at the counter.

Kenny Rogers Roasters
855-1937, 5231 Brainerd Rd
894-0693, 2021 Gunbarrel Rd
877-3820, 5390 Hwy 153
Open daily lunch/dinner, $$
Kenny Rogers' heart is in the right place, and yours will be too, if you eat here often. These heart-smart fixings start with wood-roasted chicken, which you see turning on the spit as you enter. The literature tells about the calories, and total fat. And not to worry -- it tastes very, very good! Side dishes are potatoes, mashed, with gravy, or parslied with garlic. Honey-baked beans, rice pilaf, cinnamon apples, five types of salads and slaw are only part of it. There's a BIG chicken pot pie, and, honest, the best dish of cobbler you will ever eat. Take home Kenny's famous muffins by the dozen. Oh, and get roasted drumsticks for the kids tonight, before you have to leave for PTA. Catering available.

KFC

866-6808, 323 Battlefield Pkwy	*894-0500, 4425 Hwy 58*
267-4034, 2501 Broad St	*965-7733, Hwy 151, Ringgold*
877-2865, 3720 Dayton Blvd	*875-8168, 5323 Hwy 153*
629-5724, 2301 E 3rd	*894-7501, 5318 Ringgold Rd*
855-3958, 7428 E Brainerd Rd	*629-9652, 3401 Rossville Blvd*
332-6968, 10161 Hwy 27	*899-3972, 6851 Shallowford Rd*

Open daily, lunch dinner, $$
Could there possibly be anyone alive who hasn't had at least one picnic out of "The Bucket"? Colonel Sanders started selling his original recipe long ago; they've added lower-in-fat rotisserie style now. You know the list of sides -- beans and slaw and biscuits; watch for special deals. Stores just about anywhere you are.

Kilroys Coffeehouse
267-9301, 426 Vine St
Open Mon-Sat all day, $
"The coffee culture is taking off in Chattanooga," says Roy Whitaker, owner of Kilroys on Vine Street. "Coffee is the wine of the 90's." Unique to this tiny spot at the edge of UTC's campus is "The Clicker," a remote that allows customers access to choose the music they want to hear while sipping the brew, reading the paper, or in coffeehouse style, discussing the affairs of the world. Early morning professors listen to new age, then the Provident crowd switches to jazz. Students drift in throughout the day and tune to classic rock. True coffeehouses encourage lingering; this place runs true. Roy's bagels are shipped from New York; the desserts come from everywhere. Try espresso-laced Italian tiramisu; it comes from -- where would you think? -- Montana.

Krystal

899-9812, 5401 Brainerd Rd	*866-3071, Hwy 27, Ft Oglethorpe*
266-8273, 3407 Broad St	*894-9486, 4416 Hwy 58*
266-7228, 307 Cherokee Blvd	*935-2523, Hwy 151, Ringgold*
877-2128, 4106 Dayton Blvd	*894-7604, 6300 Ringgold Rd*
622-5484, 2304 E 23rd	*867-5627, 3701 Rossville Blvd*
894-0469, Hamilton Place Mall	*499-9304, 7300 Shallowford Rd*
875-5416, 4850 Hixson Pike	*266-1364, 621 Signal Mtn Rd*

Open daily, breakfast/lunch/dinner, $

Krystals were born in Chattanooga in 1932, during the Depression. The first restaurant was located at 7th and Cherry, downtown. Now they're in eight states, and you can get breakfast in addition to the original square-bunned hamburgers, still grilled with onions, piping hot.

La Cabriole

821-0350, 1341 Burgess Rd
Open Fri-Sat, dinner at 7:30, one serving only, reservations required, $$$$$$
You'll need directions if you're not familiar with Browns Ferry Road; leave the pavement, follow the gravel drive, wind through the gate, and park beside the double-wide. At the foot of Elder Mountain and not too far from the River, this farm-turned-classical-riding-school makes a truly lovely valley view. Did I say double-wide? Yes, tucked against the trees and overlooking the horses and the jump ring is a trailer, its four rooms lovingly outfitted with tables and linens and flowers and art, for an intimate, French-in-the-country restaurant.

Reserve in advance for this five-course one-serving-only dinner, served on Friday and Saturday nights. If you're planning a visit to the city, you may want to call before you come to town; it accommodates just 40 and fills up fast. Locals know this is a place to go for a special evening, from a wedding anniversary to new-stirrings-in-the-heart blooming love. A romantic place.

Las Margaritas

899-5084, 5845 Brainerd Rd
756-3332, 1101 Hixson Pike *
Open daily, lunch/dinner, $$$
*Mexican Music and Monster Margaritas. You get that here, among the mirrors and windows, plants and piñatas, elevated bar and outdoor patio. It's open and airy in reds and whites and blacks and greens. The atmosphere is casual, festive, and fun.

Everybody who likes Mexican food comes here. Over there a backless purple T-shirt shares a Monster, double-strawed, with her date. At a family table, the young taco-eating son allows a good-sized burp; is firmly chastised by his dad. Cozy in the corner, a couple in suits designed for business discuss the market on a bullish day over Chicken Acapulco and Mexican beer. On Wednesday, it's ladies night with local bands; cars park clear up the hill from

Hixson Pike as the crowd pours in. Saturday night, come for mariachi. Another location on Brainerd Road.

Le Doux's at Bluff View Inn
265-5033, 412 E 2nd
Mon-Fri lunch, Thu-Sat dinner, $$$$$$$
From a prominent vantage point high above the Tennessee River, the Inn at Bluff View overlooks one of the loveliest vistas in the city. And if you want atmosphere, this southern dining place with a French twist is nicely elegant. The house was built in the 1920's; upstairs are bed and breakfast rooms. You're welcome in the parlor; browse the books or have a glass of wine. The wines are mostly French, the list includes Californias too; or you may select from more than 30 beers.

Three small dining rooms are intimately home-like; service is warm and very attentive. The menu changes weekly, but at lunchtime, there's always quiche; also entrées such as Grand Marnier French Toast with a mixed berry compote, mesquite-grilled chicken salad served on a brie mango quesadilla, and hickory-grilled Colorado lamb chops with little niceties like mint tea and tiny carrot-raisin rolls. A dinner menu might begin with garbure paysanne (country vegetable soup) and feature chicken, beef tenderloin, veal or red snapper, carefully prepared as they might do it in France, touched with vermouth, mushrooms, herbs, or goat cheese. Dine here with friends or just pamper yourself; you'll be charmed by the graciousness you find on the Bluff.

Little Caesar's Pizza
332-3330, 1061 Dayton Pike   *875-0300, 5510 Hwy 153*
899-9457, 7401 E Brainerd Rd   *866-1000, 1968 Lafayette Rd*
899-2650, 4801 Hwy 58   *238-5600, 9231 Old Lee Hwy*
490-8448, 4976 Hwy 58   *698-1300, 3728 Ringgold Rd*
Open daily, lunch/dinner, $$
Little Caesar's is a little nook of a place where you can choose your own toppings and even get crazy bread and salad, or a sandwich. Try it in a baby pan, or sample by the slice. Neatsa, neatsa! Some stores deliver; call and see.

The Loft
266-3601, 328 Cherokee Blvd
Open daily lunch/dinner, $$$$
A table by the softly flickering fireplace, highbacked chairs, candles, and someone special to hold hands with; a booth along the side for four, a platter of appetizers, and your friends from work in a finally-it's-Friday mood; two tables bunched together to seat 10, and grandmother's birthday party underway, balloons and all -- this popular restaurant has been the scene of countless heartwarming occasions for more than twenty years.

There's a friendly, gracious air about the place; the community-minded owner, Hamid Andalib, is so well-liked that when the place burned a few years back, folks around town pitched in to help get things going again. Customers appreciate him too; photos in the lobby show smiling faces with notes of appreciation from such famed-names as Nadia Comaneci, Reggie White, and Don Knotts, who penned "Best food in Chattanooga!"; you'll hear the same from local regulars too. Really good prime rib here, plus lobster and steak and salmon and more; Mississippi mud pie is their best-known dessert; there's a children's menu too. The separate bar is very pleasant; a recent expansion added a huge space for private parties; meeting rooms here too.

Longhorn Steaks of Chattanooga
490-0573, 5771 Brainerd Rd
Open Mon-Fri lunch, daily dinner, $$$$
If you like meat and taters, scoot your boots past the rocking-chaired porch, cross over the planked-wood floor, and set yourself down at a red-checked table in the Longhorn Steakhouse, where the jukebox music is country-flavored and you can get your steak sprinkled with Prairie Dust. This place has been voted "best steak" in several contests the past few years, Flo's Filet being the most popular choice. Or you can fire up with Texas chili in a room decked out with deerheads and neon cactus. The menu offers salmon, chicken, and burgers too. There's a full (long) bar, and happy hours. The key lime pie is right good.

Los Reyes Mexican Restaurant
855-8809, 5773 Brainerd Rd
Open daily lunch/dinner, $$$
The stuccoed walls are washed in pastel pinks and blues, flowering baskets hang from wooden beams, clay pots of flowers sit on curving, shuttered window sills. Just off busy Brainerd Road you can step into this lush courtyard atmosphere and relax with a Mexican beer. Then order your steak Ranchero or Tampiquena, ribeyes with spices; or would you prefer a sizzling skillet of fajitas, beef or chicken, piping hot? No need to stick to tacos, the back of the menu can take you far. Several desserts include standard sopapillas and caramel custard flan. There's a separate bar in another room, so the dining area is quiet, with background sounds of Mexico's music. The restroom is unique -- stall walls are corrugated tin.

Madhatters
267-0747, 201 Frazier Ave, upstairs
Open daily lunch/dinner, $$
At the very north end of Walnut Street Bridge, don't go down into the rabbit hole; climb the staircase and tunnel the right hallway to the Madhatters new place. Not just for tea parties, you get real meals here; best of all you can take a table in one of the two front rooms and gaze across the river towards downtown and Lookout Mountain; a view so wonderful there should be a cover charge. There's a bird-a-rarium for your enjoyment and hats on every wall in this former apartment building. They're expecting to have a lemonade stand by the bridge for summer-thirsty walkers.

Mandarin Garden
877-8899, 5450 Hwy 153
Open daily, lunch/dinner, $$$
This Chinese restaurant is popular with the north-of-the river crowd. Diners enjoy sitting around the big square fountain and ordering lemon fried chicken and charbroiled ribs, Mandarin style. Tall pitchers of iced tea on the serving cart confirm the fact, however, that this Mandarin garden is in the southern USA! A display case up front is set with plastic versions of menu fare; in case you're still not sure, the printed menu offers pictures which can help decide. House specialties are king crab, walnut shrimp, orange beef, and General Tso's chicken -- a hot dish of chicken and peppers, garlic-ginger flavored. Choose your meal from among ten appetizers, nine soups, and 99 entrees; even glacéd lychee fruit for dessert. Pretty good! There's a small bar.

Margaret's Luncheonette
267-9233, 15 E 7th St
Open Mon-Fri lunch, $
"Welcome Home!" says the sign on the back wall. Many a downtown luncher chose this diner when it was in the basement of Loveman's, then Proffitt's, until the store was closed in 1993. It's back in a new spot now, and the crowd is too, coming in at noon for turkey clubs, homemade vegetable soup, chunky beef stew, cottage cheese and a peach. They feed you fast in here, where you can cluster around two counters or grab a small booth.

Marriott Hotel at the Convention Center Restaurants (see cover)
756-0002, 2 Carter Plaza
This newest, tallest, glass-and-shine-modern downtown hotel adjoins the Convention and Trade Center; a great location for visitors or locals to make a dining choice.

Ashley's
♦ *Open Mon-Sat, dinner, $$$$$*
♦ Make reservations in advance at the front desk -- this elegant, intimate dining room on the second floor only seats 40. It's the kind of place you want when a relaxing evening is what you need; select from appetizers of escargot or oysters royale to entrees of salmon, lobster, swordfish, steak, lamb, and even southwestern duck; service is attentive in this rose-and-burgundy softly lit and very private setting.

Cafe Chattanooga
♦ *Open Tue-Sat, all day, $$*
♦ Just off the main lobby, this small spot lets you catch the news on CNN with your cappuccino and morning muffins; your late-day glass of wine or favorite bottled water is accompanied by soft-and-grand piano sounds; you overlook the indoor pool below.

Kicks
♦ *Open daily, afternoon/latenight, $$*
♦ Main lounge of the hotel; street and lobby entrance; hot hors d'oeuvres

every night; big-screen tv and dancing to top-40. Order from the room service menu if you want to eat here too.

The Terrace

♦ *Open daily, breakfast/lunch/dinner, $$*

♦ Stop in at The Terrace for whichever meal you happen to need; it overlooks the lobby and offers buffet and table service -- handy if you're in a hurry and comfortable if you want to stay a while and talk. Popular with downtown workers as well as hotel guests.

Mary's Deli and Bake Shop
266-1356, 724 Market St
Open Mon-Fri lunch, $
The red and blue wallpaper border leads around the corner into the tiny back room. Red valance on the window, twelve red chairs at tables for two. Pleasant, and it smells so-o-o-o good. But most of the business is takeout. The styrofoam boxes get loaded and stacked, as downtown workers on the go grab a solid meal to eat deskside while going over reports. "I'm a creature of habit," a downtown banker said. "Wednesday, it's turkey and dressing. So today, I eat at Mary's." The warming trays bubble with sweet potatoes, green beans, and homemade dressing, as the friendly staff spoons it up. Her desserts are wonderful too; cheesecake, pecan pie, strawberry cake and cookies are wrapped and ready. When you're downtown, check out Mary's. On Thursday, it's pot roast.

McDonald's

756-3593, 3620 Broad St	*866-9581, 329 Lafayette Rd*
870-2660, 2003 Dayton Blvd	*892-1976, 6220 Lee Hwy*
622-8318, 2105 E 24th St Pl	*756-4927, 813 Market St*
875-5045, 4123 Hixson Pike	*894-7911, 6401 Ringgold Rd*
894-9619, 4608 Hwy 58	*867-2345, 4502 Rossville Blvd*
877-0263, 5440 Hwy 153	*899-3630, 7020 Shallowford Rd*

Open daily, breakfast/lunch/dinner, $
Has anybody ever been able to drive all the way home with an untouched bag of McDonald's french fries in their lap? This long-time favorite place has good burger deals; light eaters can get salads, healthy muffins, non-fat yogurt in a cone. Happy Meals for kids; many stores have playgrounds; will do birthday parties.

Mom's Italian
266-2204, 1257 Market St
Open Mon-Sat lunch/dinner, $$
There's a certain beat-up charm about Mom's. The chairs don't match and the wallpaper's peeling, but the food is cooked up fresh. Mom arrives at 5:30 every morning to begin preparing her lasagna, ravioli, manicotti. By the time you arrive with your appetite, she's ready to bake you a pizza or turn out a piled-high sub. Maybe for lunch you'll want basil-kissed minestrone and hot garlic bread. Now, Mom's not really Italian, but she is somebody's mom --

check the picture wall of grandkids. Open late every day except Sunday, this downtown place is tucked in an old brick building on Market, across the street and partway between Warehouse Row and the ChooChoo. Don't drive by too fast, or miss it if you're riding the shuttle. Stop at Mom's. Somebody in there will talk to you, and bring you something good to eat. Sweets-lovers, try the cheese cake and the cream cake. They're Mom-made.

Morrison's Cafeteria
892-4909, Hamilton Place Mall
Open daily, lunch/dinner, $$
Located in Hamilton Place Mall right next door to Sears is Morrison's Cafeteria. Walk the line here; admire the display and select what you want from a tantalizing variety. Treat yourself to something you never take the time to fix at home, like the fruit-layered congealed salad. The servers are friendly and eager to dish up the roast beef, broiled fish, spaghetti, and southern-style vegetables. You can't pass dessert, can you? That coconut pie surely has your name on it; check and see. This is a very popular after-church-on-Sunday place.

Mozzarella's Cafe
855-8454, Hamilton Place Mall
Open daily, lunch/dinner, $$$
With a name like a good Italian cheese, would you expect good Italian food? You'll find some here; this mall-entrance restaurant recently refurbished and now has an Italian-cafe look and food to match. Walls here are dark-gold dazzle and tables have that black-and-white mod-Italian-city-country style; shelves are stacked with jars and rows of pastas, peppers, virgin olive oil. If you love ordinary pizza, you'll go into a smiling frenzy over what you get here; pasta dishes are as snazzy as the decor; exciting treatments too for seafood, chicken and beef. There's a small bar and an outdoor dining area; a nice spot for meeting friends early on a spring evening.

Mount Vernon Restaurant
266-6591, 3509 Broad St
Open Mon-Sat lunch/dinner, $$$
The Mount Vernon has been pleasing Chattanooga residents and visitors for 40 years. At the foot of Lookout Mountain and on the city side, it's convenient for people staying in a mountain B & B, and as near the Riverboat as Ruby Falls; but mostly you'll find local ladies meeting there for lunch, a business get-together group, or families come for supper, and dessert. The amaretto cream pie is a Mount Vernon creation, and who can resist? Before dessert though, try the broiled rainbow trout, aged New York strip sirloin or veal cutlets topped with Mount Vernon's own tomato sauce. For a lighter lunch, get the cold shrimp plate or a spinach salad bowl. It's quiet, but with a friendly kind of buzz. Booths to sit in, sequestered in several cozy rooms; private enough for three-year-old Matthew to catch a few Z's after a tromp around Rock City with his grandma and his dad.

Mudpie Coffeehouse and Newsstand
267-9043, 12 Frazier Ave
Open Tue-Sun lunch/dinner, $$
Some would call it funky. Surreal striped snakes and strange-but-interesting art adorn the walls, orange-red here, light blue on that side of the room. There are counters to prop your paper on while you sip a slow espresso; wooden tables when you bring a crowd and want to eat. Old chairs with stuffing you can see make a front-room sitting place; facing the street are a few marble-topped tables for two.

There's a newsstand with the promise: "Pay for the magazines before you sit down or we'll be forced to cane you"; buy *Mother Earth News, Village Voice,* the *Washington Post* or *Time;* kids like the basket of toys in the corner. Veggie pizzas, sandwiches, and a few fancy desserts complement the coffees; beer is available too. This new spot in an old brick building is a great place to end a walk across the Walnut Street Bridge or a browsing binge in the galleries on the artsy north shore. There's a tiny patio out back; the Little Theatre is just across the parking lot. As to the humor that makes the place, the owner, Bridgett Huckaby, used to work with Letterman; ask her about it.

Nikki's Drive Inn
265-9885, 899 Cherokee Blvd
Open Mon-Sat breakfast/lunch/dinner, $$
It's been called the best little seafoodhouse in town. Right at the tunnel on Cherokee, this smallish place has been a favorite stop for years of fried-shrimp devotees. The shrimp, you might guess, are enormous, the onion rings are huge, and the burgers are big and fat. It's a neon-and-juke-box place; if you're by yourself, you have to sit on a counter-stool; a big red sign warns that tables are reserved for two or more. Takeout is available if you love shrimp but don't like stools.

Noodles
886-1889, 1223 Taft Hwy
Open Mon-Fri lunch/dinner, Sat dinner, $$
Noodles is a quaint little restaurant located in a shopping-center nook on Signal Mountain. It's well-known to the mountain folks; for over ten years it's been cooking up everything from steaks to seafood in warm and friendly southern style. Lunches offer burgers, grilled chicken salad, and a different type of quiche every day. Cheesecake is so good they can hardly keep up with the demand; word does get around.

O'Charley's
877-8966, 5031 Hixson Pike
892-3343, 2340 Shallowford Village Dr
Open daily lunch/dinner, Sun brunch 10:30, $$$
There are a lot of things to like at O'Charley's. It's comfortable; massive booths let you sink right down. It's pretty; plants everywhere complement

the greens and browns and brick walls. It's interesting; there's a full wall of historical pictures of the city. And, it may be important to mention, it has very good food. Pastas to prime rib, sandwiches to seafood, everything has a special twist; chicken salads are Cajun style, southern fried, or fancied with pecans and grapes. Everybody's talking about the caramel pie; ask them how you can do it at home. Items to note: there is a large separate bar; the place is lively, yet somehow, maybe it's the plants, it is quiet enough to talk. And parents, kids under 10 eat FREE. What did I tell you? There's a lot to like at O'Charley's.

Old Country Buffet
499-0964, 2020 Gunbarrel Rd, Hamilton Village
Open Sat breakfast, daily lunch/dinner, $$
Travelers will recognize this fine buffet restaurant; it's in 33 states. Locals appreciate it too; it does so many things so well. There's a comfy sofa by the front door, in case there's a wait. Pay as you enter, you're given a card which keeps your table reserved; go through the line as many times as you want. The dining room is wallpapered in pretty blues and whites; everything sparkles and shines.

And now to the food! It's American-style cooking, with carved roast beef, turkey and ham for dinner every day. Step up and ask the carver to slice it thick or thin, rare or well; your plate is looking good. The salad bar alone is a meal -- greens and pastas, potato salads and slaw; several soups. At the vegetable table, choose from marshmallow-topped brown-sugared yams, big fat baked potatoes, green beans, greens, corn, squash, and more. Move ahead for breads, desserts, and drinks. Kids Birthday Club entitles them to a free meal; discount cards available for over 55.

Olive Garden Italian Restaurant
899-7707, 2200 Hamilton Place Blvd
Open daily, lunch/dinner, $$$
The door is opened by your greeter, and you are ushered into a lobby filled with the smell of Italian saucery. Olive oil? Garlic? Sausages and cheese? Tomatoes bubbling in a pot? Conversations creep around the corner; everyone who got there before you is already having fun. Sit down and have a glass of wine or raspberry lemonade. The salad bowl is endless; tasty greens tossed with parmesan and olive oil; they'll bring you all you want, with breadsticks too. Then take a tour of Italy with combination chicken parmigiana, lasagna and fettucine alfredo; steak siciliano is tomato-sauced, steak tuscany grilled with olive oil. There's veal, seafood, and specialty pastas such as straw and hay -- spinach and egg fettucine with ham, peas and mushrooms, cream sauced. Everything is freshissimo!

If you didn't grow up in an Italian home, it's not too late to become addicted to tiramisu, a most incredible dessert of ladyfingers, mascarpone (Italian cream cheese), chocolate, and espresso.

Outback Steakhouse

899-2600, 2120 Hamilton Place Blvd
Open daily, dinner, $$$$

You'll be walking around the outback for sure, if you don't get here before the crowd. But this way to the tucker (that's food). No worries. Start off with the Kookaburra wings, mild, medium or hot, or the walkabout soup. While you're eating that, for sure they've put some shrimp on the barbie, just for you. All that waiting may have you craving the Crocodile Dundee 14-ounce strip steak, or the 20-ounce Melbourne. They come with salad, bushman bread, and jacket potato or Aussie chips. The Joey menu offers the little ones a Boomerang Burger or Grilled Cheese-A-Roo.

Don't go away without dessert, mates! Try Sydney's Sinful Sundae, or Chocolate Thunder from Down Under, brownies and ice cream with chocolate all over. Wooden booths, a big bar at the back, casually dressed servers who really take care of you, and a steady buzz of noisy chatter keep the mood auss-some here. Beer, wine (some Australian) and even a Wallaby Darned -- frozen schnapps, champagne, rum and very secret mixers.

Padrino's Mexican Restaurant

877-3675, 3805 Hixson Pike
Open daily lunch/dinner, $$$

There's only one bad thing about Padrino's. It's hard to get back onto Hixson Pike at that nasty curve. But go ahead, just look both ways. It's the pretty stucco building with the lovely scenes of Mexico painted outside, mural style, for you to see. Inside, it's darkly Spanish; deep-red booths, and tables, and a separate room with a bar.

The service is warm here and the food is fresh, tasty, and interesting. They brag about their margaritas; you'll brag about the guacamole. Some folks are partial to the tostada Linda; they have a fine selection of chicken, beef and pork dishes prepared with the Mexican touch; the menu also explains how the Indian and Spanish cultures combined to create the foods we enjoy today. Next time you drive by, slow down and admire those murals; then flip your blinker and pull in.

Panda's Chinese Cuisine

870-9563, 5137 Hixson Pike
Open daily, lunch/dinner, $$

Pink cherry blossoms catch your eye in this unassuming place in the old Hixson shopping center; you like it before you even sit down because of its panda-bear name. The extensive menu has all the Chinese standards; what's different is this: they have American-style too, such as tuna and chicken salad; they have a yogurt bar with a variety of toppings; children under 6 eat free; and they will deliver any order over $20.

Send us your feedback and tips on the form at the end of this book.

Papa John's

861-4100, 776 Battlefield Pkwy   *877-5777, 3908 Hixson Pike*
855-0606, 5210 Brainerd Rd   *855-8889, 7000 Lee Hwy*
Open daily lunch/dinner, $$$

Just call your Papa. He'll bake you a fabulous pizza, and bring it to your door. Delivery is limited to the areas near the four locations, but check and see. And this pizza franchise is growing fast, thanks to exceptionally good food at a good price. Maybe you'll want the family special next Friday night when you rent a bunch of movies and stay in out of the cold. And the tailgate pak -- four large ones -- will feed the whole team after Saturday's soccer.

Peking Restaurant

899-2225, 5911 Brainerd Rd
Open daily lunch/dinner, $$$

Fire-breathing golden dragons loom large behind the big red doors. Swirls and whirls of design oriental treat your eye while you dine at white-clothed tables in this favored spot on Brainerd Road. There's a large and somewhat separate bar and a separate non-smoking room. So please enjoy.

Princess beef is hot, with peanuts and vegetables, Szechuan style; Peking shrimp in tomato sauce come on sizzling rice; chicken with plum sauce is spiced just right to make you smile. Peking Dinners can be ordered for two to ten -- the combinations allow you to try many different flavors, in customary Chinese style. Don't overlook the appetizer list. If you've never tried potstickers or steamed bao, go ahead; the meat-stuffed dumplings are even better than eggroll! And how about Peking banana for dessert?

Piccadilly Cafeteria

875-6115, Northgate Mall
Open daily, lunch/dinner, $$

After 23 years in Chattanooga, the Piccadilly is still packing them in. Shoppers drop by; so do crowds after church or before the movie. As you make your first pass on the outside line, you visualize your finished tray; it's nice to see what you're about to eat. They have some theme specialties, such as Chinese, Mexican, Italian, and Seafood night; count on chicken and roast beef every day, lots of salad and vegetable selections, plus fruit compote and lemon chess pie. A recent remodel freshened it up real pretty; there are booths for two or family-wide.

Pickle Barrel Restaurant

266-1103, 1012 Market St
Open daily, lunch/dinner, food until 1:45 AM, close 3 AM, $$$

Up the spiral staircase you'll find the finest outdoor eating spot in the city. It's great because it puts you tree-top like a bird, it's handy to Miller Park and next door to The Times, and they serve good food and drink until the wee, wee hours. It's the place to hang, downtown. Corned beef, pastrami, roast beef, clubs, and the Big Cheese (5 cheeses with sprouts and tomato) come with a pickle, of course; homemade chili, stuffed spuds and a variety of salads make good lunchtime fare. They have steaks and chicken too; beers from all around the world; wine and cocktails. Also hot spiced cider, buttermilk, and chocolate peanut butter shakes. Downstairs seating in this historic triangular building is unique; get the point?

Pizza Hut

Dine-In
899-1088, 5002 Brainerd Rd
756-8961, 3505 Broad St
332-9460, 10043 Dayton Pike
894-4835, 7801 E Brainerd Rd
877-9350, 3884 Hixson Pike
894-1461, 4511 Hwy 58
866-6513, 1905 Lafayette Rd
892-4791, 7003 Lee Hwy
875-5493, 776 Mtn Creek Rd
877-9065, 252 Northgate Mall
892-1189, 5908 Ringgold Rd
Open daily, lunch/dinner, $$$

Delivery
866-6700, 1068.Battlefield Pkwy
698-3500, 4011 Brainerd Rd
870-8181, 4104 Dayton Blvd
855-9900, 2121 Gunbarrel Rd
267-5588, 1224 Hixson Pike
842-7744, 6218 Hixson Pike
894-9044, 4850 Hwy 58

Pizza Hut's Book-It program over the last ten years has rewarded more than 19 million children in grades K-6 for READING. Children can earn coupons for pizzas through incentive programs set at their school. Pizza Hut has long been known as a family place, offering family-night-out deals and special kids treats. Good eating-in spots before the movie, or after; juke-box music and free refills on drinks. The home-delivery stores pretty well blanket the city.

Pizza Place

886-3761, 1309 Taft Hwy, Signal Mountain
Open daily, lunch/dinner, $$
In a neat little blue and white pizza shop on the top of Signal Mountain you'll find some out-of-this-world pizza; they throw their own dough and it can be whole-wheat if you like; vegetables are fresh and cut there. Choose from 19 different pizza toppings or lasagna or stuffed shells. There is a small dining area if you can't wait to get home to eat. Salads and bread sticks are on the menu too.

Porkers Uptown

267-2726, 1251 Market St
Open Mon-Fri lunch/dinner, $$
Porkers claims to be the uptown barbecue spot in Chattanooga. But don't let that make you nervous. The BBQ plates all come with baked beans and Texas toast; the hamburgers have plenty of onions, and you can get taters smothered with chili and cheese. If that's the kind of eating you're looking for, you'll find Porkers in an old brick building on Market, just uptown from the ChooChoo. It's a fairly large place, with a let's-hang-this-on-the-wall decor. Desserts: oreo cookie, lime, and coconut pie. They serve milk shakes and old-

time malts; beer is available too. The promise on the menu reads "Pig Out at Porkers. We won't squeal!"

Provident Cafeteria
755-1011, Fountain Square
Open Mon-Fri 7-9, 11-1, for Provident employees and open to public
They've done it right here; easy for employees or the general public to get to, just pop through the lobby off Walnut; it's that big building between 5th and 6th and Cherry and Walnut, of course. Daily specials are listed on the board; the cafeteria is well-arranged. You're greeted with salads -- chunky Waldorf or rounded mounds of tuna, or potato, or bowls of fruit; desserts tempt too -- thick slices of chocolate cake, apple pie, caramel creme; other lines for the big pots of soup, a grill, a deli, a meat/vegetable section, and in the middle of the room, a giant salad bar.

Now to the best reason for coming -- choose a spot under a bright yellow umbrella in the sunny skylit atrium, or sit with your friends in a curved, softly upholstered booth on the carpeted side by multicolored walls, with a view that makes you glad you left the house today. Over there -- Aquarium peaks; straight across on Cameron Hill -- cannons in Boynton Park. The First Baptist steeple points skyward; there's the business end of Raccoon Mountain. Many pluses: great view, pleasant atmosphere, reasonable prices.

Radisson Read House Hotel Restaurants
266-4121, Broad St & M L King, Read House
Since 1847 people have been gathering at this Broad Street location; it faced the railroad station and offered food, lodgings and a place to meet; 150 years later it continues to do the same, sans railroad but on the electric shuttle route.
Broad Street Bistro
♦ *Open daily breakfast/lunch/dinner, $$*
♦ Featuring pasta dishes and special wines, this hotel front-corner spot can serve you every meal, every day; you'll like the open, airy look and the very-center-of-town location; fair-weather days you can dine outdoors.
Green Room
♦ *Open daily, dinner; Sun brunch, $$$$$*
♦ The Green Room's city-landmark distinction continues as it has been since this building was constructed in 1926; new owners are carefully preserving the lavish carved-and-gilded woodwork, recessed mirrors, and glittering chandeliers, plus the elegance that's always existed within the hushed softness of the pale green walls. The paneled bar between the lobby and the dining area is new and so is the menu; it's steak, on the truly upscale side, aiming to be the finest in the city. Reservations suggested.
Yogurt and Coffee Shop
♦ *Open daily, $*
♦ Accessible from the lobby or an outside counter on the street; ice cream, fine coffees and snacks.

Red Lobster Restaurants
894-5846, 5709 Lee Hwy
870-2371, 8 Northgate Office Park
Open daily, lunch/dinner, $$$
Seems like there's always a special seafood feature at Red Lobster; sometimes it's three kinds of shrimp, sometimes it's all-you-can-pile-on-a-plate shrimp; or shrimp mixed with chicken or steak or other seafoods. Lines are often long on weekends, and you know what that means: people like the food, and they are geared up to serve you fast. Small separate bar; special menu for the little ones, and of course, red lobsters swimming in a tank near the front door.

Rembrandt's Coffeehouse
267-2451, 204 High St
Open Mon breakfast, Tue-Sun all day, $$
This newest segment of the Bluff View Potera complex is as beautifully done as the others: an old house restored to even-better-than-the-original; lovely furnishings and art for pleasing the eye; and a good -- make that great -- selection of pastries, candies, coffees, coffeemakers, and gifts. From inside there's a nice view towards downtown; outside one of the nicest patios you'll find anywhere, sort of New Orleans style.

Rib & Loin Old Southern Bar-B-Q
499-6465, 5946 Brainerd Rd
Open daily, lunch/dinner, $$
The phone number is 499-OINK. Next door to the animal collection of Sir Goony Golf, pink piggies wearing chef hats dance around the building, urging you in. Inside it's more sedate. This large, long dining place is done in no-nonsense new brick and gray beams, with blond wood chairs and benches by picture-window walls. When they bring you that big pile of napkins, you figure you're about to get something good to eat. If you're with someone you don't mind porking out with, order the Rack of Ribs for 2. Dinner plate combinations of chicken, pork and beef are available, and barbecue-stuffed baked potatoes. Top it off with an unusually fine cobbler, or pecan pie.

It calls itself Chattanooga's #1 Bar-B-Q Restaurant and someone else must agree -- like Southern Living, Chattanooga Times "Best of" contest readers, and the folks that went to Pig Out On the River. They also have drive through, and catering -- for parties of 10 or 3,000 up, no problem.

Riverside Catfish House
821-9214, Hwy 41, 18039 Cummings Hwy, Central Time Zone
Open Thu-Fri dinner, Sat-Sun lunch/dinner, $$
Mainly a weekend place, this restaurant has been serving up catfish since 1963. On the south side of the Tennessee River, diners have a beautiful view of the River Gorge. Window-sit and watch big-time barges floating along, fishermen intent on their task, or boulders up to their neck in fall foliage on

the steep banks across the way; it's a favorite stop at Color Cruise time. The catfish special is all-you-can eat of the grainfed fingerlings or boneless strips, with cole slaw, hushpuppies, and potato. Chicken and shrimp available too; the children's menu offers a combo plate and all the ketchup they can eat. They're pretty famous here for their homemade buttermilk pie, but don't overlook that coconut cake.

Roy Peppers Porch
877-7590, 5450 Hwy 153
Open daily, lunch/dinner, $$$
If you go at off hours, you may not get to sit on Roy's porch, an indoor place with old-timey swings and wisteria climbing latticed trim. The porch is for waiting and relaxing when the lines are long at this popular Hixson spot. There's also a separate bar with happy hours.

Roy Pepper's is known for its delta-style barbecue, smoked with three different aromatic woods, and its flower-pot bread, baked in a little clay pot and honey-butter glazed. Famous skewers include steak-on-a-stick and Cajun chicken; dinners for the truly hungry are a full rack of smoked ribs and a delta feast -- chicken, pork and ribs. The less hungry, or lunch-time diners, can have a simple steak or one of many sandwiches. Sides are salads, baked beans, potatoes, and a try-it-at-least-once south Georgia Brunswick stew. The one dessert, porch pudding, is cheesecake gone wild, and comes topped with berries or caramel and nuts.

Roy's Grill
866-0290, 116 Chickamauga Ave, Rossville
Open Mon-Sat, breakfast/lunch/dinner, $$
Do you ever long for the good old days? Back when, well, you know. You can find a few of them at Roy's, where they've been serving burgers since 1934. Grab a stool in this chrome-trimmed diner and listen to music in High Fidelity sound. Or sit in the tiny front room on a heart-backed red vinyl chair. Black-and-white photos of earlier years can help you reminisce. As for the food, "Ingest the Best: Roy's chili speaks for itself." There are burgers big, and the Little Roy. There's breakfast beginning at 5 AM with steak: ribeye or chicken-fried; and blue-plate specials every day. Looking for chicken livers, or meatloaf? The sign says it all: *Eat At Roy's. Do It Today.*

Ruby Tuesdays
892-4628, Hamilton Place Mall
Open daily, lunch/dinner, $$$
The salad bar greets as you enter the door. Its fresh bounty puts you in a proper mood for a pleasant meal; soon they've brought you a nice basket of hot bread, and you are on your way. This is a wood-brass and stained-glass place, at a main mall entrance, a formula type of restaurant. But it's a formula that works, and people seem to enjoy coming back again and again for the pastas, smokey mountain chicken, blackened fish, and steaks. A wide variety

of sandwiches and burgers; the bar has an equally wide variety of drinks, with and without alcohol. Booths are almost private; this is a great place to park when you can't shop another minute, and a good starting-off-point for an evening out.

Ryans Family Steak House
875-8135, 5104 Hixson Pike
855-5443, 6734 Lee Hwy
894-0592, 5326 Ringgold Rd
Open daily, lunch/dinner, $$
The name tells it all -- a family steakhouse indeed. Line up the crew, make your choice from the menu on the wall, get your tray and start loading up. You can custom-order steak or chicken, but the salad, vegetable, and dessert bars are center-stage and easy to go back to. Pretty much anything you can think of to eat here; kids love it and parents do too; prices are reasonable, highchairs are handy, and the staff keeps checking to see if you need anything else.

Sandbar Restaurant
622-4432, 1011 Riverside Dr
Open daily, lunch/dinner, $$$
A lot of people go to the Sandbar for big-screen TV-watching or for the nighttime music -- weekend rock to all-ages-love-it blues on Monday. But some people go to the Sandbar for the halibut, as their sign proclaims.

Handy to downtown, the rustic Sandbar sprawls backwards from the road to the river in random-planked style, with a bar and TV here, glass-enclosed porch there, an upper deck and a patio, river side. Pick your place. Then order that halibut, grilled, or a seafood platter or catfish fillets; maybe jumbo fried shrimp. If you really came for eating, you'll probably finish with key lime pie, homemade. Kids love the informal atmosphere; there's a menu for them too. Did I mention the view? Unbelievable! You can't watch the sun set behind Walden Ridge without wanting to come back tomorrow for a replay in show-me-again-slow-mo.

Do you prefer dinner before your walk, or after? A section of RiverWalk begins here and takes you past the homebase boathouse for the U. S. Women's National Sweep Rowing Team; catch them working-for-the-Gold daily between 4 and 7, Olympics-training in their sleek steel shell. Speaking of boats, Sandbar has a dock for water travelers. There, as the palm-trimmed sign informs, you've arrived at the Sandbar Yacht Club.

Shapiro's Gift Pantry and Delicatessen
266-3669, 723 Cherry St
Open Mon-Sat, lunch, $$
It's as close to New York as you can get around here, with a strictly southern twist. Claiming to be Chattanooga's first and finest deli, this Cherry Street

institution is a kick; shelves and coolers are stocked, stacked and crammed with coffee beans, chocolates, vinegars, mustards, jellies, soups, crackers, spices, New York cheesecake and Coca-Cola cake (that twist I mentioned); even t-shirts with the owner's picture on them. Keep going to place your order, it's kosher; choose from roast beef, corned beef, pastrami, knackwurst, Polish sausage, German sausage, turkey, liverwurst, salami, Polish ham, even veggies or lox and cream cheese; next choose your bread; rye, pumpernickel, French, onion roll, egg roll. Homemade salads stare at you from inside the cooler; another choice to make.

The back eating spot is a regulars' comfort zone; a phone on the wall for public use; a chalkboard with today's birthdays; people know their way around. Ralph Cheek and Bob Dial own the place; it's been in business since 1931 and is as famous for its fruit baskets as the Battlefield is for its cannons.

Shoney's Restaurants
861-4616, 325 Battlefield Pkwy   *892-1491, 6515 Ringgold Rd*
870-2361, 3510 Dayton Blvd   *894-5917, 2318 Shallowford Village Dr*
870-1146, 5235 Hwy 153   *894-8288, 4604 Skyview Dr*
267-5548, 401 M L King Blvd   *266-6186, 3606 Tennessee Ave*
Open daily, breakfast/lunch/dinner, $$

The bar is always open at Shoney's. The breakfast bar, that is. Or the soup and salad bar, or seafood bar; watch the marquee. There are things for the children to color and special prices for seniors. Shoney's strawberry pie has been a loved and trusted standby for years. A good place for coffee after a night on the town, or an early-morning breakfast if you got to bed at a decent hour; some Shoney's never close, some shut down midnight-to-6; check.

Shuford's Smokehouse
267-0080, 924 Signal Mtn Rd
Open daily, lunch/dinner, $$

For over nine years Chattanoogans have been coming here for genuine hickory-smoked barbecue. It's tucked against the foot of Signal Mountain; in summer you enter through a screened-in porch set with picnic tables; in winter, a closed-in space is warmed up for your feast. Whether winter or summer the barbecue is always good; buy it by the sandwich or by the pound. Shuford's offers onion rings and fries, Brunswick stew, and banana pudding; open every day, they also cater any size party you need.

Sneaker's
266-1125, 301 Market St in the Sports Barn
Open daily, lunch/dinner, $

Sneakers are visible everywhere in this restaurant-in-a-health-club on Market Street. Open to the public, it's on the shuttle stop; even if you work on the other end of town you can drop in daily for a kill shot -- pineapple juice, honey, coconut syrup, and a banana, frozen and energy-packed. They have homemade turkey chili; turkey, chicken, tuna, and veggie sandwiches; salad plates and pasta plates; even PB&J with banana for the kids. Reasonable prices and very pleasant clean-cut surroundings. What do you bet that after observing those hard-hitting racquetball shots you'll make yourself walk back to work rather than take the shuttle?

Sonic Drive-In
861-6705, 1010 Battlefield Pkwy
877-3355, 3508 Dayton Blvd
842-9982, 6216 Hixson Pike
Open daily, lunch/dinner, $

697-7200, 4348 Ringgold Rd
855-4900, 6915 Shallowford Rd

Nobody's on rollerskates, but somebody does bring your food to your car on a tray, just like the 50's, in this modernish red and white Sonic-booming chain. This place gets my Mom's vote for BEST hamburger. More good stuff: foot-longs loaded down with chili and cheese, big fat onion rings, limeades.

Soup Kitchen
756-2517, 21 E 7th
Open Sun-Fri, lunch, $$

Here's a local treasure, an institution among Chattanooga office workers, who form fast-moving lines every day for delicious soups, salads, sandwiches, and desserts. The Soup Kitchen is located where the Home Plate used to be, and has a warm-cozy-comfy look, like if you'd grown up in the country and your ma made ruffled tie-backs for the windows and ruffled cushions for the straight-backed chairs. You first reach the big pots of soup; state your choice and they'll ladle it up and start your tray; keep going past fresh-made sandwiches and salads and fine, fine desserts. See the sign over there, by the antique hat-rack? It confirms what you thought: "It's a Souper place." Packed at Sunday lunchtime too.

Soup's On
267-1555, 3103 Broad St
Open Mon-Fri, lunch, $

"Over 390,000 bowls delivered to downtown", the marquee boldly proclaims. It's enough to make you want to stop and pop in. Pay up and get your tray and bowl. It's an all-you-can-eat soup bar, with three different kinds every day, such as hearty spaghetti, beans and ham, or chunky vegetable. Three different muffins too, corn, cinnamon bran, homemade rolls. Oh, there's a salad bar, and sandwiches made to order. Near WDEF-TV and other offices, the lunchtime place fills quickly with people come to sit, as well as people taking out soup by the quart and salads by the pound. Soup's On does deliver; with a minimum order of $20, they'll prepare box lunches or trays done up to your request.

Southside Grill
266-6511, 1400 Cowart St
Open Mon-Sat lunch, daily dinner, $$$$$

First you take an old empty building, on a block that's looking a bit shabby.

Then you clean up the inside, paint the outside a classy charcoal gray, hang red awnings, and build a patio. Next you install a fine kitchen, fill several rooms with linen-clothed tables, and set huge vases of fresh flowers all over the place. Hire a top-rate chef, develop a splendid menu, and hang out your shingle: Southside Grill.

That's all it took. That block is now the brightest spot in the neighborhood, very near the ChooChoo, and delighted crowds come for lunch and dinner to enjoy "southern foods reinterpreted," such as appetizers of fried green tomatoes with rock shrimp and cherry tomato vinaigrette or entrees of grilled quail with grits and roasted Georgia peach sauce.

The menu changes frequently, but you can count on special treatment for any old standard, such as ribeye, mustard-grilled with rosemary blue cheese butter, or salmon with roasted pepper glaze and crispy artichoke hearts, or a baby lettuce salad with Stilton cheese, smoked bacon and toasted pecans. Desserts are oh, so rich.

Sportsman's BarBQ
265-1680, 231 Signal Mtn Rd
Open daily, lunch/dinner, $$
Located on Signal Mountain Road is some real southern Tennessee Bar-B-Q. Owned and operated by the third generation of Sweeneys, Dee Sweeney figures he has it down pat by now. In this down-home setting you can get sandwiches or plates -- beef or pork; or chili and cornbread. Brunswick stew is available in summer months, which is when you'll be by for takeout to feed your 4th-of-July-picnic crowd.

S & S Cafeterias
855-0554, 2343 Shallowford Village Dr
Open daily, lunch/dinner, $$
100 items on the serving line; on your table, Protestant, Catholic, Jewish and Greek Orthodox prayers of thanks. S & S is truly a place of all-Americans' tastes, with the bonus of a pleasant atmosphere and an attentive staff. Must be why they had to expand after just the first year. This great Shallowford Village location is handy for folks staying in the nearby hotels, but locals seek it out too, especially the after-church lunch bunch.

Steak and Ale Restaurant
892-7775, 5751 Brainerd Rd
Open Sun lunch, daily dinner, $$$
Do you like intimate, cozy spaces with high-backed chairs that invite you to relax? Do you like a variety of choices, and courteous service? In case you do, you'll probably be comfortable at the Steak and Ale. Their Kensington Club steak, sweet-sauce marinated, has been pleasing customers for years, as has their slow-roasted prime rib. The place is English-pub in tone, with dark plank walls and fireplaces made of stone. But the salad bar is standard

American fare. And in addition to all the beef choices, there's plenty of chicken and seafood, such as lobster tails and stuffed shrimp. Mile-high mud pie for dessert. There is a large bar, in its own room near the front door.

Steak Express
870-9608, 5450 Hwy 153
Open Mon-Sat, dinner, $$$
Tonight, maybe, you aren't in the mood to order pizza or Chinese; you're too tired to go out; and a glance in the cupboard confirms that if you cook, it will be oatmeal. Steak Express can come in like the cavalry, brightening your mood and your dining table by bringing steak cooked to order, crisp salad and a piping-hot baked potato. They have chicken and shrimp on the menu too; call to find out if you are in their Hixson-area delivery range.

Steak-Out
629-8834, 3507 Ringgold Rd
899-2528, 6940 Lee Hwy
Open daily lunch/dinner/late, $$$
Just like Steak Express described above, Steak-Out is the mothers-little-helper place for folks living near Ringgold Road or Lee Hwy. If you're outside the delivery area, they'll fix it for you to pick up, fast. A lifesaver!

Steamboat Supersandwiches
756-8388, 812 Broad St
Open Mon-Fri, lunch, $
Come in off the street and line up to order lunch. Get a sandwich made on fresh-baked Steamboat bread. Get the Steamboat specialty -- smoked ham, Genoa salami, pork roast, Swiss cheese, special sauce, mayo-mustard, lettuce, pickle and tomato. For real! There's also chicken, tuna, and egg salad or a three-cheese; sides of slaw or red beans and rice. Try the fresh-squeezed lemonade. Box lunches available.

Subway Sandwiches and Salads
899-3460, 5505 Brainerd Rd *877-0941, 5251 Hwy 153*
756-3850, 3401 Broad St *866-1679, K-Mart Plaza, Ft Ogle*
821-4070, 115 Browns Ferry Rd *499-3814, 1456 Mack Smith Rd*
870-8793, 3714 Dayton Blvd *265-3022, 850 Market St*
265-7395, 1129 E 3rd *629-2991, 3713 Ringgold Rd*
698-2877, 2113 E 23rd *867-3776, 3416 Rossville Blvd*
499-6303, 7550 E Brainerd Rd *894-7526, 5717 Shallowford Rd*
899-8039, 4420 Hwy 58
Open daily, lunch/dinner, $$
Order your sub or salad as you walk along the counter; they'll build it just the way you want and serve it hot or cold. Get turkey, ham, chicken, steak, cheese, barbecue, or BLT; add a big cookie and a bag of chips. Eat in or on the go; you should be able to find one of these cheerful little spots near wherever you live or work.

Taco Bell

756-2423, 3151 Broad St
892-9034, 7796 E Brainerd Rd
899-1197, 2100 Hamilton Pl Mall
877-9557, 3877 Hixson Pike
899-6118, 4786 Hwy 58
875-6198, 5439 Hwy 153
Open daily, lunch/dinner, $

866-0630, 422 Lafayette Rd
499-0815, 6210 Lee Hwy
899-8257, 6200 Ringgold Rd
867-4226, 4115 Rossville Blvd
899-8416, 7304 Shallowford Rd
965-8226, 403 S Hwy 151

Jeffrey, who's nine, claims The Bell as his favorite fast-food place. And who doesn't love to munch a crunchy taco? New in '95 are health-conscious, low-fat lights; free drink refills here, and always deals on special; you can get a lot for just a little cash. Mix it up with burritos, tostadas, pintos and cheese, even a pint-sized Mexican pizza; what's your pleasure? Family packs are great to take-home from the border. Or eat-in, quickly, in this bright, efficient eatery by the bell.

TGI Fridays

855-8443, 2215 Hamilton Place Blvd
752-8443, 2 Broad St
Open daily, lunch/dinner, $$$

Any day of the week is a fine day to go to Fridays. The staff is dressed in red striped shirts, suspenders are decked with buttons and pins from the wearer's private collection, and everybody wears a zany hat. Toys and signs and odds and ends hang from every corner of every corner in this upbeat, have-fun spot. Pastas are popular; there's steak-on-a-stick or vegetarian burgers with corn salsa; fish and chicken and beef done every way, but with a slightly different flair.

Desserts are good, and there's a separate, lively bar. The location by the Aquarium is so busy it had to expand after its first year to accommodate the crowds.

Thai Food at Chattanooga

267-4433, 340 Market St
Open Mon-Sat, lunch, $

Chantana Israngkul Lane, the owner of Thai Food, teaches physics at UTC, which is why the restaurant isn't open for dinner. "There's only so much time," she explains. Meanwhile she varies the daily buffet menu so Chattanoogans will get a chance to try many Thai foods.

Pud Thai, a dish as standard to the cuisine of Thailand as fried chicken and mashed potatoes are to Chattanooga, is a good place to start: it's stir-fry with rice noodles, veggies, and a hint of peanuts, coated with tamarin juice and special spices. Other almost-southern dishes are Panang Beef, a stew with tender beef chunks, potatoes, and peanuts in coconut milk with curry paste, and Tod Mun Corn, a southern-looking fritter, served with a little cup of cucumber/onion/vinegar sauce.

In this inexpensive 10-table paper-plate spot you're likely to meet downtown workers, families with kids, or foot-weary tourists; the Market Street location is handy to lots of things.

Town and Country Restaurant
267-8544, 110 N Market St
Open daily, lunch/dinner, $$$

Raise your hand now -- how many of you have had a birthday officially solemnized by Marvin Trew at the organ of the T & C as the smiling waitress brought the candle-topped slice of cake to your table amidst stares and applause all around? Depending on your age, you were either very pleased and made your wish, or you had a fit. Remember?

If walls could talk, how many stories could be told? There have been marriage proposals in the Bridge Tender bar and last dates over broiled red snapper and homestyle green beans; business deals that changed employment patterns in the town over luncheon sandwich platters; and thousands upon thousands of gatherings, over ribeyes and vegetable plates, when families or friends met simply to visit and keep in touch.

Nobody will say it's the best restaurant in town, though their steaks continue to rank with the finest you can find; yet everybody goes there, a lot. It's not a fancy place, it's love; a part of people's lives in Chattanooga for more than 40 years; a cornerstone of the north side of town.

Trip's Seafood Restaurant
892-6880, 6715 Ringgold Rd
Open Sat-Sun lunch, daily dinner, $$$

Walk the plank and board the old clipper ship for a jolly good trip; a place where a land-or-water-lubber's seafaring food-needs can be met. Dark wooden booths, high ceilings, and huge seascape paintings await you inside, where your view looks pond-ward to the home of big white geese and quacking ducks; a pleasant waterside scene in East Ridge near South Chickamauga Creek, which sometimes meanders over into the pond. A few times the Creek has reached the parking lot; ask the owner about his rowboating days.

Center stage are two buffet tables; order all-you-can eat salad and seafood and forget about the menu; or select from a big variety of menu items if you're in a lesser-eating mood. Popular items are shrimp, deviled crab, oysters on half shell, and catfish; ribeye steak and grilled chicken if you aren't out for seafood. Allow enough time for a walk by the pond with the kids; they'll love feeding the waterfowl. There's a small playground too, especially good if you've been traveling all day.

Inspectors and reviewers for Chattanooga Great Places *accept no free meals or favors; the book has no sponsors or advertisers.*

Two Twelve Market St
265-1212, 212 Market St
Open daily, lunch/dinner, $$$$
Location: perfect. Decor: perfect. Service: perfect. Food: Exquisite! The 212 gets high marks for doing what it does so well: serving fine international cuisine and providing an interesting dining spot at the north end of town. Across the street from the Aquarium complex and at the south end of the Market Street Bridge, it's handy if you're coming from the north, or downtown, or wherever else you might be when you're ready for lunch, afternoon cocktails, or a splendid dinner.

It's not large, but it's spacious; a main dining area and another farther back; an upstairs balcony, an outside deck, a small bar. Colors are muted, tables are prettily set; it leans towards southwestern, designed to be pleasant with no pretensions anywhere. World-traveled Maggie Moses and her equally-traveled daughters oversee every aspect of this restaurant, from Sally's greeting at the front to the food on your plate, created and prepared by chef Susan. Ask them about the art; all is original, much of it was created especially for 212.

The wine list is extensive, and the food, ah, yes -- start with fried artichoke hearts with lemon tarragon vinaigrette, then have pan-seared sea bass, boursin-stuffed veal chop served with champagne mushroom sauce, or grilled New York strip. The menu features specialty items from every corner of the globe. Maggie was nutrition director for the Tennessee Department of Health for a number of years; combine that with her years of living in Europe and Puerto Rico and you'll understand the focus on freshness and variety -- the vegetable plate here is not mac-and-cheese, it's what's in season and it's not fussed over, or fried. Get on the mailing list for the newsletter; keep up with the special wine-tasting dinners and the cooking classes they regularly offer. They'll do your catering or arrange private parties there. Live music weekends; jazz for Sunday brunch.

Typhoon of Toyko
875-6142, 3913 Dayton Blvd
Open Mon-Sat, lunch/dinner, $$
Order on the phone and pick up on your way home. There are 16 selections on the menu, all served with fried rice and vegetables: teriyaki chicken, sukiyaki steak, hibachi steak; or mix it up with steak and chicken, shrimp and chicken, surf and turf. Portions are large; if your day isn't too much of a whirlwind, there are tables and booths to eat in at the Typhoon.

Uncle Bud's Catfish
855-0900, 6303 Ringgold Rd
Open Sat-Sun lunch, daily dinner, $$$
A giant catfish circles the air above Uncle Bud's, possibly one of the few that got away. Uncle Bud is in the catfish business. In ten years, he has served 300

tons of them, with 2 million hushpuppies on the side. He collects ball caps too; look at the ceiling when you go inside. Take him one of yours, he'll trade. And that's just the first of many deals. Children under 6 eat free, and there are grab bags of surprises for all children who bring an adult.

Have a seat in a straight-backed chair at a checkered table, already set for you with a big roll of paper towels for keeping your fingers wiped clean. Immediately they start hauling out the fixin's -- a bowl of white beans, slaw, crispy hot hushpuppies. Now choose: will you have all-you-can-eat catfish, or chicken? Or a regular dinner, maybe oysters, shrimp, or chicken-fried steak? A bayou platter gets you froglegs, gator tail, and catfish fillets. All-you-want beverages come in a quart jar: sweet or buttermilk, iced tea, soft drinks or lemonade. Beer is served too, in mug or pitcher size.

The overall-clad staff provides very attentive service, and Uncle Bud guarantees everything. If there's something you don't like, they'll fix it or take it off your bill! It's that kind of attention, plus the public's recognition that those grainfed catfish from Mississippi farms are high in protein, low in fat, and taste darn good, that accounts for the growth of Uncle Bud's places: from Franklin, Tennessee to Nashville, to East Ridge, to Smyrna, Georgia.

Veg-Out
867-5517, 4801 English Ave
Open Mon-Fri, lunch, $
Whatever is fast food coming to, anyhow? Vegetables? You're headed south on Rossville Boulevard, almost to the Georgia line. Make a right across the railroad track, and drive up to the tan and green square building with the Veg-Out sign. Order mashed potatoes, corn, turnip greens, squash. Or peas, or beans, or okra, if you please. The cooking pots are lined up in a row; the menu changes every day. Oh, yes, they do have meats: tender chicken, country steak, three a day.

The styrofoam box is passed to you with fork and napkin, and a gift of banana pudding, for dessert. On a sunny day you may choose to sit at the picnic tables out front. Grandma would be proud, to see you eating your veggies like that.

Vine Street Market
265-4339, 735 Broad St   *267-0162, 414 Vine St*
Open Mon-Fri lunch, $ *Open Mon-Sat lunch/dinner, $$$*
The Vine Street location is near UTC; wander through the store to the back counter to order lunch, deli-style; on your way out go back through the store to pick up that unusual item you can't find anywhere else. Evenings are for relaxing; they offer table service then, with several beef, seafood or pasta choices, American gourmet style. The setting is unique: wooden tables and straight-backed chairs fill one side of the room; specialty grocery items the other; a nice place for an early evening wine-over-candlelight with a friend

while you talk over the day. The James Building location is a handy spot for downtown workers needing lunch on-the-go.

Vittles
886-3982, 1210 Taft Hwy
Open Mon-Sat, breakfast/lunch/dinner, $
Breakfast vittles served all day: old-fashioned French toast dusted with cinnamon and powdered sugar, a 6-oz ribeye with grits and biscuits, an egg sandwich with lettuce and tomato; get-you-going stuff. It's just a little nook, there on Signal Mountain, but they can feed you three squares a day, six days a week. Good food, not fast, is the promise; carried out with soups, salads, seafood, steaks, and daily specials; all to happy Rockola sounds, for feasting with a smile.

Waffle House
899-9998, 4903 Brainerd Rd	*899-9999, 6513 Ringgold Rd*
821-5908, 3805 Cummings Hwy	*899-7218, 6007 Shallowford Rd*
622-9396, 2023 E 23rd	*899-3888, 7018 Shallowford Rd*
892-9994, 4503 Hwy 58	*756-9547, 102 Signal Mtn Rd*
899-2516, 7705 Lee Hwy	

Open daily, 24 hours, $
The waffles must be good here, they've sold over 260,000,000 of them since 1955. And they claim to be the world's leading server of cheese 'n eggs, grits, raisin toast, and apple butter. You can get golden hash browns six different ways: scattered, smothered, covered, chunked, topped, and diced! This 24-hour eatery with the plain brown decor is more than breakfast, though; grab a stool or a booth when you want a burger, sandwich, or just a piece of pie.

Warehouse Row Food Court
265-7820, 1100 Market St
Open daily, lunch/dinner, $
One good thing about eating in Warehouse Row mall is the eating area, an atrium of white-chaired tables surrounded by brass-trimmed banisters, an elevator with a view, and two layers of balconies overhead. The finery beyond is priced to please, a thought that keeps your mood set on pleasant. The other good thing is the food itself.

Taiwan Express
♦ At a pretty red-tiled counter you can order an Express Platter; you'll get rice, eggroll, and a choice of such goodies as cashew chicken or garlic beef.
Cozzoli's Pizza
♦ Behind the brass rail pizzas bake, spaghetti sauce bubbles, and a sign proclaims "here is the baked potato that will change your life forever."
Larry's Deli
♦ At one counter you order sandwiches, subs and salads. At another, Gourmet Burgers. Under the huge "Your Way" sign are platters of fresh-sliced tomatoes, lettuce, pickles, and all the fixings.

Mr. Cappuccino

♦ Summer or winter, this specialty wagon is there to serve you, parked outside between the main buildings. As you order your mid-morning latte, you are reminded "Life is too short to drink bad coffee."

Way It Was Cafe

870-9768, 4047 Hixson Pike
Open daily, lunch/dinner, $$$
The way it is in The Way It Was is this: every wooden booth has its own chandelier, and no two are alike. Old-timey farming and fishing implements hang on dainty-blue walls. There's not much privacy, and the view is just the traffic on Access Road and Hixson Pike.

But does this smallish restaurant ever have the food! Listen to this: for dinner, choose between Austin steak, Santa Fe steak, or a filet; grilled salmon, shrimp, chicken piccata, veal piccata, chicken divan, veal parmesan, linguini, lasagna, spaghetti, fajitas or old-fashioned fried fish. Everything, even the croutons, is made from scratch, and cooked to order.

The 13-cakes-and-pies dessert list tempts with ambrosia cake, black-bottom pie, and a poppyseed cake with sherry topping. And we haven't even talked about lunches, or appetizers, or the specials every day of the week. Or the homemade bread! Most famous of all is Oktoberfest, the month-long celebration featuring hearty German foods. Get started; it will take you quite a while to work your way through the 110 items on this big, big menu.

Waycrazy's Bar-B-Que

332-1347, 10180 Dayton Pike
886-3283, 3720 Taft Hwy*
Open Mon-Sat, lunch/dinner, $$
*Things are kinda crazy here, at this modernish log cabin with the big front porch on Signal Mountain. The staff scurries around taking orders, bringing out jars of tea, checking to see if you like your food. Every time the swinging door flaps, you hear loud music coming from the kitchen. What's going on in there?

Maybe a barbecue chef is like the Maytag repairman, patiently waiting for the 24-hour slow-smoking time to elapse before hand-pulling the juicy, tender meat. Maybe they need the music to while away the time! Whatever, it works. You'll be crazy about the food that's set before you — bar-b-que platters, bar-b-que sandwiches, or burgers, chicken, shrimp. Pies come in pecan, coconut, or a loverly bunch of chocolates. Locals line up at the take-out counter every day; catering is available too. Also on Dayton Pike.

Looking for a particular place? Check the index at the back of this book for individual restaurants, attractions, events, galleries, museums, recreational places, sports, tours, stores, lodgings, churches, schools and business services.

Wendy's Old Fashioned Hamburgers

861-4411, 106 Battlefield Pkwy	*875-8610, 4516 Hixson Pike*
899-9060, 5200 Brainerd Rd	*894-3587, 4510 Hwy 58*
267-0754, 3116 Broad St	*899-6552, 7019 Shallowford Rd*
875-2618, 1868 Dayton Blvd	*622-0270, 4124 Ringgold Rd*
629-1080, 2103 E 24th	*867-1773, 4704 Rossville Blvd*

Open daily, lunch/dinner, $
An all-round food place, you can count on Wendy's for old-fashioned burgers, potatoes with just about anything on top, and bars with salads, taco fixings, and even chocolate pudding; ready for you to help yourself. The many sandwich combos get big ad time on TV; watch for specials, done just the way Wendy wants them; good prices for you.

Yellow Submarine Rock-n-Roll Cafe
266-8999, 347 Broad St
Open Mon-Sat, lunch/dinner, $
The downtown Yellow Sub is a neat treat after a visit to the Aquarium's underwater scenes. Enter the front room on Broad Street, you'll find some stools and booths there; wander through the sub-like halls to the back dining rooms, where jade-green walls are trimmed in red and yellow, and 60's sound surrounds. Listen to the music while Frankie Valli, the Shangri-Las and Jimi Hendrix watch over you from album covers on the wall.

The subs, cold and hot, are served on 8-inch Italian rolls; pepperoni and cheese, mushroom cheese steak, chickaPhilly, meatball, tuna torpedo, ham and swiss. There's a breakfast sub too -- scrambled eggs with onions, bell peppers and provolone cheese, bacon topped. A Guppy Meal for the little ones; soft drinks, tea and beer from the beverage port.

Food for Thought
A message to non-southerners.
As the young man says in the illustration on p.13, "Southern cooking makes you good looking." This widely-held belief is expressed in some foodstuffs that look a bit quirky to people from other parts of the country. "Sweet tea" is just what it says, and is served over lots of ice. (When you ask for "tea" in the south, it always comes iced!) Biscuits and cornbread are two staples; biscuits are most popular at breakfast time, slathered with butter and homemade jam or sorghum syrup. Cornbread is usually the bread of choice with country vegetables; it turns into hushpuppies when you're having fish. Don't let "grits" frighten you; grits are simply finely-ground corn. Sometimes grits are served as hot cereal, with butter, sugar and milk; sometimes, with salt, pepper and cheese added, as a side dish with your eggs and ham. Try it! But to really gain the Southern Cooking Badge of Honor, one eventually must acquire a taste for the most truly southern food of all -- okra. Put this on your refrigerator door for daily study:

Okra is a fuzzy pod, it's full of seeds and slime;
But chopped and battered, then deep fried; it's southern food sublime!

People Who Love Chattanooga
Russell Linnemann

"I started collecting blues albums when I was about ten," Russell tells when you ask how it all began. "And then I followed my heart and went to where the music was." Over the years his quest has led to southern backroads and northern ghettoes; to roadhouses and juke joints and cafe backrooms; sharing the black man's bottle and his blues; a white man seeking understanding through music. "It's the most gorgeous music in the world," Russell says simply, "for nothing tells of the human condition like the blues."

New Jersey-born and Michigan-schooled, he arrived in Chattanooga in 1970, a new face at a newly established university; UTC's second year. For more than a quarter of a century, as more than 7,000 students have come into his classroom, this historian has shared his knowledge of the history of the world, the British Empire, the African continent, and more recently, the blues. He's put down stay-here-forever roots, making Chattanooga his home, raising his children, working for his community, and bringing the blues to the people.

Dubbed "The Blues Doctor" by dee-jay Bobby Q. Day because of his University-PhD status and in-depth musical knowledge, he was involved with the Riverbend Festival for a while, working to make the Bessie Smith Strut more purely blues flavored, in keeping with the music the legendary singer brought to the world; his legacy there continues. Twice a week you can catch his smoky, speak-easy voice on WUTC-FM as he leads listeners into the land of the blues, telling how his life has twined with the lives of the artists; airing their stories and their songs up-close and Have-Mercy-Baby personal. And Monday nights, you can find him emceeing the blues show at the Sandbar.

"The Traveling Riverside Blues Caravan at the Sandbar is the finest blues Monday between the Chameleon Club in Lancaster, PA and Buffett's Club in Key West, Florida," Russell is quick to tell you. "Our unique geographical location at the crossroads of freeways makes it easier to bring people in." Since he knows and works with blues artists around the country, his behind-the-scenes hours on the phone result in such quality talent as Tinsley Ellis, Koko Taylor, Magic Slim, Kim Wilson, Marcia Ball, and Lil' Ed and the Blues Imperials stopping here on Mondays as they travel from one big-city weekend gig to the next; Chattanoogans troop to the Sandbar to reap the benefits.

Dr. Russell J. Linnemann is a professor in the History Department at the University of Tennessee at Chattanooga, serves on the Board of Directors of the National Blues Foundation, is Vice President of the Board for Bessie Smith Hall, hosts two blues shows on WUTC-FM 88.1, and books and hosts Blues Monday at the Sandbar Club, working tirelessly to bring quality music to Chattanooga.

Why the emphasis on bringing blues music to Chattanooga? "It's another way to teach," is Russell's answer. "It allows me to share with others what has touched my life. And understanding helps us come together." His wish list? "I want more people to discover the joy of live music. I'd like to see Chattanoogans supporting it in every way they can."

Arts & Entertainment

Contents

G-Kid 1: After we get our books, let's go to the Museum.
G-Kid 2: After that, I want to go to the Fair. Can we?
G-Kid 3: I'm tired. Carry me, please.
G-Mom: I can feel my legs getting shorter.

Organizations & Information

Allied Arts of Greater Chattanooga
756-2787, 20 Bluff View
Call ARTSLINE 756-ARTS 24-hours a day for information on what's happening in the community. For goodness sake get a membership; support the arts and get on the mailing list for *Connections*, a newsletter/calendar that guides you to the city's arts events. Member agencies in this umbrella organization include arts education resources, community arts, museums, parks and natural resources and interpretive centers, performing arts and visual arts organizations.

The variety is astounding; among the 60 groups are Authors & Artists Club, Ballet Tennessee, Chattanooga Boys Choir, Chattanooga Girls Choir, Chattanooga Anthropological Association, Chickamauga National Military Park, Creative Discovery Museum, Dance-Theatre Workshop, Friends of the Library, Hamilton County Department of Parks and Recreation, Mountain Opry, Reflection Riding, Shaking Ray Levi Society, Senior Neighbors, and WUTC-FM.

Visitors, call ARTSLINE before you get to town. Plan your stay around upcoming events.

Arts and Education Council
267-1218, 100 Woodland Street
The Council presents educational and cultural programs for students and adults, including an international film series, Tivoli dramas for student audiences, the Chattanooga Conference on Southern Literature, City Lights Musicfest, and Point of View, the nation's longest-running local TV program addressing topical issues.

Association for Visual Artists (AVA)
265-4282, 1303 Hixson Pike, Ste C
AVA's Artist-in-Residence program promotes interaction between art, artist, and community. Artists demonstrate and exhibit their works in Waterhouse Pavilion at Miller Plaza during summer months; there's an All-Member show in the fall. AVA also sponsors Artstravaganza (see p.80), which includes a children's festival. If you fly into Chattanooga's airport, you'll be treated to changing exhibits there, courtesy of AVA.

Ballet Tennessee
265-8930, 18 Frazier Ave
Two public performances annually: *Dracula* at the end of October, and a mixed-works selection of ballets in the spring; catch them at UTC Fine Arts Center. Directors Anna Baker-Van Cura and Barry Van Cura offer a summer workshop and classes for children and adults: ballet, pointe, modern, jazz.

Chattanooga Area Friends of Folk Music
775-2996, 7566 Dayton Mtn Hwy, Dayton 37321
This nonprofit organization has its sights set on preserving and promoting traditional music, arts and dance in Chattanooga and the surrounding area. The newsletter keeps you up-to-date on concerts and festivals; social events usually include informal "front-porch picking" sessions. Storytelling and collecting are part of it too.

Chattanooga Area Square Dance Association
886-3090 local; 615-367-0796 state
Square dancing is the official folk dance of Tennessee; this group is one of many within the state Association of Square and Round Dance Clubs. Square dancing is a family activity; fun and good exercise for all ages. Contact above for information about dances/classes in the area.

Chattanooga Ballet
755-4672, 615 McCallie Ave, UTC campus & branch locations
They produce *The Nutcracker* during the holiday season with a cast of 220 performers -- guest artists and students from Chattanooga Ballet and other area dance schools, accompanied by the Chattanooga Symphony Orchestra. Instruction in classical ballet, pointe, modern, jazz, and pre-ballet.

Chattanooga Boys Choir
265-3030, 1206 Market St
A tradition of choral performance and training for more than 37 years; Choir is comprised of more than 200 boys from 70 area schools. *The Singing Christmas Tree* in December and the spring concert are popular annual events.

Chattanooga Downtown Partnership
265-0771, 850 Market St
Defining itself as "the gatekeeper" of downtown, this organization works to promote the center city as a beautiful, safe and fun place to live, work, shop and play. Credit them with the Building Lights program (downtown buildings outlined in twinkling lights), plus seasonally changing banners, sidewalk planters and music at Miller Plaza, the Waterhouse Pavilion, and Ross's Landing Plaza, call or watch the paper for scheduling.

Chattanooga Girls Choir
755-4737, Cadek Conservatory, 615 McCallie Ave
The Girls Choir was started in 1987; now includes 160 girls in the training and performing choirs and has performed in Washington, DC, Vienna and Wales. Spring performance and Christmas show.

Chattanooga Mass Choir
265-0406
About 100 members in this gospel group, representing more than 23 churches

in the city. They do a benefit every Thanksgiving to raise money to feed needy families; call to find out where you can hear them sing.

Chattanooga Symphony & Opera Association
267-8583, 630 Chestnut
The full year's slate includes classical concerts, full-staged opera productions, a cabaret pops series, and chamber music concerts. To be sure you've got a ticket when the production begins, purchase a package for the type of music you prefer -- Pops, Opera, Symphony or Fanfare; also, join the Guild to participate in support activities -- that will get you the monthly newsletter too.

Chattanooga Traditional Dance Society
855-0401, 706-539-2485
Contra dancing and some square dancing to live music on the last Sunday of the month at 3 PM; beginner's workshop at every dance; partner not required; children welcome; held at Tyner Recreation Center.

Chattanooga Visitors Center
800-322-3344 or 756-8687 for visitor information by phone; located at 2 Broad St, open 8-5:30 daily, second location in Oasis area of Hamilton Place Mall, open daily, mall hours
This is your one-stop shop for just about everything Chattanooga has to offer. Call to find out what's going on in town and where it is. Visitors are people who are visiting, so even if you live here, any visit you make to a place that's not your house entitles you to Visitors Center services. Hundreds of brochures, books about area available here; also movie, *Marks on the Land*, great for school groups and everyone who's interested in knowing more about Chattanooga.

Choo Choo Kids
757-5000, Phoenix High School for Performing Arts, 1301 Dallas Road
This 18-member musical theatre touring company sings, dances, and acts its way through more than three dozen performances a year, traveling to conventions, charity events, and schools. Selected by audition from the vocal music department at Phoenix III High School for the Performing Arts, they've appeared on *Good Morning America* and *CBS This Morning*; their repertoire includes everything from Mickey Mouse Club tunes to New York dance club numbers. Members of the group learn how to build and paint sets and design and sew costumes -- and they still have to do their homework.

Choral Arts Society
238-6533
This 32-member professional chorus performs great choral music throughout the year from classical oratorios to pops concerts; specials have featured all-Jewish music, all-folk music, etc. Catch them at the Tivoli, UTC, or various churches in the area.

Choral Society for Preservation of AfricanAmSong
755-5204, UTC Music Dept, 615 McCallie Ave
This group of approximately 60 performers puts on several shows a year
featuring music by African-American composers. Call for schedule.

Civic Ballet of Chattanooga
894-1406, 8126 E Brainerd Rd
They produce *The Nutcracker* at holiday time, utilizing area dancers and more
than 200 students from Massari-Wood Dance Center in leading roles.
Massari-Wood offers classes in classical ballet, pointe, jazz, tap.

Contemporary Performing Arts of Chattanooga (CoPAC)
825-5914, 1307 Dodds Ave
This nonprofit organization focuses on cutting-edge performing arts and
oversees the Barking Legs Theatre; membership brings you discounts for
performances and members-only events. Strong community outreach
program works with schools and other groups interested in the arts.

Dance-Theatre Workshop
756-1942, 1222 Tremont
Chattanooga's improvisational group has workshops and performances.
Theatre and dance classes for children and adults; jazz, tap, modern, ballet,
scene study, improvisational acting. Home of Chattanoodle, the improv
comedy group.

The Disciples
622-4120, 265-4910
Ferdinand Sanders directs this group of eighteen gospel singers representing
several churches in the area; they rehearse at New Jerusalem Baptist. Watch
the paper or call to see where they'll be performing; they've appeared for
Coffeehouse Series and other bookings in the south.

Friends of the Festival
756-2211, Box 886, 37401
Organizers and planners of annual Riverbend Festival and Kaleidoscope for
children. (See pp.84,86)

Friends of the Library
757-5425, 1001 Broad St
Spring and fall series of bi-weekly book reviews at noon at the downtown
branch of the Chattanooga-Hamilton County Bicentennial Library; bring your
lunch. Friends also assists with "Let's Talk About It," a lecture and discussion
theme-series -- previously they have covered Great American Classics,
Mysteries, the Civil War. Friends sponsors an annual Book Sale, a huge
springtime event with proceeds going for support of Library; held in '95 at
Northgate Shopping Mall.

Mary Walker Foundation
629-7651, call between 10-4
Mary Walker was born a slave in Union Springs, Alabama in 1848, moved to Chattanooga in 1917, and lived here until her death in 1969. The Foundation has a collection of artifacts which belonged to Mary Walker, such as the Bible she was given in 1869 -- it was a treasured possession and what inspired her to learn to read in 1964, at the age of 116. The Foundation also has a collection of books on slavery, and interpretive texts and photographs of African-Americans during the Civil War. An exhibit entitled *Bright Ideas* shows the contributions of African-American inventors such as Garrett Morgan, Andrew Beard, and Granville T. Woods, who was granted over 150 patents; their inventions include the traffic light and automatic railroad coupler. Civil Rights exhibit too; all are available for display, call to make arrangements.

Positive Christian Singles (PCS)
756-2021, 419 McCallie Ave, First-Centenary Church
This non-denominational organization has something going on just about every day: Monday evening dinners include several choices of programs, bridge and volleyball; weekends are cram-packed with dances, music, travel, or service projects; dinner-gatherings every Friday; brunches and walks on Sunday; various support groups throughout the week. Only prerequisite is single-hood; Singles I for up-to-mid-thirties, PCS for all ages. Organized in late '70's, this is one of the largest such groups in the country with over 800 members. Call for information and newsletter of activities.

Ripe and Ready Players
755-6100, Senior Neighbors, 10th and Newby
Also known as "Saturday Night Live for Older Adults," this group of actors-over-60 does original material with a satirical-musical twist, focusing on the joys of being "mature." Directed by Suzanne Carter, who teaches in UTC's drama department and writes most of the material, this group does a three-performance home-show at Senior Neighbors, but mostly they're on-the-road, appearing at Barking Legs Theatre, Cumberland County Playhouse, and churches and conferences everywhere. Call for info on catching a performance or becoming part of the group.

Scenic City Chorus of Sweet Adelines
842-6197, 899-8865
International organization of women's barbershop singing -- that's four-part unaccompanied music. Public show once a year; regional contest over five states; perform at civic groups, banquets, fairs such as Hamilton County Fair and Praters Mill Country Fair. 35 women in group; contact Lois Long or Joyce Stanberry.

Looking for a particular place? Check the index at the back of this book for individual attractions, events, galleries, museums, recreational places, sports, tours, stores, lodgings, churches, schools and business services.

Society for Preservation and Encouragement of Barbershop Quartet Singing in America (SPEBSQSA)
706-937-5051
The 58 male members of the local chapter make up a chorus and six quartets. Call for schedule; funds earned from performances go to the support of musical education programs.

Shaking Ray Levi Society
267-6688, Box 21534, 37421
A center for improvisational music, performance and recording since 1986. Accomplishments: educational programs reaching more than 7,000 children of all ages in the schools, bringing professional musicians for jazz instrumentation, composition, improvisation workshops; spoken word performance series *All Talk*; and WUTC's radio program *Outside Pleasures*, with multi-ethnic music, live original music, storytellers, poets, and conversation.

Recognized nationally for its work in Chattanooga, this hardworking, highly active society is completely volunteer. A membership helps to keep the group going and gets you notices of all upcoming performances and festivals AND a 15% discount.

Tivoli/Auditorium Promotion Association (TAPA)
757-5042, 399 McCallie Ave, 37402
TAPA is the booking organization for the Tivoli and the Auditorium; they bring in touring performances throughout the year too. Tickets can be purchased for individual shows; prices lower for packages or matinees. Call to get on mailing list for advance ordering.

Art is Everywhere

We are lucky in Chattanooga. The art of nature gave us a world made of softly-rounded mountains framing a usually-sky-blue sky and a curving, meandering river outlining tree-studded ridges. The nature of art keeps us busy interpreting our world; we paint it, sculpt it, stain-glass it, sing it, write it, weave it, and then, quite proud, hang it out for someone else to see.

This from-the-heart expression is everywhere, from the preschoolers majestic scribbles magneted to the refrigerator door to the flower-bedded yard in front of our house. It's in the letter we write to a friend, the song we sing to a child-in-arms, the tapping of a toe to a rhythm we silently hear, the needlepoint from Granny, Shelagh's handwoven scarf, Aunt Minnie's quilt.

Watch for this human-art wherever you go; you'll find it under your feet, above your head, and right before your eyes, in the most everyday, ordinary places.

It's inside our office buildings, such as the **Blue Cross and Blue Shield Building,** *755-2184, 801 Pine St, open Mon-Fri 8:00-4:15.* Step into the lobby of the beautiful bronze building and enjoy the work of various art groups and individuals; exhibits change the first of each month; and stop at the **Market Court Building,** *537 Market Street, open Mon-Fri 7:00-5:00;* in a spacious lobby you'll see a two-story marble fountain surrounded by lush greenery, and Dad, Mom, Sister, Brother, and Dog out for a stroll; it's *The Family,* in copper by local sculptor Jim Collins, 1989.

Look inside our hotels and restaurants. At the **Radisson Read House,** *ML King Blvd and Broad Street, open daily,* see local artist Debbie Baker's **portraits of Civil War officers** posted in the main lobby -- Sherman, Grant, Longstreet, Bragg and more, looking full-regalia stern. Behind the registration desk hangs a reproduction of James Walker's *Battle Above the Clouds;* see the 13' x 33' original at Point Park on Lookout Mountain. On every floor of the hotel events of the Civil War period are depicted in various form. **Two Twelve Market Street Restaurant,** *212 Market St,* and **Mudpie Coffeehouse and Newsstand,** *12 Frazier Ave,* have high-flying kites, made-just-for-that-wall sculptures, rugs, tapestries, furnishings, paintings, and little surprises; look high, and low, and even in the restroom.

Many of our churches have outstanding art inside, such as the stained glass and gold windows at **First-Centenary United Methodist Church,** *756-2021, 419 McCallie Avenue.* This church traces its roots to an 1839 beginning as the first church in Chattanooga; still serving the community from a central-city location, the present building was dedicated in 1973. You are welcome to step into the chancel during weekday business hours from the Oak Street entrance to see the 18 windows. The brilliantly-colored glass is an inch or more thick, cut and faceted; for the main 50-foot-high chancel window, glass was covered with sculptured lead, then 23-karat gold leaf. Both the message and the medium are breathtaking in stained glass by day and brilliant gold leaf shining under lights at night. Beautiful from the outside too; drive down Oak Street after dark. Literature available which explains each of the windows.

And there are **14 Stations of the Cross** and **14 Tiffany stained glass windows** at **Saints Peter and Paul Catholic Church,** *266-1618, 214 E 8th St.* The history of this church is as awesome as its art; the Civil War playing a major part. Construction began in 1858, but the Union Army demolished it in 1863, using the stone for fortifications. After the war a claim was presented to the War Department; in 1888 the Federal government paid the church $18,729 for damages. On June 29, 1890, the building which stands today was dedicated. The Stations of the Cross were seventeen years in the design; the 30-foot high stained glass windows were made by Louis Comfort Tiffany, contain over 12,000 pieces of glass, and represent major events in the lives of Saint Peter and Saint Paul. Due to staff limitations, church is only open half-hour prior to services, which are Saturday 5:30 PM and Sunday 8:30 and 11 AM; plan your visit then. Literature available which describes Stations and windows.

Crane your neck and look up and up at the beautiful **interiors and domes** in some of our buildings. The **Tivoli Theatre**, *709 Broad Street* is the Jewel Box of the South; the magnificent, ornate interior is worth gazing at, no matter what the show; sit back and look around. The **Hamilton County Courthouse** is largely unaltered inside since construction in 1912; don't dash in and grab that license plate; stop and see the egg-and-dart molding, terrazzo floors, and three-story stained-glass domed vault. The **Chattanooga ChooChoo Terminal** was built between 1906 and 1909; its Grand Dome rests on four major steel supports, each 75 feet apart, and soars over the general waiting room; visit at Christmastime when the huge 60-foot wreath is hanging high.

Outside, there's wildlife to be seen. How many **eagles** can you spot on these buildings? **Chattanooga Bank Building,** *Market & W 8th*, was built in 1928 and features Art Deco detail; along about the third-floor level facing 8th you'll find eagles, a motif that was popular during the Depression; the eagle symbolized security and stability. More eagles at the entrance area of the **Maclellan Building,** *721 Broad St*, which was built in 1924, and at the 1932-built **Federal Post Office Building,** 10th and Georgia, which is the most outstanding example of Art Deco architecture in the city.

While you're outside, take a walking tour to see these items: Indian statue at Ross's Landing, named simply *Cherokee*, or Tsa-la-gi, this bronze life-size piece was created by sculptor Jud Hartman in 1992. The strong, proud-featured man faces the river, a fine catch of fish in hand. Note the fishing implements he carries. The plaque below reveals these heart-thought words: *"Among these people everyman is a king unto himself and no man is above any other."* Lovely benches are near for sitting right over the water.

Ross's Landing Park and Plaza functions as an environmental art piece, a buffer between the river and the city. Pick up the folder explaining the bands of history; pre-1600's to the 1990's. A lance head reminds of Spanish explorers; effigy pots represent the Creek Indians; names of Cherokee clans are recorded in the Cherokee language. Moldings of Civil War relics are embedded in stacked stones; castings of tools used by early industries and coiled rope used by river barges are tucked underneath the arch. Railroad track frames the lyrics to the Chattanooga ChooChoo; bottle bottoms cast from the original molds remind that Chattanooga was home to the first Coca-Cola bottling plant. Tribute is paid to Appalachian quilters and to native-born blues artist Bessie Smith; plantings of cypress, sycamore, river birch, red oaks, and red maples represent the flora from valley to mountainside. And just before you reach the city streets, watch the fountain art; rows of water jets trace the profile of mountains you can see in the distance.

Scattered through downtown are Masonry Works in Public, sidewalk art in brick for sitting, leaning or slouching! AVA selects the artist and the design, the Chattanooga Masonry Association awards the prize to the winner and builds the piece; a new one is added each year in the spring; look for these:

The Couch by Katherine Neuhardt-Minor, corner of 2nd and Broad near Aquarium, has the distinction of being listed in the Smithsonian catalogue (have a seat on this big brick sofa and get your picture took!); *The Boat* by Jim Collins, on Broad Street in front of Big River Grill; *The Water Mill* by Terry West on Market Street between bridge and Aquarium; *Cat-Fish Fantasy* by Jane Yelliot, on Market in front of Market Street Performance Hall (ceramic-tiled cats are swimming underwater, a fantasy indeed); and *An Opportunity for Conversation* by Lawrence Mathis in the 10th Street block of Market, across from Miller Park; see the window in the wall?

Older examples are the **Fireman Fountain** on Georgia, between the Hamilton County Courthouse and Brass Register; see the red-white-and-blue memorial to the first firemen to lose their lives in the city, dedicated June 9, 1888; and the **Fischer-Evans Clock** at 801 Market St, a tall and graceful cast-iron timepiece built by Fischer-Evans Jewelers in 1883, still telling Chattanooga time.

A three-piece **sculpture** by John Geoffrey Naylor ushers you to the **Bicentennial Library** at Broad and 10th; 80 crosscut slabs of stainless steel went into it; sheets of water cascade down into a pleasant pool; it was erected in 1976. Inside, of course, an art-feast of **words, ideas and don't-forget-the-past remembrances,** bound and clipped and stacked in orderly form. Across the street, *Tennessee Panorama* by Ron Pekar winds around two sides of the block; lowlands and mountain strata and sky in vivid yellows, blues and greens along the wall that's part of a TVA park.

Driving home, notice the **Folk Art Fence** surrounding the yard in North Chattanooga on Barton Avenue; the boards are carved with Civil War cannons, the Dome Building, the Aquarium, and even a replica of the Walnut Street Bridge. And what more folk-artsy thing exists than the **Little Red Birdhouses** you'll find everywhere in the city, post-perched and hanging from trees, reminders of the by-gone era of *See Rock City* **southern barns?**

Events & Festivals

Artstravaganza
265-4282, Hunter Museum of American Art and Bluff View Art District, mid-May weekend, Sat 10-10, Sun 12-7; sponsored by Association for Visual Artists
This properly named event offers much: the juried exhibition stays at the Hunter Gallery all month, accompanied by lectures and artists-dialogue; the weekend explodes with music for all and hands-on arts for the children. Local high-school music groups, the Youth Symphony, and out-of-town acts keep you entertained; the children keep themselves entertained, blowing big bubbles, testing the water-splash, painting and drawing and sculpting and singing-along, and mostly, smiling big smiles because it's so much fun to be alive, on a fine May day, on the grassy front lawn of the high-bluffed Hunter.

Battle of Chickamauga Anniversary
866-9241, Chickamauga Battlefield, Ft Oglethorpe, weekend nearest actual battle date of September 19-20, call for exact times, free
Visit the site of the battle where 18,000 Confederate and 16,000 Union soldiers lost their lives; Confederate General William Bates called the carnage a River of Death. Encampments and re-enactments, demonstrations, artillery firing of cannons, and ranger-led tours are staged by volunteers with authentic uniforms, weapons, and utensils. A great way to understand the strategy behind the battles, and the human-ache of war.

Battles of Chattanooga Anniversary
821-7786, Point Park, Lookout Mountain and Bragg Reservation, Missionary Ridge, weekend nearest actual battle dates of November 23-25, call for exact times, free
Encampments and demonstrations from two main points which overlook the valley and the city of Chattanooga. General Ulysses S. Grant arrived in Chattanooga in mid-November 1863; on November 24 the Confederates were pushed out of their defenses around Cravens House on Lookout Mountain; on November 25 Union soldiers left Lookout Mountain and broke through Confederate lines on Missionary Ridge, ending the siege and battle of Chattanooga; Union armies controlled the city from that time on. At this time of year your view across the valley is unobstructed; Civil War buffs will want to visit other historic sites on Lookout Mountain and Missionary Ridge.

Bessie Smith Traditional Jazz Festival
266-0944. Held first weekend in May. All-weekend badges $85; local admission Fri or Sat night $22.50, Sat or Sun afternoon $17.50. ChooChoo City Jazz Society
It may not be Bessie's music, but it's done in Bessie's honor: the wide-ranging effect of the festival serves to remind music lovers all over the country that Chattanooga was Bessie Smith's hometown, and funds are raised to support the Bessie Smith Hall. This three-day feast of vintage jazz feeds hearts and souls of traditional Dixieland jazz lovers; folks flock in from Boston, Seattle, San Diego, New Orleans and all points in between to hear the best bands available in the country. Past years have brought Grand Dominion, Buck Creek, High Sierra, Black Eagles. Held at the ChooChoo, the music is served cabaret style in the Centennial Ballroom, along with food and drink.

Bessie Smith Strut
Along Martin Luther King Jr Boulevard, Monday during Riverbend, mid-June, late-afternoon/evening
The Strut is officially part of the Riverbend Festival, but wow, what a whopper bopper in its own right! It's a bigger-than-giant street party, named after Chattanooga-born legendary blues singer Bessie Smith; it covers ten blocks along MLK, from Miller Plaza on Market, past the Bessie Smith Hall, the Whole Note, Memo's Barbecue, Olivet Baptist Church, and Live and Let Live Barber Shop and Laundromat, ending near Magnolia. You'll find five stages along the way with non-stop blues and jazz; even though the music is hot, all that smoke you see is coming from barbecue tents, block-sized fish

frys, and dancing, dancing, dancing. Listen to such talent as Junior Wells, Luther Johnson, Keri Leigh & the Blue Devils, Doc Paulin and His Dixieland Jazz Band; watch the people; a solid sea of Chattanoogans, come together to celebrate, on a beginning-of-summer Monday night.

Children's Autumn Festival

756-7030, Riverpark, held mid-October, Sat 10-4, Sun 1-5. Admission free, charge for games, benefits the Ronald McDonald House
A two-day carnival-in-the-park for younger children; pony rides and hayrides, a gyroscope and games, clowns and entertainment, children's art tent and stage performances. Parents and grandparents, take the little ones you love; you'll feel good seeing them have so much fun and knowing you're helping other families with little loved-ones.

Conference on Southern Literature

267-1218, 100 Woodland Street, 37405, Arts and Education Council, held spring 1995, next in spring 1997
The south is famous for its writers; this event celebrates the legacy and brings together those who enjoy the results and those who are turning out the work in today's fiction and non; plays for stage and screen, and curl-up-in-a-corner poems, stories and novels. Designed to appeal to the general reading public as well as scholars of southern literature, this biennial conference began in 1981; it brings distinguished southern authors to Chattanooga for lectures, informal discussions, book signings; includes films, dramas, music.

April '95 included a musical interpretation of Faulkner's *As I Lay Dying* and readings of award-winning plays; poet-actress-writer **Vertamae Smart-Grosvenor**, a commentator on NPR's *All Things Considered*; Atlanta novelist-screenwriter **Terry Kay**, author of award-winning *To Dance with the White Dog*; playwright-novelist **Marsha Norman**, who has won both the Pulitzer Prize and a Tony Award; total lineup of fourteen authors. Events at UTC Fine Arts Center, Tivoli Theatre, Trade Center and Market Street Performance Hall.

Fellowship of Southern Writers meets during conference with archives open at UTC Lupton Library; Fellowship recognizes and encourages literature in the south through awards and prizes.

Fall Color Cruise & Folk Festival

892-0223, 1000 Alhambra Dr, 37421 for info, event I-24 exit 158, Nickajack Reservation, Shellmound Recreation area. Usually last two weekends in October, free admission, fee for parking
Since 1968 folks have been gathering to celebrate Tennessee autumn in an area with more than 300 species of trees and 900 varieties of wildflowers, but that's not all there is to please you. There's music: traditional, bluegrass, country and gospel, matched with dancing and clogging and vocal and instrumental competitions. Folding chairs and the picnic blankets are rowed up on the ground in front of every stage; every size, shape and type of boat can be

found moored at the dock; booths are set up along the waterfront and among the trees, some filled with the works of artisans and craftspersons, some filled with southern-style foods -- fried peach pies, barbecue, corn-on-the-cob.

If you own a boat, it's a great time to be on the River, even with the crowds, as weather is usually perfect for the event. If you don't, it's a fine drive from Chattanooga via US Scenic 41 and you can take short excursions on the Chattanooga Star once you arrive -- it gets you out on the water for a while. The Southern Belle will transport you from Chattanooga through the gorge to Shellmound, a super choice, but book way, way in advance as the cruises fill up fast. This is one of the Top Twenty Annual events in the southeastern United States -- don't worry about the crowds, just go! It's a well-planned festival and there's plenty of room for everyone.

Hamilton County Fair

842-0049. Chester Frost Park, Sat-Sun 9-6 4th weekend September. Fair free, Shuttle $1.00, Chattanooga Star $5 adults, $2.50 children
Great old-timey fair fun; animals and exhibits and demonstrations and entertainment and games and food; set among the trees and along the lake-banks in our out-of-the-ordinary county park. It's the time to show off what you can do: grow the biggest pumpkin, can the greenest beans, sew the prettiest quilt, raise the fattest calf, or sing and clog your way into the hearts of hand-clapping crowds. Tents and pavilions and stages are bursting with home-grown talent and things-for-show; a true celebration of ourselves.

If you go just to be part of it all, play hum-along with the pickers on the Picking Porch, meet an udderly charming eight-gallons-to-the-day milking cow, pet a Miss-Piggy look-alike, get sticky-fingered with cotton-candy fluff, or walk around smiley-eyed because the season is autumn, and you are you. Catch the shuttle at Northgate Mall or Middle Valley Recreation Area, or catch a boat at Harrison Bay -- the Chattanooga Star will transport you cross-river to the fair.

Ketner's Mill Fall Country Fair

Box 1477, Chattanooga 37401 for info, usually held middle weekend in October, admission fee, parking free
It's worth the drive just to visit the old mill. On the banks of the Sequatchie River in Marion County, parts of it date to 1824; the new addition 1882. It's still working, pick up some stone-ground cornmeal after you've admired the simplicity of this water-driven operation. The country fair has all the things you'd expect: country cooking, more than 150 artists and craftspersons, and music and dancing. You can catch a wagon ride around the place or canoe the peaceful Sequatchie waters.

Many folks have been making this annual trek as far back as they can remember; if you've never been, let this be your year. It's the loveliest setting for a country fair in the world (see if you don't agree!), at least on a golden autumn day. Near Whitwell, Tennessee, from Chattanooga you can take the scenic drive on Hwy 27 over Suck Creek Mountain to Powell's Crossroads and follow the signs. Another route is I-24, exit 155, Hwy 28 north for 8.4 miles, turn right.

Kaleidoscope
265-4112
A new event beginning in May '95 as this book goes to press; it's planned as a creative festival for children, with international, national and local performing arts; educational and interactive activities and displays; professional theatre performances and arts activities. In '95 held in conjunction with opening of Creative Discovery Museum and right next door; may be later in summer and in a different location in future years, call.

Miller Plaza Series: Coffeehouse, Nightfall, and Nooners
265-0771, Chattanooga Downtown Partnership, 850 Market St, 37402, free
Going for nearly ten years now, the **Nightfall** concert series is unquestionably the best mixer in town. The location is central, at the intersection of Market Street and ML King Boulevard, the music begins before dark and ends by little-ones-bedtime, and the range of talent is broad enough to tickle even non-musical fancies.

Erase every notion you've ever had about going out to hear music and start fresh. It's FREE, no strain on any budget. It's out-in-the-open, kids-in-strollers and audience-in-casual fun-for-all informal. It goes on for 17 weeks; every Friday from the end of May till the end of September. A local group kicks off the show at 7 PM, at 8 the headliner comes on. '94 brought this kind of variety: C. J. Chenier and the Red Hot Louisiana Band, with energetic zydeco; Robert Earl Keen, with his songs of the American West; Wolfstone's metal-meets-Celtic folk music; the Klezmatics, a Yiddish world-beat fusion band, always a sell-out in Europe and South America; Laurie Lewis and her champion fiddle from Grand Ole Opry and Prairie Home Companion; and Hugh Masekela's South African jazz trumpet.

Never-mind your race, age, gender or marital status! This is a truly something-for-everyone kind of gathering; it's come-by-yourself safe if you can't drag someone with you; and parents, what a wonderful way to begin exposing your children to live music and developing their young musical taste-buds. Don't play hunker-in-the-suburbs at the end of the week; come downtown! Bring a folding chair, grab a bench, hang your feet over the fountain-wall, circle through the crowd and visit your friends, or press near the stage and dance your cares away. Visitors to the city, please join in. What a way to kick off your weekend!

The **Coffeehouse** series is shorter, but provides a warm spot in the week for the get-dark-early months of January and February. Come inside the Pavilion on Tuesday nights: two 45-minute acts, beginning at 7:30; coffee too. Great variety from gospel to folk to country to jazz to probably just what you like best. Family crowds here too.

Daytime weekdays offers **Nooners** at Miller Plaza, one-hour variety concerts with local talent; another feature of this is the **Bach's Lunch** series of the classical stuff. If you work downtown, you're lucky indeed. If you don't, plan your downtown trips so you can take advantage of the free music. Visitors to the city, call; they'll be happy to tell you what's happening while you're in town.

National Folk Festival
756-2787, Bluff View, First weekend in October, free
The National Folk Festival began in 1934, and has been held in many cities throughout the United States. 1995 will be its last year of a 3-year stint in Chattanooga, and it is FREE to the public. It celebrates the diversity of American culture, brought together from each and every continent, with food, music, crafts, folklife demonstrations, and special exhibitions spread along the city's riverfront from the Aquarium Plaza to the Hunter.

For information, contact Allied Arts. It takes a lot of work to put the weekend together and festival planners welcome volunteers; give a call if you can offer foreign language help, as well as office or field assistance.

Pat Boone Bethel Celebrity Spectacular
842-5757, mid May
The celebrities come to play golf at Valleybrook Country Club; guests pay to play with the celebrities; the proceeds go to benefit Bethel Bible School. This Pat Boone-led event has brought in football great Bart Starr, astronaut Capt. Jon McBride, actor Steven Shortridge, Congressman Zach Wamp and many, many more over the years; for a good cause. There's also a concert at the Tivoli and a bid-high-if-you-please auction, all done for the school.

Pops in the Park
267-8583, Chattanooga Symphony at Wilder Tower, Chickamauga Battlefield, Saturday nearest July 4th, free
Catch the Chattanooga Symphony Pops Concert at Chickamauga Battlefield's Wilder Tower on the Saturday evening closest to July 4th. It's the undisputed favorite gathering place for patriotic family picnics on the ground and flag-waving march-dancing to a rousing Sousa tune; topped off by a let's-stay-till-the-end fireworks show. Yes, there's traffic, but it's well-managed and Hwy 2 or 27 gets you home fast. Anyhow, it's a holiday, what's the rush? It's too much fun to miss; and besides, it's tradition.

Prater's Mill Country Fair
706-275-MILL, I-75 Exit 138, north 4.5 miles to Hwy 2, right for 2.6 miles to Prater's Mill, 10 mi NE of Dalton, GA, open 9-6 on a Sat-Sun in May and October
It takes two sides of the road to handle all there is to do at this fair; there's so

much, in fact, they have it twice a year! It's an old-fashioned country shindig: lots of music and fiddling and clogging to keep your spirits high; food booths filled with barbecue and country cornbread and fried pies and homemade ice cream; hundreds of craftsy and artistic things to look at, or to buy; demonstrations of every kind of thing, including a Civil War encampment and a "Peacock Alley" display. All this along the banks of Coahulla Creek and in the historic mill; built in 1855, it's on the National Historic Register.

Riverbend Festival
265-4112 info-line, held mid-June annually
You can rent three videos and get six hours of taped entertainment to go with your home-popped-budder-corn, or you can spend your $15 for a Riverbend Pin and wear it to nine days of the real live stuff: world-class entertainment on five stages, street performers, fine arts exhibits, food booths, and even a fireworks finale, set to music and lighting up the city with a blast into summer. Over 100 artists from all over the country perform for you, and for the more than half-a-million others who come with folding chair or blanket in hand for the southeast's hottest festival. Splayed along the Tennessee River from Ross's Landing to the Hunter Museum, it feeds and entertains you, exposes you to wider wonders of the world, and starts your summer right.

A sight-at-night is the Coca-Cola stage, a floating contraption anchored on the river so the audience can have all the land. A smaller stage beyond the Hwy 27 bridge marks the end of food-booth row; the smokestack flags the stage in the parking lot across the street; the street, of course, turns into a nine-day festival-space. A RiverWalk stroll gets you to the Amphitheatre, a clever under-the-highway construction of graveled tiers; a stone support of the Walnut Street Bridge makes a backdrop for the stage -- remember this sheltered spot in case of rain. Keep walking up the hill to the Hunter Museum and stage five; tables and intimate sit-down-under-a-canopy dining here, for when you want to get away from crowds for a while.

It has to last nine days; you can't possibly do it all and see it all in less. The talent is mind-boggling, only-a-tiny-portion of previous-years lineups go from big-stars B. B. to Willie; Glenn Frey & Joe Walsh, REO Speedwagon, Oak Ridge Boys, Natalie Cole, Travis Tritt, Tanya Tucker, Bill Cosby, Chicago, Mel Torme, Pete Seeger, Judy Collins, Jerry Lee Lewis, Barbara Mandrell, Smokey Robinson, Lyle Lovett, Gatlin Brothers, Judds, Sarah Vaughn, Ray Charles, Pointer Sisters, Dizzy Gillespie, Cab Calloway, Roberta Flack, Arlo Guthrie, Neville Brothers, Crosby, Stills & Nash, and the Fabulous Thunderbirds.

But don't let the star-power turn your head; what's really special about this event is the chance you get to see and hear the up-and-coming, the newer talent, the less-well-known. The smaller stages let you get close; the variety helps you develop a wider appreciation for different styles. Some folks go for the whole thing; some select special acts or an area-a-day; some simply walk along the bridges or cruise by in their boat, needing to be near the energy of the event. The Monday night Bessie Smith Strut is part of the festival; it's held near the Bessie Smith Hall on M L King Boulevard; (see p.101); there's also a 5K Fun Run, street performers everywhere, and a major visual arts show near the Hunter Museum.

Although there's a year-round planning staff, much of the work during the festival is carried out by an army of volunteers. Donate your time to roll tokens, work the entrance gate, or any of a zillion tasks; for your help you're gifted with nice expressions of appreciation.

Winter Holidays in Chattanooga
See individual attractions or call for specific times, details
Chattanooga moves quickly from glorious autumn fairs and Thanksgiving's bounty to **Winter Days and Lights**; the stars are brighter and clearer in the evening sky, the dark-hours sparkle as we hang light-strings on buildings and trees all over town and far into the countryside. Downtown, 25 of the tallest structures are outlined in light; beautifully decorated store windows and strolling musicians slow our pace; the family gathers for an early-evening **Nightlight Parade** and **Christmas on the River**.

There's an **Appalachian Christmas** at the Waterhouse Pavilion and a **Victorian Christmas** at the ChooChoo; you'll hear singing on the Courthouse steps; in the Tivoli the Boys Choir forms a **Singing Christmas Tree**; go to Lookout Mountain for **Madrigal Dinners** at Covenant College and to Rock City for **Christmas Legends**. The Southern Belle offers **Christmas Carol Cruises** and lunch with Santa; the Hunter Museum is open for **Moonlight Mansion** tours; many communities have parades with shiver-in-the-cold marching bands and Scouts-on-floats and Santas tossing cellophaned candies to the kids.

Hotel lobbies are pretty spots to see -- the taller the lobby, the taller the tree; the same thing happens at **Warehouse Row, Eastgate, Northgate**, and **Hamilton Place**; gorgeous mall-ways of greenery and red-satin ribbons and flowers and lights, set to music; **Santa** is waiting for you; sit on his lap and get your picture made beside a holly wreath. Bakeries are filled with gumdrop-roofed **gingerbread houses** and **sticky buns**; baskets of **hickory-smoked ham** and **pecan-cheese balls** arrive at the office; you deliver hand-whipped **fudge** and almost-wouldn't-set **divinity** to the neighbor who always waves from across the street; **churches and community kitchens** roll up their sleeves, boxing canned goods and baking turkeys and wrapping **special gifts**; hoping to make a little difference in someone's life.

Red poinsettias seem to follow you home, multiplying as the winter goes on. You set out candles for the season; eight in the menorah for the **Hanukkah Festival of Lights**; five for the **Christmas Advent** wreath; a single candle in each front window just for the glow it brings.

Galleries

These arts-and-artists stay in place for you year round, to browse, to study, and to buy. Two interesting and artsy areas just happen to be on either end of the Walnut Street Bridge: Bluff View Art District on the downtown side and the North Shore District on the other. Some galleries began in the mountains, but opened an in-town for convenience. Local artists are well represented, but you will find items from all over the world, as well. The art becomes more personal when you are able to meet with and watch the artist at work; call to see. A new group is planning gallery-walk evenings; watch for them.

Bluff View Art District
Spring and High Streets
This quiet location is only a pleasant riverside stroll from the Aquarium downtown. Perched on a bluff above the Tennessee River, you'll find the **Hunter Museum of American Art** and the **Houston Museum**, plus the **River Gallery** areas which have been meticulously restored and are operated by the Potera family, in one of the prettiest areas of the entire city; when you add the restaurant deck of the Back Inn Cafe or the patio of Rembrandt's Coffeehouse, it's a stay-the-day place.

River Gallery Sculpture Garden
♦ *267-7353, 214 Spring St, open daily, daylight hours*
♦ Beautiful outdoor gallery featuring regional, national, and international artists. This peaceful spot is a fitting turnaround for a river walk or a worthy destination itself. Benches and fountains, green-grassed lawns and pebbled paths, inscriptions to ponder, sun and shade to warm and cool, sculptures in every style, and the magnificent Tennessee River, guarding the wildlife on Maclellan Island, just below.

River Gallery
♦ *267-7353, 400 E 2nd St, open Mon-Sat 10-5, Sun 1-5*
♦ A red-geraniumed path guides you to the door, a jingling bell welcomes you in. Everything is strikingly displayed in this lovely gallery; room-to-room in intimate or expansive space it's filled with original fine art and crafts, from American impressionist and contemporary paintings to wood carvings. You'll find sculpture, basketry, ceramics, textiles, art furniture, art glass and handmade books. Regularly changing exhibits; call for a calendar of events. An outdoor clothesline show summer and fall features works of the area's emerging artists. **Working Artists Studios** open for occasional observation; check with the Gallery.

North Shore Art District
Frazier Avenue
Creativity is virtually bursting at the seams on this end of the Walnut Street Bridge. In addition to the galleries, **Ballet Tennessee** studios and the **Little Theatre** are here; get antique toys at **Needful Things**, contemporary

furnishings and designs at **Elements,** art supplies and frames at **Art Creations,** and used books at **Books by the Bridge;** up the hill on Forest, Joe and Billie Moan are busy cranking out Chattanooga's **CityScope** magazine, and at #408, **Notch-Bradley** is doing its thing as one of the most creative ad agencies in town.

Art'est

♦ *267-8159, 40 Frazier Ave, open Tue-Sat 11-9, Sun 1-6*

♦ This cooperative offers studio and exhibit space to potters, painters, wood carvers, and custom jewelers; custom framing and creative matting too. A good place to see in-house artists working; classes are available for all ages. They give free classes to people with life-threatening illnesses and to Scouts working towards art badges, all supplies provided, call to make arrangements.

In-Town Gallery

♦ *267-9214, 26 Frazier Avenue, open Mon-Sat 10-5*

♦ This is a cooperative gallery, committed to featuring regional artists. The 40 members' works are exhibited at all times; In-Town Plus One shows bring in nonmember guests. Founded more than 20 years ago, you'll find works of well-known locals from Ann Aiken to Jane Yelliott; includes Mary B. Lynch, Chester Martin, Herschel Pollard, Terry West, Carolyn Wright, Jim Wright.

Tafachady Red Feather Gallery

♦ *756-2797, 800-648-1165, 101 Frazier Ave, open Tue-Sat 10-6*

♦ Founded in 1988, this gallery features Native American musical instruments, weaponry, and art. Original prints by Native American artists; carvings, pottery, bead work, Navajo rugs and turquoise and silver jewelry. Native American demonstrations, storytelling, and performances by appointment at your school or organization; southeast tribal information.

Touch of Mandingo

♦ *756-2368, 24 Frazier Ave, open Mon-Sat 11-6, Sun 1-6*

♦ This African art gallery specializes in authentic African artifacts. You'll find paintings, wood carvings, jewelry, handwoven wall hangings, hand-painted clothing, and musical instruments in this new gallery; best of all, owners Diane and Mohamed Doumbouya will take the time to tell you the story behind the pieces. Mohamed handcrafts the cowrie shell-leather jewelry.

Mountains and All Around Town

At the bottom of Lookout Mountain find the **Clay Shop** and **Horsin' Around;** there are reminders of Lookout Mountain at the now in-town **Plum Nelly;** on top of Signal Mountain is **Mole Hill.** Downtown is **Rising Fawn, Sweetly Southern,** and UTC's **Cress;** along the river CSTCC's **Sculpture Garden;** lucky locations for us wherever we live, whenever we have some time to go.

Chattanooga State Technical Community College Sculpture Garden

♦ *697-4400, 4501 Amnicola Hwy*

♦ Changing exhibit of work by some of the finest indoor and outdoor sculptors in the US. Twenty-five works on display representing artists from

CA, OR, PA, NC, AL, GA, FL, TN. Self-guided tour programs available of the Garden; stay and see this beautiful riverside campus, near Riverpark.

Clay Shop & Outlook Gallery
♦ *821-5212, 3815 St Elmo Ave, open Tue-Sat 10:30-5:30*
♦ At the foot of Lookout Mountain, near the Incline, see the work of more than 60 fine artists from the region: pottery, jewelry, photography, hand-blown glass, furniture, weaving and more. In the Clay Shop, watch Vaughan Greene work the potter's wheel and see the process -- wet clay to fired and finished.

Horsin' Around
♦ *825-5616, 3806 St Elmo Ave, open Mon-Thu 9-8, Fri 9-5, Sat 9-6*
♦ Certainly the most unusual artists' work-to-watch in town; in fact, just about anywhere in the US you may travel. It's a birthing-room for carousel animals; months of labor go into lovingly designing and carving and hand-painting these beauties to life. People come from far and wide to learn the art form and to see the results. Annual show in the studio at the foot of Lookout Mountain, but always pieces to see, in progress or on display.

Mole Hill Pottery
♦ *886-5636, 1210 Taft Hwy, Signal Mtn, open Mon-Sat 9:30-6*
♦ In case you were looking for an excuse to drive up Signal Mountain, use this one: in Signal Plaza Shopping Center you'll find a small but exciting gallery specializing in locally-and-regionally-made pottery and other fine arts and crafts, such as jewelry, weavings, paintings, metal works and woodcarvings. Owner Kathy Owens is a potter, go in and watch her working at her craft.

Plum Nelly Shop & Gallery
♦ *266-0585, 1101 Hixson Pike, open Mon-Sat 10-6, Sun during holiday season*
♦ "Plum out of Tennessee and nelly out of Georgia" is where we used to find the Lookout Mountain clothesline art show; Fannie Mennen and friends opened an in-town gallery in the 70's; since 1985 owned by Joy Mullins-Storey and husband Joe, still carrying some of the artists of Mennen's days; over 400 artists represented today; handthrown pottery, hand-woven baskets, handbound books, wind chimes, furniture, throws, metal works, bird carvings. Potters, weavers and other artists regularly come in for demonstrations; there's an annual jewelry show.

Rising Fawn Folk Art
♦ *265-2760, 212 High St, open Wed-Sat 11:00-5:00. Near UTC and downtown*
♦ American folk art here, primarily southern. Visionary or "outsider" artists generally have no formal training and use what is available to them, often painting on barn boards with mud and sugar, or perhaps on an old slipcover. Much of the Outsider Art movement is centered in Alabama; see the world-renown work of Jimmy Lee Sudduth from Fayette and Myrtice West from Centre in this very interesting, specialized gallery. Paintings, wood cuttings, quilts; more than 30 artists represented.

Sweetly Southern
♦ *265-6582, 1400 Market St, open Mon-Sat 10-6, Sun 12:30-6, longer summer hrs*
♦ This small-but-nice gallery-shop faces the promenade alongside the

ChooChoo gardens; inside find original works by over 100 artists; pottery, wood, glass, weavings, jewelry; owner is glass-blower, you may catch work-in-progress.

University of Tennessee at Chattanooga Cress Gallery
♦ *755-4178, Vine/Palmetto UTC Fine Arts Center, open Mon-Fri 9-4*
♦ Two galleries here; this means two shows running simultaneously most of the time. Exhibits change monthly; artists featured from all over the country; paintings, sculpture, photography, quilts, furniture. UTC graduating seniors have show in spring.

Movies

Battle of Chickamauga Dramatization
404-866-9241, Chickamauga Battlefield Visitor Center, Ft Oglethorpe, open daily, 8-5:45
This 30-minute media show depicts the people and events of the Battle of Chickamauga and is shown hourly at the Visitor Center. See this before beginning your drive around the park.

IMAX Theatre
Opening May '96, 265-0695, Chestnut and Second
There are only six of them in the United States; 14 in the world! Chattanooga's IMAX 3-D will have a screen that is six stories high and will have seats for 400 lucky people. And what a spot: located right between the Tennessee Aquarium and the Creative Discovery Museum; you may want to get in line soon.

International Film Series
267-1218, Arts and Education Council
For more than 28 years critically acclaimed international films have been brought to the city by AEC; you won't find these treasures in the mainstream flick-of-the-month theatres. The fall series is on the UTC campus weekends beginning Labor Day through the first part of December; February through March catch the series weekends at Chattanooga State and Thursdays at the Hunter Museum. Eighteen shows during the year; you can order series tickets; call to get on the mailing list.

Marks on the Land, Story of Chattanooga
266-7070, 2 Broad St, open daily 8:30-5:30, shows every 30 minutes in Visitors Center Theater
Twenty-seven projectors lay out the story of Chattanooga in splendid form, transporting the viewer from the legend of how the mountains were formed by Big Crow's wings through the shaping of the valley by the dams of TVA. Follow the Cherokee Trail of Tears, the battles of the Civil War, Bessie Smith's blues, economic and community development, and a taste of what the city is

today. A fine beginning to a city visit; but not to be missed by everyone who lives in the area. Great insights!

Movie Houses
Mainstream movies and the must-buy-a-bag smell of popping corn; stand in line at prime-time or catch the off-hours at discount prices; several complexes offer film for 99 cents a flick.

♦ **East Ridge Cinema 6,** 892-7141, *5088 S Terrace, Kmart Shopping Center in East Ridge, Carmike; open daily 12:45*

♦ **Four Squares Cinema 3,** 877-2490, *1200 Mtn Creek Rd, Four Squares Shopping Mart, Carmike, open 7 pm Mon-Sat, Sun 1, 99C*

♦ **Hamilton Place Cinemas 10-17,** 855-0064, *2200 Hamilton Place, outside the mall on Perimeter Rd behind Grady's Goodtimes, Regal, open daily 11:45*

♦ **Hamilton Place Mall Cinemas 1-9,** 899-6695, *Hamilton Place, inside the mall at the Oasis entrance, Regal, open daily 11:45*

♦ **Northgate Cinema Eight,** 875-0990, *622 Northgate Mall Park, Carmike; open daily 12:45*

♦ **Northgate Crossing Cinemas,** 870-3334, *5131 Old Hixson Pike Northgate Crossing, Regal, open 6:45 weekdays, 12:45 Sat-Sun*

♦ **Plaza Theatre,** 892-7932, *Plaza 58 Shopping Center, 99C, two shows every evening, weekend matinees also*

♦ **Southgate 5 Theatres,** 866-0044, *532 Battlefield Pkwy, Ft Oglethorpe, Carmike, weekdays evening, weekend matinees*

♦ ****NEW IN '96.** Carmike Theatres downtown seven-screen complex near the Aquarium on 3rd and Broad Street, in the ground floor of the new CARTA parking garage. Telephone and hours are not available as this book goes to press, but plans call for one screen devoted to art and foreign films.

Movie Rentals
Some nights you just want to stay in with your favorite person for a non-stop movie fest. No busier spot in town than a Blockbusters late on a Saturday afternoon. In addition to box-office biggies, you'll find plenty of the classics, documentaries, foreign titles, music and travel; a catalogue indexes by actor or title -- find, for instance, all the works of your favorite movie star.

♦ **Blockbuster Videos,** 861-6309, *101 Battlefield Pkwy, Ft Oglethorpe; 499-9748, 5659 Brainerd Rd; 265-3411, 1748 Dayton Blvd; 877-3298, 5035 Hixson Pike; 499-3001, 4531 Hwy 58; 622-2691, 3714 Ringgold Rd*

Planetarium Show, UTC Clarence T. Jones Observatory
622-5733, 10 Tuxedo, just off Brainerd Rd, Friday nights 8:30, free
Maybe it's not really film, but it is images projected onto the domed ceiling, surrounded by silhouettes of Lookout Mountain and Chattanooga ridges, with a sunset and sunrise accompanied by heavenly-sounding music, narrated by a constellation-expert.

On top of that, on clear nights you can view the real thing through the 20-inch telescope upstairs; see a sky filled with lions and bears and mighty warriors; Orion the hunter with his belt and sword, Pleiades, Leo, Ursa Minor and Major, Dippers Little and Big. School-age children and adults, come here and get truly starstruck. There's a winding stone path through the trees to the top of the hill; it's unlighted so take your flashlight and watch your step.

Theatres

Most frequently featuring live performances, you'll find screen scenes in these theatres some nights during the week.

Barking Legs Theatre, *624-5347, 1307 Dodds Ave, evenings 3rd Mondays*

♦ Art videos, featuring rare dance, visuals artists and musicians, call for schedule.

Market Street Performance Hall, *267-2498, 221 Market St*

♦ Here's where to go to see the Rocky Horror Picture Show, as well as film classics, call for weeknights schedule.

Travel and Adventure Series by Kiwanis Club

267-6568 for info, performances at Memorial Auditorium, 399 McCallie Ave
No better way to spend your movie dollars: support Kiwanis efforts for Boys' and Girls' Clubs, Boy Scouts, Bethel Bible Village, Senior Neighbors, and Contact Ministry while you spend seven Monday evenings throughout the year traveling the world; some of the past-season features were Russia, England, Israel, Czechoslovakia, and the High Arctic Islands.

Narrators tell about their visit while you check out the puffins, harp seals, and walrus in their natural icy-cold environment without getting your feet wet; go all the way to Russia and back with no luggage lost, or best of all, begin planning your own next adventure, faraway places having been brought a little nearer through film; the itch to travel firmly planted and needing to be scratched.

Museums

Battles for Chattanooga Museum

821-2812, 3742 Tennessee Ave, open daily 8:30-8:30 June 1 through Labor Day; open 9-5 rest of year
If you have even the slightest, tiniest interest in the Chattanooga area or in Civil War history, you'll learn something at this museum. From Lookout Mountain to Missionary Ridge, the 3-dimensional electronic map lays it before you in clear (though at the height of battle a bit smoky) detail. 5,000 miniature soldiers, 650 lights, and battle sound effects keep children interested too. The battles for Chattanooga changed the outcome of the Civil War; Sherman used Chattanooga as his base as he started his march to Atlanta and the sea. After viewing the area in miniature here, you can drive around the city and visit the spots where it actually happened. Many homes on Missionary Ridge have historic markers or cannons in their yard.

Bluff Furnace Historical Park
From the RiverWalk between Walnut Street Bridge and Hunter Museum of American Art, a path leads to the Park
University of Tennessee at Chattanooga archaeologists began research in 1977, recovering thousands of artifacts and exposing some of the major foundations of the Bluff Furnace of 1854, site of the first heavy industry in Chattanooga. Placed on the National Historic Register in 1980, foundations of the stack and casting shed can be seen today by taking the RiverWalk. An interactive computer explains the operations process; a scale model depicts the original structure.

Chattanooga African-American Museum
267-1076, 730 E ML King Blvd, open Mon-Fri 9:30-4:30; Sat by appointment only
Here are housed cultural and historical documents and artifacts portraying African-American contributions to the growth of Chattanooga, and the nation. African art, original sculptures, paintings, musical recordings and local African-American newspapers. "Evenings at the Museum" programs highlight various areas of the African experience; research library available. Guided tours for all ages; school groups welcome with advance reservation.

Chattanooga Regional History Museum
265-3247, 400 Chestnut St, open Mon-Fri 10-4:30, Sat-Sun 11-4:30
The building used to be a school; it still has that schoolhouse feel, with things-to-learn-about everywhere. More than 10,000 years of area history here; you'll enjoy the hands-on Discovery Gallery as well as the award-winning exhibit, *Chattanooga Country, Its Land, Rivers and People.* Changing exhibits include Civil War, sports history and period clothing. Call for group rates. Across the street from the Creative Discovery Museum and two blocks from the Aquarium in a learning-is-great section of town.

Chief John Ross House and Park
706-866-5681, Spring Street, Rossville, GA, open Thu-Tue afternoons, summer only
John Ross was born in 1790 in Indian Territory; one-eighth Cherokee, he was brought up among the Cherokee and called Tsan-usdi, or Little John. This two-story log house was built in 1797 by John McDonald, Ross's maternal grandfather, and was the first school in north Georgia. Ross lived here as a child, and came back after completing his education, operating the supply depot and warehouse at Ross's Landing on the river five miles away; the river settlement grew into the city of Chattanooga. The house was one of the first post offices in the area; Ross was appointed postmaster in 1817.

John Ross became tribal leader of the Cherokee Nation in 1819, making numerous trips to Washington, DC on behalf of the Cherokee. He was Principal Chief until 1866; although he worked to protect their land, in 1838 the last of the Cherokee in Georgia were forced to march to Oklahoma on what was called the Trail of Tears. Ross survived the march and established a new home in Oklahoma; he died in 1886. The original house is a National

Historic Landmark and contains Ross's furniture, some was in his Oklahoma home; also an old post office desk and items from his years as tribal leader. Next to Poplar Spring, there is a pond and small park. Donations welcome.

Creative Discovery Museum

756-2738, 4th & Chestnut St, open daily summer, 10-5; Tue-Sun rest of year

You don't have to be a kid to be at kid at the Creative Discovery Museum. Imagination sparks are everywhere, designed to ignite that little stroke of genius in every artist, inventor, musician and scientist that resides in all of us. Oh, the things you can do! The exterior looks like something Dr. Seuss might have built: a lookout tower, slightly askew, with rounded things here and jutting-out things there; a building with brighter-than-a-rainbow colored walls and lots of glass that lets you see inside. What is that contraption of green and yellow gears and pulleys in there, stretching to the ceiling? You've never seen a building like this one before, anywhere in the world!

Inside, you see. It's a water sculpture; move it around, you have the power. Water splashes and pushes, falling into tubes and holes and trays. Make a whirlpool, spinning faster than a top; the forces of nature are in your hands. Oops! Have you turned into Alice? Suddenly you are tiny, looking at musical instruments towering above your head. Pass the giant guitar and push the button; it speaks to you in guitar-ese; when you go inside you'll find mikes that let you change your voice; make up a song, just as the guitar suggested. There's a recording studio, for real.

Or would you rather be a scientist? Tyrannosaurus Rex is in a room filled with dinosaur tracks and a field office for getting your working party organized. See the fossils in the sandstone over there? Do some fossil rubbings, because, actually, you are feeling more like an artist today. Alice-sized again, you walk through a split-in-half painting into a studio. There's a glass wall to paint on, and a computer that lets you look at different styles of art. You are feeling very creative, and you have an urge to build something; there's a room full of see-through cars and magnets and problem-solving tables; very inventive. Have you forgotten your little brother and sister? Don't worry, Dad has taken them into the play area; there's a kitchen and porch that look like home, and a wonderful make-believe tree to play under. What's behind all the little doors, hidden in the wall? You go back and dig for dino-bones until Mom takes you away. You've got to eat sometime, OK?

Opened May '95, this HANDS-ON arts and sciences museum for children of all ages has four core learning environments: an artist's studio, an. inventor's workshop, a musician's workshop, and a field scientist's lab; all are geared to show people how they can express themselves; a real *possibilities* place. Also changing exhibits, theatre, observatory, science lab, and more, call 756-2738. Locals, you'll want a family membership so you can come regularly. Visitors, this museum is only two blocks from the Aquarium; allow plenty of time to visit both plus the Regional History Museum; it's just across the street.

Houston Museum of Decorative Arts

267-7176, 201 High Street, Open Tues-Sat 10-4:30; Sun 2-4:30

They say Anna Safely Houston was maybe a little kooky, collecting husbands in high numbers, and walking around town with bags full of stuff. She and the husbands are gone now, but the stuff remains, an incredible collection left for the public to enjoy. It's displayed in a charming 1890's house in the Bluff View Art District, and you've never seen the like: glassware includes cut, pressed, satin, nouveau and cranberry in a variety of forms; china is American and international -- English lustreware, old blue Staffordshire, Wedgwood, Bennington, Parian, and 19th century Chinese. Dolls, toys, music boxes, quilts, coverlets, furniture and more are shown on the guided tour. A fine place to visit if your interest is art or psychology; it's inspiration if you happen to be a collector too! Group tours welcome, arrange in advance.

Hunter Museum of American Art (see cover)

267-0968, 10 Bluff View. Open Tue-Sat 10-4:30, Sun 1-4:30

Everything about the Hunter is wonderful. A fine collection of American art, from pre-Revolutionary times to the present, is permanent, with the likes of Andrew Wyeth, Mary Cassatt, John Singer Sargent, and Winslow Homer hanging around. A catalogue of the American collection is available. More than 30 touring shows come into the five galleries each year along with exhibits, lectures, and films. Nothing stuffy here; get in and get active. Find your niche, whether it's Moonlight Mansion Tours at Christmastime, Birds in Art carvings, teacher workshops, or camp for the kids. A membership supports Museum activities and gets you the monthly newsletter, invitations to special preview receptions, discounts on classes, and registration priority for tours and children's activities.

The classical 1906 mansion was once the home of Coca-Cola magnate George Thomas Hunter, who donated it to the Chattanooga Art Association in 1951. Carefully restored, its handsome architectural details and high-bluff setting make the building itself worth a trip. It was added to the National Register of Historic Landmarks in 1980. The newer addition of 1975 is modern, its squared-off shape almost becoming part of the limestone bluff; perched 90 feet above the river. The bluff was used as a lookout and garrison by both Confederate and Union armies during the Civil War; it borders Bluff Furnace archeological site (see).

Group tours available with advance reservation; also can schedule meetings/parties inside or on the huge over-the-river patio. No prettier spot in town!

National Knife Museum

892-5007, 7201 Shallowford Rd, open Mon-Fri 9-4, Sat 10-4

Owned and operated by the National Knife Collectors Association, there's an amazing collection of more than 5,000 knives, swords, razors and cutlery items of all kinds to see here.

National Medal of Honor Museum
267-1737, 400 Georgia Ave, open Mon-Sat 9-4:30
Opened in 1990, this museum is already looking for larger quarters. Dedicated to preserving the history of events and heroes of all US uniformed services from the Revolution to the present, it presents an array of military memorabilia. Uniforms, videos, pictures, and weaponry recall the Indian Wars, World War I, the Holocaust, Korean, Vietnam and Persian Gulf conflicts. Unusual items include the first cannonball fired at Chattanooga during the Civil War. The all-volunteer staff is composed mostly of veterans. Library of military history available to public.

Siskin Museum of Religious Artifacts
634-1700, 1 Siskin Plaza, Located in Siskin Rehabilitation Complex, behind Chattanooga School for Arts and Sciences, open Mon-Fri 9-4
Containing over 400 objects, the collection has items ranging from the 16th to 20th centuries in stone, wood, ivory, silver and porcelain. Religions and philosophies represented include Islam, Buddhism, Hindu and Confucianism; 140 objects are Christian, 247 are Judaica. Operated by the Siskin Memorial Foundation, many of the items were located by Rabbi Harris Swift in the 1950's. Considered to be one of the most representative collections of religious artifacts in the United States; guided tours by appointment.

Tennessee Aquarium (see cover)
265-0695, 1 Broad St, open daily 10-6, extended summer hours
Two living forests and 7,000 animals made up of 400 species in the largest freshwater aquarium in the world -- a living museum. Many maps, schematics and photographs of the Tennessee River Valley as well as rivers of the world. See p.155 for full description. Family memberships available.

Tennessee Valley Railroad Museum
894-8028, 4119 Cromwell Rd, and 220 N Chamberlain Ave, open longer hours, more days in summer, call. Parking, museum free, fee for rides
The largest operating historic railroad in the south, with a superb collection of engines and rail cars in fixed position, and a huge shop area where volunteers are constantly restoring locomotives, rail cars, push cars, and other rail memorabilia. See p.156 for full description.

TVA Energy Center
751-7599, 1101 Market St, open Mon-Fri 8-5, closed Federal holidays, free
This little corner of the gigantic TVA Office Complex downtown is the place to find out about electricity and energy. How is electricity made? How do we get energy? How does energy travel? Displays, exhibits and wall-sized maps explain the Tennessee Valley Authority and its programs. Kids will enjoy the touchy things; adults will learn about the vastness and scope of TVA. A nice downtown spot to visit; also enjoy the gorgeous landscaped park outside. Across the street from Warehouse Row.

TVA Sequoyah Energy Connection
843-4100, Hwy 27, Sequoyah Access Rd, Soddy-Daisy, open Mon-Sat 10-4, free
Out by the twin towers on the lake, you're invited to visit the Energy Connection, an education center for students, families or anyone interested in learning more about energy. Church groups, Scout troops, social clubs -- call for group reservations, they'll set you up. This high-tech spot lets you tour a nuclear plant by way of interactive computer video, try balancing energy supply with demand, and give your opinions on energy issues.

Music and Dance

Big Venues
These large facilities are the scene of locally staged concerts, symphony, opera, theatre, and dance performances, as well as productions from out of town. Watch newspapers or call box office.
National Guard Armory, *634-3022, 1801 Holtzclaw Ave*
♦ State-owned facility, leased for concerts, shows.
Soldiers/Sailors Memorial Auditorium, *757-5042, 399 McCallie Ave*
♦ City-owned facility, bookings by TAPA.
Tivoli Theatre, *757-5048, 757-5050, 709 Broad St*
♦ City-owned facility, bookings by TAPA.
UTC Arena, *266-7469 ShowLine, 266-6627 Box Office, 4th at Douglas*
♦ University roundhouse, concerts, sporting events.
UTC Fine Arts Center, *755-4269, Vine St at Palmetto*
♦ Roland Hayes Theatre for Dorothy Patten Fine Arts Series, many organizations perform here; University productions also.

Churches and Sunday Morning Song
In a town blessed with over 800 churches, a good place to find great music is the Sunday morning hour; **many churches have special musical programs throughout the year**, especially during holiday times. Watch newspapers and outdoor signs. The cost to you is the contribution you choose to put in the plate; be generous. Two are mentioned.
First-Centenary Church, *756-2021, 419 McCallie Ave*
♦ Walker Breland mans the organ at the 10:45 AM Sunday services, backing up an extraordinarily fine choir; the reverent, lovely music is imbued with a get-you-through-the-week positive energy. Many quality musical programs are offered throughout the year; they have a handbell choir and children's choirs too. Check paper or call for schedule.
Greater Faith Temple, *756-0495, 652 E 10th*
♦ On the second Sunday of any month you can hear Willie Carter and the Gospel Songbirds at 11 AM; this trio of women has been performing together for twenty years all over the south; guaranteed to put a smile in your heart. Third Sunday is Children's Choir, Men's the fourth, and on the first Sunday of every month, combined choirs for spirit-lifting song.

Clubs and Nighttime Noises

The newest club on the Chattanooga scene is strictly jazz and is toting up a flock of kudos and raves from adult music-lovers who crave a sociable place to enjoy top-flight music. Cosmopolitan, with warmth, best describes it.

Birdland, *697-7484, 2510 E Main St, open daily*

♦ Owner John McManus likes jazz. For you, he provides it live Friday and Saturday nights, via the Paul Lohorn Trio and Ed Leamon's tenor sax. And on Mondays, the Big Band Jazz Band spills off the stage with about 32 pieces of big-band sound. Other nights, you'll be jazzed by the all-classic-jazz juke box or the satellite hookup which brings in classic, piano, vocal and lite jazz. The red-box building with the white trim is just around the corner from Barking Legs on Dodds; plenty of well-lighted parking available. There's a nice-sized bar, comfortable booths for enjoying a full meal, and tables clustered around the stage; a fine stopping-off place after work, the symphony, the ball game, or anywhere else you might have been; for many, it's become a regular weekend destination. John's Birdland club is a second career after many years with T. H. Payne; he still knows how to keep his customers happy.

Two of the top here's-where-we'll-stop clubs are downstairs at the **Sandbar** and the **Market Street Performance Hall.** A poll of UTC students in a music class showed these two leading the pack by a hefty margin as favorite places for the college set; depending on the music, though, you'll find a generation-mix; music-lovers of every age who like their sound-and-sight up close. Both offer a wide array of quality musical talent; they generally keep the cover small.

Market Street Performance Hall, *267-2498, 221 Market St*

♦ "It ain't your Daddy's music," the sign proclaims. Unless your Daddy grew up on the likes of Leon Russell. Leon appeared at the MSPH in March '95; still untrimmed, and sold out, of course. And Gentle-on-My-Mind John Hartman, assisted by his son John, was there the next weekend. In the old bus-barn right square in the middle of the Aquarium-and-restaurants development that has opened up the river-end of town, the MSPH goes for performance-hall variety, booking comedy improv and film and just about every kind of music that's out here today. Michael Hedges, Jason & the Scorchers, Cigar Store Indians, Webb Wilder, Tuck & Patti, Nashville Bluegrass Band, The Back Doors, David Grisman Quintet and Dub Mystic have graced the stage; your kind of music ought to be there somewhere. Full bar with deli menu; occasional nonsmoking shows.

Sandbar, *622-4432, 1011 Riverside Dr*

♦ Everybody in town knows about Monday's Traveling Riverside Blues Caravan; everybody knows about the rock-and-roll weekends; and most especially, everybody knows about the giant patio. No place in town puts you so up-close-and-personal beside the mighty Tennessee; inside, the informal stage-and-dance-floor has picture windows facing the big backyard waterway. Special events often are scheduled for Sundays or Wednesdays; otherwise watch for weekend or Monday talent such as

Catfish Jenkins, Ridge Farm, Janie Grey, the Rev. Billy C. Wirtz, Keri Leigh and the Blue Devils, and even Koko Taylor; watch the paper or call for who's on. Bar downstairs in the club; full restaurant upstairs; RiverWalk path and boat dock out back.

Two other extremely popular musical spots are the **Brass Register** and **Yesterdays.** These restaurants are busy at noon with downtown lunchers, but the evening scene turns musical, especially on weekends.

Brass Register, *265-2175, 618 Georgia Ave*
♦ If you're looking for music, the BR provides it almost every night. Mondays for big band sounds and jazz; on weekends it's classic R&R; watch for Ladies Nights and Gents Nights and $ drinks. Folks really love this in-the-moment downtown place with the old-fashioned look.

Yesterdays, *756-1978, 820 Georgia Ave*
♦ Just a few blocks down Georgia, another what's-happening-now place with an old-fashioned look; enthusiastic crowds who like their music loud pack it full every weekend.

Since they offer music on different days and at different times, you can get a nice mix over a week's time at these pleasantly packed favorites.
♦ **Clearwater Cafe,** *266-0601, 1301 Chestnut*
♦ **Durty Nelly's,** *265-9970, 109 N Market*
♦ **Grizzly's,** *875-6013, 3600 Hixson Pike*
♦ **Las Margaritas,** *756-3332, 1101 Hixson Pike*
♦ **Stone Lion,** *266-5466, 418 High St*
♦ **T-Bones Cafe,** *266-4240, 1419 Chestnut*

You'll find country music at these places, packed on weekends.
♦ **Governors Lounge,** *624-2239, 4251 Bonny Oaks Dr*
♦ **Palomino's,** *624-9274, 2620 Rossville Blvd*
♦ **Rock and Country Club,** *894-9921, 6175 Airways Blvd*

Spots to check for live-music-and-dancing and a nice lake-and-dinner scene.
♦ **Aris' Lakeshore,** *877-7068, 5600 Lake Resort Terrace* at Lakeshore complex
♦ **Rivermont,** *877-5433, 1101 Meadowlake Rd* at the Golf and Country Club

And if you like to hear yourself sing, you can find karaoke all over town almost every night.

Not Clubs, But Plenty of Music
From halls to boats to mountaintops, you can find music behind many different kinds of doors.
Allemande Hall, *843-2850, 2548 Gunbarrel Rd*
♦ Six nights a week local square dancing clubs spin and twirl from 8:30 to 10 pm. Exercise, fellowship, and classes too. Small fee.

Bessie Smith Hall, *267-6053, 200 M. L. King Boulevard*
♦ Scheduled to open sometime in '95, plans call for weekend blues shows, cabaret style, with drinks and a light menu. Hall will offer programs to bring music to the community through classes and performances.

Opera Above the Clouds, *398-0545, Lions Club Community Bldg, Hwy 157, Lookout Mtn*
♦ Second and fourth Saturday of each month at 7 PM; bluegrass, traditional, gospel and old country music in family style. They'll pass the hat for your contribution.

Mountain Opry, *886-5897, Fairmount Rd, Signal Mtn*
♦ Every Friday night you can be entertained from 8-11 PM by old-time bluegrass music in the Walden Ridge Civic Center. A real fun, real family show; no charge but drop your contribution in the hat that is passed.

Lake Winnepesaukah, *866-5681, 1115 Lakeview Dr, Rossville*
♦ Ride the ferris wheel and then settle in every Sunday at 3 or 8 mid-May through August at Jukebox Junction for an afternoon of music; this 70-year-old park has staged Patsy Cline, Roy Acuff and Ernest Tubbs; summer '95 talent includes Billy Joe Royal, the Bellamy Brothers, Ronnie McDowell, Dallas County Line, and Chattanooga's own Dalton Roberts and his Chattaboogie Band. Show is free with admission to park.

Southern Belle Riverboat (see cover), *266-4488, 201 Riverfront Parkway, open daily, schedules fluctuate seasonally, call*
♦ Do your riverboat rambling on the Southern Belle; outside there's a beautiful calliope to circus-tune your mood; inside, book your musical choice. Do you want gospel, Dixieland, or the country sound? Different types on different nights, a matching meal and an outing on the river. See p.154 for full description.

Series for a Season

Many opportunities for a season-full of music; get on the mailing list so you'll get first crack at ordering tickets every year. If you're visiting the city, call to see what's playing while you're in town and grab that last good seat for your favorite type of music.

Chattanooga Symphony and Opera Series, *267-8583, 630 Chestnut St*
♦ Robert Bernhardt, music director of the Chattanooga Symphony & Opera Association, has a charming, engaging smile and a devilishly energetic style. The Symphony's annual Halloween costume party is a hoot, the Tivoli filled with butterflies, hoboes, fairy princesses, red-hot flappers, and parrot-on-the-shoulder pirates, vying for prizes in every age group; then settling down for a pops concert led by a conductor wearing vampire teeth and a long, flowing cape. On the floor beside the third violinist, a head stares placidly at the audience, waiting for its owner to finish the piece.

♦ Don't think there's not serious attention paid to the classical style; in addition to the cabaret pops series, the full year's slate includes seven symphony performances, three opera productions, and chamber music concerts. Visiting artists are splendid: Ani and Ida Kavafian, a violin and viola duo; John Wallace, on trumpet; and Lee Luvisi, pianist, guested in 94-95. You can start your evening out with pre-performance "Concert Conversations," led by Maestro Bernhardt or equally-spirited Walker Breland, music professor at UTC, they're a great way to learn more about the music, composers, and performers. Special events in '95 sparkled: Isaac Stern for the UTC Chancellor's Concert, stars from "Miss Saigon," "Les Miserables," and "Phantom of the Opera" for the Broadway pops, Banu Gibson and the New Orleans Hot Jazz for the benefit concert.

♦ You can purchase packages for the type of music you prefer -- Pops, Opera, Symphony or Fanfare -- to assure that you've got a ticket when the production begins. The Youth Symphony does two concerts a year, spring pops and fall classics. New in '95 was the Family Concert, aimed for children under seven. Two-year-old Justin was intrigued with his exposure to the various instruments, yet when the conductor lifted the baton and the swell of music began, whispered "I want to be the one with the stick."

Dorothy Patten Fine Arts Series, *755-4269, Vine St at Palmetto, UTC Fine Arts Center on campus*
♦ This series runs September through April; live performances by nationally recognized artists. Music and dance performances in past seasons included Corky Siegel's Chamber Blues, the Shanghai Quartet, Ohio Ballet and Aman International Music & Dance. Usually nine shows a year, including theatre; good discounts for multi or full-series packages.

TAPA Series, *757-5042, 399 McCallie Ave*
♦ This autumn/winter series brings touring performances to the Tivoli and Memorial Auditorium. The 94-95 season included such diversity as Boys Choir of Harlem, Della Reese, the Rockettes, and *Will Rogers Follies*, and such standards as *Camelot* and *Fiddler on the Roof*. Tickets can be purchased for individual shows; prices lower for packages or matinees. Call to get on mailing list for advance ordering.

Stay at Home
Want to own your own? The **Blockbuster's** and **Peaches'** stores at Hamilton Place are two great places to spend an afternoon listening and selecting your personal favorites. If they don't have it, they'll gladly order it for you.
Blockbuster Music, *855-4533, 2114 Gunbarrel Rd , open daily*
♦ Busts of the famous from Ludwig Beethoven to James Brown are perched on posts all over the store; in the center you'll find circular seating with more than 20 listening stations -- no waiting till you unwrap the package at home to decide if there's more than one track you like. This store is well organized and well stocked; there's enough Mozart to sweep you off your grand piano bench; there's a fine international section; and of course plenty of blues, country, jazz and rock.

Peaches Music, *499-6433, 2209 Hamilton Place Blvd, open daily*
♦ As soon as you enter the door someone offers to help you; there's a touch-and-find computer screen for locating any title or artist; and plenty of listening stations. Everything is clearly marked and easy to find in this pleasant store; they have music books, storage cases, other supplies too. Good selections in show tunes, boxed sets.

Check the **Organizations and Information** section, p.72, and **Events and Festivals** section, p.80, for more **Music and Dance.**

Theatre

Back Stage Dinner Theatre
629-1565, 3264 Brainerd Rd, open Fri-Sat, dinner 6:30, play 8:15
It's the only dinner theatre in town, and draws crowds from all over who love the food; of course the play's the thing; producer-director Bettye Elmore has been turning out musical comedies, mysteries, and dramas for over 15 years. "We use all-local talent," brags Bettye, "because Chattanooga is loaded with talented people. Auditions are open to the general public; we run ads in the paper when it's time to begin a new production."

Plays are offered year-round, every Friday and Saturday night; come early for dinner -- you're liable to be greeted by husband Bob Elmore, former head of the Convention and Visitors Bureau and TV travel-show host, still charmingly promoting the people and places of a city he loves. The theatre is available for private parties during the week, it accommodates 125; on the east side of the tunnel in the Ridge, it has ample parking in back.

Barking Legs Theatre
624-5347, 1307 Dodds Ave
They used to manufacture draperies in this building; now there's a curtainless stage in this comfortable, classy black box theatre, an intimate 80-seat house perfectly designed for music, theatre or dance. Ann Law came here from New York just a few years back and has worked diligently within the community to establish CoPAC, the nonprofit arts organization that oversees Barking Legs. Twofold purpose here: they bring in performers from out of town and they encourage and present local work. Incredible variety includes poetry, acoustic music, dance, and film; out-of-town performers also participate in community outreach by taking art to schools and other groups that might not get the opportunity to see the work otherwise. Audiences are treated to Question-and-Answer sessions after performances for a chance to meet and talk with the performers.

Comedy Catch
622-CAFE, 3224 Brainerd Rd, shows Wed -Sat, Sun open mike
Live at Chattanooga's comedy nightspot, comedians who've appeared on

Letterman and the Tonight Show, Showtime and HBO; check the paper or call for who's on today. In between shows big-screen TV plays comedy and music videos, or you can have dinner in the Cafe Restaurant. Smokefree show Friday at 8. Sundays are Chattanooga Variety night; if you have your own act, arrive at 7:15 for sign-up in this open-mike venue; if you just want to watch, get there about 8.

Club Kid
870-2777, 3224 Brainerd Rd at the Comedy Catch, shows Sat 11 am, children $6, adults $4, luncheon menu $
For children 4-12, interactive theatre; they must bring an adult. Lunch is at 11, burger style, with cartoons playing on the big screen; then kids get a chance-and-a-choice; take to the stage, help with the props, be the audience; no experience necessary. Michael Alfono, owner of the Comedy Catch, makes sure the space is good-for-kids safe; TV-personality Jed Mescon handles the mike; Jo Walters writes the plays, designs and makes costumes-for-all, and discovers the undiscovered talent that arrives on Saturday mornings; she's a former teacher at the Phoenix School for the Performing Arts. Each month a different theme: ground hogs and cupids, snakes exiting Ireland, Shakespeare's dreams. Kids wear capes and hats and forked-snakey-tongues, flinging out glitter-dust when it's imagination time; then, true to technology, watch themselves in replay via video.

Dorothy Patten Fine Arts Series
755-4269, Vine St at Palmetto, UTC Fine Arts Center
The Dorothy Patten Fine Arts Series is September through April; live performances by nationally recognized artists. Since 1980, it has brought music, dance and theatre to the University and to the city. Past theatre performances: North Carolina Shakespeare Festival in *Taming of the Shrew*, and the Acting Company in *A Doll's House*. Good discounts for multi or full-series packages.

Little Theatre of Chattanooga
267-8534, 400 River Street
Before the year is over, Managing Director Jeffrey Brown will have done something or other to lure you to the Little Theatre, you can bet on it! Maybe you'll buy season tickets and attend every production, as more than 50,000 people are doing annually. Maybe you'll bring your children to the Youth Programs; over 7,000 people came for just one play last year. Perhaps you'll attend one of the eight FREE dress rehearsals that are open to the public; over 500 did last year. Or maybe you'll heed the call and sign on as actor, crew, musician, choreographer, stage manager, usher, or box office assistant.

"The Little Theatre is the community getting together to produce theatre, one of the true non-elite art forms," says Jeffrey. "We draw from a 100-mile radius here, performers come from Alabama and Georgia too. For our Youth Program, we're hoping to have five satellite classrooms soon." In continuous operation since 1923, our Little Theatre is one of the oldest in the country. Major expansion in 1995 is adding 27,000 square feet; look for a truly fine facility with a 400-seat auditorium and plenty of parking by '96; right there on the north shore of the river. Eight shows a season, plus shows for the entire family in the Youth Theatre Program. Offerings in 94-95 ranged from *Guys and Dolls* to *The Front Page; You're a Good Man, Charlie Brown* to *Tartuffe*. Get a Flex pass for four anytime admissions during the season and save some bucks; or, if you know where you like to sit, go ahead and spring for fully reserved seats for all eight plays; the season runs all year. Special group rates.

Little Theatre Youth Program
267-8534, 400 River Street
In addition to being available for families, this school performance program offers four plays during year to school groups, with grade recommendations. In '94-95 season presented *Prince and the Pauper, Princess and the Pea, Adventures of Peter Rabbit,* and *OPQRS, Etc.* Performances priced low, usually last one hour. Sponsored by Allied Arts, this program is supported by various businesses. Public schools are eligible for ticket/transportation subsidies; contact Allied Arts at 756-2787.

Oak Street Playhouse
756-2024, 419 McCallie Ave
The all-volunteer staff in this highly-regarded community theatre located in First-Centenary Church stages three major productions a year in a 120-seat gem-of-a-theatre. Suzanne Smartt directs and Flo Summit produces a springtime play, usually in May, and a Christmas dinner theatre show; general auditions are open to the public. In the fall, it's puppet time; creator Fred Arnold adapts classic tales to the puppet stage and actors do the sound track; 10 shows plus three "school days" when area schoolchildren field-trip in. The puppet plays are great for all ages; dialogue and nuances keep things interesting for adults and older children, the color and action keep the little ones entertained; good family stuff.

Out of Town
We have some wonderful theatre opportunities just a pleasant drive away. Get on the mailing list and watch the paper for what's going on.
- **Dalton Little Theatre,** *706-226-6618, Dalton, GA*
- **Parnassus Theater Company,** *800-767-2480, 335 W Main St, Monteagle, TN*
- **Cumberland County Playhouse,** *615-484-5000, Crossville, TN*
- **Tennessee Performing Arts Center,** *800-333-4849, Nashville, TN*

Check the **Organizations and Information** section, p.72, and **Events and Festivals** section, p.80, for more **Theatre.**

People Who Love Chattanooga
Habte Churnet

To see Lookout Mountain is to love it; on the list of those who do are artists, historians, archaeologists, tourists, homeowners, realtors, hikers, bikers, hang gliders, spelunkers, and those who simply appreciate a pretty scene; but perhaps no one loves it more dearly than geologist Habte Churnet. To Habte, it's a giant layer cake, 500 million years of Ordovician, Silurian, Devonian, Mississippian, Pennsylvanian effort, piled and stacked and faulted and folded and eroded and weathered; a marvel to study and to enjoy.

Dr. Habte Giorgis Churnet was born in Ethiopia, obtaining a first degree in geology there, a Masters degree in geophysics from Leeds University in Great Britain, and a Ph.D. in geology from the University of Tennessee at Knoxville. Now a UC Foundation Professor and head of the Department of Physics, Geology and Astronomy at the University of Tennessee at Chattanooga, Habte has lived in Chattanooga since 1980. He and wife Enat have two children who were born here; son Dargaye is a student at Chattanooga School for the Arts and Sciences, daughter Beth is a student at Rivermont.

In the classroom, Habte asks his students to construct a Betty-Crocker-basic stacked cake. Push it slowly from the right against an obstacle; watch it fold into a gentle downwarp, or syncline; the layers curve, concave side up. Hold it in place and cut it with a sharp knife, angled downwards; push until the right slides over part of the left. The curved layers have been displaced along the cut, or fault line. Habte is smiling now. "That is what happened in nature 300 million years ago when Africa and America collided. Now," he gestures with a flourish, "take your knife and carve the top surface of the cake until it resembles Lookout Mountain. That's the weathering and erosion that have happened since."

You can read more about "Lookout Cake" in Habte's book about the geology of the area, available in 1996. Lookout Mountain is Habte's workshop, his proving ground. But so are Raccoon Mountain, Walden Ridge, Laurel Ridge, Godsey Ridge, the Tennessee River gorge. He directs his students to look, look, look; often driving his class around the city; pointing at the natural features there to see. "North Chattanooga's Stringers Ridge and Lookout Mountain are part of the same structure," he explains. "Stringers Ridge has simply eroded more. Look at the rocks of Stringers and you can see what is inside Lookout Mountain!"

His specialty is the geology of the southeastern United States, although he knew little about Tennessee before his arrival in Knoxville. After a year of "settling in" to his new surroundings, he began to truly appreciate the beauty of the southern environment -- both its geology and its people. He was delighted when the opportunity came to teach in Chattanooga, and his enthusiasm for living here grows with every discovery he makes, every student he inspires, and every paper he writes as he examines and explains the mystery of the very ground beneath our feet.

"This is my home now," Habte proclaims, not able to contain the sparkle in his eyes as he speaks of it. "I expect to be here the rest of my life."

Recreation & Sports

Retired Father: After we finish cleaning all these fish and cleaning and putting away the boat, I'm taking the day off tomorrow to rest. What about you?
Working Son: I think I'll climb the T-Wall.

Contents

Organizations & Information

Adventure Guild
266-5709, 100 Tremont Street
Provides outdoor educational services; ropes course programs, rock climbing, backpacking, team development; works with businesses/schools to promote development of character, technical expertise. Guide service for hiking, rock climbing, backpacking, and caving expeditions; such as 100 miles on the Appalachian Trail.

Barnard Astronomical Society
629-6094, 622-4762, 848 Belvoir Hills Dr, 37412 for membership information
Since 1923 this group has kept its eye on the sky; members meet monthly and also gather for star parties and field trips; learn astronomical photography. Annual event is early-May Astronomy Day; all-day events at Clarence T. Jones Observatory, a star-gazing evening at the Nature Center. Membership brings newsletters from the Society and the national Astronomical League.

Blue and Gold Club
755-4053, UTC athletic department
Join the Blue and Gold Club and support the athletic scholarship fund at the University of Tennessee at Chattanooga and a fine Division I athletic program. Call for an application, a season ticket order form, and information on minimum donations for select seating in the arena.

Chattanooga Audubon Society
892-1499, 900 N Sanctuary Rd
This organization manages Audubon Acres and Maclellan Island, as well as a farm at Sale Creek. Over 12,000 school children a year benefit from educational programs through CAS; classes include *As the Indians Left It*, focusing on Native American culture and history, and *Gifts From the Earth*, taught by an Audubon naturalist.

Chattanooga Bicycle Club
PO Box 21843, Chattanooga, 37424
Monthly club meetings, programs and newsletter; weekly rides; trips out-of-state and out-of-country; and frequent get-togethers. Safety promoted on club rides; helmets are required; children under 18 must be accompanied by adult.

Chattanooga Grotto of the NSS, Inc.
875-9804, PO Box 11506, 37401
The local chapter of the National Speleological Society meets monthly; offers training and safety programs; involved in conservation; keeps caves protected and clean; has regular caving trips. Members of the Chattanooga-Hamilton County Cave, Pit and Cliff Rescue Team are Grotto members too.

Chattanooga Hiking Club
899-0287, Box 1443, Chattanooga, 37401
Get involved for regularly scheduled hikes, day, weekend, and more; work trips for trail maintenance and construction; environmental/recreational programs. Call for information, membership, newsletter.

Chattanooga Lookouts Booster Club
499-8814, Box 91191, Chattanooga, 37412
Baseball lovers can get to know the Lookouts through family-oriented activities; bus trips, golf and bowling tournaments, picnics, covered dish parties and more throughout the season.

Chattanooga Nature Center
821-1160, 400 Garden Rd
The Nature Center is a comprehensive environmental education facility on the western side of Lookout Mountain; some activities take place at the city-owned Greenway Farm in the Hixson area. You'll definitely want a family membership; it supports the work of the Center and gets you a monthly newsletter advising of upcoming events and classes. Summer camps for kids, hikes for every age, bird watching, meteor watching, plant and flower ID.

Chattanooga Parks & Recreation Department
757-PLAY for activities, 697-9700 for reservations
If you live in the Chattanooga city limits, this is where you need to start when you want information about any type of league play; they will provide contact names and numbers. They can advise you about all city-owned recreational facilities and parks, as well as year-round activities.

Chattanooga Visitors Center
800-322-3344 or 756-8687 for visitor information by phone; located at 2 Broad St, open 8-5:30 daily, also in Oasis area of Hamilton Place Mall, open daily, mall hours
This is your one-stop shop for just about everything Chattanooga has to offer. Call to find out what's going on in town and where it is. Brochures, books about area available here; also movie, *Marks on the Land*, great for school groups and everyone who's interested in knowing more about Chattanooga.

Friends of North Chickamauga Creek Greenway
870-8575, PO Box 358, Hixson, 37343
North Chickamauga Creek begins on Walden Ridge and winds 32 miles through the heart of the Hixson community before flowing into the Tennessee River just below the dam. This group's purpose is to promote community involvement in protecting and preserving the Creek and increasing accessibility for the general public. Call for information; be a Friend.

Why are fall colors so brilliant around here? There are more than 50 types of deciduous trees and shrubs in the Chattanooga region.

Greater Chattanooga Sports and Events Committee
756-8689, 1001 Market Street
The goal: Chattanooga -- Amateur Sports Capital of the South. GCSEC brings sporting events into the city, working to attract regional, national and international sports teams and events, and to encourage sports facility development. With a board comprised of business, political and sports leaders of the community, this group brings together civic pride, natural resources and a great knowledge of sports; some 1995 events were the SEC Women's Basketball Tournament, World Cup of Freestyle Wrestling, National ASA Softball Girls Fast Pitch, and BASA Softball Slow Pitch World Series.

Hamilton County Department of Parks & Recreation
842-0177
They will direct you to the baseball, soccer and football leagues in your area of Hamilton County; also call to find out where county tennis courts and jogging tracks can be found, free for public use. There are 23 sites county-wide, usually near a school; Riverpark on Amnicola and Chester Frost Park on Chickamauga Lake are part of the county system too (see).

National Handicapped Sports, NHS
See SPARC for membership information

North Chattanooga Cycling Club
265-6116 for trip info, 7524 Eric Dr, 37421 for membership information
Two major groups in this organization: mountain bikers and road cyclists; check the Taco Bell/Litespeed Road Racing Schedule and Mountain Bike Schedule; travel and ride in everything from the Knobscorcher Spring Circuit to the Tour of Dead Leaves. Weekly rides; training; member newsletter.

Scenic City Kite Club
267-5858, 842-6748
Learn how to make them and fly them; compete at the Lions 'n Lambs Kite Fly held at Camp Jordan each spring; age divisions under 13 and over.

Sports, Arts and Recreation of Chattanooga, SPARC
697-4400, Chattanooga State, 4501 Amnicola Hwy
This community-based program provides opportunities for persons with or without a disability to participate in sports, arts and recreation. It is the only chapter of National Handicapped Sports (NHS) in the state of Tennessee. All individuals, regardless of age, can enjoy the activities offered. Benefits: use or rental of adapted equipment, bi-monthly newsletter, NHS membership and newsletter, and discounts on various conferences, events and seminars.

Tennessee Environmental Education Association, TEEA
800-342-1340 for information
TEEA is committed to working towards solutions of current environmental

problems and the prevention of new ones; membership brings a newsletter and an opportunity to promote environmental education in Tennessee.

Tennessee Ornithological Society
238-4969 for membership information
Expert guides conduct seasonal bird walks along the RiverWalk. Educational information covering habitat and identification is available. Some of the wildlife you might see: eastern screech-owls, great blue herons, beaver, wood ducks, eastern bluebirds, luna moths, frogs, muskrats and raccoons.

Tennessee River Gorge Trust
266-0314 for membership information
A land conservation organization dedicated to preserving the Tennessee River Gorge, a 25,000-acre area from Williams Island to the old Hale's Bar Dam, through education and promotion of good land stewardship. Join and help.

Tennessee Valley Canoe Club
706-375-2783, PO Box 11125, Chattanooga, 37401
Canoeists meet regularly; concerned with conservation issues and safety training; also numerous group trips. Call for information; newsletter.

U. S. Coast Guard Auxiliary
478-1587, call for information, class schedules
This organization offers classes for anyone who plans to be out on a boat; basic boating safety to more complex aspects of being on the water: power boat operation, sailing, skiing; taught at community colleges and at Coast Guard Base near Chickamauga Dam. Provide periodic free boat inspections.

Astronomy

Clarence T. Jones Observatory
622-5733, 10 Tuxedo, just off Brainerd Rd, open to public Fri 8-10 pm, free
Planetarium show begins at 8:30 each Friday; the 20-inch telescope is available for viewing when weather permits; groups call for advance setup. Get away from the bright lights with Star Parties and other activities through Barnard Astronomical Society (see); they head for mountaintops and prime countryside viewspots for optimum stargazing.

Auto Racing

Stock Car Racing
Cleveland Speedway, *479-8574, 2420 South Lee Hwy, Cleveland, TN*
♦ Joe Lee Johnson won Charlotte's first World 600 during a 30-year racing career; he left the NASCAR circuit in 1977 and opened the Speedway in

1978. Go there for **Stock Car** racing; five divisions race at this dirt track every Saturday night beginning at 7:30: late model, sportsman, late model stock, hobby, and pony class. All cars American-made.

Baseball/Softball

AA Southern League, Chattanooga Lookouts Baseball
267-2208, 1130 E 3rd St, Engel Stadium
Eight tons of hot dogs? That's what it took to feed the 292,920 people who came to see the Lookouts in '94, in Historic Engel Stadium. Unlike Mudville, there's plenty of joy here, with visits from The Famous Chicken, bat and glove give-aways, fireworks bursting in air, and bazzball, bazzball, bazzball. The fun-loving spirit of Joe Engel lingers; president of the club for many years, he was called the Barnum of the Bushes for his unusual promotions, such as giving away a house; the 17-year-old female pitcher he signed, Jackie Mitchell, struck out Lou Gehrig and Babe Ruth in an exhibition game on April 2, 1931!

The Lookouts were chartered into the Southern League in 1885; former Lookouts in the National Baseball Hall of Fame are Kiki Cuyler, Clark Griffith, Burleigh Grimes, Rogers Hornsby, Ferguson Jenkins, Harmon Killebrew, Willie Mays and Satchel Paige. The stadium went up in 1929; it's the oldest in the Southern League and still considered one of the finest, with major renovations in 1989; it's classy and clean; Birmingham, Carolina, Greenville, Huntsville, Jacksonville, Knoxville, Memphis, Nashville and Orlando come in to duke it out, call for home schedule.

Go for the season tickets and save big; get your favorite seat each game, a monthly newsletter, a Meet-the-Team picnic and a year-ending autograph party. A Lookouts game is a great-for-groups activity for your office party, church group, or family reunion; big discounts for 25 or more; also Lookout Cookouts, along the leftfield line; all-you-can-eat burgers and dogs plus your game ticket; book early, these go fast.

Make sure you take a kid to a baseball game this year; maybe bat night?

Batting Practice
There's the story of the young boy who loves baseball. He goes into the yard alone, tosses the ball into the air, swings, and misses. "Strike One!" he calls. Second pitch, another strike. The young boy straightens his shoulders, takes a deep breath, clenches his teeth, and vows to get a hit. He tosses the ball up, swings as hard as he can, and misses again. "Strike Three!" he calls on himself. "You're out!" A big smile goes ear to ear as he exclaims with delight, "Wow! What a pitcher!"

If you have no one to pitch to you, head for the practice cages at these places.
♦ **Northwest Georgia Batting Cages,** *861-1355, 600 Battlefield Pkwy*
♦ **Sir Goony's Family Fun Center,** *892-5922, 5918 Brainerd Rd*

League Play, All Ages
City of Chattanooga, 757-PLAY; check for other municipalities, counties
Chattanooga Parks and Recreation Department has 22 facilities for baseball and softball, but that's not all there is. Each municipality manages facilities, and Hamilton County does too. Generally, the governing body manages the facilities, but associations within a community manage their own league play. There are plenty of opportunities to get involved; boys and girls and men and women, if you want to play you'll be able to find a league that will welcome you. Call the Parks and Recreation Department in your area for starters; they have lists of the leagues using their facilities, and a contact name and number.

Tournaments
GCSEC, 756-8689
The Greater Chattanooga Sports and Events Committee can give you information about softball and baseball tournaments scheduled in the area; from high school Spring Flings to Fast and Slow Pitch Softball. Thousands of enthusiastic sports fans are involved annually; over 10,000 visitors came for the National Softball Association Youth Girls Fast Pitch World Series in '94.

Basketball

University of Tennessee at Chattanooga
266-6627 for individual game tickets; 755-5285 for season tickets
The **Southern Conference Men's Basketball** team has won seven Conference Championships, the last three in '93, '94 and '95. They play in the UTC Arena, otherwise known as the Roundhouse, from November to March. Catch the Lady Mocs in Maclellan Gym for some fast-moving **Women's Basketball**. See UTC.

League Play, All Ages
City of Chattanooga, 757-PLAY; check for other municipalities, counties
You can find Pee Wee basketball, zone basketball league play, city-wide basketball tournaments. As with baseball, leagues are separate from facilities; call the Parks Department in your area as a starting information point; also check with the YMCA, see p.124.

Check under **Playgrounds**, p.135 for open courts for shootin' hoops.

Biking/Cycling

The macadam road in Chickamauga Battlefield is great for biking; there's trail riding at Prentice Cooper State Park and Pigeon Mountain in Georgia on single-track fire roads. There is a cycling route in the city but remember, you are competing with cars for road space; for children there is safe riding at Riverpark, with a 5 mph speed limit on track. *(contd.)*

For clubs in the area, see Organizations, p.108. The **Taco Bell/Litespeed Road Racing Schedule** runs February-October, with races in Tennessee, Alabama, Georgia and South Carolina; the **Mountain Bike Schedule** is March-November and goes to North Carolina too; plenty of mud and dust and glory for all. Special events include a **Safety Council Kid's Bicycle Rodeo**. Can you guess what the **BRAT** and the **BRAG** are?

You can purchase bikes, have them serviced, and get information about bike clubs and upcoming races at these commercial establishments.

Bike Shop, *267-1000, 201 Frazier Ave, open Tue-Sat*
♦ Clothing, shoes and accessories, fitness equipment; service all makes.

East Ridge Bicycles, *894-9122, 5910 Ringgold Rd, open Sun-Fri*
♦ Clothing, parts, accessories; repair all makes.

Owen Cyclery, *875-6811, N Point Blvd Hixson, open Tue-Sat*
♦ Large bicycle shop carrying major brands.

River City Bicycles, *265-7176, 104 Tremont St, open Sun-Fri*
♦ Specializing in bikes for mountain, racing, triathlon, and recreation.

BRAT: *Bike Ride Across Tennessee.* **BRAG:** *Bike Ride Across Georgia.*

Billiards

Billiards are hot in Chattanooga, attracting new people and a renewed interest in a sport that's been around for years. There are numerous clubs around town; two popular downtown ones are mentioned that offer a full range of afternoon-to-late-evening entertainment, along with food and drink. Check them out; and check your phone book for other locations.

Chattanooga Billiard Club, *267-7740, 725 Cherry St; East location 499-3883, 110 Jordan Dr; open Mon-Sat 11AM-3AM; Sun 1PM-3AM*
♦ The downtown location of this club is home of the Tennessee State 9-ball Championships. Lessons and leagues are available, a pro and repair shop too. Pocket billiards, snooker, darts and big-screen TV are other options for play; at the East location there is full-swing indoor golf. Offering lunch, dinner, late-night snacks, desserts, beer, wine, espresso.

Parkway Billiards, *265-7665, 35 Patten Parkway, open daily 4PM, closes 3AM Sun-Thu, 6AM Fri-Sat*
♦ Billiards, darts and an assortment of video games. Lessons, leagues and very late-night hours. Restaurant and full bar.

Boating/Sailing

Real boating country here, with TVA's Nickajack, Chickamauga and Watts Bar Dams near Chattanooga; Chickamauga Dam is within the city limits and backs up a 35,000-acre lake. Skiers like the lake's wide-open spaces; sailing is popular too. Did you know Ted Turner spent countless hours perfecting his sailing skills on Chickamauga Lake while attending McCallie School? And, you recall, he went on to win the America's Cup in 1977 at the helm of the Courageous.

Waters here are suited to any type of boat, from sailboats to the larger cruisers, and numerous commercial resorts and boat docks are available along the mighty Tennessee's 625 miles of navigable waters from Knoxville to Paducah, Kentucky.

Before you get out on the water, get your U. S. Coast Guard certification; a good idea before you even select the boat.
U. S. Coast Guard Auxiliary
478-1587, Call for information, class schedules
This organization offers classes for anyone who plans to use a boat; basic boating safety to more complex aspects of being on the water, information about power boat operation, sailing, skiing, weather; taught at community colleges as well as at **Coast Guard Base** near Chickamauga Dam, *3551 Harrison Pike, 622-2101*. Auxiliary provides periodic free boat inspections too.

Register. It's the law!
Tennessee Wildlife Resources Agency
800-262-6704, 615-484-9571, 216 E Penfield, Crossville, TN 38555 for Region III
Tennessee Boating Safety Law requires the registration of all vessels propelled by sail or motor. Nonresidents may operate a boat with proper homestate registration for 90 days before being required to register in Tennessee. Contact TWRA for information.

Then, to find your way around the water, you'll want information from TVA.
TVA Maps and Survey Information
751-6277, 311 Broad St, 37402, open Mon-Fri 8-4:30
Navigation charts for all TVA waters are available; get the folio of everything from Knoxville to Paducah, or select a single map of the area you are interested in. Recreation maps show all boat launching sites, other helpful information. A catalogue of maps and a basic Great Lakes of the South recreation map are available at no charge.

TVA Lake Information Line
615-751-2264
Call for the latest information on lake levels and stream flows.

Here are the places that provide lake access upriver and downriver from Chattanooga.
Chickamauga Dam south to Nickajack Dam on Nickajack Lake
♦ **Nickajack Lake is 46 miles long, has a maximum width of 2.7 miles, a surface area of 10,900 acres, and a shoreline of 192 miles.** *(contd.)*

River Mile 470.0, Tennessee River Park
River Mile 463.5, Ross's Landing Park
River Mile 438.1, Walker's Landing
River Mile 431.2, Hales Bar Resort
River Mile 429.5, Marion County Park
River Mile 429.0, Camp on the Lake
River Mile 425.1, Maple View Recreation Area
River Mile 425.0, Nickajack Dam Reservoir

Chickamauga Dam north to Watts Bar Dam on Chickamauga Lake

♦ **Chickamauga Lake is 59 miles long, has a maximum width of 1.7 miles, a surface area of 35,400 acres, and a shoreline of 810 miles.**

River Mile 471.0, Chickamauga Dam Reservoir
River Mile 471.5, Chickamauga Marina
River Mile 471.7, Lakeshore Marina
River Mile 472.8, Gold Point Marina
River Mile 473.5, Booker T. Washington State Park
River Mile 475.2, Big Ridge Yacht Club
River Mile 477.5, Loret Marina
River Mile 479.0, Harrison Bay St Pk
River Mile 479.8, Chester Frost County Pk
River Mile 481.9, Lakesite Marina
River Mile 482.0, Harbor Lights Marina
River Mile 485.0, Skull Island Rec Area
River Mile 487.5, Pine Harbor Boat Dock
River Mile 487.7, Shady Grove Harbor
River Mile 490.0, Possum Creek Rec Area, Grasshopper Creek Rec Area
River Mile 495.0, Sale Creek Rec Area, Sale Creek Marina Multi Boating
River Mile 500.5, Hwy 58 Boat Dock; B & B Marina
River Mile 504.4, Dayton Boat Dock, Blue Water Campground
River Mile 512.9, Cotton Port Marina & Campground

To get from one lake to the next by boat, you have to go through the locks.
U. S. Army Corps of Engineers
875-6230, Chickamauga Lock, call Lockmaster for information, booklet
Even the smallest boat can lock through; but priorities put US Government vessels first, then commercial passenger vessels, commercial tows, and lastly, recreational boats. If there's a big backup, they promise to put you through every third lockage if possible. You've got to have at least 50 feet of line and proper deck fittings for tying up, know all buoys, markers, and lock traffic signals, and follow safe speed and mooring procedures.

If you want to rent, buy, repair or store a boat, these Marinas are open year round. Call to see if they offer what you need.
Chickamauga Marina, *622-0821, Chickamauga Boat Harbor*

♦ River Mile 471.5. South side of lake by Dam, wet and dry storage, full service. 450 slips, ships store, maintenance and repairs. No rentals.

Hales Bar Resort and Marina, *942-4040, Old Hales Bar Rd, Nickajack Lake*

♦ River Mile 431.2. Houseboat and pontoon rental, campground and covered storage.

Harbor Lights Marina, *842-5391, 9718 Hixson Pike, Soddy-Daisy*
♦ River Mile 482.0. North side of lake, wet storage, fuel, pontoon boat rentals, and picnic supplies. Baywatch Restaurant.

Lakeshore Marina, *870-2000, 5600 Lake Resort Terrace*
♦ River Mile 471.7. North side of lake by Dam, dry stack storage to 26 feet, wet slips, ships store, gas/diesel.

Loret Marina, *344-8331, 6701 Hwy 58*
♦ River Mile 477.5. South side of lake at Harrison, full-service marina with wet and dry storage, travelift service to 40 tons, boat and motor sales and service, complete refinishing service.

Pine Harbor Marina, *615-332-3963, 1145 Poling Circle, Soddy-Daisy*
♦ River Mile 487.5. North side of lake, 200 slips, ships store, open year round, full time maintenance facility, launching ramp and travel lift. Dockside Restaurant, transient parking for craft up to 60 feet.

Sale Creek Marina, *332-6312, 3900 Lee Pike, Soddy-Daisy*
♦ River Mile 495. Wet storage, 100 slips, north side of lake.

Bowling

When it's too cold and rainy to be outside, you can go bowling. When it's too hot and muggy to be outside, you can go bowling. When you want some buddies to meet up with regularly, you can join a league and go bowling. And no fooling, for man and woman, girl and boy, it is fine exercise. From south to north, here are some nice lanes. Get your two-toned shoes and matching ball and knock down some pins.

AMF Fort Lanes, *866-6563, 2029 Lafayette Rd, Ft Oglethorpe, open Mon-Sat 9AM-11PM, Sun 1-11PM*
♦ Automatic scoring, game room, snack bar, complete pro shop.

Holiday Bowl, *894-0503, 5518 Brainerd Rd, open Mon-Sat 8:30AM-4AM, Sun noon-1AM*
♦ 48 lanes with Brunswick automatic scoring in colorvision; gameroom, snack bar, lounge, pro shop, balls, bags, shoes, leagues and bowling parties, cater children's birthday parties, banquet and meeting rooms available, free learn-to-bowl classes, free playroom for children of league members.

Holiday Bowl, *843-2695, 5530 Hixson Pike, open Mon-Thu 9AM-1AM, Fri-Sat till 3AM, Sun 10AM-midnight*
♦ 24 lanes, same features as above.

Tri-State Lanes, *867-2281, 3636 Ringgold Rd, open Sun-Thu 9AM -1AM, Fri till 2AM, Sat till 3AM*
♦ 32 lanes with automatic scoring, snack bar, lounge, game room, professionally staffed pro shop, bumper bowling, open 7 days a week, certified bowling instruction, banquet room, birthday parties.

Camping/Hiking/Trails

There are hundreds of places within a hundred miles of Chattanooga for hiking and camping, so pick a cove, a meadow, or a mountaintop; lace up your boots; grab the trailmix, and go. If you have a house full of kids get a family-size tent; you'll have a ball introducing your children to the wonders of the out-of-doors. And if you've reached those now-I-have-enough-time retirement years, what glory is in store for you! Pitch camp beside a mountain stream, and relax. This is one activity no one ever outgrows.

See **Organizations**, p.108, for a hiking group; see **Recreational Equipment** in the Shopping section, p.207, for where to find the boots and tents you might need; see **Parks** in this section, p.130, and **Campgrounds** in the Lodgings section, p.209, for other places to camp and hike in addition to the ones below; also check the bookstores for books of trails and campgrounds in the Tennessee-Georgia-Alabama-North Carolina area.

Bluff Trail
Point Park, Lookout Mountain, TN
The Bluff Trail is the main hiking trail from Point Park on Lookout Mountain. Start at the metal steps left of the Ochs Museum, where Kentucky Volunteers climbed to plant their flag during Civil War times. Many trails lead away from the main one; Rifle Pits, Cravens House, Gum Springs, Skyuka, Jackson Gap, and Upper and Lower Truck Trail; get a map at the Park Visitor Center.

Cloudland Canyon State Park
706-657-4050, I-59, Exit 2, 8 miles east of Trenton, GA on SR 136
This 2,219-acre park straddles a deep gorge cut into Lookout Mountain by Sitton Gulch Creek. Elevation goes from 800 feet to 1,980 feet; ridges and valley offer rugged geology and beautiful vistas. 75 tent/trailer sites, 30 walk-in campsites, four pioneer campsites; West Rim and Waterfalls Trail; backcountry backpacking trail.

Cumberland State Scenic Trail
Signal Point, Signal Mountain, TN
Start your hike at historic Signal Point and see some of the most scenic areas in the state; Chattanooga section of trail begins in Prentice Cooper State Forest, winds along escarpments and stream valleys 20 miles northward to the rim of the Sequatchie Valley. Two primitive campsites on trail.

DeSoto State Park
205-845-5075, I-59, 7 miles northeast of Ft Payne, AL on SR 35
One of the deepest gorges east of the Mississippi River is 27-mile Little River Canyon in 5,067-acre DeSoto State Park on Lookout Mountain. DeSoto Falls plunges 110 feet from a mile-long lake; dense woodlands, wildflowers and spectacular views. Modern and primitive campsites; campstore. Miles of

hiking trails -- mountaintop and in the gorge.

Fall Creek Falls State Resort Park
615-881-5241, near Pikeville, TN on SR30
Majestic cascades, deep chasms and gorges, a waterfall plunging 265 feet; here are 16,000 acres of the most spectacular scenery in Tennessee. This resort park has an inn and restaurant with convention facilities, cabins and group lodge, tent sites, nature center and numerous hiking and backpacking trails; 345-acre lake has yielded record-size fish.

Fort Mountain State Park
706-695-2621, I-75 Exit 136, 7 miles east of Chatsworth, GA on SR52
An ancient 855-foot rock wall in the park is said to have been built by Indians; it stands on the highest point of the mountain. The 2,532-acre park has 70 tent and trailer sites and 14 miles of foot trails; swimming beach and boating.

Great Smoky Mountains National Park
615-436-1200, 44 miles SE of Knoxville, TN on US441
Half of this 800-square mile park is in Tennessee, half in North Carolina. The Appalachian Trail follows the state line for 70 miles along the high ridge of the park. Hundreds of miles of hiking trails; numerous campgrounds, reservations taken at some sites. Appalachian Mountain peaks surround many coves -- Cades Cove is one of the most popular; there are hundreds of species of plants; rhododendron, mountain laurel, and flaming azalea bloom in summer months; in autumn deciduous trees provide stunning foliage.

National Forests
404-347-4191, U. S. Forest Service, Southern Region
Contact the Forest Service for information about hiking and camping in your National Forests. These are not too far from the Chattanooga area.
♦ **Bankhead National Forest, Alabama,** *205-832-4470*
♦ **Chattahoochee National Forest, Georgia,** *404-536-0541*
♦ **Cherokee National Forest, Tennessee,** *615-476-9700*
♦ **Nantahala National Forest, North Carolina,** *704-257-4200*
♦ **Talladega National Forest, Alabama,** *205-832-4470*

North Chickamauga Pocket Wilderness
Montlake Rd, Off Dayton Pike, Soddy-Daisy, TN
North Chickamauga Creek is a major watershed for the Chattanooga area. This 1100-acre wilderness is an outstanding scenic and natural area where you'll find waterfalls, interesting rock formations and breathtaking overlooks; also a variety of wildlife such as turkey and deer. Nature lovers and historians will enjoy the trails; Stevenson Trail runs along the north slope of the Creek for four miles, allow 5 hours for the roundtrip; Hogskin Branch Loop is 1.5 miles from the parking lot and back, an hours walk. There are picnic areas and handicapped accessibility to the creek. Primitive camping

allowed in designated areas. Bowater maintains the land for public usage.

South Cumberland Recreation Area
615-924-2980, I-24, Exit to SR41, Tracy City, TN
Seven separate areas, five natural, make up the 12,000-acre South Cumberland. The Visitors Center on State Hwy 41 between Monteagle and Tracy City provides information on each component. Stone Door and Savage Gulf contain spectacular vistas, waterfalls, hiking and backpacking trails and forests; Fiery Gizzard Trail, one of the nation's most outstanding, connects Grundy Forest and Foster Falls; swim in Fiery Gizzard Creek. Carter Natural Area is part of an 18,000-acre enclosed valley sinkhole, Lost Cove, with forests, streams and caves; overlooking Lost Cove is Sewanee Natural Bridge, a sandstone arch. Grundy Lakes near Tracy City offers swimming, fishing, hiking and picnic areas.

Canoeing/Kayaking/Rafting

Our mountains and ridges create some interesting waterways, from scenic to swift. Depending on your skill, opportunities for all three types of paddle boating abound. Use your own, rent, or go on guided adventure trips.

Hiwassee River
This State Scenic River is perfect for beginners; lots of safe, fun rapids; go by raft or innertube; this river connects the Ocoee and the Tennessee.
♦ **Hiwassee Rafting Center**, *800-338-8133*. They'll rent you the raft, the funyak, or the tube, and of course lifejackets and paddles. The "put-in" is in the Cherokee National Forest; then float downriver. The Center has a campground, bathhouse, cabins, a group bunkhouse, and snack bar.

Lookout Creek
This pretty waterway is on the west side of Lookout Mountain, and winds its way through the Chattanooga Nature Center; canoe explorations can be scheduled through Center, *821-1160*, with the naturalist.

North Chickamauga Creek
This creek is normally placid and flows gently through the Hixson community as it nears the river. The Chattanooga Parks Department schedules canoe trips from Greenway Farm, call **OutVenture 842-6629**, or put in your own canoe at the Greenway area near the dam. Farther upstream, where the creek begins falling off Walden Ridge, the steep-creek boaters rush in when there are rapids-making heavy rains. Yes, they paddle these raging channels of whitewater, with incredible drops through narrow boulder-choked canyons. Would you put yourself over a 22-foot waterfall? The creek boaters descend Bear, Soddy, North Pole, and Falling Water Creeks too. It takes the right boat and the right brand of adrenaline.

Ocoee River
We've always known we have good water around here; the '96 Olympic whitewater competition exposes our long-loved Ocoee for all the world to see. The Olympic slalom in previous years was held on man-made concrete rivers; the upper Ocoee is a first in a natural setting. TVA manages the three dams here; water in the upper section is normally diverted through a tunnel to a hydroelectric plant; the riverbed is almost dry. For the 1,700-foot "Olympic River," huge rocks were added to narrow the channel; waterflow below Dam #3, not dependent on weather conditions, can be carefully controlled.

The competition: U. S. Slalom Team Trials, May 1995; Olympics Slalom, July 27 and 28, 1996. Whitewater slalom racers wind through 25 gates suspended over the water along a 600-meter course; gates are two striped poles -- red for upstream, green for downstream -- suspended over the course by a cable. There's a five-second penalty for touching a gate with body, paddle or boat. The four classes are men's single kayak, women's single kayak, men's single canoe, and men's double canoe.

None of this affects the commercial rafting farther downstream, below Dam #2. If you want your own wild ride, there is a five-mile stretch of Class III-IV rapids to challenge you; take it from Grumpy to Hell Hole; keep this in mind:

♦ Guided raft trips are available between March and November; call ahead for information and reservations.

♦ You must be at least 12 to raft the Ocoee River; it's a Tennessee law.

♦ When it's warm, wear your swimsuit or t-shirt and shorts; cooler weather bring wool sweaters, socks and windbreakers; bring a change of clothes.

♦ Leave non-waterproof watches and cameras behind; anchor your glasses.

♦ Use of alcohol or drugs is strictly prohibited.

Here are a few Ocoee River outfitters:

♦ **Adventures Unlimited,** *800-662-0667.* This wilderness adventure company provides professionally-trained guides and self-bailing rafts; photo services too. The 12-acre base camp has hot showers, a campground, picnic areas, and volleyball and basketball courts.

♦ **High Country,** *800-233-8594.* In business for 15 years; staff is expertly trained on river safety, ecology, geology and local history. Their facilities are spacious; 27 acres of meadow and forest, spacious changing area, hot tub, store, picnic pavilion, and group camping area.

♦ **Ocoee Inn Services,** *800-272-7238.* Everything you need here; family-style restaurant, rustic motel rooms, cabins on the water, boat dock, pontoon boats, fishing boats, canoes, photo services, and rafting too! Hiking trails, swimming holes, picnic areas and campgrounds just around the bend.

♦ **Ocoee Outdoors,** *800-533-7767.* They've logged 35,000 trips and 175,000 miles on the River; for sure they know their way around the twenty rapids they'll guide you through. Changing area and showers, store and picnic area, private campground. Live music weekends.

Bonus: there are mild-mannered float trips below Dam #1.

Sequatchie River
This is a Class I float stream; from north of Dayton to south of Jasper it decorates a got-to-see-it-to-believe-it beautiful valley. Take your own or rent.
♦ **Canoe the Sequatchie,** *615-949-4400, Chattanooga 855-4961, Hwy 127 south of Dunlap, open weekends April-October, daily Memorial Day to Labor Day at 8 AM, Central Time.* Scott and Ernestine Pilkington want to get you canoeing; they have over 100 canoes available, and at least twice that many paddles; choice of trips lengths available for any part of a day.

South Chickamauga Creek
This in-the-city creek is peaceful; it winds through Audubon Acres and now stays inside the Brainerd levee; paddle while you bird-and-people watch; arrange canoe trips through City Parks at **OutVenture 842-6629**.

Caving/Spelunking

If you like caves, you'll be pleased to hear there are more than 5,000 of them in the state of Tennessee alone; that doesn't include what's inside Lookout Mountain as you head south into Georgia and Alabama. There are numerous commercial caverns in the area you can explore with a guide; lighted pathways are clearly marked. For the more daring, guided wild cave tours are available in many of these same commercial caves; you generally tote your own light. Expect to get a little wet, as Jeffrey and his Dad and his Scout Troop did the weekend they got baptized in mountain-cave glop and thousand-year-old darkness, elbowing their way into the hole with more courage than a bat. After all, radar never fails; batteries sometimes do.

The genuine I'd-rather-do-it-myself spelunker can spend a year of Sundays exploring the abundance of caves in the limestone bedrock of the rugged Cumberland plateaus on Chattanooga's western edge -- Walden Ridge, Raccoon Mountain, Lookout Mountain and past the Sequatchie Valley. This activity calls for the buddy-system and plenty of know-how. Being prepared is critical; extra food, clothing, a first-aid kit, and 3 different sources of light are essential and may save your life. **Wear a hard hat and ALWAYS let people know where you will be exploring.**

Call to see which of the following commercial caverns have wild cave tours.
In Tennessee
Cumberland Caverns, *668-4396, McMinnville*
Forbidden Caverns, *453-5972, Sevierville*
Raccoon Mountain Caverns, *821-9403, Chattanooga*
Ruby Falls, *821-2544, Lookout Mountain*

The Lost Sea, *337-6616, Sweetwater*
Tuckaleechee Caverns, *448-2274, Townsend*
Wonder Cave, *467-3060, Pelham*
In Alabama
Russell Cave National Monument, *205-495-2672, Bridgeport*
Sequoyah Caverns, *205-635-0024, Valley Head*

If you want to see something interesting in a cave you can't enter, go with a group from the Chattanooga Nature Center, *821-1160,* for a **bat-watching trip** to **Nickajack Cave**.

See **Organizations**, p.108, for non-commercial **caving groups** to join.

Climbing/Mountaineering

Start at the Walnut Street Wall. This stone support post holding up the Walnut Street Bridge on the north shore has been fitted with holds, anchors and ropes. Managed as a cooperative effort by the City of Chattanooga and the Adventure Guild, it's a controlled environment where you can learn the basic climbing moves. Where to go then? Sandstone-capped mountains just begging to be climbed are all around; there are thousands of routes within thirty miles of the city. **Sunset Rock** on Lookout Mountain offers easy accessibility and 250 routes. The **Tennessee**, or **T-Wall**, stretches two miles along the rim of the Gorge, and has more than 200 routes, ranging from intermediate to extreme in difficulty; want to try Psycho Path or Finger Locking Good? Check the bookstores or Rock/Creek Outfitters for books outlining area climbing routes.

Adventure Guild, *266-5709, 100 Tremont St*
♦ Get certified with the Guild at the Walnut Street Wall; they also offer classes in more difficult climbing and organized trips when you're ready.

Rock/Creek Outfitters, *265-5969, 100 Tremont St*
♦ Don't be chintzy about climbing equipment; you'll need shoes, harness, rope, webbing, carabiners, a helmet and a pack, and most of the items directly affect your safety on the face of a wall of rock.

Exercise/ Fitness

Concentrate on strength and endurance and flexibility; determine your body fat percentage and cardiovascular efficiency and get it where it ought to be. A fit body takes a little work, and it needs to be regularly done. Here are a few choices.

Powerhouse Fitness Center
697-9720, 1254 E 3rd St, inside Warner Park Fieldhouse, free
Operated by Chattanooga Parks Department, there's a wide range of fitness programming available at no cost to the user. Indoor track, aerobics floor, stationary cycles, stairmasters, weight machine, barbells, free weights. Call for schedule of classes; aerobics are also offered at neighborhood recreation centers.

(contd.)

YMCA (5 locations)
Check with each location for fees, services provided, classes offered. Some classes are available to non-members.

- *266-3766, 301 W 6th*, Downtown Branch
- *877-3517, 4138 Hixson Pike*, North River Branch
- *266-4844, 915 Park Ave*, Henry Branch
- *858-0590, 1503 Lafayette Rd*, Ft Oglethorpe, N Georgia Branch
- *821-8307, 4900 Edingburgh Dr*, Pineywoods Branch

Fishing

Fishing is permitted all year in TVA lakes, but spring and fall will bring you some of the best results. Chickamauga Lake has good bass fishing March through June; bluegill fishing is great in July when the willow flies are hatching. In winter and early spring, the tailwaters just below the Dam provide some of the best fishing anywhere in the state; you're liable to catch white bass, white crappie and sauger; in May and June it's mostly blue, channel and flathead catfish. You'll need to go to the cooler mountain waters for your trout, but they are there in abundance, just waiting; the Hiwassee River is legend and the Tennessee Wildlife Resources Agency transplants about 2,400 one-pound trout into the Tellico River every week during spring and summer.

Before you go, get your license.
Alabama Division of Game and Fish, *205-242-3829, 64 N Union St, Montgomery 36130*
- Licenses may be purchased for 7-days, a year, or a lifetime. Not necessary if you are over 65 or under 16. There is an open season for game fish all year in Alabama waters.

Georgia Department of Natural Resources, Game and Fish Division, *404-656-4992, 205 Butler St SE, Suite 135B, Atlanta 30334*
- License required for all fresh-water fishing, may purchase season or 5-day; trout stamp required to keep trout.

Tennessee Wildlife Resources Agency, *800-262-6704, 615-781-6622, 216 E Penfield, Crossville, TN 38555*
- There are some exceptions, but basically, if you are 13 or over you must have a license to fish Tennessee waters. You can purchase your license from most county court clerks, sporting goods stores, hardware stores, boat docks, and all TWRA regional offices. Call for a booklet on fishing regulations; they will mail to you. The booklet is packed with useful information on where and when to fish, and what you're likely to catch.

For information about TVA waters, you'll want to contact the following places.

TVA Maps and Survey Information
751-6277, 311 Broad St, 37402, open Mon-Fri 8-4:30
TVA and TWRA began installing fish attractors in 1977; piles of brush anchored to the bottom of the lake to create an artificial "cover," which greatly increases the anglers catch rate. TVA recreation maps show the fish attractor locations, boat launching sites, and other helpful information. Navigation charts for all TVA waters are available too; get the folio of everything from Knoxville to Paducah, or select a single map of the area you are interested in. A catalogue of maps and a basic Great Lakes of the South recreation map are available at no charge.

TVA Lake Information Line
615-751-2264
Call for the latest information on lake levels and stream flows.

Check with these commercial establishments for your fishing supplies.
ChooChoo Fly & Tackle, *875-0944, 739 Ashland Terrace*
♦ Complete fly fishing equipment, Orvis, Sage, Cortland, Hodgeman; rainwear, waders, tying supplies.
Osprey Trading Company, *265-0306, 1101 Hixson Pike*
♦ Orvis dealer, flies and tackle, guided trips, fly fishing schools.
Reeves Tackle & Bait Shop, *842-4519, 7322 Hixson Pike*
♦ All types of fishing supplies, live and artificial bait.
Sportsman's Supply & Services, *875-4868, 4824 Hixson Pike*
♦ All fishing needs, rod and reel repair.

The marinas have supplies too, see **Boating,** p.116 for a complete listing.

Are you looking for a guided fishing trip, or fly-fishing lessons?
Osprey Trading Company, *265-0306, 1101 Hixson Pike,* has several offerings. For fly fishing, a walk-in day trip to the Cherokee National Forest gets you fishing on the Tellico, Ball and North Rivers; or go all day on the Hiwassee River in a McKenzie drift boat, 1 or 2 people on some fast water. They conduct fly fishing instruction every weekend from February through August; when you're done you'll be able to handle any trout stream anywhere. If you're looking for bass fishing on Chickamauga Lake, they'll connect you with Billy Bartlett, guide extraordinaire; if you want far-away fish, they can send you to Montana, Wyoming, or the Florida Keys.

Football

College
No need to pontificate about SEC football; folks in the south are born into allegiance to one team or another. Tennessee, Alabama and Georgia fanaticism is legend; watch for loyalty flags attached to car windows as horns

beep to make sure you know which team is best; orange or red shirts hover nervously in front of the TV on any Saturday afternoon in the fall, pulling for the Big Orange, the Crimson Tide, and those Dawgs.

In Chattanooga, the Saturday game is Blue and Gold, the Moccasins; crowds for the Southern Conference confrontations don't compare with SEC, but count that a blessing! You can get a good seat for a fine afternoon of college ball. Get season tickets and support your community's athletics.

University of Tennessee at Chattanooga, *266-6627 for individual game tickets; 755-5285 for season tickets.*

High School
Friday nights the bright lights shine above the high school scene; these training grounds have turned out a few pros; Reggie White, called the greatest defensive player in football, played at Howard High School; John Hannah, now in the Pro Football Hall of Fame, played at Baylor.

But the game's more than the fame; it's fun! In the cold-weather night the crowd and the players work as one; the yelling, stomping force in the stands pushes energy towards the team, knowing that enough noise-and-desire will propel the glory-bound quarterback safely past every tackle, till he's spiking the ball from the magic side of the goal line, and the scoreboard lights up a win. Local media give good coverage; film at 11; stats in the Saturday papers.

Youth Leagues
City of Chattanooga, 757-PLAY; Check for other municipalities, counties
As with baseball, you'll need to search out the leagues in your area. Start with the Parks and Recreation Department and the YMCA's.

Golf

The same crowd that hollers itself sick at a football game watches golf in holier-than-church silence, showing whisper-hushed respect for Masters-giants like Jack and Arnie and other winners of the prized jacket-of-green. This genteel game is as much loved in the south as barbecue and lemonade; the only thing that causes a true golfer to give-it-up is a flood on the fairway; they make orange balls, you know, for playing in the occasional snow.

If golf is your game, Chattanooga has a good lineup of public and private courses, pleasing golfers and attracting many fine tournaments to the area, contact the **Greater Chattanooga Sports and Events Committee,** *756-8689,* for information on upcoming ones. Public courses are listed below; check your phone book for the many excellent private courses we have. Many participate in reciprocal arrangements with clubs in other cities; if you're coming for a visit, your home golf club can advise you in advance.

Chattanooga City Parks Department courses
- **Brainerd Golf Course,** *855-2692, 5203 Old Mission Road*
- **Brown Acres Golf Course,** *855-2680, 406 Brown Rd*
  Open daily 8 AM till dark. These two courses are city-owned, feature fully stocked pro shops, snack bars, practice facilities, locker rooms and seven-day tee times.

Public courses
- **Concord Golf Club,** *894-4536, 7 Radmoor Lane*
- **Eastgate Golf Center,** *892-5464, Eastgate*
- **Hickory Valley Golf Course,** *894-1576, 2453 Hickory Valley Rd,*
- **Moccasin Bend Public Golf Club,** *267-3585, 381 Moccasin Bend Rd*
- **Montlake Golf & Country Club,** *332-3111, 9104 Brow Lake Rd, Soddy-Daisy*
- **The Quarry,** *875-8888, 1001 Reads Lake Rd*
- **Rivermont Golf & Country Club,** *877-8506, 1101 Meadowlake Rd*
- **Windstone Golf Club,** *894-1231, 9230 Windstone Dr*

Practice Ranges
- **Hixson Golf Driving Range,** *842-0923, 6801 Middle Valley Rd*
- **Mountain Meadows Golf & Driving Range,** *961-2343, 11004 Ooltewah-Georgetown Rd*
- **North Georgia Golf & Driving Range,** *861-0913, 1390 Battlefield Pkwy*
- **Wilcox Golf Range Center,** *622-0426, 4247 Shallowford Rd*

Hang Gliding

This land of flat plateaus and wide valleys seems as though it was designed for hang gliding. Choose Lookout Valley or Sequatchie Valley for a beautiful flight.

Lookout Mountain Flight Park
706-398-3541, 800-688-LMFP, Rt 2 Box 215H, Rising Fawn, GA 30738, open daily
This hang glider's heaven is not too far from downtown Chattanooga, perched on the western edge of Lookout Mountain. Non-flyers gather round to watch the brave assemble multi-colored wings; it's simple after that -- walk to the edge of the big flat rock, warn "Clear," and step out to start the thermal ride. The valley below welcomes with a 45-acre landing field.

This training facility is USHGA certified, has been around more than 15 years, offers tandem training, a completely stocked pro shop, and repair facilities. There's aero towing from the 2,200 foot runway below.

Sequatchie Valley Soaring Supply
800-34GLIDE, 949-2301, Hwy 127, Dunlap, open daily, weather dependent
In the Sequatchie Valley you can soar from the east or the west, near Dunlap

or Whitwell; it depends on which way the wind is blowing. Hang gliding flight instruction is available here; tandem flights available. There are onsite lodging and camping facilities.

Want to try a simulator to see if you will like it?
Raccoon Mountain High Adventure Sports
825-0444, 4117 Cummings Hwy, 37419, Off I-24 exit 174, open daily Memorial Day to Labor Day, 9AM-11:30PM
Hang gliding simulator for 800-foot flight, with cable, to a sawdust landing area, suitable for all ages.

Horses/Riding/Stables

Tennessee Walking Horse Breeders' and Exhibitors' Association
800-359-1574, PO 286, Lewisburg, TN 37091
The Tennessee Walking Horse is famous around the world today; a tough breed with great stamina, they have a graceful walk which provides a smooth, comfortable ride. Very intelligent and gentle, they are the ideal horse for men, women or children. Get information from the Association; there are many farms in the middle-Tennessee area; perhaps you can arrange a visit.

If you are interested in riding, training, or boarding your horse, check with these farms to see if they offer what you need.
Cedar Creek Farm, *706-673-4040, Old Hwy 2, Varnell, GA*
♦ No rentals, boarding, training, lessons, 3 arenas, jumps, x-country course, 300 riding acres, hay rides/parties, round pen, tack store.
Classical Riding School, *821-0350, 1341 Burgess Rd, Chattanooga*
♦ Dressage jumping, combined training, riding lessons, training for competitions, boarding.
Creek Bend Stables, *861-3682, Battlefield Pkwy, Ft Oglethorpe*
♦ No rentals, indoor and outdoor arena, training, equitation, lessons, youth club.
Peavine Creek Farm, *706-937-5359, 2 mi off I-75, open daily*
♦ School of riding, lessons, training, sales, beginner, intermediate, advanced, day programs, parties, camps, certified teacher, instructor, member United Professional Horseman's Assn, 38 yrs exp.
Trail's End Ranch Riding Stables, *706-375-4346, Hwy 27 S at Trail's End Road, near Chickamauga Park, open daily summer, weekends and by appt rest of year*
♦ Rentals here, $10 for a 45-minute guided trail ride along Chickamauga Creek and the border of the Park; instruction available; suitable for children and adults; boarding and training also. 27 yrs exp.

Looking for a particular place? Check the index at the back of this book for individual restaurants, attractions, events, galleries, museums, recreational places, sports, tours, stores, lodgings, churches, schools and business services.

Hot Air Ballooning

High Touch Balloon Company
267-3751, 900 Manufacturers Rd
Early morning and late evening flights, to take advantage of the proper winds. Do you want to fly over downtown Chattanooga, Signal Mountain, the southern valley area? You pick the spot (within safety limits). Room for two passengers; see the sun set from the air; end the flight with a champagne toast. Call for reservations. No hot air balloon races to watch in the Chattanooga area, but some are held nearby, in Nashville and Knoxville. High Touch can advise you regarding racing schedule.

Hunting/Target Practice

The woods and waters of Tennessee, Georgia and Alabama are filled with game and waterfowl, the white-tailed deer being the number one game animal. State parks often serve as operation bases for organized hunting parties. Small game includes squirrel, rabbit, coyote, beaver, bobcat, muskrat, weasel, bullfrog, raccoon, opossum, grouse, quail, dove, woodcock, duck, Canada goose; big game is deer, wild boar and bear.

Before you go, get your license.
Alabama Division of Game and Fish, *205-242-3829, 64 N Union St, Montgomery, 36130*
♦ A hunting license is required if you are between 16-65; if you hunt on deer and turkey management areas, you must buy an additional license. Call for information, seasons.
Georgia Department of Natural Resources, Game and Fish Division, *404-656-4992, 205 Butler St SE, Suite 135B, Atlanta 30334*
♦ License required, 7-day or season; preserve license; bow hunting license; waterfowl stamp; call for information, bag limits, seasons and hunting areas.
Tennessee Wildlife Resources Agency, *800-262-6704, 615-781-6622, 216 E Penfield, Crossville, TN 38555*
♦ Contact TWRA for hunting information. They'll explain licenses required; most are available from county court clerks, sporting goods stores, hardware stores, and all TWRA offices. The Hunting and Trapping Guide tells you seasons, limits and where you can hunt. Hunters must wear fluorescent orange, such as hat and vest, when hunting big game.

You can get supplies and information from these commercial establishments; gun safety classes offered at both.
Sportsman's Supply & Services, *875-4868, 4824 Hixson Pike*
♦ Shotguns, pistols, rifles, guns, ammo, accessories, black powder supplies, reloading supplies, gunsmith services; gun safety and marksmanship

instruction, 50-ft indoor pistol range.

Montlake Shooting Center, *332-1195, 2009 Mowbray Pike, Soddy-Daisy*
♦ Rifles, pistols, shotguns, ammo, accessories; Gun Safety & Marksmanship Instruction, trap, skeet, sporting clays, rifle, pistol.

Karate/Martial Arts

Check with Greater Chattanooga Sports and Events Committee, *756-8689,* and the commercial establishments for information about tournaments in this field of highly-disciplined training of body and mind. For instruction, the following establishments may provide what you need.

Powerhouse Fitness Center, *697-9720, 1254 E 3rd St*
♦ Inside Warner Park Fieldhouse, Chattanooga Parks Department

Bridges Tae Kwon Do, *899-2850, 2 locations Chattanooga & Ft Oglethorpe*
♦ Self defense, self confidence, positive thinking; men, women, children

Champions All Karate, *894-3910, 6242 Perimeter Dr*
♦ Self defense, self discipline, instructor is 5-time national champ; ages 4-18

Chu's Tae-Kwon-do, *698-2410, 3704 Ringgold Rd; 877-5661, 3835 Hixson Pike*
♦ Men, women, children, free intro classes; self defense, confidence, discipline, positive thinking

Park's Tae-Kwon-Do Institute, *396-2505, 9413 Apison Pike*
♦ Develop positive attitude, instill confidence and discipline

Rick Hall's TaeKwonDo, *892-7557, 2260 Gunbarrel Rd; 877-3451, 5147 Hxsn Pk*
♦ Self defense, karate for men, women and children, free intro class, free uniform with enrollment

Kite Flying

Some good kite-flying spots are the TVA reservation at Chickamauga Dam, the meadow at Tennessee Riverpark, and the open space at Camp Jordan; compete in the Lions 'n Lambs Kite Fly in the spring.

Scenic City Kite Club, *267-5858 or 842-6748*
♦ Contact the club for kite-flying friends.

Chattanooga Depot, *622-0630, 3701 Ringgold Rd*
♦ Get your kite materials at this hobby and model shop.

Parks/Playgrounds

Audubon Acres, aka Elise Chapin Wildlife Sanctuary
892-1499, I75 Exit 3A, right 2nd light to Gunbarrel Rd, 1 2/3 mi, follow signs, open Mon-Sat 9-6; Sun 1-6; closes 5 PM Thanksgiving through March
Little Owl Village. Spring Frog Cabin. Raccoon Point. Chickadee Lodge. Meadow Lark Run. Dragging Canoe Trail. In the midst of massive city

development over the years, this historic and beautiful spot has been preserved. This 130-acre floodplain-to-ridgetop area bisected by South Chickamauga Creek has over 8 miles of walking and hiking trails, a swinging bridge to an area once populated by Native Americans and visited by DeSoto in the 1500's, and a cabin dating back to 1754.

Yes, 1754! Still nestled in the woodlands, the cabin housed two famous naturalists over the centuries. Built and occupied first by Cherokee, the well-known naturalist Tooantuh, also known as Spring Frog, is believed to have been born there. He lived in the cabin, and grew up exploring the banks of Chickamauga Creek, observing the tsisk wa (birds) , tagaya (insects), and tsugni (standing trees). When the Cherokee were forced to leave in 1838, the house was occupied by white settlers. In 1872, William Thomas Walker moved his family into the abandoned cabin, and there Robert Sparks Walker was born, developed his love of nature, wrote *Torchlights to the Cherokees, Lookout, the Story of a Mountain, As the Indians Left It* and more, was nominated for a Pulitzer Prize, became a well-loved story-teller, and helped to found the Chattanooga Audubon Society. His wish was to be buried on the property, and you can visit his grave-site today.

In Little Owl Village, archeological digs by UTC Field School in 1993 and 1994 have unearthed black tumble beads that offer further support to the belief that DeSoto was in the area in the 1500's. The Sanctuary has an eagle aviary with bald eagle and golden eagle exhibits; free-flight program. Numerous school programs available, ex: Native American crafts, games and ceremonies; World of Raptors, Field Classes, Discovery Hikes to study soil cycle, observe wildlife and plant habitats. A property of the Chattanooga Audubon Society, it offers picnicking spots, wildflowers and trees, and South Chickamauga Creek. On National Historic Register.

Booker T. Washington State Park
615-894-4955, 5801 Champion Rd off Hwy 58
Named for famous educator Booker Taliaferro Washington, this 353-acre park on the south side of Chickamauga Lake is a perfect setting for boating and fishing; has swimming pool, picnic areas, and group camp lodge for 40, complete with kitchen. Boat launching ramp, play fields, nature trails for hiking.

Camp Jordan
867-7711, 1517 Tombras Ave
This East Ridge park has 16 softball/baseball fields, five lighted soccer fields with spectator seating, two sand base volleyball courts, a BMX track, a model airplane flying field, and a walking/jogging track. The 34,000 sq ft Arena seats 4,000 and hosts a 100-team indoor soccer league; it's also home to the Chattanooga Express semi-professional soccer team. The Camp Jordan Amphitheater is lighted for evening activities; has dressing rooms, covered kitchen, picnic pavilion.

Chattanooga Nature Center & Reflection Riding
821-1160, 400 Garden Rd, Lookout Mtn, 37419, some activities at Greenway Farm in Hixson, open Mon-Sat 9-5, Sun 1-5, closed holidays

Explore Nature! The Nature Center is a comprehensive environmental education facility featuring a crawl-in beaver lodge and mammal burrow, a wildlife diorama, a wildlife rehabilitation hospital, a 1,200-foot wetland walkway, and numerous wildlife exhibits at the edge of Reflection Riding on the western side of Lookout Mountain; some activities take place at the city-owned Greenway Farm in the Hixson area. A family membership supports the work of the Center and gets you a monthly newsletter advising of upcoming events and classes. Summer camps for kids, hikes for every age, bird watching, meteor watching, plant and flower ID. Special programs can be provided too, call to discuss. Reflection Riding is a 300-acre botanic garden adjacent to Lookout Mountain. Driving, biking and hiking trails encompass the park and adjacent land. You'll see Father Rock and the legend of the dying Chief along the way; spectacular wildflower gardens.

Chattanooga Parks & Recreation Department
757-PLAY for activities, 697-9700 for reservations

Over 25 centers available for recreation purposes, call for brochure.

Parks for Public Use
♦ **Boynton Park,** *Cameron Hill.,* A one-acre park with civil war cannons, scenic overlook of city.
♦ **Confederate and Citizens Cemetery,** *East 5th & Palmetto S.* Burial grounds for Civil War soldiers and Chattanooga citizens, including John P Long, first postmaster at Ross's Landing, from 1837-45, he suggested changing the city's name to Chattanooga.
♦ **East Lake Park,** *697-9710 for reservations, 3108 E 34th St.* 16-acre park includes duck pond, playground, tennis courts, senior adult building, amphitheatre, picnic pavilions.
♦ **Miller Park,** *697-9710 for reservations, 10th & Market St.* A one-acre park in the heart of downtown; outdoor amphitheatre, large fountain, grassy areas and plants. Popular with downtown lunch crowd, many activities scheduled here.
♦ **Montague Park,** *1141 E 23rd St.* This 45-acre park has 6 ballfields, concession stands, a playground, and grassy areas. One of city's two major softball parks.
♦ **Portland Park,** *Corner of Signal Mountain and Suck Creek.* Passive open area.
♦ **Rivermont Park,** *Lupton City Dr.* 61-acre park across the river from downtown; picnic pavilions, scenic walking/jogging trail, tennis courts, boat ramp, 4 ballfields.
♦ **Riverview Park,** *Barton Ave.* Built in 1939, this 1.5 acre park has been revitalized with new outdoor amphitheatre, playground, tennis courts, basketball courts, picnic tables, grills, large grassy area for open play.
♦ **Ross's Landing Park,** *On Tennessee River across from Aquarium.* A marina,

boat ramp, dock area, restrooms, two official size sand volleyball courts. Use of some facilities may require fees; call two weeks in advance to reserve. Connects to RiverWalk.

♦ **Ross's Landing Plaza,** *Surrounds Tennessee Aquarium.* Outdoor museum, paved history bands move back in time, stream winds through regional history eras; benches, plants, concessions. Connects to RiverWalk.

♦ **Walnut Street Bridge,** *Walnut Street at River.* This half-mile linear park is the world's longest pedestrian bridge; only such facility in southeastern US. Part of RiverWalk.

♦ **Warner Park,** *1254 3rd St.* Largest of the city's major softball facilities; 53-acres with 7 ballfields, 12 tennis courts, a paddle court, playground, rose garden, horseshoe pits, picnic facilities, public swimming pool, many grassy areas. Home to Power House Fitness Center, ArtHaus, PAL and Warner Park Zoo.

Chester Frost County Park

615-842-0177, 2318 Gold Point Circle, Hixson
This wonderful park on Chickamauga Lake's north side has boat ramps, fishing, a lake swimming and beach area, showers, snack bar, grills, a playground, and tennis courts; at the edge of Big Ridge it's loaded with dogwoods in the spring; fall foliage is fantastic.

Greenways System

266-5948 for info or to get involved
Volunteer to help build a trail, clean up a streambank, work with a citizen's group!
The term "greenway" came about in the twenties, when Benton MacKaye proposed creation of the Appalachian Trail. Today, all across the country, these protected corridors of open space can be found along river banks or ridgelines, linking wildlife refuges and neighborhood parks and historic sites.

Chattanooga, working hard to become the nation's "Environmental City," has joined the Chattanooga Parks Department, Chattanooga-Hamilton County Regional Planning Commission, and the Trust for Public Land into a new partnership for creating a network of greenways throughout the metropolitan area. The system will connect many points of interest and will provide protected trails for bike riding, jogging, walking and canoe access to beautiful streams.

♦ **Lookout Creek Greenway,** anchored by the Chattanooga Nature Center and Reflection Riding, will be a canoe trail stretching from the Tennessee River south into Georgia.

♦ **North Chickamauga Creek Greenway,** off Lake Resort Drive north of the Dam, has two miles completed; plans are to extend northward to the wild and scenic Chickamauga Gorge.

♦ **Old Wauhatchie Pike,** now closed to motorized vehicles, will link St Elmo and the South Chattanooga commercial district to Lookout Creek; offers spectacular views from Lookout Mountain.

♦ **South Chattanooga Greenway** will develop safe walks along public roads, offering alternative routes to school or work.

♦ **South Chickamauga Creek Greenway** will be anchored by the existing Brainerd Levee, and will connect the Chickamauga National Military Park in Georgia with the Tennessee Riverpark.

♦ **Tennessee Riverpark** is the central spine of the network. On the south side of River, enter near Dam and further west on Amnicola. Several segments are completed, eventually it will extend from the Dam through downtown.

Hamilton County Dept of Parks & Recreation
842-0177
Call the number above and they will direct you to the baseball, soccer and football leagues in your area of Hamilton County; also call to find out where the many county tennis courts and jogging tracks can be found, free for public use. There are 23 sites county-wide, usually near a school; Riverpark on Amnicola and Chester Frost Park on Chickamauga Lake are part of the county system too (see).

Harrison Bay State Park
344-6214, 8411 Harrison Bay Rd, Harrison, TN 37341
On the south side of Chickamauga Lake, this 1200-acre state park has campsites, some waterfront; a marina with one of the finest launching ramps in area; 140 slips available for boats up to 48 feet; boat rental, fishing, picnic shelter, pool, snack bar, showers, playground, tennis courts. Planned activities include arts and crafts, campfires. Park's name derived from bay of main channel of Tennessee River that covers the old town of Harrison; parklands have historical significance, covering site of last Cherokee Campground, 3 villages ruled by Chief Joe Vann, one of the great Cherokee chieftains. Park is haven for campers, boaters and fishermen, also picnickers and day-use visitors.

Maclellan Island
892-1499 for Audubon Society; island is near Walnut St & Veterans Bridges
When you're walking the Walnut Street Bridge you get a good view of the island below. From the back patio of the Hunter Museum, binoculars offer close-ups of great blue heron nests. The Veteran's Bridge speeds you over the island by car. How to get ON it? Call the Audubon Society, number above, and make arrangements for a charter trip on the Chattanooga Star. Plus, plans are for regular summer runs on weekends from Ross's Landing and the dock under Walnut Street Bridge, call to confirm.

This 20-acre wildlife sanctuary has meadows, wetlands, an observation deck, picnic shelter and restrooms. A wildlife blind allows for observation of a nesting colony of Great Blue Herons. Platforms built at both ends of the island provide homes for osprey nestlings. Many, many species of birds on the island, and a number of different animals. Bring your binos, bring your lunch, and wear your walking shoes for a great visit.

Playgrounds
Chattanooga Parks Department Playgrounds for Public Use
♦ **East Brainerd Park,** *Benham and Williams,* swings, slide and picnic area.
♦ **Church Street,** *next to Chattem Drug,* basketball court, swings, picnic tables.
♦ **Fort Negley,** *17th and Mitchell,* playground equipment and basketball court.
♦ **Clifton Hills,** *Brannon & 33rd,* swings and fun center.
♦ **Greenwood Terrace,** *3056 Dee Dr,* swings, playground equipment, basketball court.
♦ **Montague Park.** *23rd and Long.* Picnic area, swings, slide.
♦ **Pringle Park,** *26th & Long,* picnic area, swings, slide.
♦ **Piney Woods,** *Hooker Rd,* swings, slide, basketball court.
♦ **Park City,** *Cannon St,* swings, slide, activity center.
♦ **Park Place,** *10th & Fairview,* swings, slide, basketball court.
♦ **Rivermont,** *1100 Lupton Dr,* adaptive playground for physically challenged children; special equipment; swings, slide.
♦ **Riverside Park,** *Crutchfield St,* picnic shelter, tables, basketball court, swings, slide.
♦ **Riverview,** *Barton Ave,* swings, slide.
♦ **Ridgedale,** *2712 E 13th St,* swings, slide, activity center.
♦ **Silverdale,** *Silverdale & Bonny Oaks,* swings, slide.
♦ **Tacoa Circle,** swings, slide.

Call City Hall in your municipality for playground information; also call Hamilton County Parks Department at *842-0177.* Don't forget the wonderful playground at Tennessee Riverpark.

On a more commercial note here are some fine indoor play places. Think about it when the weather's really nasty!

♦ **Discovery Zone (2 locations),** *855-5020, 2020 Gunbarrel Rd; 870-9955, 5239 Hwy 153,* these bright and colorful indoor play areas have a separate play zone for smaller children, party rooms, careful supervision of access.
♦ **Chuck E Cheese's,** *870-3215, 22 Northgate Park,* it's a pizza parlor but the kids love the indoor play area.

Red Clay State Historic Park
615-472-2627, Off State Hwy 60, Cleveland, 37311
An Indian council house and reconstructed Indian farmstead depict the life and tragedy of the Cherokee; banned from meeting in their nearby capital of New Echota; Red Clay was the site of the last Cherokee Councils before the infamous Trail of Tears. Interpretive center, large amphitheatre, picnic area, several miles of trails; some leading to the Eternal Flame and the enchanting Blue Spring. Off US Hwy 60 south of Cleveland, on the Georgia border.

Tennessee Riverpark
842-0177, 4301 Amnicola Hwy, managed by Hamilton County Parks

Take a hike! Fly a kite! Do it at the Riverpark, phase one of a planned 22-mile development along the river. Its all-weather walking-jogging trail is two miles long, tucked nicely on the riverbank; and that's not all. For the boated crowd, there are two launching facilities; pole toters can while away an afternoon at one of the five fishing piers, which get you 50-feet out over the river. The Hubert Fry Center has a meeting area, bait shop, snack bar and restrooms.

Maybe you like parks for picnicking. You'll love this one, with tables and pavilions scattered about, just right for church socials, family reunions, or a simple sandwich on a fine spring day when the redbuds are in bloom. And what a great place for kids! The playground swings and climbing gyms are kid-safe design. A large meadow is fine for flying kites, or playing tag. There's a native American exhibit at one end, giving a glimpse of the river's historic past; along the Woodland Trail you'll discover native plants and animals in their natural habitat. Concerts in the summer, beginning about Memorial day, call 842-6748 for information.

Rollerskating/Rollerblading

Maybe you have a good sidewalk where you live; if not, there's the paved path at Tennessee Riverpark and other sections of RiverWalk.

These commercials establishments make for smooth skating in any weather.
Roller Coaster Skate World (2 locations), *861-1100, 1711 Lafayette Rd, Ft Oglethorpe; 842-6817, 5301 Hixson Pike*
♦ They'll schedule birthday parties, private parties, and fund raisers for your group. Skate sales.
Skatin' Jakes, *870-0000, 4300 Access Rd*
♦ There are public sessions, and private parties for your birthday, church, club, or fundraisers; games, snack bar, skate sales.

Rowing

We have a big river in Chattanooga just made for rowing, and plenty of people doing it. This sport is manageable by persons of any age or gender; Lookout Rowing Club's membership list includes both a 13-year-old girl and an 84-year-old man -- what's important is a love of the water, the fresh air, and the exercise.

High School and College Teams
At the **University of Tennessee at Chattanooga**, Robert Espeseth coaches

over 130 students in the rowing program, and, he proclaims "There are more women rowing than in all women's sports combined." **High schools** that have rowing teams are **McCallie, Baylor, GPS, Chattanooga School for the Arts and Sciences, and Howard.**

National Team

A major coup occurred in 1993 when the **U. S. Women's National Sweep Rowing Team** moved here, based at the Chattanooga Rowing Center. Coached since 1990 by Hartmut Buschbacher, you can spot the team rowing on the river twice every day, in intensive training for the '96 Olympics, coxswain Yaz Farooq firmly leading from the strategist's seat. These women have only three free days a month; otherwise they're rowing two hours every morning, with two hours in the weight room or on the track; then they spend four hours at a "regular" job, followed by two hours of afternoon rowing, beginning about 4:30.

The Team claimed seven medals at the Pan American Games in Argentina in March '95; three gold for the straight pair, lightweight quadruple sculls, and lightweight straight pair; four silver in the sculling competition. Salute!

Rowing Clubs
Chattanooga Rowing Center
622-6846, 1001 Riverside Drive
Several clubs row out of this facility, including the U. S. Women's Team, several of the high schools, and Lookout Rowing; there's boat storage, a training room, locker room, change room, showers, and access to the river.

If you want to row, contact **Lookout Rowing Club** at the Center. A prerequisite to membership is learning how to row; after that you may use the club's boats. There are three levels of rowing you may choose: competition, recreational, and the fitness/weight control program. The Club also schedules fun trips such as the 24-mile Gorge Row.

Competitions to watch for: Bridgefest Regatta first Saturday in May, ending at Ross's Landing; and Chattanooga Head Race in early October, both sponsored by the Lookout Rowing Club.

Skiing

Water Skiing
For **water skiing,** you need to get behind a big power boat; there is fine open water for great skiing on Chickamauga Lake; supplies can be purchased at most boating and sports equipment stores. You are required to wear an adequate and effective life vest or belt and you must have a person on board (other than the operator) who is at least 12 to watch the skier. Skiing is permitted only in daylight hours.

Snow Skiing

Cloudmont Ski and Golf Resort, 205-634-4344, atop Lookout Mountain near Mentone, Alabama

♦ The southern-most ski resort in the United States; nine machines generate enough powder for about 50 days of skiing a year, mostly in January-February. Two 1000-foot slopes.

Ober Gatlinburg, 615-436-5423, Gatlinburg, TN

♦ Offers winter skiing plus an ice rink. The tramway picks you up in downtown Gatlinburg.

You can get training, trips and equipment at the following places:
Leisure Time Snow Ski Center, 622-1335, 3520 Brainerd Rd
Play it Again Sports, 855-4672, 6227 Lee Hwy

Advanced skiers, book your trip to Vail or Vermont through local travel agents; the south, after all, is famous for **not** having snowy winters.

Soccer

Soccer has definitely made inroads in the Chattanooga area; some of the Youth Leagues have more than doubled in size, such as Middle Valley's incredible leap from 400 to 1000 children in the program in one year; Camp Jordan boasts a fabulous new $2 million indoor soccer facility. If you didn't grow up with the sport, you've got lots of opportunities to learn about it now.

Chattanooga Express
267-5425, 1300 Carter St
This semi-professional team is a member of the U. S. Inter-regional Soccer League, and plays at the Camp Jordan Soccer Arena. The 34,000 sq ft facility seats 4,000; winter season is mid-December through February.

League Play, All Ages
City of Chattanooga, 757-PLAY
As with the other team sports, you'll need to search out the leagues in your area. Check the city Parks and Recreation Department, the YMCA, and the Redoubt, Middle Valley, East Ridge, Signal Mountain, and Lookout Mountain recreational areas; there's a lot of soccer activity for the kids and there are three adult indoor soccer leagues.

You can get equipment and information at these commercial establishments.
♦ **Front Runner,** 875-3642, 3903 Hixson Pike, open Mon-Sat
♦ **Premier Soccer,** 875-5051, 1920 Northpoint Blvd, open Mon-Sat

Wondering what we look for in a Great Place?
See "How to Use This Book."

Swimming

With long-hot-summer weather, hundreds of jump-in-the-creek swimming holes, beaches dotting the riverbank, and enough swimming pools to out-patio Hollywood, you'd expect this to be the one outdoor activity for everybody. It doesn't take a lot of equipment, like rappelling or snow skiing. It doesn't take a group of people who know the strategy, like football or soccer. You can have a good time by simply holding your nose and jumping in feet first. **That is, AFTER you learn to swim. Do it early in life.**

American Red Cross, *265-3455, 801 McCallie Avenue.* Learn to swim, lifeguard, or teach swimming; classes at UTC pool, call for schedule.

YMCA's throughout area (see p.124) offer swimming and water safety instruction; some have indoor pools for year-round swimming.

City, County and State parks (see Parks) have pools or lake swimming beaches; in summer there's a lifeguarded beach on the TVA reservation at the south side of Chickamauga Lake by the Dam. The YMCA and the Parks Departments can advise you about **swim leagues** too, if competition is your thing.

Tennis/Paddleball

Call Chattanooga Tennis Association, 843-2456 for league information. They periodically offer free lessons for youth.

City of Chattanooga Tennis Courts

Lighted courts

- ♦ **Avondale,** *1305 Dodson Ave*
- ♦ **Brainerd,** *1016 N Moore Rd*
- ♦ **College Hill,** *12th and Grove*
- ♦ **East Brainerd,** *Jenkins Rd and Batters Place Dr*
- ♦ **East Chattanooga,** *2409 Dodson*
- ♦ **East Lake,** *3601 Dodds*
- ♦ **Glenwood,** *3rd and Glenwood Circle*
- ♦ **Hixson Tennis Center,** *5401 School Dr*
- ♦ **Hixson High School,** *5715 Middle Valley Rd*
- ♦ **Lakeside,** *4800 Swan Rd*
- ♦ **Lookout Valley,** *350 Lookout St*
- ♦ **Rivermont,** *1100 Lupton Dr*
- ♦ **Riverview,** *Barton and Riverview*
- ♦ **Tyner,** *6838 Tyner Rd*
- ♦ **Shepherd,** *5711 Talladega Ave*
- ♦ **St Elmo,** *4921 St Elmo Ave*
- ♦ **Warner Park Tennis Center,** *1301 McCallie Ave*

Unlighted courts

- ♦ **Alton Park,** *45th and Central*
- ♦ **Carver,** *600 N Orchard Knob*
- ♦ **Colville St,** *406 Colville*
- ♦ **East Lake Courts,** *27th and 6th*
- ♦ **Elbert Long,** *6579 E Brainerd Rd*
- ♦ **Ridgedale,** *2710 E 13th*

Hamilton County Parks Department
842-0177
Call and ask for the location of tennis courts in your area; there are many county-wide.

Red Bank, East Ridge, Fort Oglethorpe, Rossville and other communities have tennis facilities available too, call City Hall in your specific area for information.

Tennis has some private membership clubs.
Manker Patten Tennis Club, *266-6767, 100 Douglas*
♦ 18 courts, located alongside the Tennessee River
Racquet Club, *842-9622, 4932 Adams Rd*
♦ 15 courts; located in the Hixson area

Warner Park Paddle Court
757-7020, 1254 E 3rd St
This unique sport from South America is catching on fast. Combining the best elements of tennis, racquetball, and squash, it is played by two teams of two, with scoring the same as tennis. An indoor and outdoor court available; call to reserve; equipment may be checked out free.

UTC Sports

University of Tennessee at Chattanooga
266-6627 for individual game tickets; 755-5285 for season tickets
They're the Blue and Gold, the Mocs, Chattanooga's own. Do you like to watch Basketball, Football, Golf, Track, Softball, Tennis, Volleyball, and Wrestling, college style? If you're not already hooked, read on. UTC is a member of the Southern Conference, along with Appalachian State, The Citadel, Davidson, E Tennessee State, Furman, Georgia Southern, Marshall, VMI, and Western Carolina.

Men's Basketball has garnered seven Conference Championships since the University of Chattanooga became a branch of the University of Tennessee in 1969, the last two in '94 and '95. They're hot; better get those season tickets early. The Roundhouse seats 11,200 for round ball; from November to March this is a really great family winter watching event.

Women's Basketball is the Lady Mocs; catch this fast-moving sport in the 4,200-seat Maclellan Gym.

Football is at Chamberlain Field, seating capacity 10,500; home to Moc's football since 1908; tentative plans call for a new stadium by '97. Ask around for stories about Scrappy Moore, coach for 35 years, inducted into the

National Football Hall of Fame in 1967.

Wrestling and "dominated" go together when you speak of UTC's power in the Conference; they've taken the championship in 78, 79, 80, 81, 82, 83, 86, 87, 88, 89, 90, 91, 92, 93, 94 and 95! You'll find them in Maclellan Gym about once a month for a home match between November and March.

Call for a schedule for Moc's other athletic events too; there's track and tennis, softball and volleyball; something is happening throughout the school year; good entertainment for you and a great way to support your community, the students, and your home-town University.

Walking/Jogging/Running

You can keep it simple, by tying your shoes and heading out the door in your own neighborhood; thousands of people do that as a regular beginning or ending to their day; notice too the hundreds of downtown walkers in their office attire, walking shoes a nice accessory.

Some folks pick up the pace, dressed in shorts and a cap for a daily jog across the bridge or a climb of RiverWalk's up-the-bluff stairs. If you notice anyone wearing a stop-watch, step out of the way! Time-keeping marathon runners-in-training are the most dedicated of all; this 26-mile endurance test calls for the ultimate in discipline, since no one has to catch a buffalo for food anymore.

See **Parks** p.130, **Greenways** p.133, and **Great Walks** p.169, for good walking, jogging or running paths outside your neighborhood; check with the YMCA and the **Exercise and Fitness** section, pp.123-124, if you're looking for an indoor track. Remember too, the **malls** are good bad-weather trails; most open early in the morning for exercise buffs; call and verify their hours and policy, pp.187-188.

Watch for public service announcements for fun or fund-raising walk-or-run races; they're well-promoted by the media, and there are quite a few during the year.

Wildlife Viewing

Wild Watch
Look for the brown-and-white road signs with the binoculars logo identifying Watchable Wildlife sites. And follow these tips for good viewing: know migration patterns, visit in morning or evening, move slowly and quietly, and bring your binoculars so you can enjoy from a distance. Don't feed or touch the wildlife. A patient wait may bring enjoyable rewards. *(contd.)*

Our area is blessed with some excellent viewing spots. Within the city limits:

♦ **Audubon Acres** and **South Chickamauga Creek** offer opportunity to see migratory birds and many wildflowers in season, such as trillium and columbine, the careful eye may spot muskrat, or gray fox.

♦ **Big Ridge TVA Small Wild Area** has a 1.3-mile loop that takes you through 100-year old upland forest where you'll see songbirds and pileated woodpeckers.

♦ **Booker T. Washington State Park**, on the south side of the lake, where you can find more than twenty species of waterfowl.

♦ **Brainerd Levee** is where to watch for herons -- great blue, little blue and green-backed -- late in the afternoon. The federally-listed snail darter fish lives in South Chickamauga Creek.

♦ **Chester Frost Park**, north of Chickamauga Lake, has the tall pines that are home to nuthatches and woodpeckers; along the shore see osprey and sandpipers.

♦ **North Chickamauga Creek Greenway** has a paved trail beside the creek; see great blue herons, kingfishers and turtles.

♦ **Raccoon Mountain Pumped Storage Plant Reservoir** is south of the river; you'll see hawks here, and in the wintertime, bald eagles.

♦ **Reflection Riding and the Nature Center** are on the west side of Lookout Mountain; along Lookout Creek you'll see Kentucky warblers and barred owls; on the wetland walkway watch for beaver. Along the upland trails markers call your attention to wildflowers in the spring.

♦ **Savannah Bay** wading birds like the mudflats of the Bay.

♦ **Signal Point Park** north of the river is fine for watching raptors, more than thirteen species have been spotted here, ex: red-tailed broad-winged, and Cooper's hawks and peregrine falcons. You'll want a scope, you are 1,000 feet above the Tennessee River with unobstructed views of the gorge.

For birds in your own backyard, go to **Wild Birds Unlimited**, *892-3816, 7630 E Brainerd Rd*, and choose from a great assortment of bird seeds, feeders, houses and baths, so you can attract the nest builders, or those who only eat and fly away.

Zoos
In Town and Close
Warner Park Zoo, *697-9722, 1254 E 3rd St, open Mon-Fri 10-4; Sat-Sun 11-5*

♦ This division of Chattanooga City Parks is a 3.5-acre facility with 150 mammals, reptiles and birds. You'll see some exotic animals from South America, Africa and North America, and threatened and endangered species, such as chimpanzee and jaguar. Though it's small, kids never tire of seeing real live animals up close. And it's growing; new projects are planned; keep watching. Your $1 donation helps support the animals.

Tennessee Aquarium, *265-0695, 1 Broad St, open daily 10-6, later in summer*

♦ This freshwater life center is home to more than 7,000 specimens, including 400 species of fish, reptiles, amphibians, birds, and mammals. (See full description p 155)

Out of Town

Atlanta Zoo, *404-624-5630, 800 Cherokee Ave SE, Atlanta, GA 30315*

♦ You'll find Willie B and 18 other western lowland gorillas in an African rainforest here. Lions, rhinos, giraffes, tigers and zebras live in natural habitats; approximately 1000 specimens here, 278 species.

Birmingham Zoo, *205-879-0409, 2630 Cahaba Rd, Birmingham, AL, 35223*

♦ Over 800 specimens and 223 species; 100 acres of park land; cheetah exhibit, sea lion feeding, educational movies.

Knoxville Zoological Gardens, *615-637-5331, Prosper Rd, Knoxville, TN 37914*

♦ Over 1000 specimens, with the largest big cat and African elephant collection in the east; also red pandas and southern white rhinoceros; elephant and camel rides.

Nashville Zoo, *615-370-3333, 1710 Ridge Rd Circle, Joelton, TN, 37080*

♦ A natural environment zoo in the country, with more than 800 animals including clouded leopards, white tigers, llamas and giraffe.

If you're really nuts about zoos, someday you'll want to visit our National Zoo in Washington, DC.

National Zoological Park, *202-673-4721, 3000 Conn. Ave NW, Washington, DC, 20008*

This zoo has 4,746 specimens, 491 species. Call or write for information.

People Who Love Chattanooga
Marjorie Higginbotham

"I sang soprano and my sister Agnes sang alto," recalls Marjorie Higginbotham. "We were Methodists but the first time we sang together in public was across the street at the Baptist Church. The Methodists asked us to sing too, after that!" Marjorie claims she "just learned" to sing in a house with six older sisters who played the organ and a father who led the singing at church.

There were 11 children in the family, and the house was filled with activity and fun. "We had a swing in the persimmon tree," tells Marjorie, "and we liked to wade around in the creek. Mother gave up telling us to stay out of it; somebody was always falling in and getting wet! When it flooded, we'd even swing across it on a vine. It's a wonder none of us ever got hurt."

The place was Madison, Georgia, a small town east of Atlanta. Known as "the town Sherman didn't burn," it has a high concentration of pre-Civil War homes and a lovely 19th-century ambiance (see p.174). Marjorie grew up, met and married Raymond Higginbotham, and gave birth to daughter Betty and son Travis there. She was an excellent seamstress, designing and making all of Betty's clothes. Sunday dinners Marjorie and Raymond cooked together, the favorite being baked hen and dressing, with peaches and pound cake for dessert.

When Raymond went to work for the railroad, they lived in other southern cities: Atlanta, Augusta, Greenville, and Birmingham. Those years Marjorie remembers with fondness. "When we lived in Atlanta we went to see *Gone With the Wind* and watched Vivien Leigh and all the stars as they went in the Fox Theatre for the premiere. It was 1939. During the war Raymond was a Special Agent for the FBI, and rode the train with President Roosevelt when he went to the Little White House in Warm Springs. We took many family trips together on the train as the children were growing up. After Betty married and moved to Chattanooga, we'd ride the train into Terminal Station to come and visit her."

Marjorie and Raymond moved back to Madison when he retired. "I was a docent at the Cultural Center," she says. "I led tours of the historic churches and antebellum homes." She returned to the same Methodist church she sang in as a girl, and also sang and danced in the annual *Madison Follies*. She continued living in Madison after Raymond died, until a stroke necessitated her move to Chattanooga, to be near daughter Betty.

Marjorie Rucker Higginbotham has two children, seven grandchildren, and three great-grandchildren. She has lived in Chattanooga since 1985, spending much time with her family; and has enjoyed attending Hixson Presbyterian Church and having lunch with her friends at the Tea Room. Marjorie is a petite and dignified lady, and her apartment is filled with treasures of the past, family pictures, and the needlepoint she has recently learned to do.

"I like for Betty to take me for drives around Chattanooga to look at the yards and flowers," comments Marjorie, who has an extraordinarily green thumb herself. "Chattanooga is such a pretty place. I'm glad to be here."

Tours & Outings

Contents

Daughter: Do you remember riding the train into Terminal Station to visit us when the children were little?
Mother: Yes, and now that they're all grown, they come visit me! It's nice to see the young people getting out and having fun.

Fifteen Favorite Places

Some places you've heard about all your life. The **ChooChoo** tune dances in the heads of people who have never been near Chattanooga, it's such a catchy little ditty. Anyone who has driven in the south has seen a **Rock City** barn, or a billboard for **Ruby Falls**. **Civil War** buffs are familiar with the area because of its importance to the overall military campaign, as the battles at Chattanooga literally opened the door to the south. The fame of Chattanooga's new-in-the-90's world-class **Aquarium** has spread so fast it boggles the minds of even the most forward-thinking city planners. Two of our newest **malls** attract people from all over the south.

Those of us who are lucky enough to live here have picked out many places we enjoy, maybe because they are handy to where we live, or they address a special interest we have -- in trains, or music, or the out-of-doors. Following in alphabetical order are fifteen of the **favorite places** of locals and visitors; if you've never been you'll want to check them out -- there's a reason they're so popular! But then, read on, because in addition to these favorites, there are **hundreds of wonderful places to go, thousands of interesting things to do, and a million memories to be made.**

Location of Fifteen Favorites

Downtown Area	Lookout Mountain Area	Other Areas
Chattanooga ChooChoo	Incline Railway	Chickamauga Battlefield
Ross's Landing Park/Plaza	Point Park	Hamilton Place
Southern Belle Riverboat	Rock City Gardens	Lake Winnepesaukah
Tennessee Aquarium	Ruby Falls	Raccoon Mountain
Walnut Street Bridge		Tennessee Valley Railroad Museum
Warehouse Row		

Type of Attraction

Caves	Malls	Tennessee Valley Railroad Museum
Raccoon Mountain	Hamilton Place	
Ruby Falls	Warehouse Row	**Rivers**
Civil War Sites	**Music**	Ross's Landing Park/Plaza
Chickamauga Battlefield	Lake Winnepesaukah	Southern Belle Riverboat
Point Park	Ross's Landing Park/Plaza	Tennessee Aquarium
Gardens	Southern Belle Riverboat	Walnut Street Bridge
Chattanooga ChooChoo	**Rides**	**Trains**
Rock City Gardens	Chattanooga ChooChoo	Chattanooga ChooChoo
Hikes/Walks	Incline Railway	Incline Railway
Chickamauga Battlefield	Lake Winnepesaukah	Tennessee Valley Railroad Museum
Point Park	Raccoon Mountain	
Walnut Street Bridge	Southern Belle Riverboat	

Chattanooga ChooChoo Complex
266-5000, 1400 Market St

This former train station, circa 1909, includes **restaurants, a model railroad museum, an antique trolley, interesting shops, beautifully landscaped gardens, a convention center** and a Holiday Inn **hotel.** In addition to regular guest rooms, the hotel has 45 **sleeping parlors** aboard **authentic rail cars;** one of the restaurants is in a rail car too. A route on the summer schedule of the **Tennessee Valley Railroad Museum** brings a passenger train into the ChooChoo for a ride to the Museum and back. The **Shuttle** bus runs from here through town to the Aquarium.

The site is on the National Register of Historic Places. **Terminal Station** has the highest dome of its kind in the world. At one time it serviced 48 passenger trains a day; when the last train left in 1970 the depot was boarded up. A group of local men formed the ChooChoo Company and saved it from demolition, opening it to the public in April 1973.

Model train lovers will enjoy a visit to the **Chattanooga ChooChoo Southern Model Railroad** located here. See the model of Terminal Station? Follow the Chattanooga landscape to the Casey Jones Control Tower, where you enter an imaginary section of the Cumberland Mountains. Signs point to Digge & Delve Mining Company, the Town of Waverag Junction, Knott & Splynter Lumber Company, and finally, Digge & Berry Mortuary, the last ones to let you down! This HO gauge railroad was started in 1973 as a joint venture between the **Chattanooga Area Model Railroad Club** and the Chattanooga ChooChoo Company. Valued at over half a million dollars, the 174-foot-long layout has 320 structures, 3,000 feet of track, 150 switches, 120 locomotives, 1,000 freight cars, 80 passenger cars, 3 major yards and 4 passenger stations.

Chickamauga Battlefield
706-866-9241, US 27 south of Ft Oglethorpe, GA, Visitor Center open daily 8-5:45 summer; closes 4:45 Sept-May; parts of auto-tour closed after sundown

The Battlefield is part of the Chickamauga and Chattanooga National Military Park, the oldest and largest military park in the nation, dedicated in 1895. Watch a 26-minute bring-events-to-life multi-media show in the Visitor Center's Centennial Theatre about the fierce Battle of September 19 and 20, 1863. There are other demonstrations, displays and exhibits, including the 355 weapons of the Fuller Gun Collection; there's a well-stocked book store and facilities for doing research.

In the park are monuments, historical tablets, hiking trails, and horse trails. Pick up a map to guide you and explain the 8 stops on the 7-mile auto tour; rent a special tape tour produced by the Eastern National Park & Monument Association.
- ♦ Stop 1: The Battle was fought in dense woods rather than typical open fields. Monuments and markers identify units and batteries -- blue for

Union, red for Confederate — positioned much as the soldiers in 1863 would have been.

♦ Stop 2: The Battle's final day opened near this spot, when Polk attacked Thomas' corps behind log barricades. Rosecrans shifted troops to Thomas' aid, weakening the right flank and setting the scene for Longstreet's breakthrough.

♦ Stop 3: A part of Brig. Gen. John Brannan's line is marked by monuments, tablets and cannons; figures represent the three arms of the military -- infantry, artillery, and cavalry.

♦ Stop 4: Wood's division pulled out of line; before Gen. Jefferson Davis' division could fill the gap, Longstreet's troops charged from the woods behind where you stand, past the Brotherton Cabin, and across the field to the Federal line. The Brotherton Cabin stands as it was in 1863.

♦ Stop 5: Monuments across the road mark troop positions on September 19.

♦ Stop 6: The imposing 85-foot Wilder Tower honors Col. John Wilder and his infantry; Wilder's 2,000-man brigade fired at Longstreet's veterans on September 20, but were unable to stop them. A platform at the top gives an excellent view of the battlefield.

♦ Stop 7: Many Federal units were surprised by Longstreet's attack, including Rosecrans. The Brotherton Cabin is beyond the woods to your right, point of the Confederate breakthrough. A monument marking the site of Rosecrans' headquarters is to your left, on the knoll beyond the field.

♦ Stop 8: Gen. George Thomas became the "Rock of Chickamauga" here on Snodgrass Hill, when he defended and stood against Longstreet's attack. A log cabin marks the site of the 1863 Snodgrass home.

Help protect our links to the past; digging, removing or damaging the Battlefield's resources is prohibited by the Archeological Resources Protection Act; for your safety no climbing on monuments or artillery pieces.

Hamilton Place Mall
894-7177, I-75 Exit 5, open Mon-Sat 10-9, Sun 12-6

More than a mall, Hamilton is truly a Place, a point of destination for eating out, catching a movie, taking a walk, browsing, and, of course, a full-fledged shopping expedition. What was way-out-of-town in the early 80's is a commercial boon today, drawing people from all over Georgia, Alabama, and Tennessee. Almost 2.5 million visits are made annually by tourists and other visitors; and, count this on your fingers and toes, 20 million shoppers hit those shops. The Honored Guest program entitles all visitors who live 75 miles or more from Hamilton Place to dozens of discounts and special offers at Hamilton Place Stores; inquire at the Visitor's Information Center by the Oasis entrance.

Inside Tennessee's largest mall you'll find five department stores, 160 specialty shops, a food court, three restaurants, and a nine-screen movie theatre; within the complex are nine more restaurants, eight more theatres, three more shopping centers, and assorted other services, with more of everything being added even as you read this book. See Shopping, p.187.

Incline Railway
821-4224, 3917 St Elmo Ave (bottom), 827 E Brow Rd (top)
Open daily, 3-4 trips per hour

"America's Most Amazing Mile" takes you to the "most overlooked place on earth," according to the literature. I've looked over it more times than I can count, the first time as an excited kid sitting by Mother and Daddy; most recently with my grandsons Jason and Matthew; most humorously some years back with my 84-year-old grandmother as she gripped the handrails, eyes tightly shut, asking me to describe the sights to her!

The facts are this: the grade is 72.7% near the top; you can see the giant cables that pull you up and ease you back down. At the halfway point the single track widens to two as you pass the other car. In the summer, shuttles bring you from the ChooChoo to the bottom-of-the-mountain Incline gate; once you reach the top another shuttle can get you to Rock City and Ruby Falls. That's quite a deal, since the Incline quickly puts you 1800 feet above your car.

If you're visiting the city, don't miss this attraction. Besides being a unique ride, it gives you time to relax and enjoy the spectacular view, something you can't do when driving winding mountain roads. If you live here, ride at least once each spring, and fall and winter. No better way to see the dogwoods, foliage, or amazing boulders that suddenly come to view when leaves are gone.

Originally built in 1895, it's a National Historic Site, and National Historic Mechanical Engineering Landmark. Snack bars at both ends of the line. Fine observation deck at the top.

Lake Winnepesaukah Amusement Park
866-5681, 1115 Lakeview Dr, Rossville, open 10AM Thu-Sun mid-May-August;
Sat-Sun April and Sept, closing times vary; fee $2 adults, $1 children, individual
ride tickets or unlimited package available, Sunday music show free with admission

Throw your arms in the air and scream at the top of your lungs. That's the proper way to take it down on the Cannon Ball, showing your roller-coaster-bravura to beat it all! Little kids can do the scream on the Wacky Worm, a pint-sized version on the lake's north side. The park is laid out almost graduation-style; near the entrance you'll find red-spotted ladybugs that take you for a gentle ride; miniature airplanes and motorcycles for a kiddie thrill. You move from the "Must Be No Taller Than This" rides to the "Must Be At Least This Tall" south-of-the-lake kind; thankful for that winter when you finally grew enough to ride the Matterhorn, the 1001 Nights Magic Carpet, and of course, the Cannon Ball.

You began as a tot in a can't-sit-still ride on the train, over the bridges and through the woods, behind the scenes and around the park. When you were a little older, you persuaded Mom and Dad to take you on the sky-ride, soaring over the lake above the seven swans-a-swimming and the boats you paddle like a duck. Remember the "Little Miss Winnie" pageant on the lakeside stage? Then there was hanging out in the arcade in your I'll-die-if-I'm-seen-with-my-parents phase. Remember when you were a teen, holding hands with your girl and measuring your strength at the Swing-a-Sledge? Thankfully you clanged the bell with an ear-piercing swing.

Newly married, a game of miniature golf seemed a joyous way to spend a don't-grow-up-just-yet afternoon. Next thing you knew, you were booking the Birthday Cake party house for your 3-year-old, snapping her smiles as she flew a plane six feet off the ground, little eyes lit with spunk and dare. The work-years passed with company picnics under the shelter on sunny afternoons; you drove your parents out for Sunday music shows on a bench in the shade. And soon, you are admonishing your can't-sit-still grandson to "Keep hands inside!" as you circle Lake Winnie on the train.

Lake Winnie is blessed with ducks and fish and at least a million memories. Native Americans constructed an earthen dam to form the beautiful little lake. It was fought over during the Civil War with thirsty troops on both sides wanting its water supply. When the Dixons purchased it in the 1920's, they envisioned a family place for boating and picnicking. Carl Dixon designed the boat chute, forerunner of the type you see in major parks today; the miniature golf course was the second ever built in the USA, just after Fairyland's Tom Thumb course on Lookout Mountain. And the park grew.

Today, nearly half a million visitors a year enjoy the Cannon Ball with its 72-foot hill and 2,800 feet of track, and more rides than most major theme parks have -- 32 in all, with standard ferris wheel and carousel, and new-fangled pirate ships for an over-the-water sling. There are 17 picnic shelters, and the Birthday Cake house, call to reserve, no charge. They'll cater your company picnic. Watch the paper for special events.

Point Park

821-7786, N End Lookout Mountain, Visitor Center open daily 8-5:45 summer; closes 4:45 Sept-May; park open daylight hours

Point Park is visible from all over the city, because it perches on the northernmost tip of Lookout Mountain. Conversely, it is the best point from which to view the city and its environs. Beautiful any season of the year, fall foliage time is especially breathtaking; and in winter the bare-limbed trees afford unobstructed across-the-valley views. No amount of counting can number the spring dogwoods on the mountain, or the redbud trees.

If you're visiting the city in summer months without a car, it's easy to get here -- the Lookout Express will deliver you from the ChooChoo to the Incline;

after an Incline ride to the top of the mountain, it's a three-block walk to Point Park; always cooler here than in the valley below.

At the Visitor Center, across the road from the Entrance Gate, you can watch an 8-minute slide program that gears you to what you'll find in the park; also see James Walker's 13x33-foot painting, *Battle Above the Clouds*. There's a bookstore and maps; during summer months rangers give daily tours, historical talks, and demonstrations.

In this portion of the Chickamauga and Chattanooga National Military Park, you can take a walking tour to the historical areas. Be sure to note the entrance gate, largest replica of the U. S. Corps of Engineers insignia in the world. Inside, three gun batteries mark a segment of the siege lines that encircled Chattanooga: two *Parrott Rifles* weighing 1,750 pounds have grooved barrels to increase their accuracy and had a 2-mile range; at *Garrity's Battery* overlooking the valley below are the howitzers, or Napoleons, used by both armies and able to fire a 12-pound charge 1,700 yards; ideal for close-range fighting on level ground, they were largely ineffective against infantry in mountainous terrain; at *Corput's Battery*, near the western overlook, you can see Sunset Rock, from which Gen. Longstreet observed a nighttime attack in Wauhatchie Valley.

In the center of the park is the 95-foot high New York Peace Memorial, visible for miles; on the top Union and Confederate soldiers shake hands under one flag. You descend 500 feet down several tiers of steps to the Ochs Museum and Overlook; dedicated in 1940, it is named for Adolph S. Ochs, publisher of *The Chattanooga Times* and later *The New York Times*. Exhibits and pictures inside tell the story of the battle for Chattanooga; outside markers explain the geography below as you look over Missionary Ridge, Signal Mountain, and the winding Tennessee River; a great place to gain a true understanding of the routes and strategies of Union and Confederate forces during Civil War times. Be careful on the rocky trail; Umbrella Rock is unsafe to climb. From metal steps at the left of the museum you access Bluff Trail, the main hiking trail in the park. Many trails branch off from this one; all are well-marked.

The park is maintained by the National Park Service of the U. S. Department of the Interior; climbing on monuments and artillery pieces is prohibited. Help to preserve history by taking care of your park.

Raccoon Mountain Attractions
Alpine Slide, Grand Prix
825-5666, 415 W Hills Dr, US 41 off I-24 exit 174
Open daily summer, limited hrs spring, fall, closed Dec-Feb, call for details
Not a water slide, the Alpine Slide is more like a bobsled. Ride the chairlift to the top; control your speed on the 1/2-mile dry-slide descent down the mountain. Do your car racing here too, but you must have a driver's license for the Grand Prix. Ten years and up can drive the Go Carts; there are Little

Indys for the younger set.

A snack bar and nice picnic tables are located on the wooded mountainside. In the distance, a grand view of the Tennessee end of Lookout Mountain. There's a campground out here, and stables too.

Raccoon Mountain Caverns
821-9403, 319 W Hills Dr, US 41 off I-24 exit 174
Open Mon-Fri 9-5, Sat-Sun 9-7

The Crystal Palace Tour takes you a half mile into Raccoon Mountain. The caves are considered to have provided shelter to Spanish explorers, Creek and Cherokee Native Americans, Confederate and Union soldiers, and frontier settlers. In the 58-degree temperature you'll see cave coral, natural bridges, soda straws and an array of stalactites, stalagmites, columns and rimstone pools on the 45-minute walk; one of the most active caverns in the southeast, new growth continues to appear from season to season.

The Wild Cave Tour is for more experienced explorers; 2, 4, 6-hour and overnight tours are available with advance reservations. Spelunkers see underground waterfalls, mountain streams, dome ceilings and more. Protective equipment is provided for the caver's safety and convenience.

Rock City Gardens
706-820-2531, Lookout Mountain, GA, 30750, Hwy TN58 to GA157
Open daily 8:30 am till sundown

"See Rock City" painted on a barn is one of the more brilliant advertising campaigns ever undertaken, and identifies with "What to do on a trip to Chattanooga" better than any other attraction. But no amount of commercialism changes one basic fact: Rock City gardens are amazingly, breathtakingly beautiful.

When Mrs. Freida Carter started planting flowers in her back yard in the 20's, she was intent on making it even prettier, preserving over 400 varieties of plant life and winning garden club acclaim on a national scale. She merely added, of course, to what nature had already started on the mountain's weathered sandstone cap. Opened to the public in depression-year '32, the paths today still wind through slivers of light between 1000-ton balanced boulders, past rocks shaped like mushrooms and tortoises, over swinging bridges and under sheltering slabs; and yes, you walk past tumbling waterfalls to Lover's Leap, where the arrow directs your gaze to those seven states. This is probably one of the most-photographed places in the world; make sure you get your shot.

My parent's honeymoon photos include a pose in front of Mushroom Rock; all generations of my family since have stopped there too. This is a true family attraction! Just about the time the kids get tired of walking, you arrive at Fairyland Caverns and Mother Goose Village, with scenarios of well-known fairy tales. The kids will be thrilled to get a "goosey hug" from Mother Goose and her traveling companion, Gussie Goose. Gift shops and food stops are there for souvenir time and a bit of rest after all that walking, but even the parking lot is pretty here, linger longer if you please.

Locals, don't dismiss this as a summer tourist place! Mark your calendar to visit for the changing foliage every spring and fall; and on a crystal-clear winters day, when all the leaves have fallen to the ground, it's a good place to see the lay of the land and the magnificent boulder-strewn hills. As our local weatherman has been known to say, "It's so clear today, I think I'll go to Rock City and count states." Call for group rates, special events such as Spring Blossoms in April & May, Fairy Tale Festival in August, and the fabulous Legends of Christmas all through December.

Ross's Landing Park & Plaza
266-7070, 100 Broad St

Ross's Landing is the "beginning" of Chattanooga, site of a ferry and warehouse established about 1815 by John and Lewis Ross. John Ross, part Scot-part Cherokee, was chief of the Cherokee Nation; his residence was five miles away, just across the Georgia state line. In 1838 the name of the settlement was changed from "Ross's Landing" to "Chattanooga."

Touted as Chattanooga's "front porch," this area around the Aquarium and along the River's edge is a good place to rest a bit and have a cool drink, which you'll want to do before and after your Aquarium visit, or your cruise on the Southern Belle. But plan to make Ross's Landing Park a destination in itself. And go back again and again. It's free! Plus:

♦ It's historical. Paved bands of concrete take you time traveling from the formation of the first rivers to the bottling of the first Coca-Cola; from trading post days to the Chattanooga ChooChoo railroad era.

♦ It's wet. Kids love to hop across the stepping-stones, somehow managing to fall in, at least on the hottest days. Along the eastern wall, sheets of water spray above a roaring stream. Children watch in fascination, hoping for a splash.

♦ It's intriguing. Start the treasure hunt. How many concrete snapping turtles can you find? How many bottle bottoms in the Coca-Cola bridge? Where are the arrowheads?

♦ It's pretty. Native trees and shrubs make sweet-scented flowering springs, multicolored autumns. Grassy green spots are good for picnics, or tickling baby toes. Benches here and there are meant for sitting, maybe with a book.

♦ It's entertaining. Musicians are tucked in likely places, playing everything from blues to bluegrass, for summer-pleasure days. And people watching is always playing on your personal "I-watch" stage.

Wondering what we look for in a Great Place? See "How to Use This Book."

Ruby Falls Caverns

821-2544, 1500 S Scenic Hwy, Lookout Mtn
Open daily 8 am, closing varies from 6-9 pm during year

Let it rain! It won't bother your visit to Ruby Falls. For more than 60 years folks have been riding the elevator down deep inside the mountain to hike the crystal wonderlands to Ruby Falls. Named for the discoverer's wife, Ruby Lambert, well-placed floodlights now play on the 145-foot waterfall to turn it ruby red. Tour guides point out the stalactite-stalagmite formations you pass; they've been given names like well-known friends. The walk to the falls is four-fifths of a mile, generally flat except for 32 steps, and takes about 70 minutes on an average day. Don't mind playing "Turn and tuck it"; you'll be asked to hug the wall as you meet up with groups going the other way.

It may be kind-of-touristy here, but so what? Its popularity shouldn't keep you away; it's a sight to see if you like exploring underground. Locals, avoid the crowds by visiting off-season; a pretty good place to take the kids on a dreary winter day. They've added outdoor stuff over the years: a tower for a stunning valley view, a fun forest play area for the little ones.

Southern Belle Riverboat

(see cover) 266-4488, 201 Riverfront Parkway
Open daily, conditions permitting, schedules fluctuate seasonally, call

You can't have a river city without a river boat. The Southern Belle has graced the banks at Ross's Landing since 1985. Two inside decks and a fresh-air upper deck can accommodate 500 friendly people, standing, or 350 for a sit-down event.

Even if you own a big boat yourself, you'll want to ride the Southern Belle. This giant friendly party place does the driving for you, tickles you with music, and feeds you well. If you choose, there's bingo, and dancing. If you're feeling more sedate, sit on the top deck with your binoculars; listen to the narrator telling tales about the river, the mountains, the herons flying by. Delight in the sounds of the calliope, a really pretty thing to see, its tune putting you in a Huck Finn mood as it pipes you back to shore.

Maybe you've ridden river boats in other cities that are perched on big rivers. But few big rivers are as scenically gorgeous as the Tennessee. In addition to the area's incredible natural beauty, you'll see that Chattanooga hasn't mucked up its shoreline. You do pass by terminals that service business and industry, but from them come long graceful barges, gliding silently except for the signals sounded by their tows, carrying wood chips, grain, and heavy equipment. You'll pass by the foot of Lookout Mountain, go to the right of Williams Island, cruise around the end of Walden Ridge.

The Southern Belle has trips to fit your timeframe and your pocketbook. There are short sightseeing-only trips, and breakfast, luncheon, and dinner cruises. Moonlight cruises are late-evening trips available for private charter by groups. Special Events cruises are planned year-round; some get you into the Little Grand Canyon and take you to Shellmound on the last two weekends of October for some real Rocky-Top jamming.

You can plan your holidays around the variety: Valentine's Dinner, Easter Sunrise Brunch, Secretary's Week Lunch, and on and on through Labor Day and Christmas Cruises with Santa. Even the evening dinner cruises change nightly: there's a Dixieland Dinner Cruise with shrimp creole and the music of the Riverboat Ramblers; there's a Gospel Dinner Cruise with chicken and dressing and a southern gospel quartet; there's a Nashville Night Dinner Cruise with barbecue and all the fixings.

The Belle is a great setting for private parties, business functions and group trips. Call for information, they're happy to help with your planning. They'll even do your wedding, in the Chapel on the River at the Barge. Packages are available or you may create your own plans with the Southern Belle wedding consultants.

Tennessee Aquarium
(see cover) 265-0695, 1 Broad St
Open daily 10-6, extended summer hours, family memberships available

Alligator eyes. Bonnet heads. Cotton mouths. **Step right up and buy your ticket.** Sloshy bogs. Splashy falls. Flooded forests. Rushing, gushing mountain streams. **Step inside and start your ride.** Birdies singing in the tree top. Catfish napping on underwater branches. Turtles digging hidey-holes at the bottom of the lake. **Glide up and up.** The escalator, four stories high, begins to change your world. **Drip, drip, drip.** Water, gathering speed, becomes a force. **You are itching to see it, but wait!**

♦ **Stop in the glass-walled room and look outside at the Tennessee River below. It's 652 miles long and houses more species of fish than any river in North America!**
♦ **See the big blue bridge to the far right. It's over 100 years old and is the longest pedestrian walkway over water in the world!**

Now go ahead. Enjoy the Tennessee Aquarium, and all its wonders, big and small.

A rock-walled passageway eases you into a cove forest. This is the **Appalachian highlands**, birthplace of rivers, filled with songbirds, wildflowers, rocks and trees. The path takes you down like flowing water, past playful otters splashing and diving, past brook trout swimming towards the current, hungrily hunting food. Like the water, eventually you reach flat **Delta country**. The air seems warm and still. Giant snapping turtles float gently under logs, not far from black-bellied ducks, napping, balanced, one leg up. Sun-splotched tree limbs are wrapped in matching snakes. The alligator pretends to sleep, but you catch him in a blink. He's watching.

Tennessee River water flows into the **Ohio**, then the **Mississippi**, and then the Gulf, dwelling place of bonnethead sharks, stingrays, grunts and porkfish, swimming before you in awesome display in the **Gulf of Mexico** exhibit, the only salt-water tank in the Aquarium. More rivers travel you around the world, to see the red-bellied piranhas of the **South American Amazon** and the tiger fish of **Africa's Zaire**. Beluga sturgeon swim in the **Yenisy of Asia**; armor-plated sturgeon, throwbacks to the Jurassic period, in **North America's St Lawrence**; both are wearing scutes instead of scales.

Pay particular attention to the **Nickajack Lake** exhibit, for this depicts the waters outside the building. Nickajack Lake extends from the dam west of the city to Chickamauga Dam east of the city. You can see largemouth bass, sunfish, and catfish swimming in the largest freshwater tank in the world -- 138,000 gallons, with windows 9 inches thick.

This is not a place of home-sized glass fish boxes at eye level, like many aquariums you've probably seen before. The darkened canyon path takes you past huge, multi-storied bodies of water, allowing views near the top, the middle, or at the bottom looking up. You get a sense of the underwater world; going nose-to-nose with yellow spotted angelfish; watching duck feet pumping at paddlewheel speed.

When you're back outside, reflect. You've just seen **two living forests** and **7,000 animals made up of 400 species**. You've seen alligator eyes, bonnet heads, and cotton mouths. You've been to the Tennessee Aquarium, the **largest freshwater aquarium in the world**. Aren't you glad you came?

Tennessee Valley Railroad Museum
894-8028, 4119 Cromwell Rd and 220 N Chamberlain Ave
Hours different summer/winter; BE SURE to call ahead for train schedules.
Museum and parking free, fee for rides. Group reservations available.
Operated by volunteer railfans; join up if trains are your thing.

This is the largest operating historic railroad in the south, with a superb collection of engines and rail cars in fixed position for climbing on and walking through at the Cromwell Road spot. Go into the **Grand Junction Depot** for a snack in the restaurant and some browse time in the gift shop, before buying your ticket to ride. No make-believe here, this is authentic railroading, and the track goes through the 986-foot **Missionary Ridge tunnel**, built in 1858 and the original right-of-way of the East Tennessee & Georgia Railroad.

Two trips are available: the shorter trip goes between Grand Junction (Cromwell Rd) and the **East Chattanooga Depot** (N Chamberlain Ave). This is interesting; you're allowed to debark here for a visit around the huge shop area, where volunteers are constantly restoring locomotives, rail cars, push cars, and other rail memorabilia. Gather round, too, to watch your engine settle on the giant turntable before reattaching itself to your railcar for a trip back through the tunnel. The other trip is offered in summer only, a nice long ride between Grand Junction and the **Chattanooga ChooChoo**. If you're visiting the city, you may want to start at this end, it's a bit easier to find if you don't know your way around.

Walnut Street Bridge
(see cover) Walnut Street and Tennessee River

This 1890's structure spanned the River before Henry built his first Ford. After the horse and buggy days, it handled cars till 1978, then sat, out-of-favor and decaying, until citizens' efforts restored it to a better-than-before charm, its brilliant blue girders and sturdy stone posts now supporting a pedestrian path that's part of **RiverWalk**. Twinkling lights outline its shape at night, pots of flowers brighten up the days. It's a half-mile walk across; stay to the right both ways and soak up all the view.

No better spot in town to watch the evening sunset, or catch the city skyline after dark. Stroll the baby, jog in stride, or ride your bike. Take a book or your guitar for relaxing on a bench, midstream and way up high. Go with your best friend, your kids, or go alone. One of the safest places in town for evening walks, it's well-populated, well-lit, and well-patrolled.

Both ends of the bridge offer pretty spots and interesting things to do; the north shore is fast becoming the art enclave, with galleries lining Frazier; there are used books, unique toys, a coffeehouse, and the well-known T & C; a juice bar, bikes and skates for rent, a health food store and Rock/Creek outfitters.

The south end has steps that move you quickly down; one path is the fast-track back to Ross's Plaza and the Market and Broad street restaurants; go river-side for a slower stroll or head uphill towards Hunter Museum and the Bluff View Art District. You also can park your car at the end of the bridge and simply drive back home when your walk is done; no steps to climb.

Warehouse Row Factory Shops
267-1111, 1110 Market Street, open Mon-Sat 10-7, Sun 12-6

This downtown gem is the jewel of Market Street and represents so much more than a place to shop; it's ChooChoo town, redefined -- appreciate the past, look to the future. The restoration angle is impressive; eight old railroad warehouses, built in the early 1900's, became a downtown mixed-use center and got listed on the National Register. The rustic old brick looks really classy now, with awnings and fountains outside and a three-story atrium inside. Splendid hardwood floors, brass railings, and a bubble elevator combine to lead you to the finest of shops -- 45 in all including Adrienne Vittadini,

Geoffery Beene, Perry Ellis, Ralph Lauren; prices are 25%-75% off retail.

Opened in 1989, six more shops went into the Freight Depot across the street in 1994; more are planned; it's spreading towards the ChooChoo; those boarded-over buildings on Market soon will be changed. The Row is a magnet for out-of-town shoppers; 20% come from Atlanta, over 40% from Nashville, Knoxville, Birmingham, and even farther away. Locals, pay attention! <u>*Woman's Day* has selected Warehouse Row as one of the top five outlet centers in the nation</u>. You don't want to miss it. Complimentary parking available in the 3-level garage, or catch the every-5-minutes electric shuttle between the ChooChoo and the Aquarium.

Great Drives Around Chattanooga

Drives designed to entice visitors and locals to "check out the view" from different perspectives. These drives take you to the city's five highest peaks and through residential areas in the valley, by the lake, and on the ridge and mountain tops. A wonderful way to see where Chattanoogans live while you're visiting the main attractions.

Lookout Mountain
Including Rossville and St. Elmo, approximately 33 miles round trip
Lookout Mountain stands like a sentinel over the city, holding memories of Civil and Revolutionary War battles; today it's the site of some of the best known attractions and most gorgeous real estate. This drive lets you approach it from the east, and then climb it!

♦ From Ross's Landing, proceed on Chestnut to 4th Street, turn right to US27 South; follow US27 South on Rossville Blvd to **Rossville** and a stop at the **Chief John Ross House**; then proceed to **Ft Oglethorpe**; at intersection of Hwy 2 West, turn right. *9 miles*

♦ Continue west on State Hwy 2 towards Lookout Mountain; the **sandstone bluffs** begin to loom large on the mountainside; you cross over **McFarland Avenue**; look to your right -- you'll see the city of **Chattanooga** in the distance, nestled in the valley like a child in its mother's arms. Hwy 2 goes north here; but you should continue west until you reach **State Hwy 193 North**. *4.7 miles*

♦ A right turn takes you into **Tennessee,** where it becomes **St Hwy 17** and **St Elmo Ave**; you're in the historic **St. Elmo** district at the bottom of Lookout Mountain. The **Incline Railway** will be just ahead on your left. You'll find eateries and galleries here too. *4.2 miles*

♦ See the **Rock City** signs? That's **Hwy 58**. Climb the winding mountain road; Hwy 58 becomes **Hwy 157** when you enter Georgia. At the top of the mountain the entrance to Rock City will be on your left. Are you planning a Rock City visit today? *2.9 miles*

♦ Proceed on Hwy 157 to intersection with **Hwy 189, Lookout Mountain**

Parkway; turn right. *1.1 miles*

♦ Proceed on Hwy 189 North; when you enter Tennessee it becomes **Hwy 148**. You are driving through a residential area of **beautiful mountaintop homes**. Turn left on N Bragg Ave to **Point Park;** right on **E Brow Rd** past the top stop of the **Incline Railway** to Hwy 148 again to begin your mountain descent. *4.4 miles*

♦ You will reach the entrance to **Craven's House,** and to **Ruby Falls,** both on your left, as you descend the mountain. At the hairpin turn, go right towards Chattanooga. *2.2 miles*

♦ The **Tennessee River** is below on your left. The road curves itself into **Broad Street.** Proceed on Broad Street to the Aquarium and Ross's Landing. *4.1 miles*

Missionary Ridge

Including Chickamauga Battlefield, approximately 33 miles round trip

Missionary Ridge was the site of fierce Civil War fighting; cannons and markers and monuments identify the spots. Today beautiful homes grace the top of the ridge, right in the heart of the city. A nice beginning to the Battlefield Tour drive.

♦ From Ross's Landing, proceed east on **Riverside Drive** Hwy 58 N to Wilcox Blvd; turn right. *2.3 miles*

♦ Follow Wilcox Blvd to Dodson Avenue, turn left and proceed to Glass St, turn right and proceed to Campbell St, turn right. *4 miles*

♦ Campbell St quickly becomes **N Crest Rd** as you climb **Missionary Ridge;** proceed to **Delong Reservation** on your right, where there is a pulloff and markers to read. *2 miles*

♦ Proceed on N Crest Rd; admire beautiful **ridgetop homes,** views of **Lookout Mountain** and city of **Chattanooga** in **valley** below; cross Shallowford Rd at 4-way stop; note **cannons** and **markers** in yards; *drive carefully,* this is a narrow residential road; cross **bridge over I-24;** check out the view both ways. *1.5 miles*

♦ **S Crest Rd** veers to right across bridge; around curve **Sherman Reservation** is on your left; area to park while you look at Illinois monument and other markers; proceed on S Crest Rd to US27 **Rossville Blvd.** *3.5 miles*

♦ Turn left on US27 South to Ft Oglethorpe and Visitor Center in **Chickamauga Battlefield.** *3 miles*

♦ Get information in Visitor Center and take **Auto Tour** of Park. *7 miles*

♦ After touring Battlefield; proceed north on US27 and Aquarium exit to Ross's Landing. *10 miles*

Big Ridge

Including the valley and the lake, approximately 35 miles round trip

Missionary Ridge continues on the north side of the Tennessee River, however there it's named **Big Ridge**. This trip takes you by it, around it, and over it, with a wonderful lake-side stop. Great valley and lake view, lovely homes to admire.

- From Ross's Landing, proceed east on **Riverside Drive** Hwy 58 North to Hwy 153 North Exit. *7.5 miles*
- Cross **Tennessee River** over **Chickamauga Dam** for magnificent views of **Chickamauga Lake** and mountains and proceed north to Hixson Pike East Exit. *2 miles*
- Follow **Hixson Pike** past **Northgate Mall**, five-lane road changes to two. Pass golf courses and follow alongside bottom of **Big Ridge** to **Gold Point Rd** and turnoff to **Chester Frost Park** and **Wildlife Viewing** area. *5 miles*
- Turn right on Gold Point Rd, proceed to Chester Frost Park picnic area, swimming beach, fishing pier, and boat ramp. *1 mile*
- Next is turnoff to camping area and **Dallas Island**. Dallas was first county seat of Hamilton County. *1 mile*
- After your park visit, continue on Gold Point Circle past beautiful **lakeside homes**, and eventually **ridgeside homes**, as you begin to climb the heavily forested ridge on a winding road; at pedestrian crossing, turn left on **Fairview Rd,** climb to top of Big Ridge. *4 miles*
- Proceed on Fairview Rd past beautiful **ridgetop homes**; see Lookout Mountain and Pigeon Mountain in distance, Chickamauga Lake to your left, and Middle Valley and Walden Ridge to your right; *drive carefully,* this is a narrow residential road; Fairview Rd becomes **Lake Resort Drive** as you descend the ridge; note sign for **North Chickamauga Creek Greenway** on your right and **Chickamauga Lock** on your left; park and look. *5.5 miles*
- Leave Dam and turn left at BOTH lights to be on **Access Rd** with Tennessee River on your left; proceed past **DuPont Plant** to **Hwy 319 South** to Chattanooga. *1.5 miles*
- Follow Hwy 319 South to Hwy 58 S Chattanooga exit; as you cross the Tennessee River look both ways for **fabulous water and mountain views.** *1.5 miles*
- Follow Hwy 58 S to Ross's Landing. *5.5 miles*

Signal Mountain
Including Stringer's Ridge, Laurel Ridge, Godsey Ridge and Walden Ridge, approximately 29 miles round trip

Signal Mountain makes up the north side of the Tennessee River Gorge. This drive goes alongside ridges and to the mountain's point through some of the city's loveliest residential areas: **North Chattanooga, Hixson** and, of course, **Signal Mountain.**

- From Ross's Landing, follow Chestnut south to 4th St and turn left; proceed uphill to exit for **Veteran's Bridge;** turn left at the light and cross the **Tennessee River;** watch for great views of numerous ridges; you'll be on **Barton Avenue** which curves left to **Hixson Pike;** watch for beautiful

homes along the way. *2 miles*
- ◆ Stringer's Ridge is on your left as you drive the winding road past residential and then commercial; exit north at Hwy 153. *5 miles*
- ◆ You are facing the sandstone bluffs atop **Walden Ridge**; at intersection with Hwy US 27 exit left towards Chattanooga. *4 miles*
- ◆ Drive southwest on four-lane highway with **Godsey and Walden Ridge** to your right, **Laurel and Stringer's Ridge** to your left, **Raccoon Mountain and Lookout Mountain** straight ahead -- this is a magnificent drive which really shows the lay of the land! Take Hwy 127 Exit to Signal Mtn Rd. *8 miles*
- ◆ Climb **Signal Mountain** on very winding road; Hwy 127 becomes Taft Hwy; at top of mountain watch for left turn to Signal Mtn Blvd towards Signal Point. *3 miles*
- ◆ Turn left, proceed to Mississippi Avenue, James Blvd, and Signal Point Rd; **Signal Point** is part of National Military Park with fabulous view of **Tennessee River Gorge**. *1 mile*
- ◆ Retrace your drive back down Signal Mountain; reaccess Hwy US27 South. *4 miles*
- ◆ Cross Tennessee River on US27 and exit right immediately at Aquarium Exit to Ross's Landing. *2 miles*

Raccoon Mountain
Including Reflection Riding, approximately 35 miles round trip
Raccoon Mountain makes up the south side of the Tennessee River Gorge. Enjoy both nature's beauty and man's ingenuity in one afternoon; this is a nice drive in any season but try to catch the wildflowers in the spring.
- ◆ From Ross's Landing, follow Chestnut, turn left at 2nd, right to Broad Street. Proceed south on Broad Street towards Lookout Mountain. Follow signs to Hwy 41 or **Cummings Hwy**, the **Tennessee River** will be below you on your right; the highway goes around the mountain. *3.7 miles*
- ◆ Watch for left turn to **Reflection Riding** and **Nature Center**. Follow Garden Rd to Center; take scenic drive through the Riding; beautiful ponds and pastures at foot of Lookout Mountain. *2.5 miles to turn; 1 mile to Center; 3 miles around Riding; total 6.5 miles*
- ◆ Return to Cummings Hwy, turn left; cross under I-24; **High Adventure Sports** on the right; **Raccoon Mtn Attractions** on your left. *3.1 miles*
- ◆ Proceed on Cummings Hwy to entrance to **Raccoon Mountain Pumped Storage Plant** on the right-hand side of the road. Turn right. *1.2 miles*
- ◆ Follow signs; pass alongside Tennessee River and drive to top of Raccoon Mountain. At the top you will reach the **Gorge Overlook**, where information is available and you can tour the facility, going deep down into the mountain. Drive around the top-of-the-mountain **lake**; there are **picnic areas** too. Turn right to an **overlook**; you can see the city in the valley and the west side of Lookout Mountain, hiking trails too. *10.1 miles*
- ◆ Proceed down the mountain following the Scenic Train markers; right at

stop sign, to **Elder Mountain Rd;** then right at **Browns Ferry Rd**. *3.3 miles*
♦ Return to Cummings Hwy, turn left and follow to Broad Street and Ross's
Landing. *7.4 miles*

Great Freebies Around Chattanooga

If your budget is in a sad state or if you're merely frugal by nature, you'll
never run out of things to do in this city! From Arts to Zoos you can find
things to see, music to listen to, and interesting things to learn about. Pack a
picnic and try these twenty very inexpensive places.

Artstravaganza, *265-4282, Hunter Museum of American Art and Bluff View Art
District, mid-May weekend,* sponsored by the Association for Visual Artists,
there's a juried exhibition, weekend music for all, and hands-on arts for
the children. Local and out-of-town acts.

Battles of Chickamauga and Chattanooga Anniversaries, *866-9241,
Chickamauga Battlefield; 821-7786, Point Park,* weekend nearest actual battle
dates of September 19-20, November 24-25; call for exact times and
reenactments of the events.

Chattanooga-Hamilton County Bicentennial Library, *757-5310, 1001 Broad
St,* in addition to the hours of entertainment you'll receive by reading the
books, call for a schedule of Sunday afternoon concerts, speakers and
story times.

Galleries, *see p.88,* for a listing of galleries you can visit; often you can watch
an artist at work. Watch for special shows and changing exhibits. Ask to
be put on the mailing list.

**Greenways, RiverWalk including Walnut Street Bridge, and Wildlife
Viewing areas,** see listings in previous chapter. Some of these are part of
the parks systems; they offer excellent entertainment if you like walking,
watching, or just being in the out-of-doors.

Hamilton County Fair, *842-0049. Chester Frost Park, Sat-Sun 9-6 4th weekend
September,* animals, exhibits, demonstrations, entertainment, games and
food; all the stuff a fair should have. The Fair is free; you must, however,
ride the shuttle to get there, *small fee.*

Historical Cemeteries: Confederate and Citizens Cemetery, *East 5th &
Palmetto St,* burial grounds for Civil War soldiers and Chattanooga
citizens, including John P Long, first postmaster at Ross's Landing, from
1837-45, he suggested changing the city's name to Chattanooga.
Chattanooga National Cemetery, *1200 Bailey Ave,* created after Civil War
battles in late 1863; over 31,000 veterans and their dependents are buried
in 120 acres of rolling hills near the heart of downtown; limestone caves on
the north side (now sealed) may have been used as receiving storage
vaults for bodies awaiting burial.

Little Theatre of Chattanooga, *267-8534, 400 River Street,* you are welcome to
attend free dress rehearsals before each new performance. A great way to
stretch your budget if you love theatre but can't swing season tickets just

yet; or to begin exposing yourself to theatre if you aren't as knowledgeable as you'd like to be.

Malls: Eastgate, Hamilton, Northgate, Warehouse Row, all the malls publish a calendar of events; stop at the information desk and pick one up. Concerts, demonstrations, and crafts fairs take place throughout the year, free of charge.

Miller Plaza Series: Coffeehouse, Nightfall, and Nooners, *265-0771, Chattanooga Downtown Partnership, 850 Market St,* for 17 Fridays in the summer, 8 Tuesdays in the winter and many days during spring and fall, there's free music in the Plaza. Call for the exact schedule, or watch the paper. Never, never say you can't go hear music because "it's too expensive" or "I'm underage." You can here!

Parades: Nightlight Parade, *Miller Plaza to Ross's Landing,* sponsored by Chattanooga Downtown Partnership, kicking off the winter holiday season, followed by **Christmas on the River,** *Ross's Landing,* brightly decorated boats parade on the Tennessee River. Most communities stage Christmas parades throughout December.

Parks

♦ **City:** in Chattanooga and the other area municipalities you will find wonderful places to picnic and play very near your own back door. **Warner Park** has a **Rose Garden** and a **Zoo.** Get a list of the ones created just for you and use them regularly!

♦ **County:** in addition to **Riverpark** and **Chester Frost Park,** there are playfields and tennis courts spread out county-wide for your use. Call in your county, get a list, and enjoy.

♦ **National:.** The **Chickamauga and Chattanooga National Military Park** is maintained by the National Park Service and includes the following sites: **Chickamauga Battlefield,** Hwy US27 in Ft Oglethorpe; **Point Park** including **Och's Museum and Overlook,** and **Craven's House** *(small fee here)* on Lookout Mountain; **Orchard Knob Reservation; Sherman, Delong, Ohio and Bragg Reservations** on Missionary Ridge; and **Signal Point Reservation** at the south end of Signal Mountain.

♦ **State: Booker T. Washington** and **Harrison Bay State Parks** are on the south side of **Chickamauga Lake;** many fine parks in **Tennessee, Georgia, Alabama** and **North Carolina** are only an easy drive away; *a few may have small entrance fees, most do not.*

Pops in the Park, *267-8583,* hear and see the Chattanooga Symphony at Wilder Tower in Chickamauga Battlefield on the Saturday nearest July 4th and end the evening with a fireworks show. Take a quilt or your folding chairs and a picnic!

Riverbend Fireworks Show, *Ross's Landing,* mid-June on the last night of the Riverbend Festival; fireworks visible from any hill around.

Ross's Landing Park & Plaza, *266-7070, 100 Broad St,* music and crafts demonstrations are frequently staged in the plaza; get the map and follow the history trail around the park.

Rowing, *622-6846,* enjoy the competition of the Bridgefest Regatta on the first

Saturday in May; it ends at Ross's Landing. The Chattanooga Head Race is early October, both sponsored by the Lookout Rowing Club.

Tennessee Valley Railroad Museum, *894-8028, 4119 Cromwell Rd, and 220 N Chamberlain Ave,* the museum is free -- there are many fixed rail cars to climb in and walk through; there's a fee only if you ride the train.

Tennessee Valley Authority, there are 10 hydro plants on the Tennessee River; the entire TVA system includes Virginia, North Carolina, Georgia, Alabama and Kentucky, with a combination of coal-fired plants, nuclear plants, and non-power dams. Start in the **Energy Center,** *751-7599, 1101 Market St,* to see system maps and how TVA produces energy. Then tour the **Dams and Power Plants** -- nearest is **Chickamauga Dam** and **Lake,** *751-4200,* on the south side you may tour the powerhouse, call for hours; on the property swim or fish in Lake Junior or enjoy a life-guarded swimming beach; on the north side watch the boats go through the locks. Visit **Raccoon Mountain Pumped-Storage Plant,** *751-2420,* where you'll find the largest of TVA's rock-filled dams, measuring 230 feet high and 8,500 feet long. Cut 1,350 feet inside the mountain, the powerhouse chamber has four of the largest reversible pump-turbines in the world. Visitor center, reservoir and picnic area atop mountain, overlooks with spectacular views of Tennessee River gorge. **Watts Bar Dam** is north of Chattanooga; **Nickajack Dam** is downstream. In addition to providing electricity, the dams provide water recreation for the entire Tennessee Valley area. At the **Sequoyah Energy Connection,** *843-4100, Hwy 27, Sequoyah Access Rd, Soddy-Daisy,* you can tour a nuclear plant by way of interactive computer video.

University of Tennessee at Chattanooga Clarence T. Jones Observatory, *622-5733, 10 Tuxedo, just off Brainerd Rd,* the observatory is open to the public on Friday nights for stargazing; the planetarium show is at 8:30.

Watering Trough, *Harrison Pike and Meadow Lane,* take your cup and have a drink of the cool water flowing from a spring on Missionary Ridge.

Great Kids Stuff Around Chattanooga

You'll find the detail in other sections of the book, but here's a third-of-a-hundred things that are especially fun for children. Some are high-up and potentially dangerous; they require discussion of responsible behavior before departing. My grandkids and I talk about which places are OK for running and when they need to hold my hand; we have a no-climbing-on-the-railings non-negotiable rule. We also decide on a place to meet if we should get separated; not a bad idea for adults too!

Artstravaganza, *265-4282, Hunter Museum of American Art and Bluff View Art District, mid-May weekend,* arts and music for grownups and for children; hands-on activities.

Audubon Acres, aka Elise Chapin Wildlife Sanctuary, *I75 Exit 3A, right 2nd light to Gunbarrel Rd, 1 2/3 mi, follow signs,* trails through the woods and across a swinging bridge; a cabin to explore; an eagle aviary.

Buck's Pit Barbeque Restaurant, *267-1390, 3146 Broad St,* kids like the barbecue sandwiches and fries in a log-cabin atmosphere.

Chattanooga Nature Center & Reflection Riding, *400 Garden Rd, Lookout Mtn,* every kid enjoys feeding the ducks and geese in the ponds; there are wide-open spaces for running and playing; a wetlands boardwalk; animals to see; indoor exhibits.

Chester Frost Park, *Gold Point Circle,* let the kids romp around the sandy beach on hot summer days, don't forget their little pail and shovel.

Chickamauga Dam, *Hwy 153,* kids can learn about electricity during a powerhouse tour; at the overlook by the lock on the north side let them watch a barge lifted or lowered on the water elevator; on the sidewalk where N Chickamauga Creek runs into the river they can see herons fishing and people fishing; the spillways are awesome after a storm.

Children's Autumn Festival, *756-7030, Riverpark,* held in mid-October, admission is free, there's a charge for games; the festival benefits the Ronald McDonald House.

Childrens Hour, *267-4284, 827 Broad St,* this store off the lobby in the Radisson Read House has a diverse assortment of children's games and books, and a kid-sized room with kid-sized chairs for reading.

Chuck E Cheese's, *870-3215, 22 Northgate Park,* pizza, rides and games; a robotics show and handshakes by Chuck E; great for birthday parties.

Club Kid, *3224 Brainerd Rd at the Comedy Catch,* interactive theatre on Saturday mornings for kids 4-12; they get to wear costumes and watch themselves on video; kids must bring an adult.

Creative Discovery Museum, *756-2738, 4th & Chestnut St,* this hands-on museum brings out the genius in every kid; a science lab, an artist's studio, an inventor's workshop and a dinosaur dig, plus more.

Discovery Zone *(2 locations), 855-5020, 2020 Gunbarrel Rd, 870-9955, 5239 Hwy 153,* indoor playground with things to climb on, in, and over.

Hamilton County Fair, *842-0049. Chester Frost Park, Sat-Sun 9-6 4th weekend September,* children and county fairs were made for each other; this one is in a beautiful location too.

Incline Railway, *821-4224, 3917 St Elmo Ave (bottom), 827 E Brow Rd (top),* ride the train up the mountain; it slants so much you can see out of the top! At the observation building, find the lower window where you can watch the big gears turning.

Kaleidoscope, *265-4112,* a creative fun festival for children, with talent from around the world; put together by the Riverbend planners and grand in scope.

Lake Winnepesaukah Amusement Park, *866-5681, 1115 Lakeview Dr, Rossville,* more than 32 rides surrounding a lake, from Carousel to Cannon Ball, games, miniature golf and the Birthday Cake picnic house.

Libraries, *see p.237,* all branches of the public library have story time for children; some have a lap-sit program for the very young beginning at 18 months, call to register.

Little Theatre Youth Program, *267-8534, 400 River St,* four plays during the year, such as 94-95's *Prince and the Pauper, Princess and the Pea, Adventures of Peter Rabbit,* and *OPQRS, Etc.*

Miller Plaza Nightfall Series, *265-0771, 850 Market St,* beginning at 7 PM on Friday nights June through September you can take the kids to a variety of exciting outdoor music performances, FREE.

Oak Street Playhouse, *756-2024, 419 McCallie Ave,* in the fall, it's puppet time with classic tales adapted to the puppet stage; actors do the sound track.

Oasis Food Court, *Hamilton Mall,* Arby's roast beef, Boardwalk Fries, Krystal burgers, Sbarro's pizza, the Taco Bell and more, placed for fun between the movie theatre and the arcade.

Point Park, *Lookout Mountain,* from the edge of the mountain kids can pick out landmarks in the city or watch the boats on the river below; in autumn it's fun to run through the big golden leaves as they fall to the ground.

Rock City Gardens, *706-820-2531, Lookout Mountain,* the swinging bridge and Fat Man's Squeeze are fun; so is Deer Park and the chipmunks along the paths; best of all is a Mother Goose hug and the fairyland scenes in Mother Goose Village.

Ross's Landing Park & Plaza, *100 Broad St,* streams to jump across and fall into; waterfalls and pools; cement turtles to track; green-grass-good-smelling lawns to sit on for a rest.

Sir Goony's Family Fun Center, *892-5922, 5918 Brainerd Rd,* baseball and softball cages, miniature golf, and cars to speed around a track when you're old enough.

Tennessee Aquarium, *265-0695, 1 Broad St,* tanks filled with otters and ducks and fish of every size and color; make sure to go at feeding time.

Tennessee Riverpark, *842-0177, Amnicola Hwy,* a fabulous playground, meadows to run in, paved paths for rollerblading, and piers to fish off with Granddad.

Tennessee Valley Railroad Museum, *894-8028, 4119 Cromwell Rd,* is it more fun to climb around on the stationary cars and pretend to be riding, or to ride a train through the tunnel in Missionary Ridge? Do both!

Trail's End Ranch Riding Stables, *706-375-4346, Hwy 27 S at Trail's End Road, near Chickamauga Park,* ride horseback here, they'll show you how and ride along with you; they'll also set up a wiener roast for your group.

Trip's Seafood Restaurant, *892-6880, 6715 Ringgold Rd,* feed the ducks or swing on the swings; walk the plank to go inside and order those little popcorn shrimp; watch the duck pond from the big windows.

UTC Clarence T. Jones Observatory, *622-5733, 10 Tuxedo, just off Brainerd Rd, open to public Fri 8-10 pm, free,* a planetarium show and a 20-inch telescope to introduce young people to real star-gazing.

Walnut Street Bridge, *Walnut St,* Jeffrey, Jason, Justin and Matthew were impressed with being so high over the water; they like to watch the boats down below and the osprey platform at the end of Maclellan Island.

Warner Park Zoo, *697-9722, 1254 E 3rd St,* talk to the gorilla and admire the big tiger; there are some animals you can pet.

Great Views Around Chattanooga

In a city with no bad views, here are twenty-five that are truly spectacular!

Aris' Lakeshore, *877-7068, 5600 Lake Resort Terrace at Lakeshore complex,* dinner restaurant overlooking Chickamauga Lake, with views of city and mountains beyond.

Back Inn Cafe, *757-0108, 412 E 2nd,* lunch and dinner restaurant with back deck overlooking the Tennessee River and the **River Gallery Sculpture Garden,** *267-7353, 214 Spring St,* which is open during daylight hours.

Baywatch Waterfront Eatery & Bar, *843-3100, 9718 Hixson Pike,* lunch and dinner restaurant with back deck overlooking main channel of Tennessee River and Harbor Lights Marina.

Blue Cross Cafeteria, *755-5969, 801 Pine St, 10th floor,* lunch cafeteria overlooking downtown, with views of distant mountains.

Boynton Park, *Cameron Hill,* view of city skyline especially good in winter when trees are bare, and to Missionary Ridge beyond.

Chattanooga Nature Center and Reflection Riding, *400 Garden Rd,* from the valley see Lookout Mountain and the puffy white clouds reflected in the duck pond where turtles sun themselves on a rock; admire the sandstone mountain bluffs above the rail-fenced pasture where the horses graze.

Chickamauga Dam, *Hwy 153, north side at Access Road exit,* from the overlook at the lock you can view Chickamauga Lake, the Tennessee River, and every mountain and ridge for miles around.

Hwy 111 South, *descending Walden Ridge to Soddy-Daisy and US27,* you have to climb the ridge first, but as you come down it's miles and miles of valley view and, far away, the Smoky Mountains.

Figgy's Sandwich Shop, *266-8675, 20 W 8th,* get the table near the door in this lunch spot for views of downtown's contrasting architectural styles.

Gardens Restaurant, *266-5000, Terminal Building, ChooChoo Complex,* look up in the adjoining lobby at the fabulous dome; look outdoors from the restaurant onto beautifully landscaped gardens, fountains, a trolley, and authentic rail cars.

Lookout Mountain Flight Park, *706-398-3541, 800-688-LMFP, Rt 2 Box 215H, Rising Fawn, GA,* stand at the edge of the mountain and watch the rainbow-hued hang gliders float gently to the valley floor; or watch an aero-tow bring one up from below. Sand Mountain is across the valley.

I-24 West, *crossing Missionary Ridge, facing the city,* you reach the ridge-cut and descend on a curve; Lookout Mountain is dead ahead and the city fills the valley below.

Incline Railway, *821-4224, 3917 St Elmo Ave (bottom), 827 E Brow Rd (top),* it's safe to gape here while comfortably seated at a slant in the glass-topped car; the same city-valley views from the observation deck at the top.

Madhatters, *267-0747, 201 Frazier Ave, upstairs,* get a front window seat in this lunch/dinner restaurant and overlook the action on the Walnut Street

Bridge below; see Aquarium peaks and mountain peaks across the River.

Miller Park, *10th & Market St,* introspectively enjoy the fountains and trees in the park; look beyond to the city's skyline; find the historic Dome Building and Read House, and all the contrasting newer styles.

Point Park, *N End Lookout Mountain, park open daylight hours,* straight ahead from the entrance gate you'll find the easiest-to-reach overlook of the city and River below; hardier souls can follow the trail to Ochs overlook 500 feet down. The meandering Tennessee River flows both north and south at the foot of the mountain -- it's Moccasin Bend and the only place in the world where you can see such a sight!

Hunter Museum of American Art, *10 Bluff View, open Tue-Sat 10-4:30, Sun 1-4:30,* several windows offer great River views, but on the giant patio you are "hanging out" over the River while admiring the outdoor sculptures.

Provident Cafeteria, *755-1011, Fountain Square,* this lunch cafeteria has windows so wide they take in half the downtown and all the mountains beyond.

Raccoon Mountain Pumped Storage Plant, *751-2420, Cummings Hwy,* three views for the price of one, all free: 1. from the observation tower overlooking the Tennessee River Gorge; 2. during your drive atop the dam as you face Lookout Mountain and watch the hawks and eagles soar over the man-made lake; and 3. from the overlook facing city-wards, with an odd end-angle view of Lookout Mountain.

Ralph Lauren, *615-267-7656, Warehouse Row,* on the 2nd floor a colorful bed layered in Lauren linens sits in a corner window, nicely framing a citified Lookout Mountain view.

Ross's Landing Park, *100 Broad St,* from a bench in the lower grassy park, watch and hear roaring streams and splashing sheets of water; look across the street at bridges in several styles.

Sandbar Restaurant, *622-4432, 1011 Riverside Drive,* this lunch, dinner and music spot has a huge patio on the Tennessee River; you look straight across at the famous Walden Ridge sunsets.

Signal Point, *off James Blvd,* you're a thousand feet above the Tennessee River, looking across at Raccoon Mountain, and watching the falcons fly.

Southern Belle Riverboat, *266-4488, 201 Riverfront Parkway,* several thousand views just from the top deck, as your cruise changes the skyline from city to mountain and back again.

Walnut Street Bridge, *Walnut St,* look down at the moving boats, look south at the bluff and the Hunter Museum, or downtown, or the Aquarium peaks; look west at Raccoon Mountain; look north at Stringer's Ridge rising above the north shore stores; look east at Maclellan Island; count the bridges and the ridges you can see. On the RiverWalk below, look up at the underside of the Bridge; admire its construction. Or look across the river as the Bridge's twinkling lights brighten the evening.

Looking for a particular place? Check the index at the back of this book for individual attractions, events, galleries, museums, recreational places, sports, tours, stores, lodgings, churches, schools and business services.

Great Walks Around Chattanooga

Indoors and out, city and country, these are safe places winter and summer, spring and fall. If you're a fast walker timing your pace or a slow stroller with time on your hands, these ten suggestions are sure to please.

Chattanooga Nature Center. There are miles of trails at the foot of Lookout Mountain, but it's nice on the wetlands walkway too; a boardwalk through the woods and into some unusual territory by Lookout Creek; benches along the way for sitting and listening to the birds and watching for beaver and muskrat.

Chickamauga Dam Overlook. It's not a long walk, but it puts you high up and out in the open; a nice fresh-air walk at sunset time.

Downtown Strolling. Walk from the River to 11th Street on Market and back on Broad beside wide, tree-lined streets; plenty of places to stop and window-shop or get a bite to eat.

Five Miles Downtown. From Ross's Landing Plaza, cross the Market Street Bridge to Frazier; right on Frazier to Veteran's Bridge; cross Veteran's Bridge and stay on Georgia Avenue to Vine Street; left on Vine to Central Avenue; right on Central to Oak Street; right on Oak to Georgia Avenue; right on Georgia to 6th Street; left on 6th to Chestnut Street; right on Chestnut to 2nd Street; right on 2nd to Market and return to your starting point.

Historical & Architectural Walks. Pick up the brochures at the Visitors Center for maps and descriptions; they tell the history of the buildings along nicely planned walks on Broad and Market Streets, Market Street and Georgia Avenue, the Fort Wood Neighborhood, and the St. Elmo District.

Mallwalking. Contact your favorite mall and find out how early they open in the morning for walkers. You won't be walking alone!

North Chickamauga Creek Greenway. On the north side of the River, across the street from the dam; a paved walkway alongside the Creek and through the woods.

RiverWalk Part 1, Ross's Landing. Start at Ross's Landing, and stroll the RiverWalk past honeysuckle scents and calliope serenades, with benches under bridges, boardwalked paths for holding hands, an amphitheater tucked beneath a busy road. From the amphitheater, you have three choices:

1. **To the Sculpture Garden.** One path serpentines uphill, flowered red and blue. Trek off the path to the Bluff Furnace historic spot; resume your walk to the Hunter Museum, and the Bluff View Art District, have a coffee on Rembrandt's patio, find the Houston Museum, River Gallery, LeDoux's fine dining, Tony's pasta, Back Inn Cafe's deck with-a-view, the charming sculpture garden at the farthest end.

2. **Across the Walnut Street Bridge.** Another path is steeper still, a winding staircase leading to the Walnut Street pedestrian bridge. It's a

half-mile walk across, and day or night, the scenery's fine. Lights outline the brilliant blue crossbeams; pots of flowers give a garden feel. Benches face upriver towards Maclellan Island and the Hunter Bluff. On the North Shore side have a Madhatter's lemonade, gallery-hop Art'est to In-Town to Mandingo to Tafachady; choose between a book By the Bridge or skates-to-rent from the Bike Shop; relish a steak from the Town and Country, an espresso from the Mudpie, or an apple from Bridge Produce. Coming back, relax on the benches facing west for views of Aquarium peaks, steeples, and mountains; catch a killer sunset too.

3.**Cross under the road** at the amphitheater, and head back west on the other side of the street. RiverSet apartments are on your left, where lucky people have downtown at their fingertips. Soon you're back in the grassy lower reaches of the Park, near cascading waters and pretty pools. Rest and talk. Step to Aquarium Foods for a snack, Friday's for a meal or a stint at the bar. Across the street is Two Twelve Market dining, inside or on the upper deck. Just up Broad, there's the Big River for a brew; it's one block more to a sandwich at the Yellow Sub. And of course, the Shuttle can drop you off free of charge anywhere along the way to the ChooChoo.

RiverWalk Part 2, At the Boathouse. Park near the Sandbar Restaurant; have your favorite kind of drink on the patio; walk to the Boathouse on the boardwalk and watch a whole lotta rowing going on; join the Club and add rowing to your walking jaunts. Cross the little bridge and go around the water tanks; you'll find a Tennessee-American Water Company interpretive park of pipes in red-yellow-blue with a five-foot-high flowing faucet and an explanation of how we get our water.

RiverWalk Part 3, Riverpark to Dam. Start at Riverpark or beside the Dam and enjoy the upstream portion of RiverWalk; you may see redbuds blooming or kites flying or someone stringing a freshly caught fish; plans call for the path to eventually connect with the Ross's Landing portion. You could probably spend the afternoon at the playground or the picnic area. Note the River Mile markers in the sidewalk. And, of course, admire the bottom-side view of the Dam's floodgates; go when they're open after a heavy rainstorm for a fabulous display of the power of nature.

Guided Tours Around Chattanooga

Sometimes it's nice to let someone else show you the sights; it's also a good idea for an introduction to the city if you're visiting or just moving in.

♦ **CARTA Electric Shuttle,** *629-1473*, a mini-tour of downtown on the free shuttle between the ChooChoo and the Aquarium, not narrated.

♦ **ChooChoo Express Tours,** *892-9758*, packaged city tours, 2 hours to full day. Professional guide service for ChooChoo and train tour, Civil War and Lookout Mountain tour, Southern Belle river tour, or a narrated drive through historic downtown. Tours can be customized to meet the needs of your group of 5 or more -- van, bus or step-on guide.

♦ **ChooChoo Scenic Drive,** follow the ChooChoo markers for a scenic drive-yourself around the city. With map in hand, you'll understand. Beginning at Ross's Landing, the tour winds through downtown, then to the Lookout Mountain area and Battlefield. Copies of the map are available at the Visitor's Bureau.

♦ **Mini-Tours Inc,** *488-9632,* this guide service offers three popular tours: Tour 1 takes you up historic Lookout Mountain for a visit to Point Park, Cravens House, and other Civil War battle sites; Tour 2 visits Chickamauga Battlefield, scene of the bloodiest two-day battle of the Civil War; Tour 3 offers evening dining plus a ride to a mountain top for an unforgettable nighttime valley view. Narrated tours pick up at downtown hotels; call for info, reservations.

♦ **Scenic Flights with Ellsworth Aviation,** *894-4930,* our varied landscape makes for interesting flight-seeing. Ellsworth will fly you over your favorite spots, and some you may not even know about.

Great Tours Out-of-Town

You have a three-day weekend? Not enough time to take a trip, you think. "Guess I'd better stay home and clean the house," you say to yourself, with a sigh. You're tired of hearing your neighbors talk on and on about their trip to Mexico. You had to put braces on the middle kid, and the oldest one takes music lessons and sings in the choir. That's quite a commitment of time and money.

Those things needn't keep you from going places! Short trips taken regularly can add up to weeks of vacation in a year's time. Every day you spend "out there" exploring and visiting someplace new, put a marble in a jar. At the end of the year, count your marbles! The experiences they represent are inside you, and experiences can't rust, won't wear out, and will still be there when you're too old to rock the rocking chair.

Look at the map on page 4. You'll see that Chattanooga is the center of the X in a crossroads of Interstates that can move us quickly to four large cities -- Atlanta, Birmingham, Knoxville, and Nashville, with Huntsville just over two hours west on excellent roads. In three days time, you can:

♦ Spend each day exploring away from the city in a different direction, and spend the nights at home.
♦ Spend two nights in one city, exploring it at leisure.
♦ Make a "loop" trip, spending two nights away, each in a different city.

This concept works just as well for a week's vacation time! Here are some suggested trips, times and mileages. Always call ahead to be sure when things are open.

Day Trips to Different Places

♦ It's just over a hundred miles to Knoxville, Atlanta and Huntsville. That's three easy trips! Take the kids to the Space Center in Huntsville, SciTrek in Atlanta, and the Knoxville Zoo. That will sharpen their minds for school! Crash in your own bed every night.

Two Nights in One Place

♦ Perhaps you enjoy sleeping late and visiting historic and beautiful old homes. Head up to Nashville and slow-tour The Hermitage and Cheekwood and Belle Meade. Learn about Andrew Jackson, stroll in beautiful gardens, think about plantation living. Maybe your reveries of the past will coax you onto a riverboat for an evening dinner. You *will* come home relaxed.

Loop Tours -- Two Nights, Two Places

Look at the X on the map.

♦ Chattanooga to Atlanta to Birmingham to Chattanooga. *420 miles, 8 hours total driving time.* Crazy about sports and TV? In Atlanta tour CNN, visit the Omni complex; in Birmingham visit the Alabama Sports Hall of Fame. Both cities host Olympic events, so have the "fever."

♦ Chattanooga to Birmingham to Huntsville to Chattanooga. *360 miles, 7 hours total driving time.* Like the great outdoors? In Birmingham camp at Oak Mountain State Park in the state's most rugged mountains; in Huntsville enjoy the scenery beyond your campfire atop 1,800 foot Monte Sano.

♦ Chattanooga to Huntsville to Nashville to Chattanooga. *370 miles, 7 hours total driving time.* Can't get enough country music? Head towards Huntsville for the Tennessee Valley Old Time Fiddlers Convention, then polish it off with a visit to Nashville's Grand Ole Opry. Get tickets ahead!

♦ Chattanooga to Nashville to Knoxville to Chattanooga. *425 miles, 8 hours total driving time.* Studying state history? Free-tour the State Capitol and the Tennessee State Museum, drive east to Knoxville, the first state capital, see Blount Mansion and Ramsey House, political centers in their day.

Remember, those driving hours are spread over three days, and you have the chance to enjoy two entirely different places and see a lot of interesting scenery.

Here's a guide to our five "sister" cities, and our own Olympic site, with a special jaunt into North Carolina. For our friends who live there, just turn the map around and come this way! Remember the change in time zones.

Atlanta, Georgia

♦ **Population 394,017. Metro Population 2,833,511. Elevation 1,050 feet. Area code 404. Time zone Eastern.**

♦ **Convention and Visitors Bureau, 222-6688, 233 Peachtree St NE, Suite 2000, Zip 30303. Welcome Centers at Underground Atlanta, Peachtree Center Mall, Lenox Square Mall.**

♦ **From Chattanooga: Main route I-75. 120 miles. 2 hours plus.**

Georgia's capital city may have been leveled during the Civil War, but it's the place to go now if you want to see skyscrapers, luxury shops, and major league sports. Its 29 colleges include Georgia Tech, Georgia State, and Emory. It's a big city filled with cultural activities, great restaurants, and entertainment for every age.

Free Stuff to Do

♦ State Capitol in Capitol Square, *656-2844, open Mon-Fri.*

♦ Georgia State Museum of Science & Industry; in capitol. Exhibits of wildlife, fish, minerals; dioramas of Georgia industry, *open Mon-Fri.*

♦ Martin Luther King, Jr. National Historic Site, *524-1956,* 2-block area in memory of famed leader of civil rights movement and winner of Nobel Peace Prize, *open daily 9-5:30.*

♦ Underground Atlanta, *523-2311,* bounded by Wall, Washington, S. Peachtree and Martin Luther King Jr Dr. The marketplace area is the birthplace of Atlanta. Six-block area with promenades, fountains, shops, restaurants, *open daily.*

Art and Museums

♦ Robert W. Woodruff Arts Center, *898-9284, 1280 Peachtree St NE.* Largest arts complex in the SE. Includes High Museum of Art, European art from early Renaissance to present; Symphony Hall, home of Atlanta Symphony, *892-2414;* Alliance Theatre Company, *892-2414.*

♦ Museum of Jimmy Carter Library, *331-0296, One Copenhill Ave.* Exhibits of life in White House, full-scale replica of Oval Office. *Open daily.*

♦ SciTrek. Science and Technology Museum, *522-5500, 395 Piedmont Ave NE.* Self-guided tour of over 100 hands-on exhibits. *Open Tue-Sun.*

♦ Fernbank Science Center. *378-4311, 156 Heaton Park Dr NE.* Exhibit hall, observatory, planetarium, 65-acre forest with trails. Hrs vary.

Historical Homes and Gardens

♦ Atlanta History Center, *261-1837, 3101 Andrews Dr NW.* 4 structures, 32 acres. Includes: McElreath Hall, where museum exhibits focus on Atlanta history, *open Mon-Sat;* Swan House, a classic example of early 20th century architecture, fountains, gardens, *open daily;* Tullie Smith Farm, an 1840 farmhouse, craft demonstrations.

♦ Wren's Nest, *753-8535, 1050 Ralph D. Abernathy Blvd SW.* Victorian house of Joel Chandler Harris, transcriber of "Uncle Remus" stories; *open Tue-Sun.*

♦ Atlanta Botanical Garden, *876-5858, 1345 Piedmont Rd.* 15 acres of outdoor gardens; *open Tue-Sun.*

Entertainment and Tours

♦ Cable News Network studio tour, *827-2300, CNN Center, Techwood Dr & Marietta St.*

♦ World of Coca-Cola, *676-5151, 55 Martin Luther King Jr Dr.* Interactive displays and exhibits trace history of Coca-Cola; *open daily.*

♦ Six Flags Over Georgia, *948-9290, 12 mi W via I-20, exit Six Flags parkway.* Family theme park. Over 100 rides, coasters, live shows. *Summer daily.*

♦ Stone Mountain Park, *498-5600, 19 mi E on US 78.* 3,200-acre park surrounds world's largest granite monolith, rising 825 feet from the plain. Monument to Confederacy depicts Lee, Jackson and Davis. Memorial Hall, Civil War Museum, antebellum plantation with 19 restored buildings; Riverboat Scarlett O'Hara provides trips around lake; railroad travels 5 miles around base of mountain. Laser show in evenings, 732-bell carillon plays concerts. Also 10 miles of nature trails, beach, tennis, golf, ice-skating. *Hrs vary.*

Events and Side Trips

◆ North Georgia State Fair, *423-1330, Miller Park. Late September.*

◆ On the Way and Off the Path you can stop at Chickamauga, LaFayette, Ringgold, Tunnel Hill, Varnell, Dalton, Resaca, Rome, Adairsville, Kingston, Cassville, Cartersville, Kennesaw, Marietta, Dallas, and Lithia Springs -- all a part of the Blue and Gray Trail. If history is your pursuit, you'll find battlefield parks, monuments and cemeteries in these towns.

Special Side Trip to Morgan County, Georgia

◆ An hour east of Atlanta on **I-20**, then north on **Hwy 441,** is the town of **Madison,** famous for something that didn't happen. In 1864, as **General Sherman** marched through on his way to a Union victory, a delegation led by native son **Senator Joshua Hill** asked him to spare the torch. Sherman and Hill's brother had been friends at West Point, and Hill had not voted for secession; Sherman honored the request and left the town untouched.

◆ As a result, Madison is blessed with a number of **lovely antebellum homes** and **historic churches** along its **tree-lined streets.** Start at the **Madison-Morgan Cultural Center,** *342-4743, 434 S Main St, open Tue-Sun,* where you can see Senator Hill's uniform and other **Civil War memorabilia,** as well as regional history and rotating art exhibits. Get a walking-tour guide here -- there are 45 points of interest you'll see as you stroll through the community. Down the street is **Heritage Hall,** you can tour this house museum; it was built in 1833, with furnishings of the period. Other homes may be toured during the May and December **Tour of Homes,** *342-4454;* some are bed and breakfasts.

◆ If you're planning on staying overnight, try **The Burnett Place,** *342-4034, 317 Old Post Rd,* where you'll be served high tea, or the **Boat House,** *342-3061, 383 Porter St,* a non-smoking establishment. There is southern gourmet dining in **Katy's on Main,** *342-1020, 270 S Main St,* located in another antebellum home. On the antebellum trail, this town was on the stage route from Charleston to New Orleans. Some of the south's **earliest colleges** were located here, and one of the first female colleges. Many **movies** have been filmed here to take advantage of its **19th century atmosphere**. Spring flower displays are worth a trip to see in this **picturesque town**.

◆ Nearby is **Lake Oconee,** a 19,000-acre lake with 374 miles of shoreline. North on **US 441** in **Athens** are many other antebellum homes which can be toured. Also in Athens is the **Tree That Owns Itself** -- a white oak tree growing on a plot deeded to it, and **Sandy Creek Nature Center,** *613-3615, off US 441,* with 200 acres of **woods, marshland, and nature trails**.

Birmingham, Alabama

♦ **Population 265,968. Metro Population 907,810. Elevation 601 feet. Area code 205. Time zone Central.**
♦ **Greater Birmingham Convention & Visitors Bureau, 252-9825, 2200 9th Ave N, Zip 35203. Birmingham/Jefferson Visitor Information Center, 254-1654, 1201 University Blvd, Zip 35233**
♦ **From Chattanooga: Main route I-24, then I-59. 155 miles. 3 hours.**

Steel City, once called the Pittsburgh of the South, is now better known as an international medical center. Staking claim to the end of the Appalachian Chain, this city's hills provide great views and the basis for recreation and sightseeing. Downtown's renaissance put Birmingham Green in this modern, progressive city. Take a trip to the heart of the south!

Free Stuff to Do

♦ Birmingham Botanical Gardens, *879-1227, 2612 Land Park Rd.* Conservatory and arboretum of rare plants and trees. Touch and see trail for disabled. Includes Japanese Gardens, bonsai complex, Zen garden. *Open daily.*

♦ Birmingham Museum of Art, *254-2565, 2000 8th Ave N.* Collection of Renaissance, Asian and American art. Remington bronzes, and pre-Columbian artifacts. Largest collection of Wedgwood outside of England. *Open Tue-Sun.*

♦ Ruffner Mountain Nature Center, *833-8264, 1214 S 81st St.* 538 acres of the last undeveloped section of this area's Appalachian Mountains. Wildlife refuge with nature trails. *Open Tue-Sun.*

♦ Sloss Furnaces National Historic Landmark, *324-1911, 20 32nd St.* An industrial museum and site for downtown festivals. *Open Tue-Sun.*

Art and Museums

♦ Alabama Sports Hall of Fame Museum, *323-6665, Civic Center Blvd & 22nd St N.* Showcase for memorabilia of Alabama sports figures, theater. *Open Mon-Sat.*

♦ Birmingham Civil Rights Institute, *328-9696, 520 16th St N,* City's historic Civil Rights District includes Kelly Ingram Park; facility's exhibits portray World War I racial separation to present-day racial progress. *Open daily.*

♦ Discovery Place, *933-4142, 939-1177, 1320 22nd St,* Museum for children, hands-on exhibits; science and technology, natural science, energy exhibits. *Open daily.*

♦ Red Mountain Museum, *933-4142, 939-1177, 1421 22nd St S,* Natural history museum located on slopes of Red Mountain. 14-ft mosasaur, geologic history displays and exhibits. Walkway carved into face of mountain exposes more than 150 million years of geologic history. Audio tours. *Open daily.*

♦ See Birmingham Museum of Art above.

♦ See Sloss Furnaces above.

Historical Homes and Gardens

♦ Arlington, *780-5656, 331 Cotton Ave SW*. Antebellum house, diverse collection of 19th century American decorative art. Located on a sloping hill in Elyton, surrounded by oak and magnolia trees. *Open Tue-Sun*.

♦ See Birmingham Botanical Gardens above.

Entertainment and Tours

♦ Oak Mountain State Park, *663-6771, 15 mi S on I-65, exit 246*. Peavine Falls and Gorge and two lakes sit amidst 9,940 acres of state's most rugged mountains. Swimming, hiking, backpacking, bridle trails, camping. Demonstration farm.

♦ Rickwood Caverns State Park, *647-9692, 20 mi N on I-65, exit 284*. 380-acre park offers swimming, hiking. One-hour tours of cave with 260-million-year-old limestone formations. *Summer daily*.

♦ Vulcan, *328-6198, Valley View Dr off US 31, top of Red Mountain in Vulcan Park*. One of largest iron figures ever cast, 55 feet tall, 60 tons. Pedestal 124 feet high. Made of Birmingham iron and cast locally. Observation deck. *Open daily*.

Events and Side Trips

♦ State Fair, *787-2641, Fairground W on Bessemer Rd US 11*. *Mid-October*.

♦ On the Way and Off the Path you'll find Ft. Payne, Mentone, Noccalula Falls Park, DeSoto State Park, Little River Canyon, and Sequoyah Caverns. Ride the Alabama Princess Riverboat on the Coosa River in Gadsden. And shop, shop, shop at 140 outlet stores in Boaz, the U. S. Flea Market Mall in Albertville or the Mountain Top Flea Market in Attalla.

Special Side Trip to Walker County, Alabama

♦ Travel a little farther west on **Hwy 78** to **Sumiton** in **Walker County**; turn left on County Road 81 and travel 2.8 miles to the **Alabama Mining Museum**, *648-2442, 120 East Street, Dora, open daily till 4*. Florence Wiley and Sarah Kate Troup will give you a tour of the facility, which depicts the **coal mines** and their development from 1890 to 1940. Lots of interesting pictures and memorabilia; plus you'll see a **coal car, mining tools,** and rooms set up to show the miner's life -- the doctor's office, post office, time office, and the company store, where small coins called **"clackers"** were used as money. More than five mines are operating in that area of the state today in fully automated style; they are not open for touring, although you'll see the heavily loaded coal-hauling trucks on the highway.

♦ Continue west on Hwy 78 to the **Black Warrior River**. Just west of the river is red-tin-roofed **Uncle Mort's** on your left, stop for a treat in this unique **Country Store-Smokehouse-Restaurant**. Open early-morning to late-evening daily, they serve breakfast all day: the ham, bacon and porkchops are cured inhouse; all served with **sorghum syrup, biscuits** and **redeye gravy**. If you don't want breakfast, order steak, catfish, frog legs, barbecue platters or a simple smoked turkey sandwich. There's a big stone fireplace and board-and-beam ceilings; family portraits mix with antique-store finds in gilt-framed charm; stop by the front door to read all the writeups about the place. Check out the store for a **coal-miner statue** carved of **southern bituminous coal**, or buy **smokehouse meat** by the pound.

♦ Continue west to the county seat of **Jasper,** where a hundred years ago there were six coal mines and four hundred **coke ovens** operating. Today a branch of the **University of Alabama** is located here on a 37-acre campus; drive through lovely residential areas; stop at **Posey's Hardware Store,** *384-4174, 1919 8th Ave,* where they say "if you can't find it here, you don't need it"; in the downtown **Methodist Church,** a plaque recalls the visit of **President Franklin Roosevelt** when he attended the funeral of **Speaker Bankhead** -- they built a special ramp to accommodate his wheelchair.

♦ If you want to stay **overnight,** try the **Old Harbin Hotel,** *697-5652* in **Nauvoo,** west on Hwy 5. A **historical landmark**, it was built in 1923, and is furnished in period antiques; pine walls are original and guest rooms have their original numbers. If you are interested in **camping,** proceed west on Hwy 78 to **Townley;** turn left on Hwy 102. Travel 6.5 miles to Frozen Hollow Road and the Bowaters-owned **Wolf Creek Forest Camp,** a primitive site adjoining the **Wolf Creek State Game Management Area.** Contact **Bowaters** in advance at *387-1214.* If you are interested in **fishing,** travel Hwy 69 north out of Jasper to **Lewis Smith Lake.** **Smith Dam** is located on the **Sipsey Fork** of the Black Warrior River and creates a 21,000-acre lake with 500 miles of shoreline. One of the largest earth and rock-filled dams in the United States, it is 2,200 feet long and 300 feet high. Continue north on Hwy 69 to its intersection with **I-65,** where you'll find the interesting city of **Cullman,** with its **German influence,** and farther north, **Huntsville.**

Huntsville, Alabama

♦ **Population 159,789. Metro Population 238,912. Elevation 641 feet. Area code 205. Time Zone Central.**
♦ **Tourist Information Center, 551-2230 or 800/843-0468, 24-hour events hot-line 533-5723, Von Braun Civic Center, 700 Monroe St., Zip 35801.**
♦ **From Chattanooga: I-24 , then US72 through S Pittsburg, Scottsboro. 110 miles. 2 hours plus.**

Huntsville is truly where the old and the new in Alabama meet. It's called the "Birthplace of Alabama" because in 1819 the constitutional convention of Alabama Territory met here and set up the state legislature. Many houses remain from that period. Today, it's a city deeply involved in space exploration -- the George C. Marshall Space Flight Center of NASA opened here on July 1, 1960. It's gracefully situated in a curving valley. Go see!

Free Stuff to Do

♦ Big Spring International Park. Spragins St W of Courthouse Square. The town's water supply, this natural spring produces 24 million gallons daily. Around this spring the town grew.

♦ Burritt Museum & Park, *535-2882, 3101 Burritt Dr.* Unusual 11-room house built in shape of cross. Exhibitions on southern women, gems and minerals, archaeology. 167-acre park also has 3 authentically furnished cabins, other buildings; panoramic view of city. *Afternoons Mar-Dec Tue-Sun.*

♦ Huntsville Museum of Art, *535-4350, Von Braun Civic Center, 700 Monroe St SW.* Five galleries, traditional and contemporary work, regional and national artists. *Open Tue-Sun.*

Art and Museums

♦ Constitution Hall Village, *535-6565, 301 Madison St.* Recreated complex of buildings commemorating Alabama's entry into the Union in 1819. Period craft demonstrations and activities, guides in period dress. *Open Mon-Sat.*

♦ See Huntsville Museum of Art above.

Historical Homes and Gardens

♦ Huntsville Depot, *539-1860, 320 Church St.* Opened in 1860 as passenger house, depot was captured by Union troops and used as prison; Civil War graffiti survives. *Open Tue-Sat, closed Jan-Feb.*

♦ See Constitution Hall Village above.

♦ Twickenham Historic District, *551-2230, Downtown, S and E of Courthouse Sq.* Living museum of antebellum architecture; contains Alabama's largest concentration of houses. Several occupied by descendants of original builders. For tours contact Visitors Bureau.

Entertainment and Tours

♦ Madison County Nature Trail, *883-9501, 12 mi SE on S Shawdee Rd.* Green Mountain. Original house on first homestead. Chapel, covered bridge, lake, waterfall, trails, Braille trail. *Open daily.*

♦ Monte Sano State Park, *534-3757, 4 mi E off US 431.* A 2,140-acre scenic recreation area on top of 1,800 foot Monte Sano (Mountain of Health). Hiking, picnicking, camping, cabins, amphitheater. *Open all year.*

♦ US Space and Rocket Center. *5 mi W on AL 20 just off I-565 at Space Center exit.* Hands-on space exhibits, tour of NASA Space Shuttle programs and domed theater. Spacedome; Space Shuttle and science films photographed by astronauts, Omnimax system. NASA Bus tours, *837-3400,* Escorted 90-minute bus trips through Space Center featuring mission control, Space Shuttle components. *Open daily.*

Events and Side Trips:

♦ Northeast Alabama State Fair. Jaycees Fairgrounds. Regional fair involving five area counties. *Early Sept.*

♦ Tennessee Valley Old Time Fiddlers Convention at nearby Athens College, *233-8100, October.*

♦ On the Way and Off the Path you'll find Bridgeport, Stevenson, Scottsboro, Guntersville, and Mooresville. This is Tennessee River country with Guntersville Dam and Wheeler Dam creating lakes for fishing and water sports, and a wildlife refuge for wintering migratory birds. Mooresville once was home to Andrew Johnson, our 17th President. Its post office has been in continual operation since 1819.

Knoxville, Tennessee

- **Population 165,121. Metro Population 604,816. Elevation 936 feet. Area code 615, after September 1995 423. Time zone Eastern.**
- **Knoxville Convention & Visitors Bureau, 523-2316, 500 Henley St, PO Box 15012, Zip 37901.**
- **From Chattanooga: Main route I-75. 115 miles. 2 hours plus.**

Today's Knoxville is these six letters -- UTK and TVA -- and it's the gateway to the Smokies. Located in the state's Mountainous East Region, it was the first capital of Tennessee, and a frontier outpost on the edge of the Cherokee Indian nation, last stop on the way west. In addition to the football and foliage, you should see its dogwood-lined streets in the spring.

Free Stuff to Do

- McClung Historical Collection, *544-5744, East Tenn Historical Center, 314 W Clinch Ave.* More than 35,000 volumes of history and genealogy covering Tennessee and the southeastern U. S. *Open Mon-Fri.*
- Old City Historic District, *522-9070, Jackson Ave & Central St.* Restored historic center of downtown.

Art and Museums

- East Tennessee Discovery Center, *637-1121, 516 N Beaman St.* Exhibits on life, energy, transportation, fossils; includes aquarium and planetarium. *Open Tue-Sat.*
- Knoxville Museum of Art, *525-6101, 410 10th St.* Four galleries, gardens, graphics, Native American paintings. *Open Tue-Sun.*

Historical Homes and Gardens

- Confederate Memorial Hall, *522-2371, 3148 Kingston Pike SW.* Antebellum mansion, headquarters of Confederate Gen. James Longstreet during siege of Knoxville. Contains collection of southern and Civil War relics, library of southern literature. *Open Tue-Fri.*
- General James White's Fort, *525-6514, 205 E Hill Ave.* Original pioneer house built by founder and first settler of Knoxville. *Open Mar-Dec Mon-Sat.*
- Governor William Blount Mansion, *525-2375, 200 W Hill Ave.* Blount was Governor of the SW Territory and signer of the US Constitution. Restored to period of late 1700's. *Open Mar-Nov Tue-Sun, Nov-Feb Tue-Fri.*
- Marble Springs, *573-5508, 6 mi S via US 441, TN 33, E on TN 168.* Restored farmhouse of John Sevier, state's first governor. 36 acres. *Open Tue-Sun.*
- Ramsey House (Swan Pond), *546-0745, 6 mi NE on Thorngrove Pike.* First stone house in Knox County; social, religious, political center of early

Tennessee; restored gabled house, period furnishings. *Open Apr-Oct Tues-Sun.*

Entertainment and Tours

♦ Knoxville Zoological Gardens, 637-5331, *E via I-40, Rutledge Pike exit.* 1,000 animals in a park-like setting; big cats, gorillas, marine animals, elephant and camel rides. *Open daily.*

♦ Star of Knoxville, 525-7827, *300 Neyland Drive.* Riverboat offers dinner and lunch cruises. *Open May-Dec.*

Events and Side Trips

♦ Artfest, 523-7543, Citywide celebration, art shows, entertainment, barbecue cooking contest, theatricals. *Late Aug-early Oct.*

♦ Dogwood Arts Festival, 522-8733, 150 events, 80 public and private gardens on display, 60 miles of marked dogwood trails for auto or bus tours. *Mid-late April.*

♦ Tennessee Valley Fair, 637-5840, *Chilhowee Park. Early-mid Sept.*

♦ On the Way and Off the Path you'll find Cleveland, Athens, Decatur, Sweetwater, Lenoir City, Oak Ridge, Maryville, Walland, Sevierville, Pigeon Forge, Gatlinburg, Townsend, Tellico Plains, Benton and Ocoee. Some are river cities, others are tucked away in the mountains. Explore your way through them all! Watch for crafts fairs during fall foliage.

Nashville, Tennessee

♦ **Population 488,374. Metro Population 965,026. Elevation 440 feet. Area code 615. Time zone Central.**

♦ **Nashville Area Chamber of Commerce, 259-4747, 161 4th Ave N, Zip 37219. Phone 259-4700, Nashville Tourist Information Center, I-65 & James Robertson Pkwy, exit 85.**

♦ **From Chattanooga: Main route I-24. 135 miles. 2 hours plus.**

When you think of Nashville, do you think of this? It's in the Heartland of Tennessee. It's our state capital. It's Music City, USA, first in the nation in country music recording. It's a city of publishing firms. It's a city of colleges, including Vanderbilt. It's a city with green trees, vista hills, the Cumberland River, great places to eat, and many fun and interesting places to see. Go!

Free Stuff to Do

♦ Fort Nashborough. *170 1st Ave N, N end of Riverfront Park.* Replica of pioneer fort, stockaded walls, exhibits of pioneer implements. *Open daily.*

♦ State Capitol, 741-1621, *6th & Charlotte Ave.* Tours. *Open Mon-Fri.*

♦ Tennessee State Museum, 741-2692, *James K. Polk State Bldg., 5th & Deaderick.* Exhibits on life in Tennessee from early man through early 1900's. *Open Tue-Sun.*

Art and Museums

♦ Country Music Hall of Fame and Museum, 256-1639, *4 Music Square E. Open daily.*

♦ Cumberland Science Museum, *862-5160, 800 Ridley Blvd.* Planetarium, live animal and science programs. *Open daily summer, Tue-Sun rest of year.*

♦ Nashville Toy Museum, *883-8870, 2613-B McGavock Pike.* Antique toys, china dolls, lead soldiers, 250 toy and model locomotives. *Open daily.*

♦ Parthenon, *862-8431, Centennial Park, W End Ave & 25th Ave N.* Replica of Parthenon of Pericles time. Houses 19th and 20th century artworks, changing exhibits. *Open Tue-Sat, Sun summer.*

Historical Homes and Gardens

♦ Belle Meade, *356-0501, Harding Rd & Leake Ave, 7 mi SW.* Mansion once part of 5,300-acre working plantation. Was considered greatest Thoroughbred breeding farm in country. *Open daily.*

♦ Belmont Mansion. *269-9537, 1900 Belmont Blvd.* Style of Italian villa. *Open daily.*

♦ Cheekwood/Museum and Gardens, *353-2140, 8 mi SW on Forrest Park Dr.* Cultural center on 55 acres, public greenhouses, five major gardens. *Open daily.*

♦ Hermitage, *889-2941, 12 mi E off I-40 exit 221A.* Residence of President Andrew Jackson. 600-acre estate. Visitor Center and museum. *Open daily.*

Entertainment and Tours

♦ Belle Carol Riverboats: Music City Queen or Captain Ann. Board at Riverfront Park Dock. Cumberland River cruises, *244-3430.*

♦ General Jackson, Cumberland River. 300-foot paddlewheel showboat, musical stage show, *889-6611.*

♦ Grand Ole Opry bus tours include houses of country music stars, Music Row, recording studios, backstage at Grand Ole Opry, *889-9490.*

♦ Grand Ole Opry, *889-3060,* Live radio show featuring the best in country music, studio seats 4,400. *Weekends all year.*

♦ Opryland, *889-6611, 10 mi E on I-40, 4 mi N on Briley Pkwy, exit 11.* 120-acre entertainment park, coasters, music, petting zoo. *Summer daily. After Labor Day, weekends.*

♦ Ryman Auditorium & Museum, *254-1445, 116 5th Ave N.* Home of Grand Ole Opry from 1943-1974. Walking tours. *Open daily.*

Events and Side Trips

♦ Tennessee State Fair, *862-8980, Fairgrounds, Wedgewood Ave & Rains. Box 40208-Melrose Station, 37204. Mid-September.*

♦ On the Way and Off the Path you'll find Smyrna, Murfreesboro, Milton, McMinnville, Fall Creek Falls, Pelham, Monteagle, Sewanee, Tracy City, Altamont, Beersheba Springs, Bell Buckle, Wartrace, Haley, Normandy, Tullahoma -- all with special historical, geographical and just plain interesting things to see. For instance, Bell Buckle has two festivals: Quilt Walk is the 3rd Saturday in September and offers a quilt exhibition and home tour, *389-6174.* Or go in October for the Webb School Arts and Crafts Festival, *389-9322.*

Inspectors and reviewers for Chattanooga Great Places *accept no free meals or favors; the book has no sponsors or advertisers.*

1996 Summer Olympics
Whitewater Competition Site in Tennessee
Plus Cherokee, North Carolina and More

The Olympic Canoeing/Kayaking Whitewater Slalom Event of the Centennial Olympic Games

♦ If you're interested in attending the event, or just enjoying a visit to the site, you'll want to know these facts. The Ocoee River is beautiful to see anytime of the year. Nestled in a hollow of the Blue Ridge Mountains, it's where Tennessee, North Carolina and Georgia come together. The Channel for the Event is a natural river bed, given an assist. The rapids were enhanced by the addition of large rocks with a mass sufficient to prevent their movement. This narrowed the Channel from a 200-foot width down to 100 feet. A bridge was constructed to allow access to the left bank of the river. After the Event, the Ocoee Whitewater Center remains. See p.121 for outfitters and lodgings in the area.

♦ **Date:** Practice July 26, Event July 27 and 28, 1996
♦ **Place:** Ocoee River, Polk County, Tennessee
♦ **Participants:** 150 athletes from 25 countries
♦ **Class:** Men's Single Kayak (K-1), Women's Single Kayak (K-2), Men's Single Canoe (C-1), Men's Double Canoe (C-2)
♦ **Layout:** 600 meter channel with Class IV rapids, 25 gates
♦ **Gate:** two striped poles suspended by a cable spanning the river
♦ **Contest:** racers wind through green-striped gates downstream, red-striped gates upstream
♦ **Penalty Points:** 5 seconds for touching a gate, 50 seconds for missing a gate, negotiating wrong direction, pushing aside a pole

Following are two choices for loop trips to get to the Olympic Site and the Cherokee Indian Reservation in North Carolina, each is approximately 325 miles, with 6-7 hours of driving time. Remember you'll be driving on winding mountain roads for much of the journey; allow yourself plenty of time to stop and smell the evergreens.

♦ **Loop 1:** Chattanooga to Cleveland, the Ocoee Site, and Ducktown, TN via Hwy 64; cross into North Carolina and continue on Hwy 64 to Murphy and Franklin; at Franklin access Hwy 441 and proceed north to Cherokee. To return, access Hwy 129 through Bryson City and Murphy; access Hwy 64 and continue past the Ocoee Site, Cleveland, and Chattanooga. *325 miles, 7 hours.*

♦ **Loop 2:** Chattanooga to Cleveland, the Ocoee Site, and Ducktown, TN via Hwy 64; cross into North Carolina and continue on Hwy 64 to Murphy and Franklin; at Franklin access Hwy 441 and proceed north to Cherokee. To return, continue north on 441 to Clingman's Dome, highest point in Tennessee, to Gatlinburg, and Knoxville. In Knoxville, access I-75 and proceed south to Chattanooga. *326 miles. 6.5 hours.*

Things to See and Do

Cleveland, Tennessee
♦ See the Cherokee Chieftain in downtown Johnston Park; carved from a tree, it's the state's only Peter Toth sculpture; he's done one for all 50 states. There are several good tours around the Cleveland area: a self-guiding Cherokee Heritage Wildlife Tour and a Cherokee Scenic Loop Tour; there's also a downtown historic walking tour. Get information at the Visitors Bureau, *472-6587, 2145 Keith St.*

Ducktown, Tennessee
♦ Ducktown Basin Museum, *496-5778,* located at the Burra Burra Mine site and listed on the National Register; traces history of copper mining in the basin. *Open Mon-Sat.*

Franklin, North Carolina
♦ Franklin Gem and Mineral Society, *704-369-7831, 2 W Main St.* Check out the 48-pound ruby here; you can dig for your own rubies and sapphires at several mines in the area and even have your rough stones cut into gems. Overnight at the Buttonwood Inn, *704-369-8985, 190 Georgia Rd.*

Cherokee, North Carolina
♦ In this little town surrounded by the magnificent Smoky Mountains, stop at the Cherokee Historical Association and learn about the 58,000-acre reservation, known as the Qualla Boundary.

♦ Museum of the Cherokee Indian, *704-497-3481, Drama Rd;* this modern museum chronicles 10,000 years of Cherokee history.

♦ Oconaluftee Indian Village, *704-497-2315,* a reproduction of how the Eastern Band of the Cherokees lived 200 years ago; demonstrations of Indian crafts.

♦ Mountainside Theatre, *704-497-2111,* the drama *Unto These Hills* has been performed for more than 45 years; it's the story of how the Cherokees were driven west on the Trail of Tears.

Bryson City, North Carolina
♦ **The Great Smoky Mountain Railroad,** *800-872-4681,* will take you through the **Nantahala Gorge** in open-air cars; the 4-hour excursion goes into remote mountain areas and crosses Fontana Lake.

♦ **Nantahala Outdoor Center,** *800-232-7238,* you can go whitewater rafting on five Appalachian rivers, have a meal, or stay the night.

Clingman's Dome
♦ This is the highest point in the state of Tennessee, 6,643 feet plus an observation tower. When you cross the North Carolina/Tennessee state line, stop at the overlook and get a picture with one foot on each side.

Gatlinburg, Tennessee
♦ Gatlinburg Welcome Center, *436-7318, Foothills Parkway,* Great Smoky Mountains National Park exhibits and information.

♦ Great Smoky Arts & Crafts Community, *436-3301,* visit shops, studios and galleries of over 80 artists and craftsmen in an 8-mile loop, or ride the Arts & Crafts Trolley.

For more places, get *Day Trips: Chattanooga Plus a Hundred Miles.*

People Who Love Chattanooga
Veda Bucher

"I used to give lots of parties at home; now I do it for the city," says Veda Bucher. She's referring to the networking mixers she plans and hosts for the Chattanooga Convention and Visitors Bureau, which give the hundreds of Bureau members a chance to get together and exchange ideas about making Chattanooga an even more welcoming and wonderful city.

Veda Harvey Bucher is Membership Director for the Chattanooga Convention and Visitors Bureau, a member of the planning committee for the Tennessee State Bicentennial, and a member of the Chamber Area Beautification Committee. Her gardening skills are evident in the lushly planted yard at her home on Big Ridge; her cooking skills evident in the special dinners she cooks for her family when they get together. Her parents Lola and Glenn Harvey live in Chattanooga; daughter Lia is pursuing a Doctor of Pharmacy degree at UT Memphis; son Bryan is studying liberal arts at Wittenberg University in Ohio.

In addition to her hostess-with-the-mostest charm, Veda literally "is" Chattanooga -- she was born here, raised in Brainerd, and went to City High when it was on 3rd Street. She grew up eating hamburgers at the Krystal, rollerskating at the Brainerd Rink, and shopping downtown at Miller's and Loveman's. "We went to the movies at the Brainerd Theatre and to Friday-night football games," Veda smiles, recalling the City-Central rivalry. "My class had over 500 and was the largest ever to graduate from City. That's why I know so many people in Chattanooga -- I went to school with a lot of them!"

After college at Middle Tennessee, Veda worked as a secretary at Combustion and TVA. Then she got married, had children, and became a full-time homemaker. "I loved taking care of my family," Veda says, "and I was a great shopper. I found good bargains at The Leader, and shopped for the children at Margaret's Children's Shop. I learned cake decorating so I could make special family birthday cakes; of course I used that in the other entertaining we did too. I took up gardening and still enjoy that -- there's hardly a nursery anywhere that doesn't know me by name!"

Veda returned to the workforce six years ago. "Not because I had great career plans," she explains, "but I became a single parent and I had to." With no background in sales, but with a flair for organization and a bandbox-pretty style, she used her love of people and knowledge of the city to become a dynamite promoter, two years ago assuming her Bureau role. "I call the Bureau members 'my extended family,'" Veda confesses. "I get interested in what they are doing and find myself pulling for them and their business. I'm glad my work keeps me so involved with people in the community. I really believe in Chattanooga and what I see happening."

"And it truly is the Scenic City," she continues with a smile. "Some cities have mountains, some have water. We have both! I love crossing Chickamauga Dam as I drive home on Highway 153. You can see for miles around from up there. This is a gorgeous place we live in. I'm very proud of my hometown."

Shopping

Contents

The Shop Till You Drop Gang: #1: I never did find that artist's brush I need. #2: I've got to grab some rolls for morning coffee. #3: I can't quit yet! I've still got money left on the credit card. #4: I hear there's good shopping on cruises.

Areas for Shopping

Downtown

General Shopping

♦ Downtown is the place for anyone who enjoys variety, diversity, and old-fashioned charm. Downtown charming? It is; park the car and walk. Don't worry about finding a spot; Broad Street is so broad there's parking on both sides of the tree-shaded median strip. There are park benches for sitting, restaurants in every price range for grabbing a bite or staying a long, long while, and a great variety of interesting places to shop.

♦ People who are lucky enough to work downtown enjoy the close-knit community feel. It's easy to pop in a shop on a lunch hour -- merchants and customers become acquaintances, and often, friends. Those loyalists who have always shopped downtown, and others who prefer the simplicity of city shopping to the bunched-up-in-a-crowd atmosphere of a mall, buy their gifts or office supplies at **T. H. Payne's**, one of the oldest businesses in the city, where they've been selling paper and stationery since 1865. Fischer's began selling jewelry about that time too, and **Fischer-Evans** is still at 8th and Market. Both stores have an impressive history of serving their customers.

♦ Browsing is good downtown; around 7th and Market you can while away the time in **Waldenbooks**, the **Junior League Bargain Mart**, or a block back on Cherry, **Shapiro's** deli potpourri. Drop off your film at **Violet Camera; Margaret's Luncheonette** is out of the basement and open on 7th, ready to serve you, counter-style. Maybe you've been getting your hair done for years at **Mr. Ellis's** on W 8th; you probably make it a point to lunch in the **Blue Cross Cafeteria**, enjoying one of the finest skyline views in town while you eat, plus perusing an ever-changing display of art in this bronze building's spacious lobby; then you stop in at **Joy's** right there on Chestnut to pick up a plant for your new neighbor's housewarming gift.

♦ Other downtown goodies are the **Children's Hour** in the Read House (the kids will really like this books-and-games store), **Martin-Thompson Sporting Goods** on Broad, and for your sweet tooth, **Brock's Candyland** on one end of Market and the **ChooChoo Candy Factory** on the other -- walk it off! Oh, don't forget **Fix's Bakery** halfway in between, at the edge of Miller Plaza facing Cherry.

Warehouse Row Factory Shops, 1110 Market Street
280,000 sq feet, open Mon-Sat 10-7, Sun 12-6

♦ Eight old railroad warehouses, built in the early 1900's, became a downtown mixed-use center and got listed on the National Register. The rustic old brick looks really classy now, with awnings and fountains outside and a three-story atrium inside. Splendid hardwood floors, brass railings, and a bubble elevator, plus 45 shops at 25%-75% off retail.

North Shore

♦ This is downtown expanded, with a collection of interesting galleries, unique new restaurants and old standards, and the place for filling most of your outdoor recreational needs; **Rock/Creek Outfitters** and **River City Bicycles** have well-stocked attractive stores at the corner of Tremont and Frazier. Book stores, art supply shops, the Town and Country shopping center and Waldorff's for women clothing are there; keep going west on **Hixson Pike** for numerous shopping pockets: The Corner at Riverview is especially nice with **CookWorks, Osprey Trading Company, Barrett Books** and **Plum Nelly.**

Shopping Malls -- Where to Go in the 'Burbs

Eastgate Mall, Brainerd Road
700,000 sq feet, open Mon-Sat 10-9, Sun 12-6

♦ It started on Brainerd Road, on the east side of the Ridge. Two 1960's strip centers were joined together to make the area's first large enclosed shopping mall. That was Eastgate, and the year was 1968. It was renovated in 1984, and today, though somewhat outsized by its larger sisters, provides space for 60 stores, anchored by **Proffitt's** and **Goody's.** Along with many strip malls and the general commercial and retail trade on **Brainerd Road,** the area remains a shopping destination. It's doggone handy, that's why!

Northgate Mall, Hwy 153 and Hixson Pike
811,000 sq feet, open Mon-Sat 10-9, Sun 12-6

♦ When Northgate Mall opened in 1972, it was welcomed by residents rapidly settling the north side of the River. It is 10 miles from downtown, but centrally located within Hamilton County. Its 1991 renovation created an inside park which attracts daily checker players and walkers, out for a bit of socializing. You'll find three major department stores -- **Proffitt's, J. C. Penney, and Sears** -- a **Belk's for Her,** and 100 specialty stores, such as **Casual Corner, J. Riggings, The Gap,** and virtually everything from antiques to video. There's plenty of parking here and restaurants, movie theaters, and numerous strip malls nearby. Hixson Pike, Hwy 153, and newly created Northpoint Road are literally exploding with shopping opportunities; notice the number of bank branches recently opened.

♦ On Hwy 153 around Northgate you'll find **Toys R Us, Goody's,** and more malls -- Kmart, WalMart, Gadd Crossing, Plaza, Bi-Lo, and Northgate Antiques; on Hixson Pike is another Bi-Lo, and Suyen Plaza.

Inspectors and reviewers for Chattanooga Great Places *accept no free meals or favors; the book has no sponsors or advertisers.*

Hamilton Place Mall, I-75 Exit 5
1,400,000 sq feet, open Mon-Sat 10-9, Sun 12-6

♦ While Eastgate and Northgate were built in areas already attracting shoppers, Hamilton Place was built in a pasture and clearly fulfills the adage: build it, and they will come. Opened in 1987, it quickly established itself as a shopping "mecca," attracting people for hundred of miles, and spawning development of strip malls, shopping villages, entertainment, and more hotel rooms than any other area in the city. Although it is 14 miles from downtown, it's the place where crowds are wall-to-wall and traffic is bumper-to-bumper. If you like being around people, you'll love Hamilton Place. There are five department stores and 160 specialty shops in the mall, but outside, well, you'll need to go often to keep up with all the new store openings.

♦ There are more shopping centers around the main mall -- **Hamilton Crossing**, with a **TJ Maxx** and **Toys R Us; Hamilton Corner**, with **Goody's** and **Michaels Arts & Crafts**, and across Gunbarrel Road **WalMart** and **Kmart**, many nice restaurants, and **Books a Million.** Strips of stores are on Shallowford Road, the other side of the freeway, and in Shallowford Village; they extend onto Lee Hwy too.

Community Shopping

East Ridge and Red Bank offer a wide range of shopping opportunities; some people prefer the park-and-run-in ease found in one-store parking lots, or the smaller strip malls. **Ringgold Road** is an 11-mile strip of shops and eateries, from the tunnel of the Ridge to I-75's Exit #1; serving Georgians, Tennesseans and visitors staying in the lodgings to be found at either end. Red Bank's **Dayton Boulevard** is dotted with shops, with the largest concentration near the Morrison Springs intersection. You'll find shopping areas in Daisy and Soddy along **Dayton Pike**, and a mall at the intersection with Hwy 27. There is a high concentration of shops and small malls on **Hwy 58** near the intersection with Hwy 153; **Rossville Boulevard** gives you chances to spend your bucks all the way into Georgia and, on Hwy 27, south to Ft Oglethorpe. In Ft Oglethorpe, **Hwy 2** east towards I-75 is a mall-dotted drive. Though there's not a lot of shopping on top of the mountains, **Taft Hwy** sports three small but interesting malls for the Signal crowd; there are a few tucked among the winding roads of **Lookout Mountain** too. And there's plenty of shopping on **East Brainerd Road, Ooltewah-Ringgold Road,** and in the **Collegedale** area. It's a safe bet that along any major arterial, you will find a collection of shops to take care of your needs; it's a chicken-egg deal -- which came first, the traffic or the shops?

Other Ways to Shop

Mass Merchandise Discounters

♦ Stores that can be counted on to save you money all the time, and which usually give birth to a surrounding mini-mall when they are built, are the

Kmart, *866-1337, 875-2511, 899-3232, 870-9515, 855-8180, 894-8970,* **Target,** *875-3100, 899-5001,* and **WalMart,** *332-2412, 861-5090, 899-7021, 870-1680,* stores; we have a number of them in our area. They stand behind their products; when they run a deeply discounted special on name-brand products, they usually beat the prices of all but used and salvage brokers; if you go for their private-label merchandise, you may save even more.

Thrift Shops, Flea Markets and Auctions

♦ Careful shoppers do well in thrift shops, and some secondhand stores operate to benefit a charity. **N-Port** is the Non-Profit Organization of Retail **Thrift stores** in the area and your support of them supports the community too. If you've got the time to forage through cast-offs, you know there are perfectly usable goods just waiting to be discovered. Not just for families on a budget, these places are popular with nostalgia buffs and savvy shoppers too. **Flea Markets** are big business around here; **Chattanooga Flea Market,** *624-7017, 23rd St, I-24 Exit 181,* has been happening every weekend for 25 years; there are more than 400 spaces. **East Ridge Flea Market,** *894-3960, 6725 Ringgold Rd,* has 220 indoor stores; it's open weekends and holidays year round. **Auctions** are plentiful too, check with antique dealers, see p.200, and watch the classifieds for special runs. Government auctions are good bargains because they do not use professional auctioneers or spend a lot of money on advertising.

Way Out of Town

For a list of places out-of-town, Call **1-800-980-SHOP.** **Dalton's Factory Stores,** *706-278-0399,* are south on I-75 at Exit 136 with a huge West Point Pepperell store plus Corning, Revere and Farberware; **Alabama's Shopper's Paradise,** *205-593-8154,* in **Boaz** on Sand Mountain is southwest on I-59 and Exit 205 at Collinsville; a few more miles on Hwy 68 and then 168, well-marked. Four **Factory Outlet Malls** plus other shopping.

Clothing

Department Stores

♦ **Belk (2 locations),** *892-1110, Hamilton Place Mall; 877-1708, Northgate Mall, open daily,* Hamilton Place store sells clothing for the entire family, as well as gifts and housewares; the Northgate "For Her" store sells women's clothing.

♦ **JC Penney (2 locations),** *894-2330, Hamilton Place Mall, 877-1301, Northgate Mall, open daily,* brands are Hunt Club, St. John's Bay, Stafford, and Arizona Jean Company; main focus is on clothing, but they carry an extensive array of home furnishings.

♦ **Parisian,** *855-7600, Hamilton Place Mall, open daily,* large clothing-only store sells name brands for the entire family.

- **Proffitt's (3 locations)**, *855-1600, Eastgate Mall, 899-3148, Hamilton Place Mall, 875-2734, Northgate Mall, open daily,* national brand names such as Anne Klein II, DKNY, Liz Claiborne and Ralph Lauren/Polo; most everything in the line of home furnishings.
- **Sears Roebuck & Co (2 locations)**, *855-9500, Hamilton Mall, 870-0400, Northgate Mall, open daily,* everything from pants to paint and lingerie to lawn furniture; OshKosh for kids; for adults Levis, Lee, Duckhead, Arrow; numerous brands in the appliance line; computer hardware, software; tools, electronics and home furnishings.

Women's, Men's & Children's Shops

- **Eastgate Mall** has many apparel shops including **Proffitt's** and **Goody's**.
- **Hamilton Place Mall** lists more than 40 apparel shops in its directory, including **Gap** and **Gap Kids, J. Riggings, Ann Taylor, Laura Ashley, Lillie Rubin**, and **The Limited**. Stop at the information booth near the **Oasis** on the way in and grab a map and full listing.
- **Northgate Mall** has more than 20 apparel shops in and around the mall; you'll find a **Belks For Her, Northern Reflections, Size 5-7-9, Stride Rite**, and more. The information booth near the central court can give you a map and list of shops.
- **Argus Big & Tall**, *899-4298, Hamilton Place Crossing, open daily,* full-service clothing store for the hard-to-fit man.
- **Bruce Baird & Company**, *265-8821, 735 Broad St, open Mon-Sat,* men's clothing and accessories.
- **CJ Children's Apparel**, *899-7373, 5770 Brainerd Rd, open daily,* name brand clothing for boys and girls.
- **Cooley's Fine Clothing**, *877-4554, 2224 Dayton Blvd, open Mon-Sat,* men's and ladies ready-to-wear; bridal and formal wear.
- **Gentry Ltd**, *265-0521, 27 Patten Pkwy, open Mon-Sat,* men's clothing, suits, sport coats, shoes.
- **Hamrick's**, *499-5011, 2020 Gunbarrel Rd, open Mon-Sat,* name brand fashions for the family; Hamrick's brands too.
- **McKenry & Co Ltd**, *265-7522, 11 8th St W, open Mon-Sat,* men's and women's clothing and accessories.
- **Pickett's**, *266-3121, 814 Market St, open Mon-Sat,* name brand women's clothing, shoes, hats, and jewelry.
- **S & K Famous Brands**, *855-7077, Hamilton Crossing, open daily,* men's clothing and all accessories, no shoes.
- **Vassey's Mens Apparel**, *866-7072, 104 Chickamauga Ave, Rossville, open Mon-Sat,* men's sports clothing, sports shirts.
- **Waldorff's Fashions**, *266-7752, 419 N Market St, open Mon-Sat,* career women's and women's sports clothing; petite and large sizes.
- **Yacoubian Tailors**, *265-0187, 829 Broad St, open Mon-Sat,* men's and ladies alterations; women's high fashion clothing and men's custom and ready-made suits.

Factory and Manufacturer's Outlet Stores

Warehouse Row Factory Shops, *1110 Market Street*

Choose from your favorite designer's product line; merchandise is mostly current season, always priced 25% to 75% below full retail. New merchandise arrives weekly in most stores. You'll want to check the store's return/exchange policy, as some offer liberal policies but others are final sale. Most of the stores sell first quality merchandise; items that are seconds, damaged or irregular should be clearly marked.

Apparel for Women

+ **Cape Isle Knitters,** *265-5787,* women's knitwear.
+ **Casual Corner Outlet,** *267-3362,* current fashions for career or casual.
+ **Chico's,** *267-4481,* casual clothing in natural cottons, rayons and silks.
+ **Danskin,** *265-6320,* dance/athletic wear.
+ **Ellen Tracy,** *756-8101,* quality women's apparel, petites to size 24.
+ **First Choice Fashions,** *267-4749,* boutique, selections from Escada, Laurel, Crisca.
+ **He-Ro Group,** *265-9772,* Oleg Cassini, Bill Blass, evening wear, sportswear.
+ **Joan Vass, USA,** *265-6761,* cotton designer knits.
+ **Kelly Stryker,** *266-7729,* sportswear in denim, cotton, rayon.
+ **Tanner Factory Store,** *265-6702,* classic ladies apparel.
+ **Westport, Ltd.,** *266-4851,* famous label suits, dresses and sportswear.

Apparel for Men

+ **Geoffery Beene,** *266-9483,* casual sports wear, dress shirts.
+ **John Henry/Perry Ellis,** *266-7763,* brand-name fashions.

Apparel for Family

+ **Bass Clothing Store,** *265-6709,* shoes, clothing, accessories.
+ **Big Dog Sportswear,** *267-3322,* sweatshirts, t-shirts, shorts.
+ **Corbin Factory Store,** *265-1306,* suits, coats, trousers, skirts.
+ **Guess? Factory Store,** *266-3717,* for men, women, kids.
+ **J. Crew,** *756-0815,* classic designer clothing for men and women.
+ **J. Peterman Company,** *266-3434,* vintage-inspired apparel, unique gifts.
+ **Nautica,** *756-5511,* casual sportswear, activewear, accessories.
+ **Polo/Ralph Lauren,** *267-7656,* clothing for men, women, boys.
+ **President's Tailor,** *267-5152,* custom-made suits, alterations and restyling of clothes for men and women.
+ **Ruff Hewn,** *267-0415,* men's and women's casual sportswear; also boys and plus sizes.
+ **Van Heusen Factory Store,** *266-0239,* dress shirts, accessories, sportswear for men, women.

Shoes, Handbags & Accessories

+ **Coach Leatherware,** *756-1772,* handbags, briefcases, accessories.
+ **Johnston & Murphy,** *266-6022,* premium handcrafted shoes.
+ **Sam & Libby Shoe Outlet,** *756-4758,* women's fashion footwear. *(contd.)*

♦ **Cole*Haan Company Store,** 266-9629, footwear and accessories for men, women, children.
♦ **Sunglass Company,** 266-1387, brand name sunglasses.

FLR Sock & Hosiery Outlet, *698-5920, 1508 Wisdom St, open Mon-Sat,* children's and adults clothing, casual and sports wear; primarily socks.

Off-Price Stores and Clearance Centers
♦ **TJ Maxx (2 locations),** *894-4190, 2200 Hamilton Place Blvd; 870-2404, Northgate Mall Park, open daily,* better brand clothing at discount prices; some household furnishings.
♦ **Goody's Family Clothing (3 locations),** *855-4687, Eastgate Mall; 894-3011, 2115 Gunbarrel Rd; 870-3575, 504 Northgate Mall Park; open daily,* family clothing, plus and petite sizes, lingerie.
♦ **Macy's Closeout Store,** *875-2345, 5450 Hwy 153, open daily,* men's, women's and children's clothing and shoes; linens.

Consignment and Resale Shops
♦ **Apple Dumplin Children's Resale,** *892-1437, 8115 E Brainerd Rd, open Mon-Sat,* new and used children's clothing; infant to pre-teen boys and girls; clearance sales at end of each season.
♦ **Fanny's Fancies,** *624-6421, 3204 Brainerd Rd, open Mon-Sat,* bridal clothes, costumes, antique clothing.
♦ **Puttin on the Ritz Resale Shop,** *499-4984, 4777 Hwy 58, open Mon-Sat,* designer brands of women's clothing; new and resale.
♦ **Second Chance Boutique,** *894-6308, 6209 Lee Hwy, open Mon-Sat,* women's clothing, accessories, jewelry, shoes.
♦ **Selective Resale Fashions,** *894-2184, 8049 E Brainerd Rd, open Mon-Fri,* clothing and accessories.

Thrift Stores
♦ **Adventist Community Services,** *892-1592, 7413 Old Lee Hwy, open Sun-Thu,* clothing for men, women and children, linens, knickknacks, furniture, appliances.
♦ **Bethel Bible Village Thrift Shoppe (4 locations),** *870-9056, 5135 Hixson Pike, 8951 Dayton Pike, 4222 Ringgold Rd, 8016 E Brainerd Rd, open Mon-Sat,* clothing, furniture, housewares, appliances, toys. Bethel Bible Village is a home for children whose parents are incarcerated.
♦ **Discovery Shop,** *870-2070, 3600 Hixson Pike, open Mon-Sat,* upscale donated clothing, jewelry, household items, antiques. Maintained by American Cancer Society.
♦ **Goodwill Thrift Stores (4 locations),** *629-2501, 776 Battlefield Pkwy, 5125 Old Hixson Pike,, 3500 Dodds Ave, 2103 Dayton Blvd, open daily;* donated clothing, furniture, appliances, housewares.

♦ **Junior League Bargain Mart**, *266-4457, 702 Market St, open Mon-Sat,* name brand clothing, formals, furniture, jewelry, children's clothes. Over 50 years.

♦ **Ladies of Charity**, *624-3222, 1800 E Main St, open Tue-Sat,* clothing for family, household items, provides emergency financial assistance.

♦ **River of Life Thrift Shop**, *821-3163, 3821 St Elmo Ave, 4716 Rossville Blvd, open Mon-Tue, Thu-Sat;* clothing, housewares.

♦ **Salvation Army**, *756-1023, 800 McCallie Ave, open Mon-Sat,* donated clothing, housewares, appliances.

Shoes and Accessories

♦ **Jaffe's Shoe Store**, *867-9044, 5004 Rossville Blvd, open Mon-Sat,* health and ortho shoes; dance shoes and accessories.

♦ **Red Wing Shoe Store**, *894-4931, 5813 Lee Hwy, open Mon-Sat,* Red Wing brand steel toe industrial shoes for men and women; also hiking boots.

♦ **SAS Shoes**, *877-0133, 5035 Hixson Pike, open Mon-Sat,* men's and women's shoes; handbags.

♦ **Sear's Shoe Store**, *866-5935, 218 Lafayette Rd, Ft Oglethorpe, open daily,* nationally advertised shoes for the entire family; discount prices.

Formal Wear and Bridal Attire

♦ **Eaves Formal Wear (2 locations)**, *899-0057, 5210 Brainerd Rd; 877-8387, 251 Northgate Mall, open daily,* formal wear including shoes for rent; formal accessories and tuxedos for sale.

♦ **La Prissy Hen**, *877-6068, 3210 Dayton Blvd, open Mon-Sat,* bridal and special occasion formal wear for sale; bridal and tuxedos for rent.

♦ **LaDean Shop**, *866-2006, 303 Chickamauga Ave, Rossville, open Mon-Sat,* wedding gowns, bridesmaid and prom dresses, some streetwear.

♦ **Mitchell's Formal Wear (2 locations)**, *894-8841, Eastgate Mall; 894-0278, Hamilton Place, open daily,* tuxedo and bridesmaid gown rentals; tuxedo, invitation and accessories sales.

♦ **Patrick's**, *892-2600, Hwy 153 & Bonny Oaks, open Mon-Sat,* complete planning for weddings, bridal and formal attire; largest bridal registry in state; no rentals.

♦ **Prado Collection**, *899-5566, 7200 Shallowford Rd, open Mon-Sat,* formal wear, including bridal attire; also sell and rent tuxedoes, new and used.

Food

Grocery Chains

A whopping amount of any household's budget goes towards the purchase of food, so careful shopping habits are important. The grocery chains advertise heavily in newspapers; coupon clipping and an eye for specials can really make a difference in the amount you spend. Our busy schedules demand that we consider convenience too; it adds up to a balancing act of best value for the money within the shortest drive. Following are some of the major chains in our area that offer quality, reasonable prices, convenient location, and special services so we can take care of a lot of business in one stop.

♦ **Bi-Lo, formerly Red Food,** *open daily, check for specific store hours,* throw a dart at the map and you'll probably find a Bi-Lo. Located for your convenience no matter where you live, they focus on keeping the prices low. Larger stores have delis, flower shops, and in-store pharmacies. Books and video rentals in many stores also.

♦ **Food Lion,** *open daily, check for specific store hours,* Food Lions can be found on both sides of the river, the mountains, and the state line. They focus on extra-low prices; find out about the MVP Customer Card for additional discounts.

♦ **Foodmax,** *open daily, check for specific store hours,* though Foodmax stores locate in attractive mall settings, the stores themselves are mini-malls, offering large deli services, floral services, pharmacies, and even UPS shipping from some stores. They accept competitors coupons, and to get you checked out fast, guarantee no more than two to a lane and let you pay by Swipeout, honoring Amex, Discover, Visa, Mastercard, Alert, and Honor cards.

Convenience Stores

As the name implies, they are convenient. Maybe the price is a little higher, and the selection a bit basic, but you can't beat it when you realize you have absolutely no milk for the kid's breakfast in the morning; favorite stops for a quick fill-up at the gas pump too. In our fast-moving lives, they fill a certain bill; you probably have one just down the street from your house. Most have the coffee-pot always at the ready, sandwich fixings and a cooler full of whatever you're drinking.

♦ **Favorite Market**   ♦ **Handy Andy Pantries**

♦ **Golden Gallon**   ♦ **Scotchman Stores**

Outlets & Thrifts

♦ **Brock Candy Outlet,** *875-0472, Hwy 153, open Mon-Sat,* a "scratch & dent" version of a candy store; fresh candy that didn't turn out as finely polished chocolate, dented boxes; also overages; all at bargain prices.

♦ **Flowers Thrift & Distribution Center,** *877-5034, 2002 Hamill Rd, open Mon-Sat,* bread, cakes, cookies, day-old and fresh.

♦ **Kerns Bakery Thrift Store,** *861-0668, 200 Lafayette Rd, Ft Oglethorpe, open Mon-Sat,* breads, rolls, cookies, crackers, snacks; fresh and day-old.

♦ **Little Debbie Thrift Store (3 locations),** *238-7111, 9515 Apison Pike; 877-5471, 5741 Hwy 153; 899-3580, 5330 Ringgold Rd; open daily except Sat,* sell fresh Little Debbies, only the boxes or cases are damaged.

Deli, Ethnic, Gourmet, Specialty

♦ **Asian Food & Gifts,** *870-1067, 3639 Hixson Pike, open daily,* no prepared food here, but everything you need to cook your own Asian meal.

♦ **Asian Market,** *870-9020, 5139 Hixson Pike, open daily,* this store is packed with foods and supplies for preparing Asian foods; some gift items too.

♦ **Cornucopia Gourmet Food & Beverages,** *820-0905, 1228 Lula Lake Rd, Lookout Mtn, open Mon-Sat,* deli with imported wine and beer, salads, sandwiches, pot pies, quiche, casseroles, breads, small gift shop; catering and deliveries on Mountain.

♦ **Fresh Market,** *499-4223, 2115 Gunbarrel Rd, open daily,* gourmet groceries, gourmet coffee, bulk food, in-store bakery, deli, full-service meat and seafood.

♦ **Honeybaked Ham,** *875-5300, 5017 Hixson Pike, open Mon-Sat,* whole or half spiral-sliced hams; spiral-sliced turkey breast or whole turkey, oven-roasted or smoked; entrees, side dishes and desserts too; sample before you buy; get a gift catalogue for future orders.

♦ **Paris Market,** *855-4107, 7804 E Brainerd Rd, open Mon-Sat,* fresh baguettes, French Country Boule; wide variety of cheeses imported from France, Italy, England, Holland, Denmark, Spain; deli meats, gourmet pastas and spices; gourmet coffees too. Gift baskets.

♦ **Shapiro's,** *266-3669, 723 Cherry St, open Mon-Sat,* kosher delicatessen; corned beef, pastrami, and kosher salami; pickles, homemade potato salad and slaw; rye and pumpernickel breads; large assortment of imported cheeses. Gift baskets, wines.

♦ **Taj International,** *892-0259, 7334 Lee Hwy, open daily,* Asian, Indian, Pakistani, Spanish groceries, spices, gifts, movies, etc.

♦ **Tony's Pasta,** *757-0118, 212 High St,* fresh pasta and sauces, gourmet vinegars, imported olive oils; also baked items for takeout.

Bakery Goods

♦ **Bread Basket (2 locations),** *886-7771, 2116 Taft Hwy, Signal Mountain; 842-9990, 5502A Hixson Pike; open Tue-Sat,* specialty breads such as sour dough, seven-grain, pumpkin, cinnamon apple, cinnamon walnut; dinner rolls and braided breads too; jumbo muffins, cakes, pies; gift baskets.

♦ **Federal Bake Shop (2 locations),** *870-2255, 5125 Old Hixson Pike; 490-0486, 7401 E Brainerd Rd, open Mon-Sat,* custom-decorated wedding and birthday cakes; wide variety of cookies, pastries and breads.

♦ **Fix's Old-Fashioned Bakery and Sandwich Shop,** *756-3497, 850·Market St, open Mon-Fri,* coffee rings, stuffed breads; cranberry, banana and pumpkin breads; sandwiches; at Christmastime, fruitcakes, pfeffernuesse and gingerbread houses. Gift baskets available.

♦ **Koch's Bakery,** *265-3331, 1900 Broad St, open Mon-Sat,* all types of baked goods including cookies; custom cakes made to order.

Wondering what we look for in a Great Place? See "How to Use This Book."

Beverages, Coffees & Teas, Beer & Wine

♦ **ABC Liquors,** *622-5915, 3948 Brainerd Rd, open Mon-Sat,* climate control cellar; ports, champagnes, fine wines.

♦ **Barnie's Coffee & Tea Company (2 locations),** *894-3998, Hamilton Place Mall; 870-5973, Northgate Mall, open daily,* specialties from around the world; beans and ready-to-drink coffee; coffee makers and accessories.

♦ **Beverage Barn,** *875-8918, 4700 Hixson Pike, open daily,* discount prices for beer, kegs, soft drinks, mixers and even ice.

♦ **Georgia Winery,** *706-937-2177, I-75 Exit 141, Battlefield Parkway, Ringgold, open Mon-Sat,* wine tasting daily; muscadine, Catawba wines; get on mailing list for fall grape stomp at the farm.

♦ **Cafe Tazza,** *265-3032, 1010 Market St, open daily,* gourmet coffee beans and coffee advice.

♦ **Rembrandt's Coffeehouse,** *267-2451, 204 High St, open daily,* pastries, candies, coffees, coffeemakers, and gifts.

♦ **Fresh Market,** *499-4223, 2115 Gunbarrel Rd, open daily,* gourmet coffee beans, other beverages.

♦ **Vintage Wine & Spirits,** *877-9474, 800 Mountain Creek Rd, open Mon-Sat,* specialty here is wines.

Fruits and Vegetables

♦ **Bridge Fruit and Produce,** *266-9257, 330 Frazier Ave, open daily,* fresh produce, fresh-cut flowers; jams and preserves; potted plants and garden plants.

♦ **Calvin Wood Open Air Market,** *875-3303, 5110 Hixson Pike, open daily,* fruits and vegetables; bedding and house plants.

♦ **Chattanooga Farmers Market,** *267-9556, 1114 Baldwin St, open daily,* three year-round produce stands: Jr. Osborne, Phillips Produce, and the Roden's; 90 covered and 24 open sheds for local farmers during summer and fall; market invites city/county schoolchildren in October for pumpkin shopping.

♦ **Fairmount Orchard,** *886-1226, 2204 Fairmount Pike, Signal Mtn, open Sept 1-Christmas Eve daily,* apple orchard with apples, jams and jellies, ciders and spices; pumpkins at Halloween.

♦ **Hamilton County Farmers Market,** *899-2723, 6628 Lee Hwy, open daily,* year round; fruits and vegetables, of course; summer flowers and plants.

♦ **McCormack's Indian River Fruit Market,** *267-4421, 1105 Baldwin St, open Mon-Sat,* season ends in June, sells Indian River fruit only.

Meat, Poultry & Seafood

♦ **Chattanooga Fisheries,** *267-4180, 1939 Central Ave, open Mon-Sat,* mostly fresh seafood from Gulf - shrimp, oysters, scallops, crab, fillets and whole fish; some frozen seafood, such as salmon.

♦ **Chick'n Farm,** *894-2143, 3907 Webb Rd, open Mon-Fri,* fresh meat market with chicken, beef and fish; also wholesale business.

♦ **Don's Meat Shop (2 locations),** *842-1256, 6402 Hixson Pike, open Thu-Sun; 698-7830, 3308 Ringgold Rd, open Tue-Sun;* variety of fresh meats, special cuts and orders.

♦ **Ed's Butcher Block,** *861-3300, 795 Chickamauga Ave, Rossville, open Mon-Sat,* special orders; grind own sausage and beef; cater plate lunches and hams for holidays; 21 years.

♦ **Rusty's Meat Market,** *866-8993, 1219 Lafayette Rd, Rossville, open Mon-Sat,* special cuts; cheeses, stuffed pork-chops; homemade sausage; 35 years.

Natural Foods & Health Products

♦ **Country Life Natural Foods & Vegetarian Restaurant,** *622-2451, 3748 Ringgold Rd, open Sun-Thu,* cooler, frozen and bulk foods, vitamins and herbs, cookbooks, health books and small appliances such as breadmakers and juicers; knowledgeable staff to answer questions.

♦ **Only One Earth,** *756-3466, 340 Frazier Ave, open Mon-Sat,* natural foods, nuts, and organic foods; environmental service goods, pet care and gardening.

♦ **Vitality Center,** *266-5016, 1202 Hixson Pike, open Mon-Sat,* natural food market carries a wide variety of bulk food, herbs and spices; frozen entrees, pastas and meal mixes. Also books on nutrition, organic baby foods, and pet products.

Sweets & Treats

♦ **Brock Candyland,** *267-4523, 200 Market Street,* wall-to-wall candy in this specialty store across from Aquarium, sugarless candy available too, as well as ice cream, breads, espresso, and gifts; kiddie birthday parties.

♦ **C. C. Loy's,** *266-2362, 141 N Market St, open Mon-Sat,* fancy candies, tins and all; gifts and cards and pretty things; restaurant here too.

♦ **Chatt ChooChoo Candy Factory,** *756-6064, 1400 Market St, open daily,* in the ChooChoo complex, they make chocolate fudge and taffy before your eyes; other candies too.

♦ **Cookie Bouquet,** *875-2354, 4812 Hixson Pike, open Mon-Sat,* custom-made cookies; pre-made flower-shaped cookies; arrangements similar to florist services with 24-hr notice.

♦ **Jim Garrahy's Fudge Kitchens,** *820-0774, 1400 Patten Rd, Lookout Mtn, open daily,* conveniently located at the Rock City entrance, fudge making here in every variety; fresh lemonade.

♦ **Russell Stover Candies,** *894-2024, 5520 Brainerd Rd, open Mon-Sat,* outlet store sells every kind of Russell Stover candy; gift boxes too.

♦ **Southern Taffy,** *821-4456, 827 E Brow Rd, open daily,* at the top of the Incline, get taffy, pralines, peanut brittle, candy apples and more, made fresh on site.

♦ **Sugar Shoppe,** *855-2051, 8000 E Brainerd Rd, open Mon-Sat,* buy supplies here for making cakes and candies; cake pans, wedding cake tops, etc.

Home Building, Remodeling and Gardening

Building Materials, Hardware & Tools

- **84 Lumber Company,** *875-8184, 5400 Hwy 153, open daily,* extensive array of lumber and building supplies.
- **Abe Shavin Hardware & Home Center (2 locations),** *265-8271, 2700 Broad St; 892-3969, 5330 Ringgold Rd, open daily;* cater to the do-it-yourselfer; hardware, tools and home maintenance supplies.
- **Ace Hardware (13 locations),** *most stores open daily,* check the phone book to find your neighborhood Ace; a hardware store with a generous variety of tools; electrical, plumbing and heating supplies; building supplies; and even sporting goods.
- **East Chattanooga Lumber & Supply,** *698-8661, 1805 Crutchfield, open Mon-Sat,* treated deck materials, masonite siding, drywall and supplies, leaded and beveled glass entrance doors and stair parts; more than 40 years, free delivery.
- **Evans Lumber Co,** *698-8521, 2700 8th Ave, open Mon-Fri,* since 1954; a complete line of supplies for the homebuilder; lumber, plywood, roofing, fencing, and insulation; dealers for Peachtree Door and Andersen Windowalls.
- **Home Depot,** *894-1001, 6241 Perimeter Dr, open daily,* working warehouse selling broad spectrum of home supplies; from lumber and hardware to plants and garden supplies; bath and kitchen supplies, lighting, anything you need for remodeling.
- **Interior Trim & Supply Co,** *855-9190, 3903 Volunteer Dr, open Mon-Fri,* hardwood and pine molding; special millwork such as fireplace mantels, arched casings, or gingerbread; stair parts including fittings, newells, balusters and handrails; free estimates.
- **Lowe's (3 locations),** *861-4120, 540 Battlefield Pkwy; 954-2400, 2180 Gunbarrel Rd; 870-3214, 5428 Hwy 153; open daily,* sells lumber, hardware, remodeling supplies; home appliances.
- **Southeastern Salvage Building Materials,** *892-5766, 6052 Lee Hwy, open daily,* close-outs, buy-backs and surplus on all kinds of items for remodeling and home decorating.
- **True Value Hardware (2 locations),** *821-8429, 3712 Cummings Hwy; 622-8755, 3903 Ringgold Rd; open Mon-Sat,* True Value claims to be the country's largest hardware chain, with stores in all 50 states; hardware, tools and general building supplies.
- **Walt's Salvage Store,** *861-9874, 1410 Lafayette Rd, Rossville, open Mon-Sat,* surplus and salvage merchandise, assorted molding styles and windows.

Wondering what we look for in a Great Place?
See "How to Use This Book."

Floor & Window Coverings; Paint & Wallpaper

♦ **Blind Place**, *855-5193, Brainerd Village, open Mon-Sat,* design consultant on staff to help with your plans; blinds, shades and shutters, custom draperies and bedspreads; free in-home estimates.

♦ **Chattanooga Paint & Decorating,** *875-6744, 5149 Hixson Pike, open Mon-Sat,* complete decorating service store; wall coverings, window treatments; Benjamin Moore Paints with computer color-matching system; designer on staff.

♦ **Gilman Paint & Wallcovering (4 locations),** *861-0663, 114 Battlefield Pkwy; 877-1395, 5111 Hixson Pike; 894-3551, 6505 Lee Hwy; 756-4285, 801 Riverfront Pkwy; open Mon-Sat,* paints, wallpapers and supplies; color matching.

♦ **Lee Paint Center,** *894-1465, 6620 Lee Hwy, open Mon-Sat,* paint and wallpaper center; Kurfee's and Benjamin Moore paints; wallcoverings; video color planner; more than 30 years.

♦ **Major Hang-Ups Wallpaper,** *499-1198, 8174 E Brainerd Rd, open Mon-Sat,* thousands of rolls in stock; discount designer wallcovering specialists; discounted book orders.

♦ **Sherwin-Williams (5 locations),** *866-2673, 534 Battlefield Pkwy; 894-4765, 5232 Brainerd Rd; 877-1204, 3613 Dayton Blvd; 624-1055, 1315 E 23rd St; 877-0571, 5112 Hixson Pike; open daily,* full-service paint stores; wallpapers, window coverings, painting supplies from caulk to cleanup.

♦ **Wallpaper Gallery,** *267-3636, 3507 Broad St; open Mon-Sat,* custom order wallpaper here; choose from Waverly, Schumacher, Imperial, Olney, Seabrooke; large in-stock selection at discount prices; full line of supplies and accessories.

Nurseries & Garden Supplies

♦ **Austin's Garden Center,** *267-6515, 241 Signal Mtn Rd; open Mon-Sat,* seeds to weed killer; complete line of garden supplies and plants; grass seeds and fertilizer for your lawn, annual flowers.

♦ **Barn Nursery,** *698-2276, 2410 S Hickory St, open daily,* top-quality plants; annuals, perennials, trees, shrubs; gardening supplies; Christmas trees in December.

♦ **Burkhart Farms Nursery,** *706-965-6677, Hwy 151 S, Rock Spring, GA;* Burkhart Farms has both container and field-grown trees and shrubs. 10 miles south after Exit 140 on I-75.

♦ **Four Season's Nursery & Bonsai,** *866-2275, 2311 Mack Smith Rd, Rossville; open daily,* shrubs, trees, seasonal plants; greenhouse and nursery on site.

♦ **Green Thumb Nursery,** *842-3892, 5431 Hixson Pike; open daily,* large selection of nursery stock here; other items for your landscaping needs.

♦ **H & L Nursery,** *842-5753, 6114 Dayton Blvd; open daily,* trees are the specialty; also have annuals, perennials and shrubs; mulches, sod and fertilizers; experienced staff.

♦ **Hillside Nursery,** *238-4743, 10111 Lee Hwy, open Mon-Fri, weekends by appt,* specializes in groundcovers and perennials for residential or commercial use.

♦ **Holcomb Garden Center (2 locations)**, *877-8782, 5513 Hwy 153; 894-7414, 5337 Ringgold Rd; open Mon-Sat,* garden items, plants, birdfeeders.

♦ **Mulch & More**, *499-0819, 5327 Hwy 58, open Mon-Sat,* bulk or bag, they'll deliver; topsoil, mushroom compost, pine straw, pine and hardwood mulch; custom soil mixes.

♦ **North River Nursery**, *877-6409, 4527 Hixson Pike, open daily,* horticulturist available; bedding plants, flowering shrubs, perennials, great selection of foliage plants. Water gardens too.

♦ **Ooltewah Nursery & Landscaping**, *238-9775, 5829 Ooltewah-Ringgold Rd, open Mon-Sat,* seeds to sod; plus shrubs, trees and bedding plants; mulches and topsoil. They will deliver.

♦ **Signal Mountain Nursery**, *886-3174, 1100 Hubbard Rd, open daily,* 25-acre nursery with over a quarter-million plants; landscape design and installation available, professional lawn maintenance too. Lawn and garden supplies for sale.

Home Furnishings

Antiques & Art

♦ **Bits of History Antique Mall**, *267-7989, 2435 Broad St, open daily,* mall has over 50 dealers offering antiques and collectibles; near Lookout Mountain.

♦ **Chase Dacus Collection**, *622-1715, 3214 Brainerd Rd; 266-3648, 47 E Main St, open Sun-Fri,* estate specialists buy, sell and trade furniture, antiques, and Persian rugs.

♦ **Chattanooga Antique Mall**, *266-9910, 1901 Broad St, open daily,* period and primitive furniture; also estate jewelry, sterling and collectibles. More than 50 dealers. Broad Street antique district.

♦ **ChooChoo City Antique Mall**, *267-3626, 1500 Broad St, open daily,* furniture, collectibles, glass, jewelry, lighting fixtures.

♦ **Clements Antiques & Auction Gallery**, *842-4177, 7022 Dayton Pike, open Mon-Fri, Sat by appt,* in business more than 50 years; pays immediate cash for estates; monthly estate auctions by insured auctioneers; call for information.

♦ **East Town Antique Mall**, *899-5498, 6503 Slater Rd, open daily,* East Ridge mall has 120 booths, wide variety of items; also offers appraisals and estate liquidations. No-fee layaways available.

♦ **Gailco Galleries**, *855-6990, 2100 Hamilton Pl Blvd; 870-1717, 1920 Northpointe Blvd, open daily,* custom framing and prints.

♦ **Hampton House Studios**, *892-0795, 6138 Preservation Dr, open Mon-Sat,* exclusive Hampton distributor; limited editions of original art.

♦ **In-Town Gallery**, *267-9214, 26 Frazier Ave, open daily,* Chattanooga's cooperative gallery with original works by more than 40 regional artists.

♦ **Log Cabin Herbs & Antiques**, *886-2663, 4111 Taft Hwy, Signal Mtn, open*

Thu-Sun, American furniture, folk art, country accents, collectibles, herbs.

♦ **Marie's Antique Mall,** *899-4607, 6503 Slater Rd, Ste C, open daily,* all types of antiques.

♦ **Northgate Antique & Auction Gallery,** *877-6114, 5520 Hwy 153, open Mon-Fri, Sat-Sun by appointment,* over 10,000 square feet of showrooms; fine antiques; monthly auction sales by licensed and bonded auctioneers; more than 35 years in business; pay immediate cash for estates.

♦ **Rugina's Afrikan Village,** *265-7714, 1394 Market St at ChooChoo,* African artifacts; art, baskets, pottery, jewelry, furniture, toys.

Bedding & Linens

♦ **Chateau Creations Outlet,** *821-2886, 3929 St Elmo Ave, open Wed-Sat,* place mats, pillows, tablecloths, tapestry handbags and luggage, yard goods; discount prices.

♦ **Supreme Products,** *894-3529, 406 Scruggs Rd, open Mon-Sat,* complete line of bedspreads, comforters, curtains and draperies, table linens at factory discount prices.

♦ **Towel & Linen Inc (2 locations),** *821-2688, 2821 Cummings Hwy; 892-9257, 6853 Lee Hwy, open Mon-Sat,* towels, sheets, bedspreads, shower curtains, tablecloths, wickerware.

♦ **Warehouse Row** (see p.186)

China, Crystal, Decorative Accessories, Kitchenware

♦ **Bombay Company,** *894-6400, Hamilton Place Mall, open daily,* reproductions of Queen Anne furniture; neo-classic, antebellum furniture and accessories.

♦ **CookWorks,** *266-6133, 1101 Hixson Pike, open Mon-Sat,* bakeware, cookware, table-top items such as placemats, glassware; bath section too.

♦ **Fischer-Evans Jewelers,** *267-0901, 801 Market St, open Mon-Fri,* in addition to jewelry, gift gallery and fine china.

♦ **Habersham Plantation,** *875-8840, Northgate Mall, open mall hours,* furniture, gifts, collectibles and accessories.

♦ **Hour Glass,** *877-2328, 322 Northgate Mall, open daily,* collectibles, fine home decorative accessories.

♦ **Lambs & Ivy,** *877-6871, Northgate Mall; 870-8002, 5226 Old Hixson Pike,* handmade bears, Fitz & Floyd collectibles, furniture, quilts, Daddy's Longlegs Dolls.

♦ **Patrick's,** *892-2600, 1-800-27 CHINA, Hwy 153 & Bonny Oaks, open Mon-Sat,* complete line of china, crystal and silver; Lenox, Wedgewood, Spode; largest bridal registry in state.

♦ **Pier 1 Imports,** *892-9778, 2130 Hamilton Place, open daily,* novelty furniture, decorative accessories.

♦ **Ralph Lauren,** *267-7656, Warehouse Row, open daily,* accessories and furnishing for the home.

♦ **Some Place,** *899-9442, 6503 Slater Rd, open daily,* consignment shop for

household items.
- **T. H. Payne Co**, *756-4000, 821 Market St, open Mon-Fri,* office supplies, plus a fine line of gifts and home accessories
- **Villeroy & Boch**, *267-3878, Warehouse Row, open daily,* European china, crystal, gifts and accessories.
- **Waccamaw**, *899-5364, 2020 Gunbarrel Rd, open daily,* home supply store; bedding and linens, dinnerware, stemware, flatware; small appliances, cookware; rugs, lamps, picture frames, wicker, brass.
- **Welcome Home**, *265-2039, Warehouse Row, open daily,* home accessories, afghans, linens, brass, giftware.
- **Wicker World**, *892-2909, Hamilton Crossing, open daily,* furniture, florals, arrangements, gift items, brass items, decorative trees, baskets.
- **Yessick's Design Center**, *892-1785, 1926 Gunbarrel Rd, open Mon-Fri,* complete interior design center; furniture and accessories displayed in two-story home setting.

Parties, Gifts & Flowers

Catering & Planning

Many, many restaurants provide catering of food services, please refer to the section and category listings on p.18 and pp.20-69 to consider them. Here are two businesses that specialize in full catering services.
- **Charles Siskins**, *624-5853, 3227 Brainerd Rd, by appointment only,* full-service event planner; invitations, flowers, tents, entertainment, food, bartenders.
- **Goetz & Associates**, *238-7799, 9220 Lee Hwy, by appointment only;* off-premises caterer; weddings, cocktails parties, etc.

Flowers & Gifts

- **Brow Gallery**, *886-5973, Signal Mtn Shopping Center, open Mon-Sat,* gifts, bridal registry, balloon bouquets.
- **Downey's Florist & Gifts**, *877-9193, 2112 Dayton Blvd, open Mon-Sat,* full-service florist, silks, gift gallery, lead crystal, rustic furniture.
- **Dry Duck**, *870-8951, 3828 Dayton Blvd, open Mon-Sat,* collectibles, brass, bird feeders and birdbaths, wind chimes.
- **Gregg's Chattanooga Florist**, *698-3303, 1701 E Main, open Mon-Sat,* centrally located full-service florist, stuffed animals, balloons.
- **Humphrey's Flowers (2 locations)**, *892-2225, Hamilton Place Mall; 629-2525, 1220 McCallie Ave; open Mon-Sat,* telephone and walk-in orders; fresh or silk arrangements, FTD.
- **Joy's Flowers & Gifts (2 locations)**, *265-4608, 841 Chestnut St; 698-5244, 1704 McCallie Ave; open Mon-Fri,* full-service florist, FTD and delivery.
- **Killian Daisy Florist (4 locations)**, *778-8010, 979 E 3rd St; 499-9132, 6309 E Brainerd Rd; 855-3630, East Ridge Hospital; 899-2440, 4727 Hwy 58;* full-

service florist.

- **Liesl's Garden,** *396-3677, 6314 Apison Pike, open Sun-Fri,* specialty gift and flower store.
- **Northgate Flowers,** *877-9885, 4844 Hixson Pike, open Mon-Sat,* full-service florist, 24-hour answering service.
- **Where the Heart Is,** *861-1079, 762 Battlefield Parkway, Ft Oglethorpe, open Mon-Sat,* gifts, decorating accessories, floral arrangements.

Party Balloons, Costumes & Supplies

- **Balloon A'Fair,** *266-6562, 113 Frazier Ave, open Mon-Sat,* pink and blue and silver and gold; balloons for the young and balloons for the old.
- **Balloon Factory,** *629-6954, 4415 Brainerd Rd, open Mon-Sat,* balloon arches and bouquets; custom decorating and table arrangements; flags, banners, party supplies; bulk balloon sales.
- **Beauty & the Beast Costumes,** *870-3510, 3708 Dayton Blvd, open Mon-Sat,* costumes for rent, accessories for sale.
- **Eaves Costume World (2 locations),** *899-0057, 5210 Brainerd Rd; 877-8387, 251 Northgate Mall; open daily,* adult theatrical costumes for rent; Halloween costumes in October.
- **Hallmark Stores,** *861-4035, 350 Battlefield Pkwy, Ft Oglethorpe; 866-3333, 1002 Battlefield Pkwy, Ft Oglethorpe; 892-2929, Hamilton Place Mall; 267-9685, 805 Market St;* gifts, cards, invitations, decorations.
- **If It's Paper,** *622-0741, 4413 Brainerd Rd, open Mon-Sat,* party supplies, plates, tablecloths, decorations.
- **Party Palace,** *499-6333, 6940 Lee Hwy, open Mon-Sat,* latex balloons to 40"; many mylars; helium rental; party and event planning with custom decorating; unique centerpieces, columns, arches.

Recreation and Hobbies

Arts & Crafts

- **Art Accent,** *267-0072, 825 McCallie Ave, open Mon-Fri,* art supply, graphic to fine arts; paints, brushes, paper; consulting for matting; artists on staff, display student work.
- **Art Creations,** *266-3626, 201 Frazier Ave, open Mon-Sat,* artists' materials and custom picture framing.
- **Corner Arts & Frames,** *842-1562, 5414 Hixson Pike, open Tue-Sat,* framing and prints; specialty conservation framing to protect heirlooms.
- **Fat Jane's Crafts & Ribbon,** *870-8276, 5141 Hixson Pike, open Mon-Sat,* beads, jewelry, crystals, craft supplies.
- **Gannon Art Center,** *622-8236, 3520 Brainerd Rd, open Mon-Sat,* custom framing, art supplies, gallery.
- **Julie's Framing & Gallery,** *875-5555, 2120 Northpoint Blvd, open Tue-Sat,* sell prints, frame heirloom items, wedding bouquets, medals.

- **Let's Make a Doll**, *875-2764, 5622 Hwy 153, open Tue-Thu, Sat, classes;* teaches how to make porcelain dolls; sells finished dolls.
- **Michaels Arts & Crafts**, *499-4095, 2115 Gunbarrel Rd, open daily,* supplies for arts and crafts, from florals and baskets to t-shirts and cross-stitch.
- **Old America**, *875-4707, 5027 Hixson Pike, open daily,* arts and crafts supplies, flowers, wicker furniture.
- **Treasure Cache**, *892-4774, Hamilton Place Mall, open daily,* local crafts and artists' items.

Books, New & Used

- **Baptist Book Store**, *629-2593, 4316 Brainerd Rd, open Mon-Sat,* children's, general, and religious books; wide assortment of Bibles.
- **Barrett & Company Booksellers**, *267-2665, 1101 Hixson Pike, open daily,* extensive children's collection; books for school reading lists; bibliographic research; special order books; will gift wrap and mail books too. In Corner at Riverview shopping center.
- **BLK Books**, *855-8898, 6503 Slater Rd, open Tue-Sun,* used, out-of-print, and rare books; over 20,000 volumes on all subjects. Appraisals available too. Staff will help you find what you're looking for. In antique mall behind Cracker Barrel, just off I-75's Exit 1.
- **Book Browser**, *855-5868, 2200 Hamilton Place Blvd, open daily,* discount family book store; Christian books, art, cards, music. New releases every day.
- **Book Company at Flea Market**, *622-1805, 1920 S Kelley St, open Tues-Sun,* used books at the Flea Market: hardbacks and paperbacks. They buy collections of any size.
- **Book Rack (2 locations)**, *877-7924, 3501 Dayton Blvd; 629-5259, 4330 Ringgold Rd; open Mon-Sat,* thousands of used paperbacks at these stores, and they'll trade you 2 for 1 of the same type.
- **Book Stop**, *870-2468, 3643 Hixson Pike; open Mon-Sat,* used paperback trading and selling here on Hixson Pike; 2 for 1 of the same type.
- **Book Store**, *877-4578, 3627 Dayton Blvd; open Mon, Wed, Fri,* most books half-price or less, guaranteed 25% off; fiction and non; hardback and paper; children's books and cookbooks; will special order.
- **Book Worm**, *870-1536, 6425 Hixson Pike, open Mon-Sat,* 2 for 1 trading here on used paperbacks; used music cassettes and CDs too; comics.
- **Books By the Bridge**, *266-0900, 201-G Frazier Ave, open daily,* used books for reading or collecting; spacious viewspot upstairs overlooking the north end of the Walnut Street Bridge.
- **Books-A-Million**, *894-1690, 2020 Gunbarrel Rd, open daily,* the bookstore that has everything: an espresso bar, benches for sitting when you want to look over your books; gifts; international newspaper stand; magazines; and, of course, about a million books. Look for the stores in our sister cities too.
- **Books-A-Million** *out of town; 205-591-0573, Eastwood Mall, Birmingham; 205-979-3046, Hoover Commons, Birmingham; 205-883-1942, Westbury*

Shopping Center, Huntsville; 205-536-1940, The Mall, Huntsville; 615-691-2665, 8513 Kingston Pike, Knoxville; 615-860-3133, 1789 N Gallatin Rd, Nashville.

- **Chattanooga State Bookstore,** *697-4425, 4501 Amnicola Hwy,* text books, school supplies, greeting cards, Chattanooga State memorabilia.

- **Childrens Hour,** *267-4284, 827 Broad St, open Mon-Sat,* educational games, books, toys; aimed at ages 13 months–13 years.

- **Christian Family Book Store,** *499-3028, 6009 Ringgold Rd, open Mon-Sat,* Christian books, boxed cards, church supplies, engraving.

- **Crabtree Booksellers,** *886-5944, 2905 Taft Hwy, open Mon-Sat,* appraisals and binding available here; title searches too, in this antiquarian and used bookstore on Signal Mountain.

- **Good News Christian Book Shop,** *698-4511, 3736 Ringgold Rd, open Mon-Sat,* this Christian book store will imprint your Bible while you wait. Music and gift items too.

- **Grace Episcopal Book Store,** *698-2444, 20 Belvoir Ave, open Mon-Fri,* books for children and adults; nice selection of cards, stationery and gifts.

- **Grist Books & Stuff,** *855-4032, 6503 Slater Rd, open Mon-Sat,* reference books, antiques and collectibles.

- **Joshua's Christian Stores,** *894-5320, 7200 Shallowford Rd, open Mon-Sat,* books, Bibles and commentaries; selection of gifts and music.

- **Lamplighter Books,** *877-3010, 404 Northgate Mall, open mall hours;* religious books and gifts, Bibles and engraving.

- **Lemstone Books,** *892-0717, Hamilton Place Mall, open mall hours,* gifts, cards and music in addition to Bibles and books in this store in the mall.

- **Little Professor Book Center,** *877-7080, 5450 Hwy 153, open daily,* bargains here; 10% for Seniors on Wednesdays, bestsellers discounted 25%; get a bonus book club membership for more savings. Magazines and newspapers plus books on tape; they'll special order for you too.

- **McKay Used Books,** *892-0067, 6401 Lee Hwy, open daily,* many books are half the original price; choose from over 65,000 non-fiction, fiction and children's books and more than 13,000 used compact discs.

- **Tuck Shop Bookstore at Covenant College,** *820-1560, Scenic Hwy, open Mon-Fri during school year,* textbooks, gifts, sweats and tees.

- **UTC Bookstore,** *755-4107, UTC Student Center, open Mon-Fri,* textbooks, literature, dictionaries, school supplies, gift shop.

- **Waldenbooks (5 locations),** *899-7557, Eastgate Mall; 894-9406, 894-6586, Hamilton Place; 265-2980, 700 Market St; 875-0195, Northgate Mall; mall stores open mall hours; downtown closes earlier;* offers wide variety of books and magazines; 10% discount for Preferred Reader Membership.

- **Wild Hare Books,** *886-1360, 1219 Taft Hwy, open Mon-Sat,* all types of books, all categories.

Looking for a particular place? Check the index at the back of this book for individual attractions, events, galleries, museums, recreational places, sports, tours, stores, lodgings, churches, schools and business services.

Collectibles, Hobbies, Games & Toys

- **American Collector's Exchange,** 265-8862, 2401 Broad St, open Mon-Sat, comics, comic-related cards, magic, posters.
- **Chattanooga Depot,** 622-0630, 3701 Ringgold Rd, open Mon-Sat, model railroading kits, kites, general hobby materials.
- **Chattanooga Magic & Fun,** 892-5682, 4738 Hwy 58, open Mon-Sat, costumes, games, magic; magic shows for parties.
- **Childrens Hour,** 267-4284, 827 Broad St, open Mon-Sat, educational games, books, toys; aimed at ages 13 months-13 years.
- **Christmas Corner,** 821-6963, 3905 St Elmo, open Mon-Sat, specializes in educational and classic toys, Brio trains; doll houses and dolls; miniatures, adult hobbies; annual customer doll house show; upscale Christmas items.
- **Hobby House,** 870-5327, 5622 Hwy 153, open Tue-Sat, model and general hobby supplies; model ships specialty.
- **Ken's Baseball Cards,** 843-1014, 7637 Middle Valley Rd, open daily, buy and sell baseball cards.
- **Toys R Us (2 locations),** 892-6555, 2200 Hamilton Place Blvd; 877-1801, Hwy 153 at Northgate, open daily, wide variety of toys and games; video games; hobby supplies.

Pets

- **Animal World,** 499-0554, 1414 Gunbarrel Rd; 629-0129, 2223 E 23rd, open Mon-Sat, boarding and grooming, all breeds dogs and cats, medicated baths, pet supplies.
- **Bermuda Triangle,** 875-5870, 5425 Hwy 153, open daily, fish and aquarium supplies.
- **Chew-Chew Pet Center,** 756-5329, 709 Signal Mtn Rd, open Mon-Sat, full-line supplies; sell all pets except dogs; specialize in fish and birds.
- **Econopet,** 855-5200, 2260 Gunbarrel Rd, open daily, fresh/salt fish; birds and small animals such as spiders, reptiles; dog and cat supplies.
- **Fish Store,** 899-3842, 6401 Lee Hwy, open daily, everything for the aquarist; reef systems, supplies; fresh/salt fish; trained staff.
- **Heavy Petting,** 855-1760, 4746 Hwy 58; open Mon-Sat, pet supplies and grooming.
- **Pet Care Warehouse,** 875-0355, 2105 Northpoint Blvd, open daily, supplies for domestic and wild animals; fish and iguanas for sale.
- **Pet Inn Boarding & Training Kennel,** 892-6725, 7112 Bonny Oaks Dr, open Mon-Sat, grooming, training and boarding -- good for visitors who stay where pets aren't allowed.
- **Pet Super Store,** 870-1097, 5035 Hixson Pike, open daily, all pet supplies; small animals for sale.
- **Petstuff,** 899-6670, 5772 Brainerd Rd, open daily, large selection of supplies; fish and small animals; grooming service.
- **Reigning Cats & Dogs,** 858-0362, 856 Battlefield Pkwy, Ft Oglethorpe, open Mon-Sat, retail store, supplies; bath and dips; boarding kennel.

Sporting Goods & Recreational Clothing

- **Allsports,** *698-4084, 3752 Ringgold Rd, open Mon-Sat,* sporting goods; sports apparel and equipment; sports medicine.
- **Eddie Bauer,** *510-9605, Hamilton Place Mall, open daily,* men's and women's clothing, luggage, backpacks, hiking boots.
- **Front Runner,** *875-3642, 3903 Hixson Pike, open Mon-Sat,* running and soccer shoes; soccer apparel.
- **Martin-Thompson Sporting Goods,** *267-3373, 627 Broad St, open Mon-Sat,* school and team sales; custom uniforms for teams; custom specialty items.
- **Outdoor Connection & Exchange,** *510-8368, 6727 Ringgold Rd, open daily,* canoes, kayaks, camping gear and clothing; rentals from pop-up tents to horseshoes; used equipment.
- **Outdoor Footwear,** *855-7309, 6209 Lee Hwy, open Mon-Sat,* large selection of boots including hiking and hunting boots; Performance shoes.
- **Play It Again Sports,** *855-4672 Hwy 153 & Lee Hwy, open daily,* buy, sell, trade and consign used sports equipment.
- **Premier Soccer,** *875-5051, 1920 Northpoint Blvd, open Mon-Sat,* soccer clothing and equipment, running shoes, warm-up suits.
- **Pro Golf Discount,** *875-8400, 5450 Hwy 153, open daily,* discounted golf equipment.
- **Pro Golf Discount,** *894-0304, 2200 Hamilton Place Blvd, open daily,* discounted golf equipment.
- **River City Apparel & Camping Outlet,** *266-4265, 14 Frazier Ave, open daily,* name brand catalog outlet; camping equipment and clothing.
- **Rock/Creek Outfitters,** *265-5969, 100 Tremont St, open daily,* camping equipment, shoes, backpacks, tents, canoes, maps, books and more.
- **Warehouse Golf,** *892-8671, 5813 Lee Hwy, open Mon-Sat,* full service retail golf center.

Note: Many Sporting Goods stores are listed in the **Recreation & Sports** section beginning on p.107 under the specific sport they support.

People Who Love Chattanooga
Ivous and Craig Burton

On June 18, 1937, in the spring of their lives, Ivous Sizemore and Craig Burton got married. The ceremony was in Jasper, Alabama, at the home of their pastor. As they tell the story, they didn't really hear the words; they were a little nervous, but happy, starting a new venture in life, together.

Craig: We got in our Model A Ford after the ceremony, and left for a honeymoon in Chattanooga. Out of Birmingham we took Hwy 11. The Model A wouldn't go very fast. It took us a while to get there.

Ivous: I was surprised when we came around Moccasin Bend. I had thought the Tennessee River was swift, but there it was, placid as Walden Pond. A lone barge was floating along, not even making a ripple.

Craig: We could see the city by now and hurried on. We didn't have a place to stay, but when we found the Read House (see p.220) we decided that's where we would stop.

Ivous: The lobby was so pretty! I remember the marble floors. Everyone was gracious to us as we checked in. Being young and shy, we thought they could probably tell we were just married. When we got to our room and saw the lovely towels and soaps and the crystal chandelier, we said "This must be the bridal suite." I walked over to the window and saw Lookout Mountain in the distance. It made me think how we were just starting out, at the bottom of the mountain, with all our life ahead. Around sunset we went downstairs for dinner. We were seated at a table with candles and a white tablecloth. We could hear soft music in the background. It was our first dinner together as husband and wife.

Craig: The next morning, we went to Lookout Mountain. Of course we rode the Incline. It was an awesome sight to a young couple, looking over the city from the top of the mountain. We visited Rock City and saw Lover's Leap and the spot where you can see seven states. After that, we went to Ruby Falls. We both liked Chattanooga a lot. The population then was over 100,000, quite a bit larger than Jasper. We went back home the next day. As I remember, we spent about $25.00 on our honeymoon weekend.

Ivous and Craig settled in Jasper. They had a daughter, built their first house, and endured the separation caused by a world war. After the war two sons were born. Linda and Craig Jr. and Hal went to school, and played, and faster than the wind, it seemed, grew up and moved on with their own lives. But the two who had started out together continued, together.

Ivous: We were so pleased when our daughter moved to Chattanooga. We said, "This gives us a good reason to visit our honeymoon city." We eventually had grandchildren and now we have greatgrandchildren in Chattanooga. It still makes me feel good every time we come around Moccasin Bend and see the Tennessee River.

Craig: We've shared a lot of things over all these years, like raising our family, running a business, and traveling around. We've been to Europe and Australia and the Caribbean. But we still love Chattanooga and fully expect to spend our 60th anniversary at the Read House on June 18, 1997.

Lodgings

She: There's so much to do here! There's swimming and hiking and shopping and dancing and museums and galleries and great places to eat. What do you want to do first?.
He: Dump these suitcases.

Contents

Visitors Services

Foreign Language Assistance

♦ **Chattanooga Area Convention and Visitors Bureau,** *800-322-3344, 1001 Market St, 37401*

Call or write in advance if you're planning a trip and know you'll be needing translation assistance; they have a language bank and should be able to arrange for an interpreter.

Where to Stay and What to Do Assistance

♦ **Allied Arts of Chattanooga,** *ARTSLINE 756-ARTS*

Call 24-hours a day for information on what's happening in the arts community.

♦ **Chattanooga Area Convention and Visitors Bureau,** *800-322-3344, 756-8687, 1001 Market St, Chattanooga, TN, 37401*

Coming for a visit? This is the place to contact! They can answer your questions and send information.

♦ **Chattanooga Downtown Partnership,** *265-0771, 850 Market St*

Call for information on events happening in downtown area, mostly free, see Arts and Entertainment.

♦ **Chattanooga Visitors Center,** *800-322-3344 or 756-8687 for visitor information by phone; located at 2 Broad St, open 8-5:30 daily, second location in Oasis area of Hamilton Place Mall, open daily, mall hours*

Already in the city? Pop in here for maps and brochures; get information about attractions and facilities in the area.

♦ **State Welcome Centers**

Great places to stop for maps and brochures, get a drink of water, use the restroom, and get a family photo by the state flag.

Alabama. *205-635-6522,* open daily 8:30-5; vending machines and restrooms available after closing; I-59 south about 9 miles from Valley Head

Georgia -- *706-937-4211,* open daily 8:30-5:30; vending machines and restrooms closed between 11:30PM and 7:30AM; I-75 south between Exits 142 and 141

Tennessee -- *615-821-4895,* open daily 24 hours, hosts on duty 8AM-8PM; I-24 east, near Exit 174, 7 miles from downtown Chattanooga

Tennessee - *615-892-7723,* open daily 24 hours, hosts on duty 8AM-8PM; I-75 north, near East Ridge and Exit 1

Write or Call with Comments

♦ **Women in Tourism Services,** *756-8687, 1001 Market St, Chattanooga, 37401*

This organization is not directly involved in providing tourist information, but its members are involved in providing tourist services. They are interested in hearing from visitors to the area. Let them hear from you.

How to Find Your Way

If you're coming from the Atlanta, Birmingham, Huntsville, Knoxville or Nashville areas, the freeways will move you quickly; roadway signs will direct you to US27 to get to the downtown area, which sits on a curve of the river. There are four major hotel/motel clusters; (1) west of and around Lookout Mountain; (2) where Tennessee and Georgia meet on I-75; (3) in the Hamilton Place area; and (4) downtown. Go a little farther off the track to find lovely B&B's and pleasant campgrounds.

Interstate 24

♦ **Exit 174** is dotted with a cluster of good motels; you're still seven miles out of town here, but are close to the **Lookout and Raccoon Mountain** attractions. **Exit 181** is nearer town; you'll find lodgings on the side of Missionary Ridge; **Exit 184** guides you through a major residential area to lodgings on Brainerd Road. Interstate 24 ends at intersection with I-75.

Interstate 75

♦ **Exit 5 (Exit 7 two miles north)** has the greatest concentration of guest rooms anywhere in the area -- over 1,000 and still growing. Tennessee's largest shopping mall is here, and the restaurants and movie theatres that make up Hamilton Place; to get anywhere else, you'll need wheels.

♦ **Exit 1** is where Tennessee and Georgia meet, and on both sides of the freeway motels, restaurants, and campgrounds can be found. The main drag here is Ringgold Road; the incorporated spot you're in is East Ridge.

US27

♦ **US27** takes you from I-24 north to the downtown area. **Exit 1A** leads to the heart of downtown, Warehouse Row, and three main hotels. **Exit 1C** leads to the Aquarium, the Creative Discovery Museum, and the Southern Belle; it's the river-end of town. There are a number of B&B's in some of the historic areas. The free shuttle runs back and forth from the river to the ChooChoo every five minutes; good walking on tree-lined streets too.

Definition of Areas

♦ **Battlefield:** south of GA 2, east of GA 193, west of I-75
♦ **Downtown:** the River to Main St; US 27 to Central Ave
♦ **Hamilton:** south of Bonny Oaks Dr, east of Hwy 153
♦ **Lookout:** south of Tenn. River, east and west of Lookout Mtn, Raccoon Mtn
♦ **Northlake:** north of Chickamauga Lake, east of Hwy 153
♦ **Northriver:** north of Tenn. River, west of Hwy 153; Signal Mtn too
♦ **Ridge:** east and west of Missionary Ridge; west of I-75 and Hwy 153; north of GA 2
♦ **Southlake:** south of Chickamauga Lake; north of Bonny Oaks Dr

Category Listings and Reviews

Location by Area

ALL LOCATIONS
About Tenn B&B RSO
Vacation Rentals

BATTLEFIELD
Best Western
Captains Quarters
Gordon Lee Mansion
KOA Campground

DOWNTOWN
Adams Hilborne
Bluff View Inn
Comfort Hotel
Days Inn
Holiday Inn ChooChoo
Marriott
Milton House B&B
Radisson Read House

Ramada

HAMILTON
Best Western
Comfort Suites
Comfort Inn
Country Suites
Days Inn
Holiday Inn
Marriott Courtyard
Marriott Fairfield Inn
Ramada
Red Roof Inn

LOOKOUT
Alford House B&B
Best Western
Chanticleer Inn
Comfort Inn

Days Inn
Holiday Inn
KOA Campground
Lookout Inn
Lookout Lake B&B
McElhattan's Owl Hill
Raccoon Mtn Camp
Ramada

NORTHLAKE
Chester Frost Park
Lakeshore Apartments

NORTHRIVER
Holiday Inn Express

OUTLYING
Cloudland Canyon St Pk
Days Inn
Hales Bar Camp

Hidden Hollow Resort
KOA Campground
Lake Ocoee Inn
Ramada

RIDGE
Best Holiday Park
Best Western
Days Inn
Holiday Inn
Kings Lodge
Ramada
Shipp's Yogi Br Camp
Shoney's Inn

SOUTHLAKE
Harrison Bay St Park

Type of Accommodation

APT/CONDOS
Lakeshore
Vacation Rentals

B&B/INNS
About Tenn B&B RSO
Adams Hilborne
Alford House
Bluff View Inn
Captain's Quarters
Chanticleer Inn
Gordon-Lee Mansion
Lookout Inn

Lookout Lake
McElhattan's Owl Hill
Milton House

CABINS
Cloudland Canyon St Pk
Hidden Hollow Resort
Lake Ocoee Inn

CAMPGROUNDS
Best Holiday
Chester Frost Park
Cloudland Canyon St Pk
Hales Bar Marina

Harrison Bay St Park
KOA Kampgrounds
Raccoon Mtn Camp
Shipp's Yogi Bear

HOTELS
Comfort Hotel
Holiday Inn ChooChoo
Marriott Hotel
Radisson Read House

MOTELS
Best Western
Comfort Inns

Comfort Suites
Country Suites
Days Inns
Holiday Inns
Kings Lodge
Marriott Courtyard
Marriott Fairfield Inn
Ramada
Red Roof Inn
Shoney's Inn

Daily Rates

UNDER $50
About Tenn B&B RSO
Best Holiday Park
Best Western
Chester Frost Park
Cloudland Canyon St Pk
Comfort Inns
Days Inns
Hales Bar Camp
Harrison Bay St Park
Kings Lodge
KOA Kampgrounds
Lakeshore Apartments*
Lookout Inn
Raccoon Mtn Camp
Ramada

Shipp's Yogi Bear
Shoney's Inn

$50-$100
About Tenn B&B RSO
Alford House
Best Western
Bluff View Inn
Captains Quarters
Chanticleer Inn
Comfort Inns, Hotel,
  Suites
Country Suites
Days Inns
Gordon-Lee Mansion
Hidden Hollow Resort
Holiday Inns

Kings Lodge
Lookout Inn
Lookout Lake B&B
Marriott Hotel
Marriott Courtyard
Marriott Fairfield Inn
McElhattan's Owl Hill
Ramada
Radisson Read House
Shoney's Inn

OVER $100
About Tenn B&B RSO
Adams Hilborne
Bluff View Inn
Captain's Quarters
Country Suites

Holiday Inn ChooChoo
Lookout Lake B&B
Marriott Hotel
Radisson Read House
Vacation Rentals

* 30-day lease
required.

About Tennessee Bed and Breakfast Reservation Service
615-331-5244, PO Box 110227, Nashville, TN, 37222
Numerous listings in Chattanooga area, such as hilltop country Victorian with Lookout Mountain view, rambling Tudor home on Signal Mountain, private suite with kitchen near lake access, downtown suite with pool near Aquarium. Thoroughly screened hosts and regularly inspected houses; full travel services; reservations by telex or fax; accommodations available in every state.

Adams Hilborne
615-265-5000, 801 Vine St, 37403
Downtown
Wendy and David Adams own the Edgeworth Inn on Monteagle Mountain and opened this small European-style hotel here in 1995. A Victorian Romanesque home, it has rooms with 16-foot ceilings, hand-carved moldings, arched doorways and Tiffany glass windows. Rooms are filled with antique furnishings and original artwork, and have private baths, telephones, cable tv, modem attachments and fax machines. Continental breakfast is served in the banquet room with Lookout Mountain views; full-service restaurant open in early '96. Grand Ballroom and other meeting rooms available for parties and receptions. The Window Shop carries unusual and elegant gifts and books; open to public. Located in the historic Fort Wood district of downtown Chattanooga, in a lovely neighborhood setting adjacent to UTC campus.

Alford House Bed and Breakfast
615-821-7625, 5515 Alford Hill Dr, Lookout Mountain, 37409
Downtown 5 miles
Lovely three-story brick home on slope of Lookout Mountain, set among the trees and boulders and deep ravines. Decorated in Victorian country, filled with antiques, family heirlooms; 3 guest rooms, one a suite with private entrance. Full continental breakfast in dining room. Gazebo, trails for mountain hiking. Conveniently located near Mountain, Battlefield and downtown attractions.

Best Holiday Trav-L-Park for Campers
706-891-9766, PO Box 9464, 37412
I-75 Exit 1, Downtown 10 miles
Campground located on Civil War battlefield site. Pool, rec room and playground; laundromat and store. Sunset Civil War ceremony for summer campers; bingo and hayrides.

Best Western Motels (4)
.800-528-1234
Best Western, *615-821-6840, 3644 Cummings Hwy, 37419*
I-24 Exit 174, Downtown 7 miles
54 units, senior discount. Pool; pets. Near Lookout Mountain attractions.

Best Western, *706-866-0222, 1715 LaFayette Rd, Ft. Oglethorpe, GA, 37042*
Jct US 27 & SR2, Downtown 9 miles
38 units. Tastefully furnished rooms; small pets only. Near Battlefield attractions.
Best Western, *615-894-1860, 6650 Ringgold Rd, 37412*
I-75 Exit 1, Downtown 10 miles
123 units, complimentary breakfast, indoor pool, meeting space up to 100. Near many East Ridge restaurants. Offers "See Chattanooga" packages.
Best Western, *615-899-3311, 7641 Lee Hwy, 37421*
I-75 Exit 7, Downtown 16 miles
100 units, senior discount. Pool; pets extra charge. Restaurant 24 hours, beer/wine. Two miles to Hamilton Place Mall.

Bluff View Inn
615-265-5033, 412 E 2nd St, 37403
Downtown
Two 1920's houses in the Bluff View Art District offer seven rooms, a parlor in each house, and two suites with elegant kitchens. All have private baths and private phones, cable TV; some have view of Tennessee River. These Colonial Revival homes have been meticulously restored and appointed with fine art and antiques. Full gourmet breakfast furnished. Fine dining room open for lunch and dinner; also Italian bistro and European coffeehouse. Patio/garden terrace. Museums and galleries, including a sculpture garden, surround this secluded, tranquil place; walk to Aquarium, Ross's Landing, Walnut Street Bridge via the RiverWalk.

Captains Quarters Bed and Breakfast
706-858-0624, 13 Barnhardt Circle, Ft Oglethorpe, GA, 30742
Downtown Chattanooga 10 miles
1902 Classic Revival home; built by the Army when Ft Oglethorpe was established, lived in until 1946 by Army captains and their families. Totally renovated; each of the six rooms has private bath, color TV; king-size rooms have original mantels with Italian tile. Full breakfast. On a quiet street with similar officers' homes, across from former parade grounds, gazebo; near enough to Chickamauga Battlefield to hear the muskets firing when make-believe skirmishes are scheduled.

Chanticleer Inn
706-820-2015, 1300 Mockingbird Lane, Lookout Mountain, 37350
Downtown 5 miles
Stone cottages nestle among fine homes on top of Lookout Mountain near the entrance to Rock City. 18 rooms, each with private entrance, cable TV; some fireplaces. Pool, stone-paved patios and courtyard, continental breakfast.

North Georgia Area Code is 706. The Atlanta Area Code is 404, although
plans are underway to add an additional Area Code.
Western North Carolina Area Code is 704.

Chester Frost Park
615-842-0177, 2318 Gold Point Circle, Hixson, 37343
Downtown 16 miles
180 campsites on beautiful Chickamauga Lake's north side; locals should buy a tent just to camp here. Fall foliage is fantastic, at the edge of Big Ridge. Boat ramp, fishing, lake swimming area, showers, snack bar, grills, playground, tennis courts.

Cloudland Canyon State Park
706-657-4050, I-59 Exit 2, near Trenton, GA
Downtown Chattanooga 22 miles
75 campsites, 16 cabins both 2 & 3 bedroom, 40-bed group camp. Full-service park features laundry, bathhouses, pool, tennis courts, bike rentals, 4.5 miles of hiking trails along deep mountain gorge, 7.5 miles primitive backpacking. Open year-round.

Comfort Hotel, Inns, Suites (4)
800-221-2222
Hotel, *615-756-5150, River Plaza, 407 Chestnut St, 37402*
27N Exit 1C, Downtown
205 rooms, 12-story. Small lobby opens into restaurant (see Seasons), and 4th Street Lounge; outdoor pool. Offers "See Chattanooga" packages. By Creative Discovery, Regional History Museums; 2 blocks to Aquarium.
Inn, *615-821-1499, 3109 Parker Lane, 37419*
I-24 Exit 175, Downtown 6 miles
60 units. Indoor/outdoor pools, pets. Near Lookout Mountain attractions..
Suites, *615-892-1500, 7324 Shallowford Rd, 37421*
I-75 Exit 5, Downtown 14 miles
62 units. Indoor pool, continental breakfast. Near Hamilton Place Mall, many restaurants adjacent.
Inn, *615-894-5454, 7717 Lee Hwy, 37421*
I-75 Exit 7, Downtown 16 miles
64 units, 2-story. Coffee, breakfast. Pool. Two miles to Hamilton Place Mall.

Country Suites by Carlson
615-899-2300, 800-456-4000, 7051 McCutcheon Rd, 37421
I-75 Exit 5, Downtown 14 miles
82 units. Lobby with country atmosphere, lovely decor in burgundy/green. Spacious suites have wet bar with microwave; deluxe suite has platform sleigh bed, platform whirlpool. Breakfast, indoor/outdoor pools, airport transportation, cable TV, recreational facilities. Opened 1994. Near Hamilton Place Mall, many restaurants.

East Tennessee Area Codes 615 will be 423 after September 1995.
This affects Chattanooga and Knoxville; Nashville remains 615.
North Alabama Area Code is 205. This includes Birmingham and Huntsville.

Days Inn Motels (5)

800-325-2525

Days Inn, *615-266-7331, 901 Carter St, 37402*
27N Exit 1A, Downtown
135 units, 3-story. Pool, cafe, lounge. In center of Downtown area, by Trade Center. Aquarium packages, on Shuttle Route.

Days Inn, *615-267-9761, 101 E 20th St, 37408*
27N, Exit 1, Downtown
142 units, senior discount, pool, pets, restaurant.

Days Inn, *615-821-6044, 3801 Cummings Hwy, 37419*
I-24 Exit 174, Downtown 7 miles
82 units, indoor pool, pets extra charge. Near Lookout Mountain attractions.

Days Inn, *615-894-0440, 1400 N Mack Smith Rd, 37412*
I-75 Exit 1, Downtown 10 miles
260 units, some suites, pool, playground, jogging track, restaurant. Senior discount. Convention facilities, 7,500 sq ft of exhibit space. Near many East Ridge restaurants.

Days Inn, *615-855-0011, 7015 Shallowford Rd, 37421*
I-75 Exit 5, Downtown 14 miles
132 units, 2-story. Pool, coffee, restaurant. Airport transportation. Near Hamilton Place Mall.

Days Inn, *706-965-5730, Alabama Hwy, Ringgold, GA 30736*
I-75 Exit 140, Downtown Chattanooga 17 miles
60 units, 1 floor, pool, pets allowed. Near access to Battlefield Parkway.

Gordon-Lee Mansion Bed and Breakfast

706-375-4728, 217 Cove Rd, Chickamauga, GA, 30707
Downtown Chattanooga 17 miles
A National Historic site, the Gordon-Lee House is one of the south's more gracious antebellum mansions. It served as Union headquarters and then hospital during the Civil War. Open year round, this 1847 Greek Revival home offers three rooms with four-poster beds, private baths; parlor, library, museum, small modern apartment, upstairs porch; 2-bedroom modern cabin in original brick building near mansion. Smokefree premises, some age restriction. No pets. Complimentary wine and cheese in evening. Elegant, yet informal, breakfast served in dining room. Several verandas, seven acres lined with oaks, elms and maples, formal garden. Beautiful facilities for weddings, receptions, parties on grounds and in Rosecrans Retreat, a separate building. In charming town of Chickamauga, across street from Crawfish Springs amphitheatre; just south of Battlefield area. Corporate rates.

Hales Bar Marina & Campground

615-942-4040, PO Box 247, Guild, TN, 37340
I-24 Exit 161, Downtown 21 miles
42 sites on Nickajack Lake, west of Chattanooga. Boat ramp, boat rental, houseboat available 2-7 days, sleeps 6; fishing, showers, laundry, ice. By former Hales Bar power plant, Tennessee River Mile 431. Central Time Zone.

Harrison Bay State Park
615-344-6214, 8411 Harrison Bay Rd, Harrison, TN 37341
Downtown 18 miles.
183 sites, some waterfront, on south side of Chickamauga Lake in this 1200-acre state park. Marina has one of finest launching ramps in area; 140 slips available for boats up to 48 feet; boat rental, fishing, picnic shelter, pool, snack bar, showers, playground, tennis courts. Planned activities include arts and crafts, campfires. Park's name derived from bay of main channel of Tennessee River that covers the old town of Harrison; parklands have historical significance, covering site of last Cherokee Campground. Park is haven for campers, boaters and fishermen, also picnickers and day-use visitors. Two-week max for camping.

Hidden Hollow Resort
706-539-2372, 463 Hidden Hollow Lane, Chickamauga, GA 30707
Downtown Chattanooga 18 miles.
A small secluded resort on 135 acres in northwest Georgia's Appalachian Mountains. Quaint country inn and cozy cabins are of logs from Hidden Hollow's own woods. Sleeping lofts, fireplaces, in some cabins. Porches, lawn games. Recreation hall for group hoedowns, workshops or meetings, a chapel for country weddings. 3-acre spring-fed lake. Near Cloudland Canyon State Park, on east side of Lookout Mountain.

Holiday Inns (5)
800-HOLIDAY
ChooChoo, *615-266-5000, 800-TRACK-29, 1400 Market St, 37402*
27N Exit 1A, Downtown
360 rooms, 48 train-car rooms. 3 pools, 1 indoor, lighted tennis. Turn of century atmosphere in restored train station, main lobby under 85-foot free-standing dome.   Shopping arcade, gardens, restaurants (see p.26) 1880 Chattanooga ChooChoo engine, trolley car. Shuttle through downtown to Aquarium.
Express, *615-877-8388, 4833 Hixson Pike, 37343*
Downtown 7 miles
57 units, 2-story. Near Northgate Shopping Mall, many restaurants. Opened 1994.
Inn, *615-821-3531, 3800 Cummings Hwy, 37419*
I-24 Exit 174, Downtown 7 miles
163 units, 2-story. Restaurant, lounge, pool, exercise room. Near Lookout Mountain attractions.
Inn, *615-892-8100, 6700 Ringgold Rd, 37412*
I-75 Exit 1, Downtown 10 miles
231 units. Restaurant, pool, playground, laundry. Near many East Ridge restaurants.
Inn, *615-855-2898, 2345 Shallowford Village, 37421*
I-75 Exit 5, Downtown 14 miles
131 units. Restaurant, pool. Near Hamilton Place Mall.

Kings Lodge
615-698-8944, 800-251-7702, 2400 Westside Dr, 37404
I-24 Exit 181, Downtown 4 miles
139 units, 2-story. On side of Missionary Ridge with view of Lookout Mountain and city in valley below. Some balconies. Pool, cafe, lounge. Laundry, some kitchen units. Small pets.

KOA Kampgrounds (3)
All have bathhouse, grocery, swimming pool, showers, laundry, playground.
Mountain Shadows, *706-398-3888, PO Box 490, Trenton, GA 30752*
I-59 Exit 3, Downtown Chattanooga 15 miles
109 sites and Kamping Kabins, located on 44 acres of beautiful native Appalachian forest. Pool, grocery, picnic pavilion, game room, playground, nature hiking with magnificent overlook of valley. Horseback riding nearby; hayrides; family-oriented activities. Sightseeing itinerary and discount coupons for Lookout Mountain attractions.
South Lookout Mountain, *706-937-4166, Rt 5, Box 12, Ringgold, GA, 30736*
I-75 Exit 141, Downtown Chattanooga 15 miles
165 sites. Exercise room, large pool and snack bar; cable tv and Kamping Kabins. Social events, hayrides, tours and discount tickets available. Near Georgia Winery, on Parkway leading to Chickamauga Battlefield.
North Cleveland, *615-472-8928, PO Box 3232, Cleveland, TN 37320*
I-75 Exit 20, Downtown Chattanooga 29 miles
80 sites. Shady campsites, Kamping Kabins, cable tv, pool, showers, store, laundry, pavilion. Near Red Clay State Park, Hiwassee River, Ocoee River, whitewater rafting (1996 Olympics).

Lake Ocoee Inn & Marina
800-272-7238, Rt 1, Box 347, Benton, TN 37307
Downtown Chattanooga 55 miles
Rustic motel rooms and cabins beside the lake on Hwy 64. Restaurant serves family-style meals; marina has boat dock, rents pontoon or fishing boats, canoes, water skis; rafting trips on Ocoee River in self-bailing rafts.

Lakeshore Apartments
615-877-1269, 5600 Lake Resort Terrace, 37415
Downtown 10 miles
48 efficiencies with lake and mountain view at this large, lovely complex north of Lake Chickamauga near the dam. Linens furnished but no kitchen utensils. Use of pool, health spa, clubhouse, tennis courts. Spacious grounds. Restaurant with dinner and dancing. Several marinas nearby; 3 miles to Northgate Shopping Mall. Excellent for long business or vacation stays or relocation house-hunting time. 30-day lease.

Wondering what we look for in a Great Place?
See "How to Use This Book.".

Lookout Inn
706-820-2000, Rt 1 Box 396, Lookout Mountain, GA, 30750
Downtown 8 miles
On top of Lookout Mountain. 16 motel rooms and cabins, pleasant gray buildings, white-shuttered, some with porch offering fabulous view east towards Chattanooga valley and city. Pool; complimentary continental breakfast. Covenant College across street. 6 miles to hang gliding at Flight Park, 14 miles to Cloudland Canyon State Park. Near Lookout Mountain attractions; however no restaurants nearby.

Lookout Lake Resort Bed and Breakfast
615-821-8088, 3408 Elder Mtn Rd, 37419
Downtown 8 miles
Lakeside setting on man-made lake at foot of Elder Mountain; some guest rooms have cooking facilities, all have private bath. Deck, solarium, swimming pool, fitness center, half-court indoor basketball court, facilities for boarding horses, floating gazebo for fishing, tennis courts, jogging trail. Continental breakfast weekdays, full breakfast weekends, room service available. Near Lookout Mountain attractions.

Marriott (3)
Chattanooga Marriott at the Convention Center
800-841-1674, 615-756-0002, 2 Carter Plaza, 37402
27 N Exit 1A, Downtown
343 units, 15-story, 16 suites. Executive Level provides deluxe accommodations, concierge services. Modern small lobby, bubble elevators, balconies, coffee shop with indoor pool below, restaurants (see p.47), lounge, entertainment, dancing, exercise equipment, gift shop. Airport transportation. Convention facilities with 68,000 sq ft of space, exhibition halls, meeting rooms, and ballroom. Center of downtown area, adjacent to Convention and Trade Center, near Aquarium, on Shuttle route.
Courtyard by Marriott,
800-321-2211, 615-499-4400, 2210 Bams Dr, 37421
I-75 Exit 5, Downtown 14 miles
109 units, breakfast, pool, dining room. In Hamilton Place Mall area; restaurants, shopping, theatres.
Fairfield Inn by Marriott,
800-228-2800, 615-499-3800, 2350 Shallowford Village, 37421
I-75 Exit 5, Downtown 14 miles
105 units. Pool, no pets. Near Hamilton Place Mall, many restaurants.

McElhattan's Owl Hill Bed and Breakfast
615-821-2040, 617 Scenic Hwy, 37409
Downtown 7 miles.
Situated on Lookout Mountain and bordering the Chickamauga Reservation, this bed and breakfast features a wildflower trail and access to other hiking. The two pleasant rooms are non-smoking, with private bath. Fresh breads

and fruits, breakfast cooked to order. Children welcome.

Milton House Bed and Breakfast
615-265-2800, 508 Ft Wood St, 37403
Downtown
Built in the early 1900's and listed on the National Register, this white-columned red brick Greek Revival home sits on a quiet street in Chattanooga's historic Fort Wood district. The grand, winding staircase leads to four bedrooms furnished with antiques, each uniquely decorated, some with fireplace, balcony, jacuzzi, day room. Full breakfast served in dining room; billiard room, terrace available to guests. Stroll the historic district, site of Civil War redoubt, see the cannons which remain. Near UTC campus, Fine Arts Building, Challenger Space Center. Corporate rates available.

Raccoon Mountain Campground
615-821-9403, 319 West Hills Dr, 37419
I-24 Exit 174, 1 mile N, Downtown 8 miles
104 sites, bathhouse, grocery, pool, laundry. Adjoining attractions: Alpine Slide, Caverns, stables, TVA world-famous pumped storage reservoir and recreation area. Close to Lookout Mountain.

Radisson Read House Hotel
615-266-4121, 800-READHOUSE, M L King & Broad Street, 37402
27N Exit 1A, Downtown
137 two-room suites, wet bars; Governor's and President's Suites have two bedrooms and views; 100 guest rooms with queen or king beds. Historic Hotel of America; listed on the National Register.

Since 1847 this corner of downtown Chattanooga has held a hotel; first as the Crutchfield House. Occupied in 1863 by Union forces, it was converted to a hospital. After surviving the war, it burned in 1867 and was rebuilt by John T. Read, opening in 1872 as The Read House. In 1926 the original structure was replaced by the 10-story building that remains today. Its Georgian style is lavish; terrazzo and marble floors, black-walnut paneling, carved and gilded woodwork. The Silver Ballroom has 25-foot ceilings and Waterford chandeliers; recent renovations focused on careful preservation of the old; you'll find Civil War history in the art on every floor. Notable people who have graced the Read House with their presence include Winston Churchill, Eleanor Roosevelt, Charles Laughton, Gary Cooper, Tallulah Bankhead, and Ivous and Craig Burton, see related article, p.208.

Central downtown location on shuttle route; 2 blocks to Trade Center and 7 blocks to Aquarium; both elegant and casual dining available, see Restaurants p.55; conference facilities offer 20,000 sq ft of meeting space.

Inspectors and reviewers for Chattanooga Great Places *accept no free meals or favors; the book has no sponsors or advertisers.*

Ramada (5)
Inn, *615-265-0551, 800-228-2828, 2100 S Market St, 37408*
27N Exit 1, Downtown
129 units. Pool, restaurant, lounge, live entertainment.
Ltd , *615-821-7162, 800-251-1962, 30 Birmingham Hwy, 37419*
I-24 Exit 174, Downtown 7 miles
80 Units.   Continental breakfast, indoor pool, near Lookout Mountain attractions.
Inn, *615-894-6110, 800-228-2828, 6639 Capehart Lane, 37412*
I-75 Exit 1, Downtown 10 miles
145 units. Pool, fishing, jogging track, restaurant, lounge, live entertainment. Near many East Ridge restaurants.
Ltd, *615-855-2090, 800-RAMADA, 2361 Shallowford Village*
I-75 Exit 5, Downtown 14 miles
44 units. Near Hamilton Place Mall, many restaurants adjacent.
Inn, *615-479-4531, U. S. 64 Bypass, Cleveland, TN 37320*
I-75 Exit 20, Downtown 29 miles
145 units. Pool, restaurant. Near Cleveland, Red Clay State Park, Hiwassee, Ocoee Rivers, whitewater rafting, (1996 Olympics).

Red Roof Inn
615-899-0143, 800-THE-ROOF, 7014 Shallowford Rd, 37421
I-75 Exit 5, Downtown 14 miles
112 units. Near Hamilton Mall, restaurants; morning coffee and newspaper, non-smoking rooms available; under 18 free with parents.

Shipp's Yogi Bear Jellystone Park Camp
615-892-8275, 6728 Ringgold Rd, Chattanooga, 37412
I-75 Exit 1, Downtown 10 miles
185 sites. Bathhouse, paddle boat and canoe rental, fishing, pool, playground, grocery, snack bar, laundry. Activities include 18-hole mini-golf, volley ball, horseshoes, basketball, wagon rides, movies. Yogi birthday cakes available for parties.

Shoney's Inn
615-894-2040, 800-222-2222, 5505 Brainerd Rd, 37411
I-24 Exit 184, E on Moore Rd to Brainerd Rd, Downtown 6 miles
95 units, 2-story. Restaurant, pool. Entertainment, many restaurants nearby, convenient to downtown and to airport. Airport transportation.

Vacation Rentals
615-886-6130, 420 White Rd, 37421
Area homes, condos, cottages, log cabins, B & B's, and more; for rent weekly or 2-night minimum on weekends; all properties completely furnished; will sleep six adults or more. One property is six-acre farm; great setting for weddings and family accommodations.

People Who Love Chattanooga
Ray Robinson

Dr. Ray Edwin Robinson is so fond of Chattanooga that in his years of pastoring East Tennessee churches, he chose to live here three times, serving at Burks and Fairview United Methodist Churches from 1960-65, as Associate Minister of First-Centenary United Methodist Church from 1969-73, and as Senior Minister from 1990-95. Ray and his wife, Jane Rusk Robinson, have retired to Walland, Tennessee, near their birthplace, and are devoting time to travel and to enjoying their family. They have two daughters and four grandchildren. Ray offers the following observations about the city he still loves.

It is impossible to talk about Chattanooga's great places without talking about Chattanooga's great people. This is a community whose people exude a wonderful spirit of friendship. The latchstring is always out for visitors and neighbors to drop in and chat awhile. The gracious old-timers invite a sharing of the good life with newcomers. The pace is slower and more relaxed in Chattanooga than in most of America, and gives people more time to enjoy the fresh, clean air and beautiful scenery, as well as one another. It's part of the reason people decide to make Chattanooga home.

I know what happens at First-Centenary every Sunday. It probably happens at each of the downtown churches, but it certainly doesn't happen in every city. Long after a service of worship is over, there will be many clusters of friends enjoying rich fellowship, and introducing other friends. There is a warmth about that experience that is impressive. There's a lot of bonding and a lot of caring. Church, for many, is the meeting and mixing place for the diverse population. It was inspiring to me to watch it happen.

There are many monuments and markers in the Chattanooga area recognizing the heroes who laid down their lives during Civil War battles, but the city is full of living heroes too, who daily give of themselves to make good things happen. It takes people with vision and commitment to bring to reality the many businesses, cultural opportunities, and community services the citizenry enjoy. Chattanooga has those people. And though most of the time things flow as smoothly as the Tennessee River on a lazy summer day, when an emergency or a special opportunity presents itself, Chattanoogans show their determination and power by rallying with creative strength to meet the challenge.

One last comment: soon after I first moved to Chattanooga, I noticed something that really touched me. I had lived in a city where funeral processions gained little respect. But in Chattanooga, the mood is quite different. Cars and trucks will stop until the mourning family passes by. One day, on the way to the cemetery, I saw a boy about eight or nine get off his bicycle and stand at attention with his cap over his heart until the very last car passed by. It may seem like a very small thing, but it made me ask: "Who taught him that kind of respect?" I believe he learned that from the community. Chattanooga has the kind of schools and churches and civic clubs and families that make for that kind of a boy. Chattanooga really does have a magic, positive way of raising kids.

Services

Contents

Boy: Daddy, do they have schools for cats?
Dad: No, son, but they do have schools for fish.
Boy: Too bad Sam isn't a cat-fish.

Basic Services

Administrative offices to the weather, plus where to get your drivers license, or renew your license plate, or register to vote -- this should help you find what you need to find.

- **Ambulance, Fire and Medic**   **911**

- **Administrative: Cities and Counties**
Chattanooga City	615-757-4926
Chickamauga GA City Hall	706-375-3177
Collegedale TN City Hall	615-396-3135
Dade County GA Commissioners	706-657-4625
East Ridge City TN City Hall	615-867-7711
Fort Oglethorpe GA City Hall	706-866-2544
Hamilton County TN Commissioners	615-209-7200
Lakesite TN City Hall	615-842-2533
Lookout Mountain GA City Hall	706-820-1586
Lookout Mountain TN Town Hall	615-821-1226
Red Bank TN City Hall	615-877-1103
Ringgold GA City Hall	706-935-3061
Rossville GA City Clerk	706-866-1325
Signal Mountain TN City Hall	615-886-2177
Soddy-Daisy TN City Hall	615-332-5323
Walden TN Town Hall	615-886-4362
Walker County GA Commissioners	706-638-1437

- **Animal Control - Hamilton County**   615-624-5302

- **Auto Registration County Clerks Office**   615-209-6505
- **Boat Registration County Clerks Office**   615-209-6500

- **Building Permits Chattanooga**   615-757-5105
- **Building Permits Hamilton County**   615-209-6460

- **Business License County Clerks Office**   615-209-6500

- **Certificate, Birth**   615-209-8025
- **Certificate, Death**   615-209-8025

- **Drivers License - Tennessee**   615-634-6218
- **Drivers License - Georgia**   706-866-1229
-
- **IRS Federal Tax Information**   800-829-1040

- Literacy/GED Hotline TN — 800-531-1515

- Marriage Licenses - Hamilton County — 615-209-6500

- Motor Vehicle - Hamilton County — 615-209-6525

- Parking Tickets - Chattanooga — 615-757-5144

- Passport Information — 615-899-9550

- Police, Non-Emergency - Chattanooga — 615-698-2525
- Sheriff's Office - Catoosa County, GA — 706-935-2323
- Sheriff's Office - Dade County, GA — 706-657-4112
- Sheriff's Office - Hamilton County, TN — 615-209-7100
- Sheriff's Office - Walker County, GA — 706-638-1919

- Social Security Administration — 800-772-1213

- US Mail - General Mail Facility Chattanooga — 615-499-8231
- US Mail - Zip Code Information — 615-499-8231

- Utilities
- Brush & Trash Service - Chattanooga — 615-757-5091
- Electricity - Electric Power Board — 615-756-2706
- Garbage Collection - Chattanooga — 615-757-5092
-                          East Ridge — 615-892-8666
-                          Fort Oglethorpe — 706-866-0962
-                          Red Bank — 615-877-1103
-                          Rossville — 706-866-1325
-                          Signal Mountain — 615-886-2177
-                          Hamilton County, arrange for private pickup
- Gas - Chattanooga Gas Company — 615-490-4230
- Recycling - Chattanooga Recycling Center — 615-697-1408
- Telephone - South Central Bell — 615-557-6500
- Water & Sewer -   City, Tenn-Am Water Co — 615-755-7650
-                    Other/County - Call Administrative Offices

- Veterans Affairs, Benefits Info — 800-827-1000

- Voter Registration - Catoosa County, GA — 706-935-3990
- Voter Registration - Dade County, GA — 706-657-8170
- Voter Registration - Hamilton County, TN — 615-209-7720
- Voter Registration - Walker County, GA — 706-638-4349

- Weather - National Weather Service — 615-855-6494

Business Services

Printing and copying, passport photos, temporary personnel, facilities information, mailing services and fax machines -- we often find ourselves in need of these, with the busy lives we lead. A few are listed.

Clerical Temporary Services

There are a number of employment services in the area to provide assistance when you need temporary personnel. Here are a few that offer bonded, insured staffing and guaranteed satisfaction.

- **Carolyn's Temporary Service,** *877-6666, 5211 Hwy 153*
- **Norrell Temporary Services**, *899-5123, 6025 Lee Hwy*
- **Olsten Staffing Services**, *855-7859, 2115 Stein Dr*
- **Southern Temp,** *266-8367, 701 Cherokee Blvd*

Copying, Fax and Printing Services

Never mail an insurance claim form without making a copy for your own records! That and other reasons for keeping records of what we do cause high demand for copy and printing services; fax machines are today's greatest timesaver; check with these businesses for that quick service you need.

- **Advantage Printing,** *266-0703, 714 Cherry St;* full-color printing, high-volume copying, laminating, free pickup/delivery
- **American Printing & Graphics,** *894-6298, 5950 Shallowford Rd;* raised and foil printing, high-speed copies, desktop publishing, free pickup/delivery
- **Kinko's,** *3 locations, 899-2679, 5749 Brainerd Rd; 877-0100, 5239 Hwy 153; 265-6309, 716 McCallie Ave;* open 24 hours, oversize copies, posters and banners, computer services, hourly MAC/IBM rentals, color scanning, mounting, laminating, collating and binding, shipping, fax, video conferencing
- **Mail Boxes Etc,** *2 locations, 499-4440, 2288 Gunbarrel Rd; 877-5568, 5251 Hwy 153;* mail boxes for rent, packing materials, mailing services, copy and fax machines, volume discounts for copies and packages
- **Quik Print,** *4 locations, 894-8674, 5250 Brainerd Rd; 266-3111, 719 Cherry St; 855-1777, 2115 Gunbarrel Rd; 870-8117, 5035 Hixson Pike;* high-speed, color and oversize copies, blueprint and computer printout copying, binding

Package Delivery and Shipping Services

When you absolutely must have it there the next day and it's too big to fax, you have several choices. Call for rates and pickup times.

- **Airborne Express,** *800-247-2676*
- **Federal Express,** *800-238-5355*
- **United Parcel Service,** *800-742-5877*
- **Mail Boxes Etc.,** see above listing for take-in mailing services
- **U. S. Postoffice,** Express and Priority Mail are good deals at the post office in your own neighborhood

Need to send a telegram, or transfer money?
- **American Telegram,** *800-343-7363*
- **Western Union Money Transfers,** *800-325-6000*
- **Western Union Telegram,** *800-325-6000*

Passport Photo Services
Get your passport photo at one of these places; for information about getting your passport, call *615-899-9550.*
- **Images,** *756-3686, 827 Broad St*
- **Express Photo,** *899-7956, 4421 Hwy 58*
- **Violet Camera Shops,** *894-2761, 5522 Brainerd Rd; 265-1012, 9 E 7th St; 877-5297, 24 Northgate Park*

Planning and Information Services for Business Development
These folks work to make Chattanooga an even greater place. They bring new business in, help businesses that are already here, and provide forums for businesses to help each other.
- **Chamber of Commerce,** *615-756-2121, 1001 Market St,* markets Chattanooga locally, nationally and internationally, offers *Leadership Chattanooga* training, and supports public policy issues.
- **Chattanooga Downtown Partnership,** *615-265-0771, 850 Market St,* coordinates downtown business efforts through cooperative programs; recruits downtown retail business; markets downtown area.
- **RiverValley Partners,** *615-265-3700, 835 Georgia Ave,* recruits industrial/commercial businesses to Hamilton County area; supports existing business; resource center for business development.
- **World Trade Center Chattanooga,** *752-4316, 605 Chestnut, Ste 210,* promotes international trade; provides electronic data-base listings of goods and services available worldwide; provides translation services, research services, and meeting, conference and exhibit space.

Planning and Information Services for Seminars, Meetings, Conferences and Conventions
Small local meetings or huge week-long conventions require a lot of preplanning and knowledge of the city. There's help available!
- **Chattanooga Convention and Visitors Bureau,** *615-756-8687, 1001 Market St, 37401,* this hardworking group of people promotes, coordinates and services conventions, trade shows, and other types of meetings; they also provide a public information center for tourists and conventioneers. Call them first; they'll get you started and help you all the way through.
- **The Meeting Company,** *855-0959, Box 80003, Chattanooga 37414,* "Putting all the pieces together" is the service this company provides; for your meetings and conventions, on hotel properties and off. Start-to-finish planning assistance includes facilities selection, equipment rental, food, decorations, entertainment, transportation, and even promotion of your

event. If you live here, but don't know all the resources that may be available, they can assist in coordinating your event; if you are out-of-town, they can be your local eyes and ears.

Spaces and Facilities for Meetings

Some of the larger meeting spaces are listed. Check also under Restaurants and Lodgings sections for spaces that have meeting rooms available.

- **Chattanooga ChooChoo Holiday Inn Centennial Center,** *800-872-2529, 266-5000, 1400 Market St,* theatre, classroom, banquet and reception space; restaurants on property; guest rooms.
- **Chattanooga-Hamilton County Convention and Trade Center,** *756-0001, One Carter Plaza,* meeting rooms, 60,000 sq feet of exhibit space, conference rooms; theatre, classroom and banquet configurations. Adjacent to Marriott Hotel.
- **Chattanooga Marriott,** *800-228-9290, 756-0002, Two Carter Plaza,* Plaza Ballroom 87 x 52; theatre, classroom, banquet and reception space; restaurants on property; guest rooms.
- **Comfort Hotel River Plaza,** *756-5150, 407 Chestnut St,* combined Chattanooga rooms 100 x 54; theatre, classroom, banquet and reception space; restaurants, guest rooms.
- **Covenant College,** *706-820-1560, Scenic Hwy, Lookout Mtn,* the Great Hall accommodates 450 for a banquet; theatre and classroom space; 198 dormitory rooms available in summer months.
- **Days Inn & Convention Center,** *800-251-7624, 1400 N Mack Smith Rd,* theatre, classroom, banquet and reception space; restaurant and guest rooms.
- **Dubose Conference Center,** *800-537-9968 (TN), 924-2353, Hwy 41 & College St, Monteagle, TN,* for meetings on a mountain, this center offers theatre, classroom and reception space; motel, dorm and cabin rooms, restaurant and outdoor pavilion.
- **Memorial Auditorium,** *757-5042, 399 McCallie Ave,* meeting rooms, exhibit space; main concert hall seats 3,866, community theatre seats 1,012.
- **Radisson Read House Hotel,** *800-333-3333, 266-4121, M. L. King Blvd & Broad St,* elegant Silver Ballroom 107 x 35; theatre, classroom and banquet space; restaurants on property; guest rooms.
- **Ramada Inn I-75,** *800-2-RAMADA, 894-6110,* theatre, classroom, banquet and reception space; restaurant and guest rooms.
- **Tivoli Theatre,** *757-5050, 709 Broad St,* jewel-box theatre seats 1,762; state-of-the-art sound and lighting systems.
- **University of Tennessee at Chattanooga Arena,** *755-4706, 720 E 4th St,* roundhouse has seating capacity of 12,000.
- **University of Tennessee Fine Arts Center,** *755-4269, Vine St at Palmetto,* Roland Hayes theatre has seating capacity of 505.

Inspectors and reviewers for Chattanooga Great Places *accept no free meals or favors; the book has no sponsors or advertisers.*

Child Care Services

Babysitters come to you; for daycare, you go to it. A few daycares have "drop-in" or 24-hour service. Listings of some of the services in the area show ages accepted, hours available. Call and visit to determine which service is right for you and your child. Hotels often can arrange services for visitors to the area.

Child Care at Home Services

♦ **Best Friends Home Care Services,** *855-4654, 6172 Airways Blvd, Suite 113,* a referral service; get baby-sitters on short-term notice or plan for a long-term contract. For any age child; caregivers are screened and bonded.

Day Care Services

♦ **Care & Play Center II,** *870-4812, 4105 Norcross Rd, open Mon-Fri 7:30AM-12:30AM, Sat 7AM-6PM;* age 6wks-12yrs; weekly contract; dropins welcome.

♦ **Central Baptist Church Child Dev. Center,** *698-3598, 901 Woodmore Lane, open Mon-Fri 7:30AM-5:30PM;* age 6wks-4yrs; weekly rate.

♦ **Child's Play Children's Play Center,** *899-1871, 6940 Lee Hwy, open Mon-Fri 7:30AM-midnight, Sat 8:45AM-midnight;* age 6mo-10yrs; daily, weekly, monthly rate; dropins welcome.

♦ **Country Brook Learning Center, Inc.,** *855-1664, 1043 Grays Dr, open Mon-Fri 6:30AM-6:30PM;* age 6wks-12yrs; weekly contract; school transportation.

♦ **Cross of Christ Lutheran Child Care Ministry,** *875-8217, 3204 Hixson Pike, open Mon-Fri 6:30AM-6PM;* age 2yrs-5yrs; yearly contracts; accepts handicapped children.

♦ **Discovery Child Care and Learning Center,** *870-4572, 621 Memorial Dr, open Mon-Fri 6AM-6PM;* age 6wks-12yrs; dropins welcome; will walk children to White Oak school; accepts handicapped children.

♦ **East Ridge Presbyterian Learning Center,** *867-2717, 4919 Court Dr, open Mon-Fri 6:30AM-6PM;* age 6wks-5th grade; weekly rate; school transportation.

♦ **Fort Lake Child Development Center,** *866-2258, 916 Carline Rd, Rossville, open Mon-Fri 6AM-12:30AM;* age 6wks-13yrs; daily, weekly, monthly rates, as can afford; dropins welcome; school transportation.

♦ **Happy House Child Care,** *698-2944, 2407 Meade Circle, open Mon-Sun 24 hours;* age 6wks-12yrs; rate as needed; dropins welcome with call ahead; accepts handicapped children.

♦ **Kiddie-Kare Learning Center,** *899-4136, 7514 Noah Reid Rd, open Mon-Fri 6AM-6PM, Sat 7AM-6PM;* age 6mo-7yrs; dropins welcome.

♦ **Kids-N-Fun Child Care Center,** *842-0886, 6712 Middle Valley Rd, open Mon-Fri 7AM-6PM;* age 12wks-12yrs; weekly contracts; school transportation; accepts handicapped children.

♦ **Kids Stop,** *344-2311, 5730 Hwy 58, open Mon-Fri 6:30AM-6PM;* age 6wks-5yrs; daily rates. *(contd.)*

- **Kindercare Learning Centers (3),** *870-1651, 1010 Gadd Rd; 894-6332, 1380 Gunbarrel Rd; 899-2821, 4650 Redlands Dr, open Mon-Fri 6:30AM-6PM;* age 6wks-12yrs; weekly contracts; dropins welcome; school transportation.
- **LaPetite Academy (2),** *842-6756, 6502 Middle Valley Rd; 899-6495, 7531 Shallowford Rd, open Mon-Fri 6AM-6PM;* age 6wks-12yrs; 3-day minimum contract; dropins welcome; school transportation.
- **Lilyland Learning Center (2),** *629-0303, 1510 E 3rd St; 894-6648, 2025 Hickory Valley Rd, open Mon-Fri 6:30AM-5:30/6PM;* age 6wks-5yrs; weekly contract; accepts handicapped children.
- **Neighborhood Christian Child Dev. Center,** *698-3769, 3661 Brainerd Rd, open Mon-Fri 24 hours;* age 6wks-5-1/2yrs; weekly contracts; dropins welcome; accepts handicapped children.
- **Northside Learning Center,** *266-7497, 923 Mississippi Ave, open Mon-Fri 6:30AM-5:30PM;* age 12mo-12yrs; weekly rate.
- **Primrose School (2),** *499-5584, 1619 Gunbarrel Rd; 870-4840, 1985 Northpoint Blvd, open Mon-Fri 6:30AM-6PM;* age 6wks-12yrs; weekly/monthly contracts; dropins if space available; school transportation; accepts handicapped children.

Churches and Community Services

General Community Services
- **American Red Cross,** *265-3455, 801 McCallie Ave*
- **Big Brothers/Big Sisters,** *698-8016, 2015 Bailey Ave*
- **Community Kitchen,** *756-4222, 727 E 11th St*
- **Goodwill Industries, Inc,** *629-2501, 3500 Dodds Ave*
- **Make-A-Wish Foundation,** *265-9474*
- **Salvation Army,** *756-1023, 800 McCallie Ave*
- **United Way,** *752-0300, 420 Frazier Ave*

Seniors Community Services
- **Area Agency on Aging,** *266-5781*
- **Family & Children's Services,** *755-2870*
- **First Call for Help,** *265-8000*
- **Older Adult Services,** *698-8214*
- **Senior Neighbors,** *755-6100*

Churches
Chattanooga is a city of over 800 churches; more than 70 denominations list themselves in the phone book. Fundamentalist to non-denominational, small congregation or large, you should be able to find the church that fits your needs and welcomes you into its community.

If you are a resident, and want a church in your neighborhood, there are locality listings in your phone book. Most churches have active outreach programs that provide immeasurable service to the community, providing food, counseling, and tutoring to those in need; many contribute financial support and personal assistance to children's homes, nursing homes, prisons, and other community agencies.

For the visitors to the city, if you are interested in a place to worship or the history, art, and music of churches, a few on the most highly traveled routes are listed below by area; call ahead for time of services; your hotel hosts should be able to assist you with directions. See p.78 for Art, p.98 for Music in churches.

Churches in Battlefield Area
♦ **Ft Oglethorpe United Methodist Church,** *866-1398, 1000 Battlefield Pkwy*
♦ **St Gerard Catholic Church,** *861-9410, 415 Lafayette Rd*

Churches in Downtown Area
♦ **First Baptist Church of Chattanooga,** *265-2257, 401 Gateway*
♦ **First Baptist Church East Eighth,** *265-3229, 506 E 8th*
♦ **First Christian Church,** *267-4506, 650 McCallie Ave*
♦ **First Church of Christ Scientist,** *266-1331, 612 McCallie Ave*
♦ **First Presbyterian Church of Chattanooga,** *267-1206, 554 McCallie Ave*
♦ **First-Centenary United Methodist Church,** *756-2021, 419 McCallie Ave*
♦ **Greater Faith Temple Missionary Baptist Church,** *756-0495, 652 E 10th*
♦ **Second Presbyterian Church,** *266-2828, 700 Pine St*
♦ **St Paul's Episcopal Church,** *266-8195, 305 W 7th St*
♦ **Sts Peter and Paul Catholic Church,** *266-1618, 214 E 8th St*

Churches in Hamilton Area
♦ **East Brainerd Church of Christ,** *892-1389, 7745 E Brainerd Rd*
♦ **Hickory Valley Christian Church,** *892-4270, 6605 Shallowford Rd*
♦ **Resurrection Lutheran Church,** *894-6345, 7429 Shallowford Rd*
♦ **Seventh-Day Adventist Church,** *396-2134, 4829 College Dr E*

Churches in Lookout Mountain Area
♦ **Church of the Good Shepherd Episcopal,** *821-1583, 211 Franklin Rd*
♦ **Lookout Mountain Presbyterian Church,** *821-4528, 316 N Bragg Ave*
♦ **Our Lady of the Mount,** *820-0680, 1227 Scenic Hwy*
♦ **St Elmo Presbyterian,** *821-1424, 4400 St Elmo Ave*

Churches North of the Lake, east of Hwy 153
♦ **Bethel Temple Assembly of God,** *842-2982, 6613 Hixson Pike*
♦ **Burks United Methodist Church,** *842-4219, 6433 Hixson Pike*
♦ **Central Baptist of Hixson,** *877-6462, 5208 Hixson Pike*
♦ **Trinity Lutheran Church,** *870-1236, 5001 Hixson Pike*   *(contd.)*

Churches North of the River, west of Hwy 153
- Grace Church of the Nazarene, 842-5919, 6310 Dayton Blvd
- Hixson Presbyterian Church, 875-0616, 1005 Gadd Rd
- Red Bank Baptist Church, 877-4514, 4000 Dayton Blvd
- St Timothy's Episcopal Church, 886-2281, 630 Mississippi Ave, Signal Mtn

Churches in Ridge Area, south to Rossville, east to I-75
- B'nai Zion Congregation, Conserv/Trad, 894-8900, 114 McBrien Rd
- Brainerd Baptist Church, 624-2606, 300 Brookfield Ave
- Brainerd Church of Christ, 698-8011, 4203 Brainerd Rd
- Brainerd United Methodist Church, 698-6951, 4315 Brainerd Rd
- First Cumberland Presbyterian Church, 698-2556, 1505 N Moore Rd
- First Lutheran Church, 629-5990, 2800 McCallie Ave
- First Seventh-Day Adventist Church, 624-9618, 400 Tunnel Blvd
- Good Shepherd Lutheran Church, 629-4661, 822 Belvoir Ave
- Greek Orthodox Church, 629-4881, 722 Glenwood Dr
- Highland Park Baptist Church, 493-4111, 1907 Bailey Ave
- Jones Memorial United Methodist Church, 624-6073, 4131 Ringgold Rd
- Korean Full Gospel Chattanooga Church, 499-8432, 5421 Ringgold Rd
- Mizpah Congregation-Reform, 267-9771, 923 McCallie Ave
- Our Lady of Perpetual Help Catholic Church, 622-7232, 501 S Moore Rd
- River of Life Church, 891-2120, 6880 Direct Connections Dr
- Unitarian Universalist Church, 624-2985, 3224 Navajo Dr

Churches in Southlake Area, south of the Lake, east of Hwy 153
- Bayside Baptist Church, 344-8327, 6100 Hwy 58
- St Thaddaeus Episcopal Church, 892-2377, 4300 Locksley Ln

Educational Services

Public and private schools, libraries and private classes are listed here.
Public Schools K-12
Catoosa County School System
- 706-965-3977-- Call this number to find out what school your child will attend
- 706-965-2297, 207 N Cleveland St, Ringgold, GA, 30736, business office; 8,000 students in system at 8 schools.

Chattanooga Department of Education
- In 1994, citizens of Chattanooga voted to merge the Chattanooga Department of Education with the Hamilton County Department of Education. It is scheduled to occur in the 1997-98 school year, but as of May 1995, plans for the merger have not been developed.
- 825-7348 -- Call this number to find out what school your child will attend
- 825-7200, 1161 W 40th St, Chattanooga 37409 -- business office
  Approximately 20,000 students enrolled in the City's system; zoning in

effect for most schools; three magnet schools by application only: Chattanooga School for Arts and Sciences, 1100+ students, grades K-12, Chattanooga School for Liberal Arts, 450 students, grades K-8, and 21st Century Preparatory School, 400+ students, grades K-9, based on Joel Barker's Ecological, Futures and Global concept.

Chattanooga Southeast Tennessee Home Education Association (CSTHEA)
- 266-4663, for information about teaching your child at home.

Dade County Department of Education
- *706-398-3548, Box 188, Trenton, GA 30752;* 2,300 students in Dade County system; special education classes available.

Hamilton County Department of Education
- *209-8500 -- information line; school calendar and Board meeting dates*
- *209-8400, 201 Broad St, 37402 -- business office*
- Call business office for brochure detailing curriculum, statistics such as average class size, food services, child care programs, exceptional education programs, zoning, and enrollment and attendance policies. Admissions at individual school. Five schools have received National School of Excellence award. Approximately 24,000 students enrolled.

Walker County Department of Education
- *706-638-1240, Lafayette, GA, 30728,* 8,600 students in Walker County system, gifted and special education classes available.

Private Schools K-12
- **Baylor School,** *267-8505, 157 Baylor School Rd, Chattanooga 37401,* Grades 7-12; coed; summer programs and camp; established 1893.
- **Boyd Buchanan School,** *624-9063, 4626 Bonnieway Dr, Chattanooga 37411,* Pre K- 12th grade; coed; established 1952 by Church of Christ.
- **Bright School,** *267-8546, 1950 Hixson Pike, Chattanooga 37405,* Pre-K through 6th; coed; extended care programs; summer academic programs.
- **Chattanooga Christian School,** *265-6411, 3354 Broad St, Chattanooga 37409,* K-12th grade; coed; interdenominational; summer camp; established 1970.
- **Girl's Preparatory School,** *634-7600, 205 Island Ave, Chattanooga 37405,* 7th-12th grades; female only; summer programs open to public.
- **Lutheran School,** *622-3755, 800 Belvoir Ave, Chattanooga 37412,* 3 yrs-8th grade; coed; summer camp.
- **McCallie School,** *624-8300, 500 Dodds Ave, Chattanooga 37404,* 7th-12th grades; male only; summer academic programs and camp open to public.
- **Montessori Children's House,** *886-5947, 302 Signal Mtn Blvd, Signal Mtn, 37377,* 18 mo-6th grade; coed; summer programs for pre-1st grade.
- **Montessori World of Children,** *622-6366, 1080 McCallie Ave, Chattanooga 37404,* 18 mo-6th grade; coed; summer programs for pre-1st grade.
- **Notre Dame High School,** *624-4618, 2701 Vermont Ave, Chattanooga 37404,* 9th-12th grades; coed; campus by Missionary Ridge downtown.
- **Senter School,** *622-3398, 1512 S Holtzclaw, Chattanooga 37404,* K-8th grades; coed; summer camp open to public; established 1892.

Colleges and Universities
Chattanooga State Technical Community College

- *4501 Amnicola Hwy, Chattanooga 37406 & Branches*
- *Admissions -- 697-4401*
- *Continuing Education -- 697-4410*
- *Dayton Branch -- 570-1104*
- *Downtown Chattanooga Branch -- 634-7700*
- *East Campus Branch -- 697-4797*
- *Kinball Branch -- 837-1327*
- *Truck Driving -- 266-5544*
- Chattanooga State's curriculum is the most extensive in Tennessee, covering general education, transfer studies, career and technical fields, and vocational training. The college offers 40 two-year associate degree programs in computer science, engineering technology, environmental science and technology, liberal arts, and nursing and allied health. The 18 one-year industrial technology programs include air conditioning and refrigeration, cosmetology, licensed practical nursing, and welding. Sixty-two courses of study for students planning to transfer to four-year colleges are offered, as well as professional and non-credit personal interest classes, and technical and corporate training packages.

- The campus has a DEC mainframe computer and two IBM AS 400's, plus more than 800 personal computers for student use. Computer-based multi-media learning is offered in several disciplines. The Wellness Program, with emphasis on helping students, faculty and community build balanced, healthy lifestyles, offers a state-of-technology fitness center and classes in backpacking/hiking, skin/scuba diving, bicycling, canoeing and international bicycle tours, open to students and the public. Financial aid, career counseling, tutoring, child care, and job placement are available, as well as a variety of services for the deaf. Co-operative education programs available too.

- Chattanooga State began operating in 1965; merged with the State Area Vocational-Technical School in 1983. Main campus facility has nine buildings on 100 riverside acres. Enrollment is approximately 10,000 at all campuses. Academic calendar runs late-August to mid-May; several summer sessions offered.

Covenant College

- *706-820-1560, Scenic Hwy, Lookout Mtn, GA 30750*
- *Admissions -- 820-2398*
- *Continuing Education and Quest Program -- 265-7784*
- *Quest campuses -- Chattanooga, Cleveland, Dalton, Ft Oglethorpe, S Pittsburg*
- Covenant is a Christian liberal arts college affiliated with the Presbyterian Church. Associate of Arts, Bachelor of Arts, Bachelor of Science, Bachelor of Music and Masters of Education degrees are offered, with sixteen

majors and several pre-professional programs. Quest offers BS in Organizational Management with evening and weekend classes. Off-study credit programs include the American Studies Program, the Au-Sable Trails Institute, the Study Abroad Program of Christian Colleges, and the American Institute of Holy Land Studies.

♦ Located atop Lookout Mountain since 1964 on a 300-acre main campus, enrollment is approximately 600, with 41 states and 21 foreign countries represented. Library holdings include 70,200 bound volumes and 27,000 titles on microfilm. Carter Hall, formerly a resort hotel, is the campus centerpiece and a regional landmark. Academic calendar late August-early May; 3-week May term. Quest enrollment is ongoing throughout the year.

Lee College
♦ *472-2111, 1120 N Ocoee St, Cleveland, 37320*
♦ *Admissions - 422-7316*
♦ Lee is a Christian college affiliated with the Church of God. Baccalaureate degrees from 27 majors in 55 programs of study; all students must complete traditional general education core including 18 semester hours of religion. Special programs include semester in Europe/Asia, studying in England, Germany, China or Ukraine; a Latin American studies program, based in Costa Rica; a Middle East studies program, with travel in Israel; the Los Angeles Film Studies Center, studying creative and business aspects of filmmaking. Musical groups Lee Singers and Ladies of Lee have toured Europe and the Far East.

♦ Located on a 45-acre campus, with enrollment of approximately 2,000, 29% are students from denominations other than the Church of God. Founded as Bible Training School in 1918, it was renamed in 1947. Academic calendar late August-early May; three summer sessions.

Southern College of Seventh-day Adventists
♦ *238-2111, PO Box 370, Collegedale, TN 37315*
♦ *Admissions -- 238-2844 or 800-768-8437*
♦ Southern College is a four-year co-educational institution established by the Seventh-day Adventist Church. It moved to its present location in 1916 and assumed its present name in 1982. The 1000-acre campus is 18 miles east of Chattanooga.

♦ Southern College offers 39 baccalaureate degree majors and 31 minors, 18 associate degree majors, and four one-year certificates. Ten departments offer secondary teaching certification. The College serves as an extension campus for Andrews University, which offers an M.S.N. degree, and for La Sierra University, which offers the M.Ed. degree; and is affiliated with two marine biological stations: Bahamian Field Station, San Salvador, Bahamas, and Walla Walla College's Rosario Beach Marine Biological Station on Fidalgo Island, Puget Sound, Washington. *(contd.)*

♦ Library holdings of 200,000 items include the Dr. Vernon Thomas Memorial Civil War and Abraham Lincoln Collection and 900 periodicals. WSMC FM90.5 is a fine arts radio station licensed to the College, providing broadcasting training for students. Academic calendar is August-May, four 4-week summer sessions.

Tennessee Temple University
♦ *493-4100, 1815 Union Ave, Chattanooga 37404*
♦ *Admissions -- 800-553-4050, 493-4213*
♦ Tennessee Temple is affiliated with Highland Park Baptist Church, and provides a traditional liberal arts program balanced with a historical Baptist position regarding doctrine and conduct. Faculty, staff and students are encouraged to be members of Highland Park Baptist Church. Associate of Arts, Associate of Science, Diploma of Theology, Bachelor of Arts and Bachelor of Science degrees available; majors in College of Biblical Studies and Church Ministries, Arts and Sciences, Education, School of Studies for the Deaf, and School of External Studies.

♦ Located in downtown Chattanooga, Temple was organized in 1946 as a 2-year college and Bible school, expanded to 4-year college and seminary, achieved University status in 1979, and was fully accredited by the American Association of Bible Colleges in 1984. Enrollment is approximately 500. Library houses 154,000 books and receives 325 periodicals. Academic calendar late August-early May.

University of Tennessee at Chattanooga
♦ *755-4111, 615 McCallie Ave, Chattanooga 37403*
♦ *Admissions Undergraduate -- 755-4662*
♦ *Admissions Graduate -- 755-4666*
♦ *Continuing Education -- 755-4344*
♦ The University's programs provide a firm grounding in the liberal arts and strong professional preparation. Seven schools and colleges with 100 bachelor's and 70 master's degree programs; baccalaureate degrees are offered in liberal arts, sciences, business, education, engineering, fine arts, health, human services, nursing, and physical therapy; Master's degrees in business, computer science, criminal justice, education, engineering, English, music, nursing, psychology, and public administration.. The College Challenge Program gives outstanding high school students opportunity to take selected college courses; there is an early admission program for exceptionally gifted students. Division I NCAA athletics with basketball, football, wrestling, 14 national fraternities and sororities, and more than 100 student organizations. Continuing Education offers an Elderscholars program for senior citizens, youth development programs, off-campus academic credit programs, and cable tv classes; also professional development and conference and program development services.

♦ In 1969 the University of Chattanooga and Chattanooga City College merged with the University of Tennessee to form the UTC campus. The University of Tennessee system has four primary campuses in the state. Approximately 8,000 students at UTC represent 70 Tennessee counties, 38 states and 35 foreign countries. Downtown 85-acre campus fronts McCallie Avenue. Library holdings of over 1 million books and periodicals. Academic calendar late August-early May; summer sessions.

Library Services

♦ **A C Kalmbach Memorial Library,** *894-8144, 4121 Cromwell Rd, open Mon-Fri 9-5,* founded to preserve the history of model and prototype railroading; collection of over 3,000 books, 35,000 magazine issues, 3,500 photographic prints, and 37,000 slides; open to public.

♦ **Catoosa County Library,** *935-3800, 404 Gum, Ringgold, open Mon-Fri 10-5, Sat 10-1*

♦ **Chattanooga-Hamilton County Bicentennial Library Downtown,** *757-5310, 1001 Broad St, open Mon-Thu 9-9, Fri-Sat 9-6, Sun 2-6 except closed summer*

♦ **Chattanooga-Hamilton County Bicentennial Library East Branch,** *855-2685, 5900 Bldg, Eastgate, open Mon-Tue 9-6, Wed-Thu 9-9, Fri-Sat 9-6*

♦ **Chattanooga-Hamilton County Bicentennial Library North Branch,** *870-0636, 5020 Hixson Pike, open Mon-Tue 9-6, Wed-Thu 9-9, Fri-Sat 9-6*

♦ **Chattanooga-Hamilton County Bicentennial Library Ooltewah Branch,** *396-9322, 9318 Apison Pike, open Mon-Tue 9-6, Wed-Thu 9-9, Sat 9-6*

♦ **Chattanooga-Hamilton County Bicentennial Library South Branch,** *825-7237, 925 W 39th St, open Mon-Thu 9-6, Sat 9-6*

♦ **Church of Jesus Christ of Latter-Day Saints,** *892-7632, 1019 N Moore Rd,* Family History Center; access to library in Salt Lake, one of largest genealogical centers in world; open to public.

♦ **City of East Ridge Library,** *867-7323, 1517 Tombras Ave, open Mon-Thu 10-8:30, Fri-Sat 10-6, Sun 2-5*

♦ **Fort Oglethorpe Library,** *866-8355, 15 Barnhardt Circle, Fort Oglethorpe, open Mon 10-5, Tue 10-7, Wed-Fri 10-5, Sat 10-1*

♦ **Rossville Public Library,** *866-1368, 504 McFarland Ave, Rossville, open Mon-Wed 9-5, Thu 1-8, Fri-Sat 9-12*

♦ **Signal Mountain Library,** *886-7323, 1114 James Blvd, open Mon 3-9, Tue-Wed 10-6, Thu 3-9, Fri-Sat 10-2*

Specialty Classes

Continuing Education

♦ **Chattanooga State Technical Community College,** *697-4410,* "College: Not for Kids Only" is a free, regularly scheduled workshop that overviews CSTCC and its many educational opportunities; panel of successful adult students who share their experience and advice; long list of Continuing Ed classes. *(contd.)*

♦ **University of Tennessee at Chattanooga,** *755-4344,* Computers to tennis, babysitting to bicycling, classes in Microsoft Word, Leadership Skills for Managers, Business Tax Workshop, Teams in the Workplace, CPR: Heartsaver, Beginning Golf and Lifeguarding are just a few of the offerings through Continuing Ed. Youth University for grades 1-9.

Cooking

♦ **CookWorks Cooking School,** *266-6133, 1101 Hixson Pike,* Two-hour classes include printed recipes and tasting session. Instructors are chefs from local restaurants; previous classes included Stocks, Sauces and Kitchen Basics, Authentic Clay Pot Cookery from the Southwest, Asian Specialties, French Pastries, Specialty Roasting and Grilling.

♦ **Two Twelve Market St Restaurant,** *265-1212, 212 Market St,* call for newsletter announcing monthly classes, events.

Driving

♦ **Haman's Driving School,** *894-9300,* teen course in classroom and in car; adult course in car.

Elderhostel

♦ **Lee College,** *472-2111,* week-long program for ages 60 and over, non-credit classes, dormitory life.

Motivation

♦ **Mother Goose,** *706-820-2531, 615-870-3887, Martha Bell Miller.* Mother Goose says "Yes" to goosey hugs and "No" to smoking, drinking and drugs; motivational programs for schools, hospitals, festivals and promotional events. She wears full costume and is accompanied by Gussie Goose; the 50-minute show can accommodate up to 500 children.

Nature, Recreation and the Out of Doors

♦ **Audubon Acres,** *892-1499,* classes include *As the Indians Left It,* focusing on Native American culture and history, and *Gifts From the Earth,* taught by an Audubon naturalist.

♦ **Adventure Guild,** *266-5709,* outdoor experiential education; mountaineering, climbing classes at the Walnut Street Wall.

♦ **Chattanooga Nature Center,** *821-1160,* basketry, eagle and sky watch, bluebird nest box building, spring hikes, owl prowl, herbal gardening.

♦ **Chattanooga Parks & Recreation Department,** *757-PLAY,* activities and classes in arts and crafts, photography, and just about every sport.

♦ **Creative Discovery Museum,** *756-2738,* classes and workshops make everything from paper to rockets; study earth, wind, fire and water.

♦ **Tennessee Aquarium,** *266-9352,* classes for members; children, family and behind-the-scenes programs.

Media Services

Newspapers and Magazines
Founded in 1869, *The Chattanooga Times* once had Adolph Ochs at the helm, prior to his years at *The New York Times.* You can start your day with this

morning daily; its watchword is "to give the news impartially, without fear or favor." Och's granddaughter Ruth Holmberg is Chairman of the Board today; publisher is Paul Neely. *The Chattanooga Free Press*, the city's afternoon daily and Sunday paper, was founded in 1936 by Roy McDonald. Frank McDonald is Chairman of the Board today; publisher is Lee Anderson. Count on both papers for good coverage of community events and support of your organization's doings. *CityScope Magazine*, published by Joe and Billie Moan, is quarterly in-depth coverage of the city's people and places. There are many fine community and specialty newspapers; a few are listed.

- **Catoosa County News**, *706-935-2621*, weekly, circulation 4,000
- **Chattanooga Business Journal**, *629-7500*, monthly, circulation 8,000
- **Chattanooga CityScope Magazine**, *266-3440*, quarterly, full-color
- **Chattanooga Free Press**, *756-6900*, afternoon daily, circulation 42,000; Sunday circulation 115,000
- **Chattanooga Times**, *756-1234*, morning daily, circulation 41,000
- **Chug Magazine**, *266-4545*, Chattanooga urban gamut, weekly
- **Cleveland Daily Banner**, *472-5041* Mon-Fri circulation 18,000, Sun 19,000
- **Dade County Sentinel**, *706-657-6182*, weekly, circulation 10,500
- **Hamilton County Herald**, *892-1336*, weekly legal paper
- **North Hamilton Sun**, *698-5306*, north county monthly
- **Scenicland Spotlight**, *855-5009*, southeast events and happenings

Radio Stations

Public station 88.1 WUTC-FM, Jazz 88, offers jazz, blues, and the BBC; weekdays it's *Fresh Air* and *Monitor Radio* 5-6, Jack Hale hosts evening jazz/blues at 6:30 featuring "The Blues Doctor," see p.70, on Wednesdays. Other programming includes *BluesStage, Worldwide, Crescent City Sounds, Portraits in Blue, Outside Pleasures, E-Town, Montreux/Detroit Great Hits,* and *Marian McPartland's Piano Jazz.*. Member support is important; join and enjoy the monthly guide alongside the great music, if you have a business, underwrite a program, call 755-4756. Other school-affiliated public stations are **90.5 WSMC**, *238-2905*, a fine arts station at Southern College affiliated with NPR; and **91.5 WAWL**, *697-4470* at Chattanooga State, which features new artists and alternative rock music.

Commercial stations offer a broad range of blues, country, rock and roll, standard oldies and top 40; you'll find numerous news/talk shows and gospel programming too. Some of the radio legends are **Luther Masingill**, who's been broadcasting more than 50 years; catch his *Sundial* show from 6-10 weekdays on **1370 AM WDEF; Blues Master Bobby Q. Day**, at WNOO for many years, now with **1150 WGOW** for blues and talk weeknights beginning at 7; and longtime **Mr. Rock and Roll Tommy Jett**, at **101.9 WSGC** with the oldies. Travel US 101 with award-winning **Hot Country Favorites** at **100.7 WUSY**; speaking of travel, catch **Terrie Edwards Frederick** and her *Scenic Center Safari* Sunday mornings at 5:30 and 10:30 on **WDOD 96.5** and **1310**.

(contd.)

Radio Stations (contd.)

AM Broadcasting	FM Broadcasting	FM Broadcasting
820, WWAM, *942-1700*	88.1, WUTC, *755-4790*	100.7, WUSY, *892-3333*
1070, WFLI, *821-3555*	88.9, WMBW, *629-8900*	101.9, WSGC, *937-4653*
1150, WGOW, *756-6141*	89.7, WDYN, *493-4382*	102.3, WFXS, *899-5111*
1240, WSDT, *332-8020*	90.5, WSMC, *238-2905*	102.7, WBDX, *899-5111*
1260, WNOO, *698-8617*	91.5, WAWL, *697-4470*	105.5, WLMX, *861-1050*
1310, WDOD, *266-5117*	92.3, WDEF, *785-1200*	106.5, WSKZ, *756-6141*
1370, WDEF, *785-1200*	94.3, WJTT, *265-9494*	107.9, WOGT, *756-6141*
1450, WLMR, *624-4200*	96.5, WDOD, *266-5117*	

Television Stations

Public station WTCI Channel 45, *629-0045*, brings great programming to the city; from *American Playhouse* to *Austin City Limits*, *Julia Child's Cooking* to *Lamb Chop's Play Along*, *NOVA* to *Scientific American Frontiers*, *Sesame Street* to *Talking with David Frost*, *Wall Street Week* to *Wild America*, *The Windsors: Royal Family* to *Yanni: In Concert at the Acropolis*; many music specials and local programming too, such as *Family Business Insight* and *Southern Accents*. The station depends on member support and volunteers; call to see how you can help and join before the fund-drive; you'll enjoy the really fine monthly magazine with insights into upcoming programs; or underwrite a program, call *629-0045*.

Cable

♦ **Battlefield Cable TV,** *866-3337*
♦ **Chattanooga Cable TV,** *855-4300*

Commercial

♦ **ABC network, WTVC Channel 9,** *756-5500, News 756-6397,* sponsors Science Theatre Mon-Fri at Northgate Mall during school year

♦ **CBS network, WDEF Channel 12,** *785-1200,* special *Point of View*

♦ **FOX network, WDSI Channel 61,** *697-0661,* carries FOX programming, no local

♦ **NBC network, WRCB Channel 3,** *267-5412, News Hotline 267-5417, Weather Hotline 265-1883, On Your Side 266-4357;* specials: *Tell Us What You Think, Trendz on 3,* Jaycees monthly show, *Kids Talk* quarterly

♦ **UPN network, WFLI Channel 53,** *825-5731,* variety programming

---

Inspectors and reviewers for Chattanooga Great Places *accept no free meals or favors; the book has no sponsors or advertisers.*

Medical Services

Emergencies 911

Bloodbank

- **Blood Assurance,** *756-0966, 700 E 3rd, Chattanooga, open Mon-Fri 8-6:30, Sat 8-2:30, non-profit community volunteer*
- **Blood Assurance Donor Station,** *756-0966, 201 Thomas Rd, Ft Oglethorpe, open Tue-Fri 10-5:30, Sat 10-2:30*

Clinic

Basic health-care and minor emergency service are offered through the Hamilton County Health Department; some other clinics are listed too.

- **Atrium Emergicare,** *495-3535, 1949 Gunbarrel Rd, Chattanooga, open Mon-Sat 9-8, Sun 9-6;* walk-ins welcome, minor emergencies
- **Hamilton County Health Department Downtown,** *209-8000, 921 E 3rd St, Chattanooga, open Mon-Fri 8-4,* children's clinic, dental clinic, STD clinic, chest X-rays
- **Hamilton County Health Department Eastside,** *493-9234, 2210 E Main St, Chattanooga, open Mon-Fri 8-4;* family planning, pre-natal, dental, women with infant children, immunizations
- **Hamilton County Health Department Ooltewah,** *238-4269, 5520 High Street, Ooltewah, open Mon 8-5:45, Tue-Fri 8-4;* birth control, dental, pre-natal, women with infant children, Dr in on Monday for children
- **Hamilton County Health Department Sequoyah,** *842-3031, 9527 W Ridge Trail Rd, Soddy-Daisy, open Mon-Fri 8-4;* family planning, pre-natal, dental, women with infant children, immunizations
- **MedSouth,** *894-5861, 4432 Hwy 58, Chattanooga, open Mon-Fri 8-6:30, Sat 9-3;* walk-ins welcome, emergencies
- **Physicians Care 1,** *899-6222, 2021 Hamilton Place, Chattanooga, open Mon-Fri 9-6;* walk-ins welcome, emergencies
- **Physicians Care 2,** *875-0700, 4490 Hixson Pike, Chattanooga, open Mon-Fri 8:30-6:30, Sat 9-4, Sun 10-4;* walk-ins welcome, emergencies
- **Physicians Care 3,** *894-3589, 403 McBrien Rd, Chattanooga, open Mon-Fri 8:30-6:30, Sat 9-4, Sun 10-4;* walk-ins welcome, emergencies

Hospitals

Erlanger medical complex is the largest facility in the area, with a trauma unit and emergency medical helicopter; the complex includes an eye center and the children's hospital.

- **Chattanooga Outpatient Center,** *622-7212, 1301 McCallie Ave, Chattanooga,* no emergencies, mammograms, MRI's, outpatient services
- **Chattanooga Rehabilitation Hospital,** *698-0221, 2412 McCallie Ave, Chattanooga,* rehabilitation for accident, stroke
- **East Ridge Hospital,** *894-7870, Emergency Room 855-3522, 941 Spring Creek*

Rd, Chattanooga, hospital services, no trauma, child birthing specialty, 100 beds

♦ **Erlanger East Surgery Center,** *778-8400, 1755 Gunbarrel Rd, Chattanooga, open Mon-Sun 8-8 for quick care, Mon-Fri 6-6 for surgery;* outpatient surgery, walk-ins, minor medical quick care

♦ **Erlanger Medical Center,** *778-7000, Emergency Room 778-2094, 975 E 3rd St, Chattanooga,* full-service hospital, teaching hospital, burn unit, kidney transplants, heart program, cancer program, child birthing, women's center, 811 beds

♦ **Erlanger North,** *778-3300, Emergency Room 778-3393, 632 Morrison Springs Rd, Red Bank,* full-service hospital, 57 beds

♦ **Hutcheson Medical Center,** *858-2000, Emergency Room 858-2161, 100 Gross Crescent Circle, Ft Oglethorpe,* full service hospital, child birthing, 220 beds

♦ **Memorial Hospital,** *495-2525, Emergency Room 495-8577, 2525 DeSales Ave, Chattanooga,* hospital services, no trauma, 350 beds

♦ **Miller Eye Center,** *778-6011, 975 E 3rd, Chattanooga,* part of Erlanger, eye surgery and care

♦ **Moccasin Bend Mental Health Institute,** *265-2271, 100 Moccasin Bend Rd, Chattanooga,* state institution for children and adults

♦ **North Park Hospital,** *870-1300, Emergency Room 875-4099, 2051 Hamill Rd, Chattanooga,* full-service hospital, 88 beds

♦ **Parkridge Medical Center,** *698-6061, Emergency Room 698-6061, 2333 McCallie Ave, Chattanooga,* hospital services, no trauma, 296 beds

♦ **Siskin Hospital,** *634-1200, 1 Siskin Plaza, Chattanooga,* physical rehabilitation hospital

♦ **TC Thompson Children's Hospital,** *778-6011, Emergency Room 778-6101, 975 E 3rd St, Chattanooga,* part of Erlanger, any service for children, 115 beds

---

Information Services

♦ **AIDS Hotline,** *267-2437, 744 McCallie Ave*
♦ **AIDS Hotline, CDC National,** *800-342-AIDS*
♦ **Alzheimer's Association, Inc,** *622-3443, 109 N Germantown Rd*
♦ **American Cancer Society,** *267-8613, 850 Fort Wood St*
♦ **American Heart Association,** *265-3466, 519 E 4th St*
♦ **Chattanooga & Hamilton County Medical Society,** *622-2872, 1917 E 3rd*
♦ **Medicare,** *800-342-8900*
♦ **Planned Parenthood of East Tennessee,** *267-7923, 744 McCallie Ave*
♦ **United Network for Organ Sharing (UNOS),** *800-24-DONOR*

Mental Health Crisis Services

♦ **Alliance for the Mentally Ill,** *615-691-3707*
♦ **Fort Wood Center,** *615-266-6751,* 24-hour emergency service
♦ **Joseph W. Johnson Jr Mental Health Center,** *615-756-2740*
♦ **VISTA Community Mental Health Center,** *615-861-3387*

Transportation Services

Unfortunately, ChooChoo town has no train service! Except for our fine Railroad Museum, you won't be able to do any boarding here. Until Amtrak begins stopping here, please come by plane, bus or automobile!

Chattanooga Metropolitan Airport is located at Lovell Field. The new terminal was completed in 1991.

♦ *Airport Authority 855-2200*
♦ *Page someone at Airport 855-2215*

Airlines for Commercial Flights

♦ **American Eagle Airlines,** *800-433-7300*
♦ **ASA, Atlantic Southeast Airlines, the Delta commuter,** *800-282-3424*
♦ **ComAir, commuter for Delta,** *800-354-9822*
♦ **Delta Air Lines,** *800-221-1212*
♦ **Northwest Airlink,** *800-225-2525 domestic, 800-447-4747 international*
♦ **USAir,** *800-428-4322*

Airlines for Scenic Flights

♦ **Ellsworth Aviation, Inc.,** *894-4930, 115 Nowlin Lane,* Contact pilot Chuck Ellsworth for a fine ride over Chattanooga's beautiful rivers and ridges.

Bus Services
Charter

These businesses have buses available for charter; call for sizes available and scheduling and pricing information.

♦ **America's Best Tours,** *629-4245*
♦ **Bestway Motorcoach & Tours,** *266-8687*
♦ **Choo-Choo Express Tours,** *892-9758*
♦ **Riverbend Tours,** *942-5139*
♦ **S & S Tours,** *624-2043*

Commercial

♦ **Greyhound Bus Lines,** *800-231-2222, 515 Chestnut St,* call for fare and destination information; no reservations - get to station 1 hour before departure time

Public

The city bus system offers several special services beyond the regular CARTA routes.

♦ **Chattanooga Area Regional Transportation (CARTA),** *629-1473,* call for schedule information; route maps available at all downtown banks, libraries, Electric Power Board; regular fee $.75, $.35 for students and senior citizens, children under 5 free
♦ **CARTA Care-a-van Service,** *698-9038,* for those who can't use regular bus service due to medical problems; call for application; city service only
♦ **CARTA Shuttle,** *629-1473, every 5 minutes, Mon-Fri 6AM-10PM, Sat 9AM-*

10PM, Sun 9AM-8:30PM *(hours subject to change), except for Thanksgiving and Christmas Day,* you can catch a **FREE** electric shuttle downtown. Park in the big garage at the **ChooChoo**; the shuttle travels north on Market to 10th, goes west two blocks to Carter, then circles the Library and proceeds north on Broad Street to the **Tennessee Aquarium** and the **Visitors Center**; reversing itself to come back to the ChooChoo. It passes by the **Marriott, Days Inn Rivergate,** and **Radisson Read House** hotels and stops at just about every corner, including **Warehouse Row**.

♦ **Lookout Mountain Express,** *629-1473, every 30 minutes between 10AM-10PM, between Memorial Day weekend and Labor Day weekend,* the Express delivers you from the **ChooChoo** to the **Incline** at the foot of **Lookout Mountain** with stops at the **Mount Vernon Restaurant** and **Battles for Chattanooga Museum**. At the TOP of Lookout Mountain, the Express runs between the **Incline, Ruby Falls,** and **Rock City**; a boon if you've ridden the Incline up and your car is still at the bottom! Small fee.

Limousine Services

♦ **Bell Limousines,** *344-6174,* stretch and superstretch limos with TV, VCR, CD player; for weddings, parties, proms, corporate, out-of-town

♦ **Limo One,** *267-LIMO,* stretch, superstretch, sedans, vans; public service commission approved; available for local or out-of-town functions

♦ **Nation Limousine Service,** *867-7001,* standard and superstretch, local or out-of-town, color TV, VCR, cellular phone, stereo, bar set-ups

Rental Car/Truck Services

♦ **Budget Car and Truck Rental, 2 locations,** *855-2224, 1705 Shepherd Rd, by airport, open daily; 698-3858, 2308 E 23rd St, open Mon-Sat,* mostly Fords available by the day, weekend, or longer, must pick up there

♦ **Dollar Rent A Car,** *855-2277, 855-5757, 1624 Shepherd Rd, by airport, open daily,* unlimited mileage within 850 mile radius, passenger vans too, extra charge for delivery

Taxi Services

♦ **Checker Cab,** *624-1410, 2016 Wilson St,* vans, out-of-town, executive cars, package delivery, 24-hours

♦ **East Ridge Cab Co,** *899-2289, 1414 S Moore Rd,* 24 hours, 7 days

Index

D

Notes

Chattanooga Great Places Feedback Form

Based on my personal experience, I wish to nominate/confirm/disapprove for listing the following restaurant, sight, shop, lodging, or other:

_____

_____

Please include address & telephone number of the establishment.

REPORT
Please describe food, service, style, comfort, value, date of visit, & other aspects of your experience; attach extra page if necessary.

I am not concerned, directly or indirectly, with the management or ownership of this establishment.

Signed: _____

Address: _____

Phone Number: _____ Date: _____

Send to: Phase II: Publications
        5251-C, Hwy 153, #255
        Chattanooga, TN 37343

Book Order Form

There's nothing like having your own personal copy of *Chattanooga Great Places*. Then you can make notes in it and refer to it whenever the need arises. If you need more copies, for yourself or as a gift for someone else, complete the form below and send with your check or money order.

You'll also want to have the *Chattanooga Great Places* companion, *Day Trips: Chattanooga Plus a Hundred Miles*, packed with information about Great Places to visit in the Tennessee, Georgia, Alabama and North Carolina area. With both books in hand, you're set!

Books $11.95 each
Shipping & Handling $2.00 for each book

I'd like _____ copies of *Chattanooga Great Places*.

I'd like _____ copies of *Day Trips: Chattanooga Plus a Hundred Miles*.

My check or money order for $ _____ is enclosed.

Name: _____

Address: _____

City/State/Zip: _____

Telephone Area Code: _____ Number:_____

Allow 4-6 weeks for delivery.

Bulk Orders Invited

For bulk quantity discounts or special handling call 615-875-4795 (after September, 1995 423-875-4795).

All guidebooks published by Phase II: Publications are available at bulk discounts for corporate gifts, conventions, and fund-raising sales for clubs and organizations.

Phase II: Publications
5251-C Hwy 153, #255
Chattanooga, TN 37343